PARTY AND PROCEDURE IN
THE UNITED STATES CONGRESS

PARTY AND PROCEDURE IN THE UNITED STATES CONGRESS

Edited by Jacob R. Straus

ROWMAN & LITTLEFIELD PUBLISHERS, INC.

Lanham • Boulder • New York • Toronto • Plymouth, UK

Published by Rowman & Littlefield Publishers, Inc.
A wholly owned subsidiary of The Rowman & Littlefield Publishing Group, Inc.
4501 Forbes Boulevard, Suite 200, Lanham, Maryland 20706
http://www.rowmanlittlefield.com

10 Thornbury Road, Plymouth PL6 7PP, United Kingdom

British Library Cataloguing in Publication Information Available

Library of Congress Cataloging-in-Publication Data

Party and procedure in the United States Congress / [edited by] Jacob R. Straus.
    p. cm.
  ISBN 978-1-4422-1172-8 (cloth : alk. paper) — ISBN 978-1-4422-1173-5 (pbk. : alk. paper) — ISBN 978-1-4422-1174-2 (electronic)
  1. United States. Congress—Rules and practice. 2. Legislation—United States. I. Straus, Jacob R.
  KF4937.P37 2012
  328.73'05—dc23   2011048721

∞™ The paper used in this publication meets the minimum requirements of American National Standard for Information Sciences—Permanence of Paper for Printed Library Materials, ANSI/NISO Z39.48-1992.

Printed in the United States of America

Contents

Preface

THIS BOOK BUILDS ON THE KNOWLEDGE of the importance of political parties in Congress and how they use procedure to influence the legislative agenda. Examination of the use of procedure by congressional political parties invites the use of numerous social science methods. *Party and Procedure in the United States Congress* highlights these varied approaches to answer questions about agenda setting, decision-making, strategy, and compromise.

Patterns of power in Congress fluctuate over time. In some periods, elected chamber leaders wield the most power and at others committee chairs control the legislative agenda. Understanding how party leaders and committee chairs utilize procedure to advance legislation is fundamental to how Congress operates.

To pass legislation, both the House of Representatives and the Senate must pass and present identical language, in identical vehicles, to the president for his signature. The process of getting from idea to introduction to passage in each chamber is governed by rules and procedures unique to each body. This volume examines how parties, leadership, and the chambers of Congress use procedure to advance their agendas.

This book would not have been possible without the support of the editorial team at Rowman & Littlefield. My coauthors and I are appreciative of the assistance of Jon Sisk and Darcy Evans, among others. Additionally, I am grateful to my colleagues at the Congressional Research Service and the Library of Congress who contributed their expertise and dedication to this publication.

This book is clearly a collective effort. I thank all of the contributors, who have provided original and important scholarship to each chapter. As editor and author, I take full responsibility for any omissions or errors of fact or interpretation. Additionally, new members were added to the families of the editor and two of the authors. Congratulations to Jennifer Hayes Clark and James Wallner on the birth of their children!

I dedicate this book to my family. Thank you to Sarah, Lillian, and Benjamin for your love, inspiration, and support.

Jacob R. Straus

1

Navigating Congress*

Jacob R. Straus

C ONGRESS IS A DYNAMIC INSTITUTION. At different points in history, political parties, the elected chamber leadership, committees, and rank-and-file members have each enjoyed periods as the dominant centers of power within the House or Senate. During these periods, rules and norms have been developed to empower those seeking authority. Shifts in the balance of power and amendments to the rules and norms are generally slow to develop. Even when it appears that the House or Senate has made a quick change to its rules or norms, in reality, the process has long been in development (Rockman 1994, 143). This is true of big institutional changes like the overthrow of Speaker Joseph Cannon and smaller, but significant, changes like the creation of the subcommittee bill of rights in 1973. The preferences of members are filtered through these institutional structures to produce their desired outcomes.

For forty years, between 1954 and 1994, the Democrats dominated Congress. When the Republicans won control of the House of Representatives in the 1994 election, observers knew the institution would change, but they did not immediately know how (Wilcox 1995; Cheney and Cheney 1996, 190–210; Fenno 1997). The changes that did occur, however, were easily categorized by scholars conducting research on the effect of regime change in Congress and how change can frame internal operations and procedure (Dodd 2001, 410), where each piece is constantly seeking to increase its own power relative to others and the effect of institutional structure is contingent on the willingness of participant actors to use institutional tools to help further their goals (Weaver and Rockman 1993, 446–47).

*This chapter reflects the views of the author and does not necessarily reflect the views of the Congressional Research Service or the Library of Congress. The author would like to thank Matthew Glassman, Colleen Shogan, and Douglas MacMillan for their comments on earlier drafts.

Shifting Centers of Congressional Power

While the role of individuals within Congress can be important, understanding how party leaders and committee chairs utilize floor procedure to advance a legislative agenda is fundamental to understanding how Congress operates. This volume explores the relationship between party and floor procedure. At different times, House and Senate rules have empowered both elected leaders and committee chairs with the ability to direct the chambers' legislative outcomes. While controlling the floor is an art rather than a science, each congressional era has had different ideas about which groups and what processes best accomplish the goals of Congress.

Historically, three main groups have come to share power: political parties, committees, and elected leaders. In the House of Representatives, this is especially true, as parties—especially party leadership—and committees dominate. Individual members cannot do much without their party's support. In the Senate, individuals have more power, but are still very much constrained by the institutional assignment of power to leaders, parties, and committees.

Political Parties

During the first several congresses, party structures were weak and individual members dominated policy. For example, James Madison wielded considerable influence in the early House of Representatives. Ellis (2000) credits Madison with "managing" Alexander Hamilton's financial plan for state debt assumption through the House.[1] The coalition that Madison built to ensure the passage of Hamilton's plan helped establish the foundation for creating political parties in the United States.

As political parties developed, the rules of Congress and the parties' place within the House and Senate changed to accommodate members' desires to organize along ideological lines (White and Shea 2000, 39–40). Both major parties of the time—the Federalists and the Jeffersonian Republicans—organized themselves within Congress to protect their respective party's self-interest and its "need to enact specific policies in an arena where real differences over public policy existed alongside perceptions of serious public danger if the wrong policies, people, or groups dominated" (Silbey 1994, 6).

Over the succeeding decades, parties became the basis for the American political experience and process (Aldrich 1995). Today, it would be hard to imagine Congress organizing or operating without a majority and minority party and the elaborate sets of operational rules that the parties have negotiated over time (Maisel 1990). Additionally, congressional parties are not only expected to set policy, but they also receive input from constituents and the White House (Reichley 1985; Sinclair 1994; Stanley and Niemi 2001).

Committees

Committee chairs have historically derived their power from both political parties and chamber rules. Since virtually all legislation introduced in the House and Senate is referred to at least one committee and most controversial legislation must be passed by the committee before floor consideration, committees wield enormous selection power. The policy stances advocated by committee chairs, therefore, can affect legislation's eventual floor success (Unekis and Rieselbach 1983; King 1997). In fact, being a committee chair can be so powerful that individual members will use political capital to try to become a chair and directly influence public policy (Fenno 1973; Leighton and Lopez 2002). Additionally, committee chairs can influence how multiply-referred legislation is considered by other committees. Baughman (2006) argues that when a piece of legislation is multiply referred and the chair of the primary committee sits as a rank-and-file member on the second committee, the chair often exerts his or her influence in an attempt to make the second committee "roll" and defer to the primary committee (137–38).

Not all committee chairs, however, are created equal. While many want the gavel as a way to control public policy, others may also perceive benefits for their constituents or themselves (Gryski 1991). Whatever the reason that a member becomes a chair, he or she cannot ascend to that position without the blessing of the party organization. This is especially true in the Senate, where the parties have, at various times, created internal rules that prohibit senators from chairing multiple committees in any given Congress (Collie and Roberts 1992). In this case, senators must choose their sole fiefdoms.

Congressional Leaders

For many members of Congress, ascending to party leadership can be a career goal. The power of the most prominent leadership role in Congress, the Speaker of the House, has been well documented (Hinds 1909; Green 2010; Grant 2011). While the Speaker and the Senate majority and minority leaders might command media and scholarly attention, other elected leaders in both chambers wield significant power over the legislative agenda and institutional resources. In fact, both the majority and minority parties elect a number of leaders, each of whom is expected to play a role in deciding which legislation is brought to the floor and therefore ensuring the passage (or defeat) of those measures as agents of the party (Rohde 1991, 35–36).

The influence of the Speaker of the House and the Senate majority and minority leaders stretches from committee assignments to the structuring of special rules in the House and crafting unanimous consent agreements in the Senate, to the assignment of members to conference committees (Lazarus and Monroe 2007). Through control of the chambers' organizational rules, these leaders can impact policy outcomes more broadly than any rank-and-file member or committee chair. As the public face of their party's caucus (or conference) within the chamber, the Speaker of the House and the majority and minority leaders in the Senate exercise that power and work to ensure the party's agenda is fulfilled.

Majority Power and Minority Rights

An examination of the various power centers—political parties, committee chairs, and elected chamber leadership—reveals two major themes that appear throughout this volume: majority power to set the legislative agenda and minority rights to attempt to amend pending legislation. In each instance, how the majority and minority use chamber rules to accomplish these goals is essential. The House and Senate can be starkly different in how the majority and minority strategize. In both chambers, however, the goals of the majority and minority parties are the same: to pass legislation that meets the goals of their party's agenda.

Majority Agenda Control

In the House of Representatives, the majority party has a virtually unimpeded ability to control the legislative agenda. Because the majority party has at least 50 percent of the chamber's members, the majority leadership enjoys the power to schedule legislation and control the House Committee on Rules—the House committee responsible for issuing special rules for legislative floor consideration. Cox (2001) reminds us of the importance of majority party status when he concludes in his study of agenda setting that "while each member's ideology (relative to the floor and committee medians) does systematically influence his or her dissent role, majority status matters above and beyond ideology and is clearly the larger effect substantively" (186).

In the Senate, the power of the majority vis-à-vis the minority is more complicated. Past research into majority party agenda setting and power in the Senate suggests that the majority party, aided by power afforded to individual senators, has a significant negative agenda control and can more easily keep items off the agenda than place items on the agenda (Gailmard and Jenkins 2007). Scheduling of legislation, especially in the Senate, however, is more than a function of just the majority party leadership's desires. It is fundamentally a reflection of the leadership's attempt to mirror its members' preferences for legislative action (Lebo, McGlynn, and Koger 2007).

Minority Rights

Few would argue that in legislative institutions minority party members must have some right to change (or attempt to change) legislation. The procedure for carrying out these rights varies from institution to institution, with some minority members having realistic opportunities to amend legislation and other minority members having only the ability to "make noise" and not affect real change (Lijphart 1999). In Congress, the ability of the minority to exert their rights has changed over time, with some scholars believing that attempts to limit minority amending power is the root cause of current partisan conflict (Polsby 2004), that minority power increases as majority cohesion declines (Binder 1997; Martorano 2004), or that if a majority is small but cohesive, the minority party rights are impinged (Dion 1997).

Regardless of whether this is true, the fact remains that the minority parties in the House and Senate have numerous procedural tools available to them to attempt to amend legislation. This volume explores many of the procedural tools available to minority members of Congress and juxtaposes them against the majority's ability to set the legislative agenda.

Organization of the Book

To address the use of procedure by political parties in Congress, this volume is divided into four sections. Section I focuses on leadership, the resources available to congressional leadership, and the role that leaders play within the House and Senate. Section II covers the House of Representatives, section III focuses on the Senate, and section IV discusses the process of reconciling legislative differences between the House and Senate. Each section provides theoretical and practical insight on the role that political parties play in using procedure to advance their legislative agenda within Congress. In its own way, each chapter also considers how modern congressional procedure compares to historical trends within Congress.

Section I: Leadership

In recent years, the importance of leadership in the House and Senate has grown. In the House, the majority leadership can control the floor agenda, and in the Senate the majority and minority leaders are expected to bring their caucuses together on "important" legislative issues. With the extra stress that can accompany these roles, why would a rank-and-file member choose to run for leadership? In chapter 2, "Congressional Leadership: A Resource Perspective," Matthew Glassman directly explores that question. He begins by examining the minority whip election in the 112th Congress (2011–2012) between Representatives Steny Hoyer and James Clyburn with an effort to understand the appeal of leadership to members. The chapter analyzes the resources—both staff and financial—available to party leaders and the power these resources impart.

Section II: House of Representatives

Section II focuses on the House of Representatives. Chapters in this section include an examination of the creating and discarding of a special rule (i.e., king of the hill and queen of the hill); an analysis of the motion to recommit; a study of appropriations limitation amendments; a look at how technology, specifically electronic voting, has changed floor behavior in the House; and a discussion of the role caucuses can play within the House.

Chapter 3 begins our discussion of the House of Representatives with an examination of special rules and their role in setting the terms of debate. In "Toppling the King of the Hill: Understanding Innovation in House Practice," James V. Saturno discusses the creation, development, and discarding of a type of special rule. In 1982, the House first used a practice that came to be known as a king-of-the-hill rule. Although its use as a procedural innovation was downplayed at the time, it proved to be a useful way for the House leadership to allow various groups and factions within the House to offer alternatives in a more controlled manner than traditional modes of consideration. This initial success led to more frequent use of king-of-the-hill rules over the next decade. This success was not without controversy, however, and shortly after the change in majority control of the House in the 104th Congress (1995–1996) its use was effectively abandoned. This chapter empirically examines the use of king-of-the-hill rules in order to assess how they served as an innovative procedural tool for House leadership, and explains why their use was discontinued.

In chapter 4, "The Appropriations Process and Limitation Amendments: A Case Study on Party Politics and the House Floor," Jessica Tollestrup examines the proposal and passage of limitation amendments on the House floor as a means of evaluating floor decision-making dynamics between the majority and minority parties during the annual appropriations process. Limitations provide a good vehicle to test theories of voting in the House because they often have important policy implications in areas of significant controversy. In addition, the extent to which individual members are able to successfully propose and pass limitation amendments can be indicative of larger patterns of partisan domination over the floor process. After a review of relevant theory, the chapter describes the history of limitations, the procedural framework in the House, and the potential impact of limitation amendments on policy implementation. Tollestrup uses an original dataset comprising over nine hundred limitations from the 97th Congress (1981–1982) through the 110th Congress (2007–2008) to analyze amendments sponsored by members of the majority versus the minority party. The chapter concludes that as party polarization in the House has increased, limitation amendments as a procedural weapon of the minority have also become more significant.

Chapter 5 discusses procedural tools available to minority party members. In "Minority Party Strategies and the Evolution of the Motion to Recommit in the

U.S. House," Jennifer Hayes Clark examines the use of the motion to recommit legislation back to committee and the role it plays in party strategy on the House floor. The motion to recommit is often regarded as one of the few minority party powers or rights institutionalized in the House rules. Although the motion to recommit a bill back to committee has been firmly established since the origins of the House, some have challenged its capacity to confer power to minority party members. This chapter examines the evolution of the motion to recommit as codified in House rules over time, the context surrounding changes to the motion to recommit, and the degree to which this tool has served as an effective means for the minority party to shape policymaking, especially in the context of conditional party government in the contemporary House.

Chapter 6 begins a shift in focus from specific procedures to more general congressional operations. In "Let's Vote: The Rise and Impact of Roll Call Votes in the Age of Electronic Voting," Jacob R. Straus examines how electronic voting has impacted House roll call voting activity. In the 1880s, legislative proposals were introduced to create an automated voting system in the House of Representatives. In 1970, with the passage of the Legislative Reorganization Act, the House adopted an electronic voting system, which facilitated the move away from the traditional oral roll call system for recorded votes and decreased the average voting time from approximately forty-five minutes per vote to fifteen minutes or less. This chapter discusses the development of automated voting proposals since the 1880s, examines the legislative history of electronic voting adoption in 1970, explores how the adoption of electronic voting fits with the role parties play in the legislative process, and discusses the effects of electronic voting on floor behavior. Using roll call data, the chapter analyzes the effect of electronic voting on the number of roll call votes per Congress and discusses the possible reasons for the increase in electronic roll call votes since 1973.

Finally, chapter 7 completes the discussion of the House of Representatives by exploring the role that member service organizations (i.e., caucuses) can have on legislative activity. In "The Caucus Process as a Catalyst for Democracy," former Congressman Major Owens examines the history of floor activity by caucuses and reflects on the role the Congressional Black Caucus (CBC) played during debates on many major pieces of legislation. As the former head of the CBC, Congressman Owens brings a unique perspective to this analysis and discusses the challenges caucuses face in coordinating floor activity within a political party. He also reflects on several successes and failures of the caucus during his tenure.

Section III: Senate

Section III covers the Senate and the specific role that party and procedure play in floor debate. Included in this section are chapters about Senate deliberation and negotiation between the majority and minority party, the procedural toolkit available to the majority party for bringing legislation to the floor, the stylized process for creating and passing defense authorization legislation, and the filibuster.

In chapter 8, "The Death of Deliberation: Party and Procedure in the Modern United States Senate," James Wallner brings his valuable insight as a Senate staff member to debunk conventional wisdom that gridlock has debilitated the Senate. Wallner argues that while most scholars maintain that the Senate either operates in a manner that is majoritarian (the majority completely controls debate and blocks the minority) or collegial (an open process allowing equal majority and minority participation), a third type of decision-making exists: structured consent. In this environment, unanimous consent agreements are used to negotiate participation by the majority and minority parties and all senators have opportunities to engage in the legislative process. The chapter explores the influence of party leaders on floor activity and how leaders employ that influence to move the policy process forward on all but the most controversial issues.

Chapter 9 continues the discussion of the power of the majority to set the legislative agenda in the Senate. In "Beyond Motions to Table: Exploring the Procedural Toolkit of the Majority Party in the United States Senate," Aaron S. King, Francis J. Orlando, and David W. Rohde begin by discussing how scholars have often concluded that parties can have little influence in determining policy in the Senate. They turn that idea on its head, however, by exploring recent scholarship that has shown that parties do have an impact on how the Senate operates. One of the means through which this is true is the partisan use of the ability of any senator to table amendments. In this chapter, the authors provide a thorough analysis of motions to table amendments utilizing a new dataset of Senate roll calls ranging from the 91st Congress (1969–1970) through the 111th Congress (2009–2010), in addition to probing the *Congressional Record* for case studies. They examine both frequency and success rates of motions to table by the majority and minority over time and find that the majority is using motions to table more often and with a higher rate of success. They also scrutinize the reasons that the use of tabling motions fluctuate over time and find that the strategy of both the majority and minority parties plays an important role. The results support and augment the existing research that demonstrates the place that motions to table hold in the toolkit of party politics in the Senate.

In chapter 10, "Defense Authorization: The Senate's Last Best Hope," Colleen J. Shogan explores why the Senate's defense authorization process appears to be immune to the partisan obstruction that has stalled the Senate's consideration of many other major pieces of legislation. The chapter begins by examining the legislative process in which defense authorization is considered annually in the United States Senate. Scholars and journalists have noted the increased use of partisan obstruction in the Senate, sometimes referring to it as the chamber where "legislation goes to die." Although obstructionism is pervasive, the defense authorization bill has achieved annual consideration, debate, and passage in the Senate without fail for decades. Using analysis of the *Congressional Record* and interviews with Senate staff, this chapter isolates some of the key characteristics of the defense authorization bill that make it the Senate's "last best hope" for legislative effectiveness.

Finally, in chapter 11, "Filibustering and Partisanship in the Modern Senate," Gregory Koger explains the partisan use of obstruction and cloture in the modern Senate. Both parties try to use the legislative process to improve their brand name reputations. For the majority party, this means trying to enact landmark legislation, to fulfill the basic tasks of Congress, and to provide benefits for individual majority party members. In response, the minority party filibusters to block majority initiatives, to force modifications so they are acceptable to minority party members, and to ensure that minority members receive their fair share of spending and other policy benefits. Also, the minority party may filibuster to take legislation "hostage" until the majority party allows votes on its hot-button proposals. This competition has fed a partisan polarization of voting on cloture.

Section IV: Legislative Reconciliation between the Chambers

Finally, section IV examines the negotiation process between the House and Senate at the end of the legislative process. The first chapter in this section briefly examines conference committees and focuses on alternatives to conference committees available to the House and Senate. The second chapter is a case study of health care legislation in the 111th Congress and describes the various methods used to produce President Barack Obama's signature legislation.

In chapter 12, "Ping Pong and Other Congressional Pursuits: Party Leaders and Post-Passage Procedural Choice," Barbara Sinclair analyzes how, when, and why alternatives to conference committees have been increasingly employed. Using an original dataset, she first reviews evidence showing that the House and Senate are almost always able to resolve their legislative differences. She then examines the mix of procedures used to resolve those differences and argues that changes in reconciliation in the last few years are the result of the majority party leadership's adaptation to changed circumstances, particularly its need to satisfy an increasingly diverse set of caucus (or conference) members. She substantiates her argument by developing and testing hypotheses on the types of major measures on which one would expect alternative procedures to be utilized.

Finally, in chapter 13, "Legislative Sausage-Making: Health Care Reform in the 111th Congress," Mark J. Oleszek and Walter J. Oleszek provide a comprehensive summation of the book's major themes through an examination of President Obama's health care reform legislation in the 111th Congress. In a detailed analysis of the legislative process, Oleszek and Oleszek explore the congressional and political landscape of the 111th Congress, summarize

President Obama's strategic approach, discuss House and Senate action, and outline the attempts to reconcile differences between House and Senate legislation. The chapter concludes with thoughts on the difficulty of passing landmark legislation and what the process used for health care might mean for future attempts to pass comprehensive measures.

Note

1. It should be noted that James Madison initially opposed Hamilton's assumption plan. Only after mediation by Thomas Jefferson was Madison willing to put aside his objections and allow the plan's passage (Ellis 2000, 48–80).

References

Aldrich, John H. 1995. *Why Parties? The Origin and Transformation of Political Parties in America.* Chicago: University of Chicago Press.

Baughman, John. 2006. *Common Ground: Committee Politics in the U.S. House of Representatives.* Palo Alto, CA: Stanford University Press.

Binder, Sarah A. 1997. *Minority Rights, Majority Rule: Partisanship and the Development of Congress.* New York: Cambridge University Press.

Cheney, Richard B., and Lynne V. Cheney. 1996. *Kings of the Hill: How Nine Powerful Men Changed the Course of American History.* New York: Simon & Schuster.

Collie, Melissa P., and Brian E. Roberts. 1992. "Trading Places: Choice and Committee Chairs in the U.S. Senate, 1950–1986." *Journal of Politics* 54:231–45.

Cox, Gary W. 2001. "Agenda Setting in the U.S. House: A Majority-Party Monopoly?" *Legislative Studies Quarterly* 26:185–210.

Dion, Douglas. 1997. *Turning the Legislative Thumbscrews: Minority Rights and Procedural Change in Legislative Politics.* Ann Arbor: University of Michigan Press.

Dodd, Lawrence C. 2001. "Re-Envisioning Congress: Theoretical Perspectives on Congressional Change." In *Congress Reconsidered*, 7th ed., edited by Lawrence C. Dodd and Bruce I. Oppenheimer, 389–414. Washington, DC: CQ Press.

Ellis, Joseph J. 2000. *Founding Brothers: The Revolutionary Generation.* New York: Vintage Books.

Fenno, Richard F. 1973. *Congressman in Committees.* Boston: Little, Brown, and Company.

———. 1997. *Learning to Govern: An Institutional View of the 104th Congress.* Washington, DC: Brookings Institution Press.

Gailmard, Sean, and Jeffery A. Jenkins. 2007. "Negative Agenda Control in the Senate and House: Fingerprints of Majority Party Power." *Journal of Politics* 69:689–700.

Grant, James. 2011. *Mr. Speaker! The Life and Times of Thomas B. Reed, the Man Who Broke the Filibuster.* New York: Simon & Schuster.

Green, Matthew N. 2010. *The Speaker of the House: A Study of Leadership.* New Haven, CT: Yale University Press.

Gryski, Gerard S. 1991. "The Influence of Committee Position on Federal Program Spending." *Polity* 23:443–59.

Hinds, Asher. 1909. "The Speaker of the House of Representatives." *American Political Science Review* 3:155–66.

King, David. C. 1997. *Turf Wars: How Congressional Committees Claim Jurisdiction.* Chicago: University of Chicago Press.

Lazarus, Jeffrey, and Nathan W. Monroe. 2007. "The Speaker's Discretion: Conference Committee Appointments in the 97th through 106th Congresses." *Political Research Quarterly* 60:593–606.

Lebo, Matthew J., Adam J. McGlynn, and Gregory Koger. 2007. "Strategic Party Government: Party Influence in Congress, 1789–2000." *American Journal of Political Science* 51:464–81.

Leighton, Wayne A., and Edward J. Lopez. 2002. "Committee Assignments and the Cost of Party Loyalty." *Political Research Quarterly* 55:59–90.

Lijphart, Arend. 1999. *Patterns of Democracy: Government Forms and Performance in Thirty-Six Countries.* New Haven, CT: Yale University Press.

Maisel, L. Sandy. 1990. "The Evolution of Political Parties: Toward the 21st Century." In *The Parties Respond*, edited by L. Sandy Maisel, 307–23. Boulder, CO: Westview Press.

Martorano, Nancy. 2004. "Cohesion or Reciprocity? Majority Party Strength and Minority Party Procedural Rights in the Legislative Process." *State Politics & Policy Quarterly* 4:55–73.

Polsby, Nelson W. 2004. *How Congress Evolves: Social Basis of Institutional Change.* New York: Oxford University Press.

Reichley, A. James. 1985. "The Rise of National Parties." In *The New Direction in American Politics*, edited by John E. Chubb and Paul E. Peterson, 175–200. Washington, DC: Brookings Institution Press.

Rockman, Bert A. 1994. "The New Institutionalism and the Old Institutions." In *New Perspectives on American Politics*, edited by Lawrence C. Dodd and Calvin Jillson, 143–61. Washington, DC: CQ Press.

Rohde, David W. 1991. *Parties and Leaders in the Postreform House.* Chicago: University of Chicago Press.

Silbey, Joel H. 1994. "The Rise and Fall of American Political Parties, 1790–1993." In *The Parties Respond*, 2nd ed., edited by L. Sandy Maisel, 3–18. Boulder, CO: Westview Press.

Sinclair, Barbara. 1994. "Parties in Congress: New Roles and Leadership Trends." In *The Parties Respond*, 2nd ed., edited by L. Sandy Maisel, 299–318. Boulder, CO: Westview Press.

Stanley, Harold W., and Richard G. Niemi. 2001. "Party Coalitions in Transition: Partisanship and Group Support, 1952–1996." In *Controversies in Voting Behavior*, 4th ed., edited by Richard G. Niemi and Herbert F. Weisberg, 387–404. Washington, DC: CQ Press.

Unekis, Joseph K., and Leroy N. Rieselbach. 1983. "Congressional Committee Leadership, 1971–1978." *Legislative Studies Quarterly* 8:251–70.

Weaver, R. Kent, and Bert A. Rockman. 1993. "When and How Do Institutions Matter?" In *Do Institutions Matter? Government Capabilities in the United States and Abroad*, edited by R. Kent Weaver and Bert A. Rockman, 445–61. Washington, DC: Brookings Institution Press.

White, John Kenneth, and Daniel M. Shea. 2000. *New Party Politics: From Jefferson and Hamilton to the Information Age.* New York: Bedford/St. Martin's.

Wilcox, Clyde. 1995. *The Latest American Revolution? The 1994 Elections and Their Implications for Governance.* New York: St. Martin's Press.

Section I
LEADERSHIP

2

Congressional Leadership

*A Resource Perspective**

Matthew Glassman

I N THE WAKE OF THE 2010 ELECTIONS, House Democrats faced a potential lead-ership contest. Losing majority control of the House meant a Republican Speaker in the 112th Congress (2011–2012), leaving the party with one less leadership position.[1] Outgoing speaker Nancy Pelosi announced she would seek the position of minority leader and, despite some rumbling from dissatis-fied elements of the caucus, no serious opponent stepped forward to challenge her (Dennis 2010c; Hunter 2010a).[2] This left three Democratic leaders from the 111th Congress (2009–2010)—Majority Leader Steny Hoyer, Majority Whip James Clyburn, and House Democratic Caucus Chairman John Lar-son—jockeying for the remaining two available positions: minority whip and caucus chairman (Hunter 2010b).

Both Clyburn and Hoyer announced they would seek the minority whip position, with Clybun specifically stating that he would not accept a demotion to caucus chair (Dennis 2010a; Hunter 2010c). A short campaign commenced. Clyburn and Hoyer both solicited—and received—public support from various representatives and member groups (Hunter 2010d, 2010e, 2010f). Meanwhile, Pelosi and others worked publicly and privately to secure a deal, hoping to avoid a divisive vote in the caucus and potential long-term scars among House Demo-crats (Palmer and Dennis 2010).

After several days, a deal was reached: Clyburn withdrew from the race, averting the need for a secret-ballot caucus election. In exchange, he was named "assistant

*The views expressed herein are those of the author and are not presented as those of the Congressional Research Service or the Library of Congress. Thanks to Jacob Straus and Colleen Shogan for their valuable suggestions and assistance.

minority leader" (Hunter 2010g). The position did not previously exist; it is a new position in the Democratic leadership structure. This raises the question: What exactly did Clyburn get in the settlement that averted the competitive race for minority whip? What did he lose? In his own words, Clyburn indicated that what he was getting was a "seat at the table" with the leadership, a chance to be part of the leadership decision-making process (Hunter 2010g). This is undoubtedly true. But such an intangible authority is hardly worth the paper it is written on. The party leaders could just as easily have given Clyburn (or anyone else) a "seat at the table" without bestowing on him a formal leadership position, and they could just as easily cut him out of the process even with the position.

One way to assess the contest for the minority whip position is from an institutional perspective, which renders it a fight over the formal authority and resources of the leadership position. Stripped to their institutional core, leadership positions in the House and Senate are a collection of formal authorities and resources, derived from statutes, chamber rules, and caucus by-laws. In the case of the Hoyer-Clyburn race for minority whip, much of the formal authority disappears. House rules make no mention of the position of minority whip, and the rules of both the Democratic caucus and Republican conference give the whip position little formal authority (Democratic Caucus 2010; House Republican Conference 2010).

Absent such formal authority, the *institutional* value of the office is largely a sum of the resources that it bestows on the individual, primarily money that can be translated into staff. The resources of the minority whip at the time of the Hoyer-Clyburn race were substantial: an appropriation of $1.69 million that supported a staff of approximately twenty-five and resided in a multi-room suite on the third floor of the Capitol.[3] Winning the post, however, would translate into a net funding cut for either Clyburn or Hoyer; the funding for their previous jobs—majority whip and majority floor leader—in fiscal year 2010 was $2.5 million and $2.1 million, respectively. Even worse, a loss in the race would mean *no* marginal resources. Once out of the leadership, a member must fall back on his personal staff and, if he is entitled to it, committee staff.

The brokered deal that created Clyburn's new "assistant to minority leader" position did not include a public announcement of the resources allocated to the new position, but it is safe to assume they are more than nothing. The creation of a new leadership position by party leaders, however, does not enlarge the size of the total resource pie. Without the unlikely cooperation of the House Appropriations Committee, funding for Clyburn's new position will have to come out of existing funding provided to the Democratic leadership, in effect forcing Pelosi, Hoyer, and the House Democratic infrastructure to make room for Clyburn out of their own resources. It is unclear, according to House expenditure reports, how much money and staff have been dedicated to Mr.

Clyburn.[4] His office space, however, has been reduced to H-133, a small office on the first floor of the Capitol.

Following from this illustration, the remainder of this chapter places the leadership structures of the House and Senate into the context of material resources. It first outlines a theory of leadership power based on resources. It then surveys the contemporary leadership resource structure of the House and Senate. Finally, it examines trends in leadership resources, using appropriations and staffing data from the past thirty years.

A Resource-Based View of Leadership Power

Theories of congressional leadership power can be grouped into three general categories. The oldest and most traditional views leadership power and success as a function of individual ability (Neustadt 1990; Ripley 1967; Caro 2002). Weak leaders do not have the necessary attributes or abilities; strong ones do. Assembling winning coalitions is a difficult task, and leaders cannot simply sit around and wait; they must use their skills of persuasion and legislative procedure to "grow the vote" (Arnold 1990). A second viewpoint—informational theories—presents leaders as clerks, greasing the institutional skids for the preferences of the median member of the chamber (Krehbiel 1991), severely limited in their independent ability to influence outcomes. Leadership may organize and manage the orderly production of policy outcomes, but it is ultimately a servant of the median member.

Finally, a third body of scholarship focuses on the institutional context of leadership (Jones 1968; Cooper and Brady 1981; Rohde 1991; Cox and McCubbins 1993; Evans and Oleszek 1999; Cox and McCubbins 2005; Sinclair 2007). Leaders are empowered as agents of the rank-and-file (Sinclair 1983); their institutional authority reflects the preferences and degree of homogeneity within the party caucus. An ideologically unified party will empower leadership with formal authority through amendment of chamber and party rules; a heterogeneous coalition will strip the central leadership of the same authority (Rohde 1991; Aldrich and Rohde 2000; Gamm and Smith 2001). Similarly, leaders are in a competitive power environment with other internal institutions. Whenever the rank-and-file choose to weaken a competing authority—such as during the committee reforms of the 1970s—leaders inherently stand to gain (Sinclair 2007).

Most contextual-institutional theories focus on the formal authority given to leaders through chamber and party rules, or the balance of authority between leadership and committee chairs, or leadership and individual members. One limitation of this perspective is that the formal authority granted to the leadership is usually limited to only the very top leadership. For example, the rules of the House grant significant authority to the Speaker, but very little to the minority leader, and virtually none to the majority leader or whips. Party rules are similarly thin on the formal powers of inferior leaders.

An alternative way to contextualize congressional leadership is through the material resources allocated to it. Previous studies (Hall 1987) have understood resources as an important factor in the strategic choices legislators make. Leadership is granted specific material resources—money, offices space, media access—not given to rank-and-file members, and such asymmetrical distribution allows leaders numerous advantages that can be leveraged to exert control over their members' legislative choices (Sinclair 1983; Curry 2011).

Most importantly, leaders can translate material resources into an informational advantage. Information, both policy and political, is valuable to members of Congress (Kingdon 1973; Hall 1987; Hall 1996; Curry 2011), and any source of cheap and reliable information will be well used by members. Leadership can translate money into dedicated and well-paid staff expertise across numerous policy areas, which can generate high-quality policy and political information for members. Rank-and-file members can then choose to rely on the leadership information, or try to gather their own. Their relatively small personal resource allocation, however, yields them fewer staff, who are often less experienced and stretched across multiple responsibilities (Curry 2011).

Leadership can also use resources to gather information and control the distribution of information. Individual members do not have the staff capacity to actively monitor the dynamics of other members' preferences across even a minimal number of issues. Leadership, however, controls the whip system, whose primary function is to gather information from individual members and distribute information back to the same members. Rank-and-file members have little ability to coordinate and share information across issues without using such a centralized, and leadership-controlled, system.

Finally, leadership has informational advantages through their public-facing operations. While the prestige and authority of their positions allow them greater media access than rank-and-file members, their resource advantage allows them to leverage this access. Individual members typically employ a single communications director, whose press relationships are typically dominated by local, district-oriented newspapers. Leadership may employ entire media teams—communications directors, deputy communications directors, speechwriters, webmasters, and even dedicated "new media" personnel.

This resource-information perspective encourages us to view leadership not just as a collection of discreet authorities given to specific individuals, but also as a capacity to dominate the production and flow of information on Capitol Hill. With such information domination, leadership can more easily enforce their preferences upon the rank-and-file, even when such preferences drift away from the caucus median. And just as the institutional authority handed to leadership ebbs and flows contextually over the course of time, so does the resource capacity of the congressional leadership. The remainder of this chapter takes an in-depth look at the primary resource advantage of leadership—money—and the principal use to which it is put—staff.

Congressional Leadership Funding

Contemporary appropriations for House and Senate leadership are contained in the annual legislative branch appropriations act, which contains funds for the operation of the House of Representatives, Senate, and legislative branch support agencies such as the Library of Congress.[5] Total leadership funding is contained in a variety of sub-accounts within the bill. In the fiscal year 2010 act, for example, there were sixteen separate line-items that contained House leadership funding, and twelve separate line-items that contained Senate leadership funding.[6]

The leadership funding structure of the two chambers is similar, but not identical.[7] As shown in table 2.1, in both chambers there are named sub-accounts

TABLE 2.1
Leadership Accounts in the FY2010 Legislative Branch Appropriations Act

House **(Under "Salaries and Expenses")* ***(Under "House Leadership Offices")*	*Senate* **(Under "Salaries, Officers, and Employees")*
Speaker's Office	Offices of the Majority and Minority Leaders
Speaker's Office for Legislative Floor Activities	Office of the Vice President
Majority Floor Leader	Office of the President Pro Tempore
Majority Whip's Office	Office of the Majority and Minority Whips
Minority Floor Leader	Conference Committees
Six/Nine Minority Employees	Policy Committees
Republican Steering Committee	Secretaries for the Majority and Minority
Republican Conference	Expense Allowance for Majority and Minority Secretaries
Republican Policy Committee	Expense Allowance for Leadership
Democratic Steering and Policy Committee	Representational Allowance for Leadership
Democratic Caucus	Miscellaneous Items
Training and Policy Development—Majority	
Training and Policy Development—Minority	
Cloakroom Personnel—Majority	
Cloakroom Personnel—Minority	

Source: P.L. 111-68, 2010, Legislative Branch Appropriations, 123 Stat. 2023

that fund the principal chamber leaders,[8] as well as named sub-accounts that fund the policy arms of the majority and minority parties of each chamber.[9] In addition, there are Senate accounts that fund offices for the vice president and the president pro tempore.[10] In both chambers, funds can be transferred between the various leadership accounts.[11]

The funding structure for House leadership provides separate sub-accounts for the named majority and minority leadership; the Senate funding is provided in single sub-accounts with report language that stipulates the funding be divided equally between the majority and minority (United States Congress 2009c). While there have been a handful of changes to the account structure in the past decades, for the most part the funding structure in fiscal year 2010 is similar to that of thirty years ago.[12]

Not all leadership positions are directly funded; while the parties are free to create their own leadership structures, the appropriations process creates a de facto official list of offices from a financial point of view. Therefore, positions such as "assistant to the Speaker," which was held by Representative Chris Van Hollen and then Representative Xavier Becerra under Speaker Pelosi in the 110th and 111th Congresses, needed to be supported through funds authorized and appropriated for other leadership positions. In practice, funding for the small assistant to the Speaker staff was provided through funds appropriated and disbursed for the Speaker's office (United States Congress 2009a). Similarly, any resources given to Representative Clyburn in his capacity as assistant minority leader will likely be funded in this manner.[13]

In fiscal year 2010, a total of $47,539,000 was appropriated to these sub-accounts, which represents just over 1 percent of total funding for the legislative branch.[14] Of the total amount, $25,881,800 was appropriated for House leadership and $21,658,000 for Senate leadership, which was slightly less than 2 percent of the total appropriation for House operations and slightly more than 2 percent of the total appropriation for Senate operations, respectively.[15]

Approximately two-thirds of House leadership funding is core funding, with one-third going to party policy operations. Funding appropriated to the majority and minority for policy operations is identical; each party received $3,064,000 for its respective caucus/conference accounts and $787,000 for cloakroom personnel and training and development accounts. Such even-handed treatment of the majority and minority conforms to theories of legislature professionalization, which suggest that a well-professionalized legislature will see fewer instances of strongly asymmetric allocations of resources between the majority and minority (Polsby 1968).

Funding for the core leadership, however, is not distributed evenly between the majority and minority; the majority received 57 percent of the total core leadership funds in fiscal year 2010. On first glance, it might appear that the funding gap is entirely due to the existence of the Speaker, who received over $5.5 million in fiscal year 2010 and who has no equivalent position in the minority party. The minority leader, however, received close to *double* the funding of the majority leader, placing him closer in line with the Speaker from a resource perspective.

Thus, it makes more sense to compare the core leadership funding by considering the majority to be composed of the Speaker, the majority leader, and the majority whip, with the minority equivalents being the minority leader, the minority whip, and the "nine minority employees" account, which has no majority equivalent. From this perspective, funding for the minority positions is approximately 81 percent, 67 percent, and 70 percent of the funding for the corresponding majority positions. This perhaps better reflects the disparity in workload between the majority and minority in the House.

Unlike House leadership funding, Senate leadership funding includes virtually no distinction between the majority and the minority. Funds for the majority and minority leaders and majority and minority whips are evenly divided, as are funds for the conference committees, policy committees, and secretaries of the conferences. This probably reflects the weaker role of leaders in the Senate, and the smaller disparity between majority and minority responsibility for crafting floor agendas and scheduling legislation.

Congressional Leadership Staffing

As a political resource, money is instrumental. In regard to congressional leadership, the primary expenditure of official appropriations is for staff. In fiscal year 2010, for example, the Speaker's office spent 91 percent of its funding on personnel (United States Congress 2010, 1–6).[16] In part, the high percentage spent on staff is explained by the resources that are provided to leadership free of charge. Office space in the Capitol is provided at no cost, and the cost of already-existing furniture is not charged against spending accounts. Most of the explanation, however, lies in the nature of the job: congressional leadership does not require much travel, and contract services for office supplies, food, and information technology resources are not particularly expensive.

In effect, the running of a leadership office is the research, production, management, and dissemination of ideas and information, and that primarily requires people. Technological advances and increases in the complexity of governing have resulted in greater demand for policy expertise (Romzek and Utter 1997). The legislative branch of the federal government as a whole saw a marked increase in staff during the twentieth century (DeGregorio 1994), and congressional staffers are perceived as having significant influence over public policy (Manley 1966; Kofmehl 1977; Malbin 1980; Rundquist, Schneider, and Pauls 1992). For congressional leaders to wield significant informational influence, they need an army that can collect, produce, and distribute proprietary information.

Identifying and counting leadership staff is a tricky endeavor, and almost any methodology needs to be taken as an estimate, especially methodologies seeking temporal consistency. Here, we employ data compiled by Petersen and colleagues (2010), who used a count of employees drawn from House and Senate phone directories. Authorizations for these positions come in two forms: statutory authorization for specific positions ("statutory employees") and statutory authorizations for the discretionary use of money to hire employees however the employing office sees fit ("lump-sum employees"). Both types of authorizations are permanent; the statutory employees system is largely an outgrowth of the historical practice of naming individual congressional employees in appropriations acts (Rogers 1941), while the lump-sum system is a more flexible design that came to prominence beginning in the mid-twentieth century. The House currently uses a mix of statutory and lump-sum authorization; the Senate has largely replaced its statutory leadership positions with an entirely lump-sum system.[17]

In addition to legal limitations, such as maximum salary, placed on these positions through their authorizations or annual chamber pay orders, party rules in both chambers may direct the use of leadership staff. For example, the conference rules of the House Republicans specifically provide for the shared use of leadership staff, under the direction of the Republican leader (Speaker or minority leader), and in particular put the Republican leader in direct authority over the Republican floor assistants and Republican conference (House Republican Conference 2010, 35–36). Such coordinated use of party leadership staff is common, and blurs the lines when differentiating between different employing offices; leadership staff may often be technically employed by one office but doing collective leadership work (Rundquist, Schneider, and Pauls 1992).

A total of 228 House and 175 Senate leadership employees were identified for 2010. This estimated leadership staff of 403 is a small percentage of total congressional staff. Peterson and colleagues (2010) estimated that a total of 9,889 people are employed by the House and 6,099 by the Senate, making leadership staff just over 2 percent of all staff in the House and less than 3 percent in the Senate. The vast majority of House and Senate staff work in members' personal offices (over 70 percent in the House and Senate) or for committees (15 percent House; 20 percent Senate).

In the House, the distribution of staff between core leadership and party organization is heavily tilted toward the core leadership. Of the 228 leadership staff, 166 were employed in the core leadership office. The Democratic Caucus and Steering Committee employed only 26 people; the Republican Conference and Policy Committee just 26 as well. Within the core leadership, two-thirds of the staff (102) were working for the majority; the Speaker's office alone employed 59 people. Senate leadership staff are distributed in an altogether different arrangement. The core leadership staff account for less than half (74) of all leadership staff; the party organizations employ a slightly larger number (84).

Leadership staff serve in a variety of capacities. For example, an analysis of job descriptions among staff in the Speaker's office produces thirty-five different job titles.[18] This diversity of positions reflects—and has enabled—trends in leadership informational power in recent decades.

Leadership Resource Trends

The institutional role of congressional leadership, particularly in the House, has changed dramatically in the past generation (Jones 1968; Sinclair 1999). As party ideologies have become more homogenous, the party caucuses have placed increased institutional authority in the hands of leaders (Aldrich and Rohde 2000). Individual leaders, particularly Speaker Gingrich (1995–1998), have been identified as transformative figures in the institutional development of the chambers (Sinclair 1999). Concepts that would have been unimaginable during the 1970s— such as the perception that a two-thousand-page bill was "written in the Speaker's Office"—have become commonplace (*Congressional Record* 2010, H761).

How have the resources of leadership changed during this period? In this section, we examine the dynamics of House and Senate leadership funding and staffing between 1982 and 2010. Data here are drawn from two sets of sources. Appropriations data on the funding of leadership accounts are drawn from House and Senate appropriations materials, including annual and supplemental bills, committee and conference reports, subcommittee prints, and chamber expenditure reports. Data on staffing of leadership offices are drawn from Petersen and colleagues (2010), who used a count of employees drawn from House and Senate phone directories. The primary conclusion is simple: leadership resources have increased dramatically in the past thirty years.

Changes in Leadership Appropriations, 1982–2010

Two key questions arise when considering the temporal dynamics of leadership funding: First, has the overall amount of funding changed over time and, second, has the distribution of the funding changed over time? In fiscal year 1982, total leadership funding in the House and Senate was $9.7 million; in fiscal year 2010, total leadership funding (in constant 1982 dollars) was $21.0 million. In effect, leadership funding has more than doubled in the past thirty years.

Figure 2.1 plots the total leadership appropriations, by chamber, from 1982 until 2010, using constant 1982 dollars.

As shown in figure 2.1, both House and Senate leadership funding has increased steadily during the past thirty years. House leadership funding, however, has shown more dramatic growth; after not increasing much at all relative to inflation between 1982 and 1989, between 1989 and 2010 it increased by 239

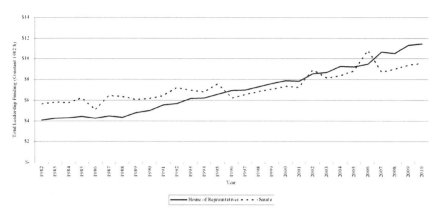

FIGURE 2.1
Total Leadership Funding, by Chamber, FY1982–FY2010 (constant 1982 dollars).
(Annual and Supplemental Appropriation Acts, FY1982–FY2010)

percent. Senate funding during the same period increased by 157 percent. In comparison, overall non-leadership House funding increased 64 percent during the same period, overall non-leadership Senate funding increased 57 percent, and the entire budget for the legislative branch, adjusted for inflation, increased 49 percent between 1982 and 2010.

Overall funding growth in the House and Senate also does not appear to be related to any specific changes in leadership. Examination of the sub-accounts, however, shows a significant change in the allocation of leadership appropriations. Figure 2.2 plots the percentage increase in Speaker, minority leader, all other core funding, and party leadership funding.

As shown, funding growth has been strongest for the Speaker and minority leader, followed by party funding and other core leadership positions. The growth, however, has not been steady over time. Initially, funding growth for the Speaker's office and the minority leader lagged behind growth for party

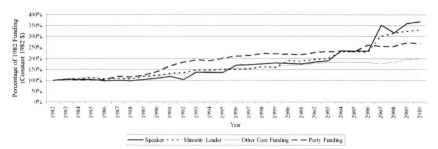

FIGURE 2.2
House Speaker, Minority Leader, Party, and Other Core Funding, FY1982– FY2010 (percentage of 1982 funding, constant 1982 dollars). (Annual and Supplemental Appropriation Acts, FY1982–FY2010)

and other core leadership. Beginning in 2004, however, the Speaker's office and minority leader's office have seen a tremendous increase in resources, with total real funding for the two offices nearly doubling between 2003 and 2010. In particular, fiscal year 2007 stands out; the Speaker's office saw an almost 50 percent increase in funding, while the minority leader's office saw a 30 percent increase. These changes have not significantly affected the balance of funding distribution; as with the 2010 distribution shown in figure 2.2, the breakdown was similar in 1982: the core majority leadership received approximately 40 percent of funds, core minority 30 percent, and the party organizations 15 percent each.

Changes in Senate leadership funding have shown a different dynamic. Almost all of the growth has been centered in the core leadership. Figure 2.3 plots the percentage of 1982 funds in real dollars, 1982 to 2010.

As shown, total core leadership funding has increased at a much faster pace than either party funding or funding for the vice president. Core leadership funding has increased 486 percent since 1982; funding for the party organizations and the office of the vice president have remained almost flat by contrast, increasing only 33 percent and 12 percent in real dollars over thirty years.

Changes in Leadership Staff, 1980–2011

The natural consequence of the increased appropriations to leadership in the House and Senate has been an increase in the number of staffers working for leadership. In 1982, there were a total of 71 core leadership employees in the House and 27 in the Senate. By 2010, there were 166 core leadership employees in the House and 74 in the Senate (Petersen et al. 2010). This represents an increase of 233 percent in the House and 274 percent in the Senate. Party leadership offices saw smaller, but still significant, growth in staff over the same period.

These figures vastly outstrip overall staffing growth in Congress. Between 1982 and 2010, total staff in the House increased just 11 percent. In the Senate, overall

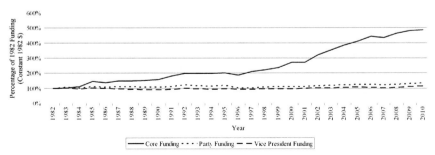

FIGURE 2.3
Senate Core, Party, and Vice President Funding, FY1982–FY2010 (percentage of 1982 funding, constant 1982 dollars). (Annual and Supplemental Appropriation Acts, FY1982–FY2010)

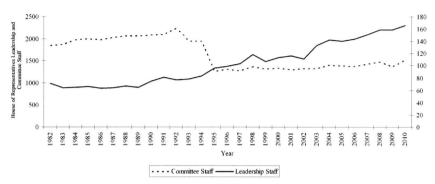

FIGURE 2.4
House Core Leadership and Committee Staff, 1982–2009. (House Telephone Directories, 1982–2009)

staff increased 52 percent. Of particular note is the continued growth of leadership staff in the House after 1995. While member office and committee staff was reduced by an estimated 11 percent and 35 percent, respectively, in 1995 and have never returned to pre-1995 levels, leadership staff continued to grow throughout the same period. Figure 2.4 plots the growth of House leadership staff against the decline in House committee staff.

In effect, the total distribution of House staff on the Hill has bent away from committee staff and toward member offices, leadership, and officer staff.

A second important finding is the large increase in staff in the Speaker's office. In 1982, the Speaker's office employed just fourteen people. By 2010, the staff had more than quadrupled to fifty-nine people. Figure 2.5 plots the growth in Speaker's office staff, with demarcations for the presiding Speaker.

As shown, the growth of the Speaker's office staff has not been steady. Instead, it has seen two significant increases. The first is the well-known increase under Speaker Gingrich in 1995, in which the staff of the Speaker's office went from ten to twenty-eight and then peaked at thirty-eight in 1998. The second is a similar increase in 2007 under Speaker Pelosi. After staffing levels were more or less constant or saw a slight decline under Speaker Hastert, they nearly doubled between 2006 and 2008, going from thirty-six to sixty-four staffers.

Conclusion

Three observations accompany this analysis. First, the substantial increase in leadership resources over the past thirty years is consistent with most accounts of congressional institutional development during the same time period, which understand the empowerment of leaders in both the House and Senate as a meaningful and durable institutional change to the structure of the legislature.

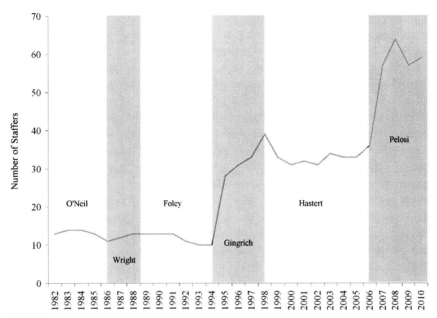

FIGURE 2.5
Staff Employed by the Office of the Speaker, 1982–2010. (House Telephone Directories, 1982–2010)

It is important, however, to differentiate resource capacity from formal authority. While both may be empowered by the same underlying contextual factors (such as homogenous majority caucuses), the processes by which each strand of leadership power is enhanced are fundamentally different. Alteration of House and caucus rules takes place almost entirely between the biennial elections and the start of a new Congress; changes in the resource capacity of the leadership take place under the appropriations process, which runs on the fiscal calendar. Furthermore, changes in leadership appropriations, while subject to chamber-wide votes on final passage of the legislative branch appropriations bill, are not widely debated or even brought up for stand-alone votes.

Second, the very existence of significant leadership resources is a (relatively) modern phenomenon. Powerful leaders (such as Speaker Cannon) existed prior to substantial material resources being available to leadership, and they relied on institutional authority to wield influence. As numerous historical analyses have shown, the relative powers of the leadership and the committee system have ebbed and flowed over the last 150 years (Binder 1997; Cooper and Brady 1981). This ebb and flow, however, has mainly been through the dynamic of formal authority under chamber rules, not through the balance of resource allocation.

Viewed in this light, resource allocation has become a second track of relative power in Congress. One difference, however, is that the rank-and-file have shown little interest over time in reducing the resources of leadership; while committee and member personal resources have at times seen drastic cuts, leadership resources have continued to grow. When combined with the separate process for producing them, it is an open question as to whether future congresses—even ones interested in empowering the committee system relative to the leadership—will seek direct reductions in the resources of the central leadership.

Finally, the establishment of a durable institutional bureaucracy under the leadership, and particularly under the Speaker, may have long-term consequences for congressional policymaking. Like the creation of the Executive Office of the President in the 1930s or the entrenchment of the congressional committee system in the postwar era, we may be witnessing a transformational period in the fundamental nature of the leadership offices. Such past expansions have had dramatic effects on the functioning of the core institutions. In the case of congressional leaders, this beefing up and entrenching of the bureaucratic structure may serve to attenuate future attempts to limit the formal authority of the institutions.

Notes

1. Neither the caucus rules of the House Democrats nor the conference rules of the House Republicans provide for a leadership position parallel to the Speaker when the party is in the minority (Democratic Caucus 2010; House Republican Conference 2010).

2. Representative Heath Shuler formally opposed Pelosi, but admitted publicly from the outset that he did not "have the numbers to win," and that his candidacy was a protest against her leadership (Dennis 2010e). Pelosi won the secret ballot caucus vote 190–43 (Hunter 2010h).

3. In fiscal year 2010, the office of the minority whip employed people in the following positions: chief of staff, two communications directors, deputy coalitions director, special assistant, press secretary, policy advisor, legislative counsel, senior advisor for defense policy, director of new media, associate director of new media, deputy scheduler, strategic communications, deputy director of coalitions, speechwriter, and a financial administrator. In addition, the office employed four staff assistants, three floor assistants, a paid intern, and three shared employees (United States Congress 2010, 17–19).

4. The 2011 House telephone directory lists two senior staff and three support staff for the assistant to the minority leader.

5. For a complete breakdown of legislative branch appropriations funding, see Brudnick (2011).

6. These figures do not include the accounts that fund agency contributions for leadership staff. *Fiscal Year 2010 Legislative Branch Appropriations Act*, P.L. 111-68, 123 Stat. 2023, October 1, 2009.

7. By long-standing practice, the House and Senate do not participate in the appropriations process for the internal affairs of the other chamber; each chamber passes the appropriations for the other without comment. See United States Congress (2009b, 2).

8. In the House, this includes the "Speaker's Office," "Speaker's Office for Legislative Floor Activities," "Majority Leader's Office," and "Majority Whip's Office." In the Senate, this includes the "Offices of the Majority and Minority Leaders" and "Offices of the Majority and Minority Whips."

9. In the House, these accounts are "Republican Steering Committee," "Republican Conference," "Republican Policy Committee," "Democratic Steering and Policy Committee," "Cloakroom

Personnel—Majority," "Cloakroom Personnel—Minority," "Democratic Caucus," "Training and Program Development—Majority," and "Training and Program Development—Minority." In the Senate, these accounts are "Conference Committees," "Officers of the Secretaries of the Conference," "Policy Committees," "Secretaries for the Majority and Minority," "Expense Allowances for the Majority and Minority Secretary," "Expense Allowances for Leadership," and a "Miscellaneous Items" account, which includes funds for conference committee expenses, consultants to the majority and minority leader, and policy committee expenses.

10. These accounts are "Office of the Vice President" and "Office of the President Pro Tempore."

11. House leadership offices have unilateral ability to transfer funds among the various offices. See *U.S. Code* 2 (1999), § 74a-11. Senate leadership offices require approval of the Senate Committee on Appropriations. See *U.S. Code* 2 (1982) § 64-2; United States Congress (2009c, 7).

12. For example, in the fiscal year 1982 legislative branch appropriations act, there was no "Speaker's Office for Legislative Floor Activities," all Republican party funding was combined into the "Republican Conference" account, there were no accounts for "Training and Program Development," and the "Cloakroom Personnel" accounts were still funded through appropriations for the clerk of the House. In the Senate, there was an account for "Floor Assistants to the Majority and Minority Leaders," which was abolished in fiscal year 1984.

13. It is also possible, but unlikely, that a new leadership office could be authorized and funding appropriated.

14. Total funding for the legislative branch in fiscal year 2010 was $4,656,031, which includes funds for the House, Senate, Joint Items, Capitol Police, Office of Compliance, Congressional Budget Office, Architect of the Capitol, Library of Congress, Government Printing Office, Government Accountability Office, Open World Leadership Center, and Stennis Center for Public Service.

15. Total funding for the House of Representatives in fiscal year 2010 was $1,369,025; total funding for the Senate in fiscal year 2010 was $926,160,000. See *Fiscal Year 2010 Legislative Branch Appropriations Act*, P.L. 111-68, 123 Stat. 2023, October 1, 2009.

16. The remainder of funds expended by the Speaker's office went to travel, supplies and materials, printing and reproduction, equipment, "rent, communications, and utilities," and "other services."

17. P.L. 95-26, 91 Stat. 80, May 4, 1977.

18. Job titles in the Speaker's office include scheduler, assistant scheduler, advance director, policy director, deputy director for policy, policy advisor, chief of staff, assistant to the chief of staff, press advisor, communications director, deputy communications director, director of protocol and special events, press assistant, researcher, press secretary, floor assistant, floor director, director of information technology, deputy director for member services, directory of member services, special assistant, personal assistant, deputy chief of staff, staff assistant, special assistant, financial administrator, director of new media, deputy floor director, chief counsel, director of intergovernmental affairs, speechwriter, senior advisor for strategic planning, and counsel to the Speaker.

References

Aldrich, John H., and David W. Rohde. 2000. "The Consequences of Party Organization in the House: The Role of Majority and Minority Parties in Conditional Party Government." In *Polarized Politics: Congress and the President in a Partisan Era*, edited by Jon Bond and Richard Fleisher, 31–72. Washington, DC: Congressional Quarterly Press.
Arnold, R. Douglas. 1990. *The Logic of Congressional Action.* New Haven, CT: Yale University Press.
Binder, Sarah A. 1997. *Majority Rights and Minority Rule: Partisanship and the Development of Congress.* New York: Cambridge University Press.

Brudnick, Ida. 2011. "Legislative Branch: FY2011 Appropriations." *Congressional Research Service.* Washington, DC: Library of Congress.

Caro, Robert A. 2002. *Master of the Senate: The Years of Lyndon Johnson.* New York: Alfred A. Knopf.

Congressional Record. 2010. 111th Cong., 2nd sess., February 24. Vol. 156, pt. 7.

Cooper, Joseph, and David W. Brady. 1981. "Institutional Context and Leadership Style: The House from Cannon to Rayburn." *American Political Science Review* 75:411–25.

Cox, Gary W., and Mathew D. McCubbins. 1993. *Legislative Leviathan: Party Government in the House.* Berkeley and Los Angeles: University of California Press.

———. 2005. *Setting the Agenda: Responsible Party Government in the U.S. House of Representatives.* New York: Cambridge University Press.

Curry, James M. 2011. "Information and Majority Leadership Power in the House of Representatives." Paper presented at the annual meeting for the Midwest Political Science Association, Chicago, Illinois, March 31–April 3.

DeGregorio, Christine. 1994. "Professional Committee Staff as Policymaking Partners in the U.S. Congress." *Congress and the Presidency* 21:49–65.

Democratic Caucus, U.S. House of Representatives. 2010. "Rules of the Democratic Caucus."

Dennis, Steven T. 2010a. "Hoyer Makes Whip Bid Official." *Roll Call,* November 8.

———. 2010b. "Pelosi Seeking End to Hoyer-Clyburn Race." *Roll Call,* November 9.

———. 2010c. "Shuler Ready to Challenge Pelosi in Contest He Can't Win." *Roll Call,* November 14.

Evans, C. Lawrence, and Walter Oleszek. 1999. "The Strategic Context of Congressional Party Leadership." *Congress and the Presidency* 26:1–20.

Gamm, Gerald, and Steven S. Smith. 2001. "The Dynamics of Party Government in Congress." In *Congress Reconsidered,* 7th edition, edited by Lawrence C. Dodd and Bruce Oppenheimer, 245–68. Washington, DC: Congressional Quarterly Press.

Hall, Richard L. 1987. "Participation and Purpose in Committee Decision Making." *American Political Science Review* 81:105–27.

———. 1996. *Participation in Congress.* New Haven, CT: Yale University Press.

House Republican Conference. 2010. "Rules of the House Republican Conference for the 112th Congress."

Hunter, Kathleen. 2010a. "Pelosi Running for Minority Leader." *Roll Call,* November 5.

———. 2010b. "Hoyer, Clyburn Pull Weekend Whip Duty to Lock in Support." *Roll Call,* November 6.

———. 2010c. "Clyburn on Chairing Caucus: Been There, Done That." *Roll Call,* November 8.

———. 2010d. "Members Supporting Clyburn." *Roll Call,* November 8.

———. 2010e. "Members Supporting Hoyer." *Roll Call,* November 8.

———. 2010f. "CBC Endorse Clyburn for Whip." *Roll Call,* November 9.

———. 2010g. "Clyburn to Serve as Assistant Leader." *Roll Call,* November 13.

———. 2010h. "Pelosi Wins Bid for Leader Despite 43 Defections." *Roll Call,* November 17.

Jones, Charles O. 1968. "Joseph G. Cannon and Howard W. Smith: An Essay on the Limits of Leadership in the House of Representatives." *Journal of Politics* 30:617–46.

Kingdon, John W. 1973. *Congressmen's Voting Decisions.* New York: Harper & Row.

Kofmehl, Kenneth. 1977. *Professional Staffs of Congress.* West Lafayette, IN: Purdue University Press.

Krehbiel, Keith. 1991. *Information and Legislative Organization.* Ann Arbor: University of Michigan Press.

Malbin, Michael J. 1980. *Unelected Representatives: Congressional Staff and the Future of Representative Government.* New York: Basic Books.

Manley, John F. 1966. "Congressional Staff and Public Policy-Making." *Journal of Politics* 30:1046–67.

Neustadt, Richard. 1990. *Presidential Power and the Modern Presidents.* New York: Free Press.

Palmer, Anna, and Steven T. Dennis. 2010. "Pressure Builds for Deal in Hoyer-Clyburn Race." *Roll Call*, November 8.

Petersen, Eric, Parker Reynolds, and Amber Wilhelm. 2010. "House of Representatives and Senate Staff Levels in Member, Committee, Leadership, and Other Offices, 1977–2010." *Congressional Research Service*. Washington, DC: Library of Congress.

Polsby, Nelson. 1968. "The Institutionalization of the U.S. House of Representatives." *American Political Science Review* 62:144–68.

Ripley, Randall B. 1967. *Party Leaders in the House of Representatives*. Washington, DC: Brookings Institution.

Rogers, Lindsay. 1941. "The Staffing of Congress." *Political Science Quarterly* 56:18–19.

Rohde, David W. 1991. *Parties and Leaders in the Postreform House*. Chicago: Chicago University Press.

Romzek, Barbara S., and Jennifer A. Utter. 1997. "Congressional Legislative Staff: Political Professionals or Clerks?" *American Journal of Political Science* 41:1251–79.

Rundquist, Paul S., Judy Schneider, and Frederick H. Pauls. 1992. "Congressional Staff: An Analysis of Their Roles, Functions, and Impacts." *Congressional Research Service*. Washington, DC: Library of Congress.

Sinclair, Barbara. 1983. *Majority Leadership in the U.S. House*. Baltimore, MD: Johns Hopkins University Press.

———. 1999. "Transformational Leader or Faithful Agent? Principal-Agent Theory and House Majority Party Leadership." *Legislative Studies Quarterly* 24:421–49.

———. 2007. *Unorthodox Lawmaking: New Legislative Processes in the U.S. Congress*. Washington, DC: Congressional Quarterly Press.

United States Congress. 2009a. *Statement of Disbursements of the House, January 1, 2009, to March 31, 2009*, 111th Cong., 1st sess., H. Doc. 111-26. Washington, DC: Government Printing Office.

———. 2009b. *Legislative Branch Appropriations Bill, 2010*, 111th Cong., 1st sess., 2009, H. Rpt. 111-160. Washington, DC: Government Printing Office.

———. 2009c. *Legislative Branch Appropriations Bill, 2010*, 111th Cong., 1st sess., S. Rpt. 111-29, 6-9. Washington, DC: Government Printing Office.

———. 2010. *Statement of Disbursements of the House, July 1, 2010, to September 30, 2010*, 111th Congress, 2nd sess., H.Doc. 111-151. Washington, DC: Government Printing Office.

Whittington, Lauren W., and Steven T. Dennis. 2010. "House Democrats Reach Leadership Deal." *Roll Call*, November 12.

Section II
HOUSE OF REPRESENTATIVES

3

Toppling the King of the Hill

*Understanding Innovation in House Practice**

James V. Saturno

I N THE SPRING OF 2011, a *CQ Today Online News* headline trumpeted, "Battle to Balance Budget May Resurrect Vintage Floor Move." The vintage procedure in question was a "king-of-the-hill" rule; a method for structuring the amendment process that had not been used by the House since 1994, and the close cousin of which, a queen-of-the-hill rule, had not been used since 2002. Despite this long dormancy, the practice nevertheless remains in the mind of lawmakers and observers as a viable and potentially useful method for the consideration of legislation. To understand why, it is necessary to look back and trace the life cycle of the practice to assess how it developed as an innovative procedural tool for House leadership, how well it worked, and why, ultimately, it has fallen into disuse. By doing so we may gain not only a more accurate view of the importance of this device, but also better insight into the forces that drive procedural innovation in the House.

The chief role of the Rules Committee in the modern House of Representatives is to regulate the consideration of major legislation on the floor. Toward that end, under both Democratic and Republican majorities, the committee has developed an arsenal of practices to assist lawmakers in navigating an increasingly difficult lawmaking environment. Limited only by their imagination for crafting procedural tools and their ability to command the support of their party, the members of the Rules Committee majority have been the chief instrument through which the majority party leadership has attempted to balance

---

*The views expressed herein are those of the author and are not presented as those of the Congressional Research Service or the Library of Congress. This chapter has benefited from the insightful comments of Richard Beth, Richard Forgette, Valerie Heitshusen, and Elizabeth Rybicki. The analysis and conclusion presented are solely the responsibility of the author.

deliberation and decision-making in the consideration of legislation by the House. Barbara Sinclair has described "unorthodox lawmaking" as the willingness to adapt the way in which legislation is considered to confront specific political, substantive, or procedural problems and suggested that a hallmark of congressional practice in recent years has been for leaders to modify or transform existing procedures and practices as necessary in order to facilitate lawmaking (Sinclair 2007, 287).

The means by which the Rules Committee performs this role is to report a resolution privileged for consideration by the House, called a special rule or, simply, a rule. When adopted by the House, the provisions of a special rule can supersede the standing rules of the House—as well as rulemaking provisions in statutes such as the Congressional Budget Act—but only in application to the specific measure named in the resolution. Special rules serve two key functions: (1) to enable the House to consider a specified measure, and (2) to establish terms for considering it, including any modifications to the amending process. In the modern era, the Rules Committee has developed and discarded numerous ways of structuring the consideration of legislation as the lawmaking environment has evolved. As is widely recognized, a key component of this development has been the increasing use of rules that restrict or regulate the offering of amendments. King-of-the-hill rules are only one example of the kind of rules that became more commonplace during the 1980s in order to exert greater control over floor consideration (Bach and Smith 1988; Marshall 2002).

To grasp the way in which king-of-the-hill rules can affect the amendment process it is useful to look at some of the potential limitations imposed by the regular amending process. House procedures do not allow for amendments that would re-amend a portion of the text of a measure under consideration that has already been amended. One recourse can be to allow a member the opportunity to offer a second-degree amendment to a pending first-degree amendment, which would then be voted on first. This can allow the House an opportunity to decide between the two alternatives. A shortcoming of this approach, however, is that if the House adopts the second-degree amendment, its text replaces that of the initial amendment, and the House never gets an opportunity to vote directly on that initial amendment. In addition, if the second-degree amendment replaces the entire text of the first-degree amendment, its adoption precludes the House from considering any further alternative to the first-degree amendment. Any attempt to do so would constitute an attempt to re-amend already amended text in contravention of House rules. The regular amending process does not permit members to adopt an amendment without simultaneously preventing a vote on others.

This principle can be particularly important in the case of an amendment that proposes a complete substitute for the text of a pending measure. Once a full substitute has been adopted, no further amendments to any portion of the measure are in order, since any would constitute attempts to re-amend already amended text.

Special rules, however, can provide that an amendment be in order "notwithstanding the adoption of a previous amendment." Such a structure can be used to afford the House the opportunity to vote in succession on each of several competing alternatives for the same text. Beginning in 1980, the House Rules Committee developed a standard form for special rules that would provide such a structure. These rules came to be called king-of-the-hill rules because they provided that, if more than one alternative were adopted, the last one that secured a majority vote would be the one considered as finally adopted.

Initially, king-of-the-hill rules were used infrequently, only once in the 96th Congress (1979–1980), four times in the 97th Congress (1981–1982), and twice in the 98th Congress (1983–1984), and many observers typically associated them only with considering amendments in the nature of a substitute for the concurrent resolution on the budget. This is not surprising, since they were first used for the consideration of a budget resolution and were used for the consideration of fourteen of the fifteen budget resolutions considered between 1980 and 1994. Over time, however, king-of-the-hill rules came to be used somewhat more frequently, and for a wider variety of measures, peaking at 13 percent of all special rules in the 101st Congress (1989–1990) when 15 out of a total of 115 special rules adopted for the consideration of bills and resolutions were king-of-the-hill rules. Special rules could also incorporate more than one king-of-the-hill structure for considering alternatives to only a portion of a measure, such as a single title or section. For example, during the 100th Congress, H.Res. 435 and H.Res. 436 together incorporated ten separate king-of-the-hill structures for considering alternatives to different provisions in H.R. 4264 (the Department of Defense authorization bill). In all, as shown in table 3.1, between 1980 and 1994, eighty-seven king-of-the-hill structures were provided in sixty-six special rules.

After the 1995 transition to a Republican majority, the Rules Committee stopped using king-of-the-hill rules. Occasionally it used a modified form in which, if more than one alternative obtained a majority, the one considered as finally adopted would be the one that received the greatest number of votes. These rules have been termed "queen-of-the-hill" or "most votes wins" rules. In all other respects, the queen-of-the-hill structure works in the same manner as its predecessor. The Rules Committee, however, reported queen-of-the-hill rules infrequently, using them on only three occasions in the 104th Congress (1995–1996), twice in the 105th Congress (1997–1998), and once in the 107th Congress (2000–2001), before discontinuing the practice entirely. In all cases, the rules provided for amendments in the form of full substitutes.

Because king-of-the-hill rules provided that only the last alternative to secure a majority vote would be considered as adopted, the perception developed that the order in which amendments could be offered had a significant effect on

TABLE 3.1

King-of-the-Hill Rules in the House of Representatives, 1980–2002

Rule	Date	Measure
		King-of-the-Hill
96th Congress (1979–1980) (1)		
H.Res. 642	April 23, 1980	H.Con.Res. 307—FY1981 budget resolution
97th Congress (1981–1982) (4)		
H.Res. 134	April 30, 1981	H.Con.Res. 115—FY1982 budget resolution
H.Res. 198	July 29, 1981	H.R. 4242—Tax Incentive Act of 1981
H.Res. 477	May 21, 1982	H.Con.Res. 345—FY1983 budget resolution
H.Res. 604	October 1, 1982	H.J.Res. 350—balanced budget constitutional amendment
98th Congress (1983–1984) (2)		
H.Res. 476	April 4, 1984	H.Con.Res. 280—FY1985 budget resolution
H.Res. 519	June 11, 1984	H.R. 1510—Immigration and Nationality Act amendments (four structures)
99th Congress (1985–1986) (8)		
H.Res. 136	April 23, 1985	H.J.Res. 247—paramilitary operations in Nicaragua
H.Res. 174	May 21, 1985	H.R. 1460—Anti-apartheid Act of 1985
H.Res. 177	May 22, 1985	H.Con.Res. 152—FY1986 budget resolution
H.Res. 186	June 6, 1985	H.R. 2677—supplemental appropriations
H.Res. 331	December 5, 1985	H.R. 2817—environmental superfund amendments
H.Res. 455	May 14, 1986	H.Con.Res. 337—FY1987 budget resolution
H.Res. 481	June 25, 1986	H.R. 5052—Military Construction Appropriations
H.Res. 531	August 7, 1986	H.R. 4428—DOD Authorization (four structures)
100th Congress (1987–1988) (8)		
H.Res. 139	April 8, 1987	H.Con.Res. 87—FY1988 budget resolution
H.Res. 156	May 6, 1987	H.R. 1748—DOD Authorization
H.Res. 160	May 7, 1987	H.R. 1748—DOD Authorization (five structures)
H.Res. 219	July 8, 1987	H.R. 2342—Coast Guard Authorization
H.Res. 410	March 23, 1988	H.Con.Res. 268—FY1989 budget resolution
H.Res. 435	April 26, 1988	H.R. 4264—DOD Authorization (five structures)*
H.Res. 436	April 28, 1988	H.R. 4264—DOD Authorization (five structures)
H.Res. 521	August 11, 1988	H.R. 5210—omnibus drug initiative (two structures)**
101st Congress (1989–1990) (15)		
H.Res. 111	March 22, 1989	H.R. 2—Fair Labor Standards Act amendments
H.Res. 135	April 26, 1989	H.R. 2072—Dire Emergency Supplemental Appropriations
H.Res. 145	May 3, 1989	H.Con.Res. 106—FY1990 budget resolution
H.Res. 165	June 7, 1989	S.J.Res. 113—U.S./Japan joint development of FSX aircraft*
H.Res. 173	June 14, 1989	H.R. 1278—Financial Institutions Reform, Recovery and Enforcement Act
H.Res. 211	July 24, 1989	H.R. 2461—DOD Authorization
H.Res. 249	September 27, 1989	H.R. 3299—Omnibus Budget Reconciliation Act of 1989 (two structures)

Rule	Date	Measure
H.Res. 382	April 26, 1990	H.Con.Res. 310—FY1991 budget resolution
H.Res. 388	May 9, 1990	H.R. 770—Family and Medical Leave Policy Act
H.Res. 395	May 23, 1990	H.R. 4636—assistance to Panama and Nicaragua
H.Res. 399	May 23, 1990	H.R. 3030—Clean Air Act amendments (four structures)
H.Res. 434	July 17, 1990	H.J.Res. 268—balanced budget constitutional amendment
H.Res. 457	September 10, 1990	H.R. 4739—DOD Authorization
H.Res. 461	September 12, 1990	H.R. 4739—DOD Authorization
H.Res. 490	October 3, 1990	H.R. 5269—Comprehensive Crime Control Act of 1990

102nd Congress (1991–1992) (15)

Rule	Date	Measure
H.Res. 105	March 12, 1991	H.R. 1315—RTC funding
H.Res. 123	April 16, 1991	H.Con.Res. 121—FY1992 budget resolution
H.Res. 156	May 20, 1991	H.R. 2100—DOD Authorization
H.Res. 162	June 4, 1991	H.R. 1—Civil Rights Act amendments
H.Res. 247	October 16, 1991	H.R. 3371—Omnibus Crime Control Act of 1991
H.Res. 266	October 31, 1991	H.R. 6—FDIC Reform Act
H.Res. 275	November 13, 1991	H.R. 2—Family Medical Leave Act
H.Res. 320	November 26, 1991	H.R. 3435—RTC Refinancing, Restructuring, and Improvement
H.Res. 374	February 26, 1992	H.R. 4210—Economic Growth Acceleration Act
H.Res. 386	March 4, 1992	H.Con.Res. 287—FY1993 budget resolution
H.Res. 447	May 7, 1992	H.R. 4990—Rescinding Certain Budget Authority
H.Res. 450	June 10, 1992	H.J.Res. 290—balanced budget constitutional amendment
H.Res. 474	June 3, 1992	H.R. 5006—DOD Authorization (two structures)
H.Res. 513	July 9, 1992	H.R. 5518—Department of Transportation Appropriations*
H.Res. 590	October 2, 1992	S. 1696—Montana National Forest Management Act

103rd Congress (1993–1994) (13)

Rule	Date	Measure
H.Res. 133	March 18, 1993	H.Con.Res. 64—FY1994 budget resolution
H.Res. 246	September 8, 1993	H.R. 2401—DOD Authorization
H.Res. 254	September 28, 1993	H.R. 2401—DOD Authorization
H.Res. 293	November 8, 1993	H.Con.Res. 170—removal of armed forces from Somalia*
H.Res. 336	February 3, 1994	H.R. 3759—supplemental appropriations
H.Res. 384	March 10, 1994	H.Con.Res. 218—FY1995 budget resolution
H.Res. 401	April 13, 1994	H.R. 4092—Violent Crime Control and Law Enforcement Act
H.Res. 429	May 18, 1994	H.R. 4301—DOD Authorization
H.Res. 431	May 23, 1994	H.R. 4301—DOD Authorization
H.Res. 484	July 21, 1994	H.R. 4604—Budget Control Act of 1994
H.Res. 509	August 9, 1994	H.R. 4590—Granting MFN status to China

(*continued*)

TABLE 3.1
(continued)

Rule	Date	Measure
H.Res. 512	August 11, 1994	H.R. 4907—Full Budget Disclosure Act
H.Res. 570	October 6, 1994	H.J.Res. 416—limited authorization for U.S. troops in Haiti

Queen-of-the-Hill

104th Congress (1995–1996) (3)		
H.Res. 44	January 25, 1995	H.J.Res. 1—balanced budget constitutional amendment*
H.Res. 116	March 28, 1995	H.J.Res. 73—term limits constitutional amendment
H.Res. 119	March 22, 1995	H.R. 4—Personal Responsibility Act
105th Congress (1997–1998) (2)		
H.Res. 47	February 21, 1997	H.J.Res. 2—term limits constitutional amendment
H.Res. 442	May 21, 1998	H.J.Res. 119/H.R. 2183—campaign finance reform
107th Congress (2001–2002) (1)		
H.Res. 344	February 12, 2002	H.R. 2356—campaign finance reform

*Indicates a case in which more than one amendment offered was agreed to

outcomes. Indeed, one recent study stated that "virtually every contemporary textbook on Congress takes at face value that the [king-of-the-hill] rule was used by the Democratic leadership to sequence alternatives in such a way as to help ensure the ultimate passage of bills in forms suitable to the party leadership." Specifically, the perception is that the structure of king-of-the-hill rules allowed electorally vulnerable members to vote in favor of two or more options, thereby providing political cover and at the same time allowing the party leadership to build winning coalitions around their preferred option. The study concluded that, based on the number of members who voted in favor of multiple options, the conventional wisdom about the use of such rules was largely supported (Miller, Moffett, and Overby 2010, 16).

Where this analysis falls short, however, is in answering the question of why king-of-the-hill rules *in particular* were used. None of the arguments regarding members voting on multiple alternatives is dependent on those alternatives being offered in a king-of-the-hill amendment structure. Some members will undoubtedly vote for more than one option in any situation in which multiple choices are available, especially if the ultimate outcome is not in doubt. Such opportunities are not unique to king-of-the-hill rules, however, and may be afforded by any rule that structures the amending process. As the historical record demonstrates, the number of occasions on which the Democratic leadership may have been pressed by marginal members to provide such opportunities is exceedingly small. In addition, concerns about electoral vulnerability did not end in the 103rd Congress. Republican majorities in the 104th Congress through the

109th Congress (2005–2006) only rarely used their queen-of-the-hill variation even though they would presumably have had the same incentives to protect electorally vulnerable members of their conference. Democrats did not revive their use in the 110th Congress (2007–2008) and 111th Congress (2009–2010). That they did not do so illustrates a need for a better explanation, one that explains why this particular form of restrictive rule was developed in the first place, and which may also help us to understand its demise as well.

One of the most salient facts about the historical record on the use of king-of-the-hill rules is the infrequency with which multiple alternatives were adopted. In 93 percent of the king-of-the-hill structures identified (81 out of 87), one or none of the alternatives were adopted. If the six queen-of-the-hill rules are added to this total, the percentage rises a bit to almost 94 percent (86 out of 93). This record indicates that despite the conventional wisdom that the sequencing of amendments allowed for the majority leadership to exercise partisan control, it rarely mattered in practice. Given that the peculiar feature of king-of-the-hill rules rarely came into play, one has to ask what advantage they offered to the majority leadership that distinguished them from other forms of restrictive rules or the regular order for the amending process and, thus, serves as a better explanation for their origin and use.

One possible answer comes from the Rules Committee itself. In the *Survey of Activities of the House Committee on Rules* compiled at the end of the 103rd Congress, the committee explained the use of king-of-the-hill rules this way:

> The procedure was created to provide Congress a fair procedural way to debate and dispose of broad policy alternatives. Most "King of the Hill" amendments are amendments in the nature of a substitute proposing competing budget priorities, foreign policy strategies, or major defense weapons options. Since the regular amendment process does not provide Members with a way to decide upon each policy choice independently, according to its own merit, the "King of the Hill" procedure guarantees that each amendment will be voted on regardless of the disposition of any of the alternatives. It gives members maximum ability to examine a range of policies and to work its will on each major policy choice. (U.S. Congress 1994, 25)

Before accepting this explanation, it is important to examine the historical record in order to put king-of-the-hill rules in their proper context. Eric Schickler (2001) posits that a wide range of collective interests drive institutional change in Congress, and that more than one interest can be significant in bringing about any change. Furthermore, different interests can be important at different points in time. The particular form and use of king-of-the-hill rules suggest that different forms of restrictive rules were developed to deal with different circumstances.

The circumstances that existed in the 96th Congress were different from those in the 103rd Congress or that exist today, and theoretical constructs developed to explain the actions of the Rules Committee or the functions of special rules are not robust over time and across legislative contexts (Marshall 2002). The procedural problems that were perceived to exist or what options were available for managing the consideration of bills on the House floor have changed over time so that choices, and their implications, in 1980 meant something different from what they meant in 1994 or would mean today. For example, other changes in rules and practices have had an impact on the minority's ability to get a vote on its preferred policy alternative. In particular, a change in House Rules in the 104th Congress effectively guaranteed the minority the right to offer a motion to recommit with "instructions to report back an amendment otherwise in order" (Lynch 2011). The historical context was changed because by providing a guarantee to the minority through the motion to recommit, the new rule changed the pressure on the Rules Committee majority to provide the minority with a guarantee through the amendment process. Perhaps the most salient thing to keep in mind then is that the early use of king-of-the-hill rules, and perception of them, occurred in an era when restrictive rules, and restrictions on the amending process generally, were far less common than they are today, and that they were designed to allow the Rules Committee to address problems specific to that time.

A partisan theory of Rules Committee behavior asserts that it uses its agenda control powers to shape policy choices in a way that benefits the majority party (Rohde 1991; Cox and McCubbins 1993; Marshall 2002). In the context of the 96th Congress, however, benefiting the majority was not just about shaping policy choices, but also about time management. A feature of structured rules is that they not only restrict policy choices, but they also limit the amount of time necessary to arrive at the ultimate choice. Restrictive rules benefit the majority party, not simply because they can be used as an instrument of party power, but also because they can improve the institutional capacity of the House to act on legislation in a timely and predictable manner. The need to establish such an instrument came about because one effect of the reforms of House procedure in the 1970s was an overall increase in amendment activity, among both minority Republicans and junior Democrats. The increase, along with the time it consumed and the unpredictability it created, caused problems for all representatives by making it more difficult for the House to reach a conclusion in the consideration of legislation (Bach and Smith 1988, 31). Representative David Bonior characterized the House of the late 1970s as "anarchy, chaos, a lot of wasted time" (Hook 1987, 2451). In 1979, Representative John LaFalce of New York, along with over forty colleagues, sent a letter to the Speaker and the Rules Committee complaining of inefficiency and suggested a "judicious expansion" of the use of restrictive rules (quoted in Bach and Smith 1988, 33). Data compiled by the Republican staff of the House Rules Committee illustrate the impact of this expansion and show an increase in the percentage of restrictive rules of all types—growing from 12 percent in the 95th Congress (1977–1978) to 70 percent in the 103rd Congress (*Congressional Record*, Oct. 7, 1994, 29203). The search for an answer to the question of why king-of-the hill rules in particular came about must begin in that context, and it also must attempt to separate them from a discussion of restrictive rules more broadly.

First Use

Consideration of budget resolutions prior to 1980 tended to be a messy affair, and House leadership seemed to regard it as a growing problem. The Congressional Budget Act (CBA) had only been put into effect in 1975, and in many ways the House was still trying to work out its implementation. In 1978, it had taken a full week and twenty-one roll call votes to get through consideration of the budget resolution. In 1979, it was even worse. Consideration had been scheduled for three days, but ended up being stretched to two weeks and thirty-six roll call votes. The difficulties of trying to consider the budget resolution in the House under an open amending process had become obvious and some complained that protracted debate on the resolution revealed a fallacy in the new budget process itself. Some representatives were concerned that debate focused on the wrong things, going beyond the intended purpose of setting overall spending and tax policies and becoming focused on specific programs. Representative Jaime Whitten, chair of the Appropriations Committee, was concerned that while line-item recommendations in the budget process had no direct binding impact, they "obscure[d] the overall macroeconomic responsibilities of the Budget Committee" and demonstrated that the House might be "losing sight of the basic objectives of the Budget Act" (*CQ Weekly Report* 1979, 878). Representative Richard Bolling, chair of the Rules Committee and one of the coauthors of the act, stated more simply that the budget process "has gotten less and less macro, and more and more micro," and "that's exactly the opposite of what I had in mind." He's further quoted as saying that "we have to devise a technique whereby those who wish to use the budget process as a means of making political points are limited to making political points on macro issues" (*CQ Weekly Report* 1979, 879; Smith 1989, 40).

In 1980, things were going to be different, and H.Res. 642, the rule reported by the Rules Committee for consideration of H.Con.Res. 307, the first budget resolution for fiscal year 1981, showed just how different. Instead of an open amending process, the rule made in order a handful of specific amendments, mostly substitutes for the full text of the resolution. In managing the rule for the Democrats, Mr. Bolling stated:

> It is obviously an unusual rule and this is an unusual situation. We spent a lot of time crafting the rule and we tried to take into consideration all of the broad interests that were present in the House of Representatives on this very difficult matter.

With the exception of a couple of amendments on revenue sharing and one particular corrective amendment to be offered by the chairman of the Budget Committee, virtually everything is a real substitute.

It is just as fair as we could make it and not leave it wide open. We had an experience with the wide open consideration of these matters that made it pretty clear that the House did not like it. (Bolling 1980, 8789–90)

In addition to shifting the focus of consideration to a limited number of broad substitutes, however, what made this an unusual rule was the provision that stated, "If more that one of the amendments in the nature of a substitute made in order by this resolution has been adopted, only the last such amendment which has been adopted shall be considered as having been finally adopted and reported back to the House."

In devising this new procedure, the Rules Committee was making it possible to expand the number of substitutes that could be considered beyond that which would normally be in order under the regular amending process. More importantly, it was to guarantee that all of the substitutes thus made in order would actually get debated and voted on.

Managing H.Res. 642 on behalf of the Republicans, Representative Del Latta, ranking member on the Budget Committee and a member of the Rules Committee, expressed qualified support. He described the rule as a compromise and stated, "Certainly, every person who would like to offer an amendment . . . could not be given an opportunity if we are going to attempt to limit debate somewhat during the consideration of this first budget resolution." Although he was sorry that additional amendments weren't made in order, he further stated, "On balance I believe it is a fair procedure and a compromise that probably should be acted upon favorably by this House" (Latta 1980, 8790–91).

Debate on the rule by other members did not even mention the novel feature that guaranteed that all of the substitutes made in order would be debated. Instead, members focused on the fact that, for the first time, the House would be allowed only to debate a limited number of substitutes. In the course of debating the rule, some representatives expressed concern with a "take it or leave it" approach that prevented them from addressing individual programs separate from a substitute for the whole budget that could contain many other decisions to which they might be opposed. Others simply criticized the limited number of alternatives. Representative Robert Bauman said:

If your name is Giaimo, Conable, Quillen, Obey, Mitchell of Maryland, Solarz, Ottinger, Holt, Latta, or Rousslot then all is well and good and you are high on the hog. I do not say that in any denigration of the Members involved. They were able to get their part of the deal arranged either for the inherent merit of their proposals, or their good looks, or talent, or whatever else commended them to the Rules Committee. But for the rest of the House of Representatives, most of the 435, they are out in the cold. They get to vote on these few propositions and nothing else, and that is all. Good luck, you can go back to your people and explain why you are not important enough to be included in this club. (Bauman 1980, 8795)

In the end, despite misgivings and uncertainty about the new approach to considering the budget resolution, the House voted 261–143 to adopt the rule, with Democrats voting 219–40 and Republicans voting 42–103.

The chief aim of the Rules Committee in this instance does not seem to have been stricter partisan control, but rather to promote the capacity of the budget process to achieve agreement on an overall budget policy and keep the debate at a big-picture level, while simultaneously allowing members from both parties to have an opportunity to be heard. The chief criticism leveled by members in this first instance, especially from the minority, was the restriction on the nature and number of amendments made in order, and not the unique procedural properties of king-of-the-hill rules (i.e., that the last alternative approved would win). The five amendments in the nature of substitutes for the budget resolution that made up this first king-of-the-hill structure, even with the other amendments allowed under the rule, concerned representatives because they represented significantly more limited opportunities than members had previously experienced or expected under an open amending process.

In looking at this rule it is notable that the two substitutes to be offered by Democrats were placed first, and the three to be offered by Republicans were placed in what has been described by scholars as the more advantaged later positions. In addition, two additional Democratic amendments (those offered by Representatives Parren Mitchell and Stephen Solarz) were second-degree amendments offered as substitutes for the Obey amendment (the first substitute to be offered), rather than as amendments to the budget resolution itself, placing them in even less-advantaged positions since they would have to survive an even greater number of votes to be successful. Ultimately, however, the order in which the amendments were offered did not play a significant role, as none of the amendments were adopted, and only the Obey amendment attracted more than two hundred votes (losing 201–213).

Early Development

The next king-of-the-hill rule was not considered by the House until the 97th Congress, and it was again for consideration of the budget resolution. In April 1981, the Rules Committee reported H.Res. 134. Like its predecessor in the previous Congress, this rule provided for a limited number of substitutes that would be in order in a specified sequence, each remaining in order even if any previous amendments were adopted, and "if more than one of the amendments in the nature of a substitute made in order by this resolution have been adopted, only the last such amendment which has been adopted shall be considered as having been adopted and reported back to the House."

During consideration of H.Res. 134, Representative Robert Walker raised a series of questions that expressed for the first time concerns of the minority with the nature of a king-of-the-hill rule. He began by stating that "another key element of it [the rule] is, that in reality, a majority of this House could vote for every one of the amendments and end up with the final amendment being adopted as the will of the House. Is that correct?" When Representative Bolling confirmed this, Mr. Walker continued, "And so, therefore, the Rules Committee has really structured the rule in a way which, by order, can very much make the difference as to how we finally come out on the determination of the House with regard to the budget. Is that not the case?" (Walker 1981, 7994). The possible effect of sequence was dismissed by Representative Bolling, but Mr. Walker continued along these lines and stated that "it seems to me that we have here the first major closed rule that we will have in the Congress, and what does concern me is the fact that by establishing the order of consideration, the Rules Committee may have set a precedent as to other kinds of rules that we will be considering of a controversial nature, and thereby present us with this dilemma at several points in the future. Could the chairman comment on that particular concern of this Member?" Mr. Bolling responded simply by stating, "This is not a new procedure. . . . This is precisely what was done with the last occasion, I believe, that we dealt with the budget. There is nothing new about this procedure. There is no precedent [being set]" (Bolling 1981, 7994).

Although Mr. Walker's concerns were framed in terms of a concerned minority, it does not appear that at this time king-of-the-hill rules were perceived in purely partisan terms. Opposition to the rule came chiefly from Democrats concerned with the limited opportunities members would have to offer amendments. For example, Representative Carl Perkins lamented, "If this package is forced down our throats, if we are denied the opportunity to amend or modify it—or even to strengthen it if the need may be shown—then we are surrendering our responsibilities" (Perkins 1981, 7994). Representative Theodore Weiss was even more direct, and suggested that the House vote to "defeat the rule and to send the matter back to the Committee on Rules, hopefully to have them report out an open rule where all amendments will be in order" (Weiss, 1981, 7995). On the other hand, Representative Trent Lott, a Republican on the Rules Committee, expressed support and stated that "by reporting a rule of this nature, the committee has insured that each significant point of view espoused by Members of this body will have adequate debate and consideration" (Lott 1981, 7997). The resolution was adopted by the House, 328–76, with Democrats voting 170–60 and Republicans voting 158–16 (*Congressional Record*, April 30, 1981, 8003).

As in 1980, the order in which the amendments were offered does not correspond to the assumption that the last amendment in the sequence would be reserved for the position supported by the majority leadership. Instead, the first two substitutes were offered by Democrats and the final substitute was offered by the ranking Republican on the Budget Committee, Representative Latta. Representative Walker's concerns notwithstanding, the two Democratic alternatives received only 69 and 119 votes before the Republican alternative, embodying the Reagan administration's first budget proposal, was adopted, 253–176, with Democrats voting 63–176 and Republicans voting 190–0 (*Congressional Record,* May 7, 1981, 9016).

A king-of-the-hill rule was next used a couple of months later for consideration of the Tax Incentive Act of 1981. The rule, H.Res. 198, made two substitutes in order, and its consideration did not give rise to any discussion of the procedure for their consideration. The rule was adopted, 280–150 (*Congressional Record,* July 29, 1981, 18045). Again, the Republican alternative, embodying the Reagan administration's tax proposals, was successfully considered in the final position, but since the Democratic alternative had previously been rejected, the king-of-the-hill provision in the rule had no impact.

By the following year, when it was again used for consideration of the budget resolution, the procedure appears to have been given a name and was being referred to in the press as a "king-of-the-mountain" rule (Tate 1982, 1174). H.Res. 477 provided a complex amending process, with seven amendments in the nature of substitutes in order, five of them subject to additional perfecting amendments. Neither the fact that the rule had a king-of-the-hill structure nor the order in which the substitutes would be considered, however, drew any significant criticism, although it was the first time that a majority-sponsored amendment (by Representative James Jones, the Budget Committee chair) would be offered in the final position. Representative Lott, managing consideration for the Republicans, did engage Minority Leader Michel in a discussion of the rule on the House floor during which the latter made it clear to members that "the last vote on a substitute is the one that is controlling" (Lott 1982, 11092). Despite the restrictions in the rule, Representative Lott said:

> It represents, in my opinion, the best efforts, although not perfect, of the leadership on both sides of the aisle to fashion a fair and equitable approach to this extremely complex issue.
>
> We [the Republicans] did get what we asked for under the rule, and that is the clear choice between our plan and the Jones bill. (Lott 1982, 11091)

The rule was adopted by voice vote. During the course of consideration of the budget resolution none of the substitutes achieved a majority vote, the closest being the substitute offered by Representative Latta, which lost 192–235.

The fourth and final time a king-of-the-hill rule was used in the 97th Congress was for consideration of H.J.Res. 350, a balanced budget constitutional amendment. H.Res. 604, the rule for its consideration, was reported by the Rules Committee to preempt another rule (H.Res. 450) following a successful discharge effort. Its provisions were discussed only briefly, and it provided for only two alternatives under a king-of-the-hill procedure. What is significant about it is the way in which the king-of-the-hill procedure was structured. The first alternative made in order was an amendment in the nature of a substitute to be offered by Representative Bill Alexander, and the second was a substitute to be offered by Representative Barber Conable consisting of the same text as the underlying measure. The rule was structured in this way because if the Alexander amendment were adopted, the House would not be able to vote on the Conable language directly, in manner similar to the regular order in which voting to adopt one alternative may have the effect of preventing a vote on another alternative. By providing that the Conable language could be offered as an amendment in the event that the Alexander amendment were adopted, the House was able to ensure a direct vote on both alternatives. This would prove to be a common use of the rule in the years to come, with the original bill language being in order as the final alternative. The Alexander amendment was rejected, however, 77–346, and the Conable language was not offered as an amendment. Instead, the House simply voted on the Conable language when it voted on the measure.

In the 98th Congress, king-of-the-hill procedures were used only twice. The first was for the consideration of the H.Con.Res. 280, the fiscal year 1985 budget resolution. In managing consideration of H.Res. 476 for the majority, Representative Butler Derrick stated:

> While the rule is not technically complex, it does involve a number of amendments and a slightly unusual procedure. Because of this, and because the matters being considered are so important, I want to take a few minutes to make sure that every Member understands what the rule does.
>
> The rule involves what some people refer to as a "King of the Mountain" procedure. House Concurrent Resolution 280 is made in order as the original text. Eight amendments in the nature of a substitute are made in order as amendments to that. . . . [B]ecause the amendments in the nature of a substitute are by definition mutually exclusive, the rule provides that, if more than one substitute is adopted in the Committee of the Whole, only one of those—the last one adopted—will be reported back to the House. Thus "King of the Mountain," where the last amendment standing is the winner. (Derrick 1984, 7772)

Debate on the rule was short, but the minority expressed a variety of opinions on its impact. Managing the rule for the minority, Representative Latta said, "As far as the Rules Committee is concerned, I think it has done a good job in reporting out a rule that everyone can live with" (Latta 1984, 7774). Representative

Walker offered no opinion on the king-of-the-hill procedure itself, but expressed concern that "this rule gives the minority a little, but it gives the majority a lot. This rule is typical of the way we operate around here all the time: Using the power of the majority to give special advantages to the majority when it comes to consideration of legislation" (Walker 1984, 7774). Representative Bill Frenzel's opinion was more mixed and he stated that, in his opinion, "the 'last passed wins' rule is not perfect, but it far surpasses last year's 'first over the top' rule which eliminated debate and amendments. But to say that this is at least not a blatant gag rule is surely to damn with faint praise" (Frenzel 1984, 7774).

Again, the last amendment made in order was an amendment that could be offered by the Budget Committee chair consisting of the text of the measure as introduced in order to ensure that the original language in the measure would get a direct vote. None of the first seven substitutes achieved more than 132 votes, so the final substitute was not offered.

The second king-of-the-hill rule in the 98th Congress was unique because, unlike all of its predecessors, it did not make in order substitutes for the entire text of the bill. Instead, H.Res. 519 provided that in four specific policy areas within H.R. 1510, the Immigration and Nationality Act amendments, the House would consider two or three specified alternatives, and that if more than one of the alternatives were adopted, only the last would be considered as finally adopted. This was done, in the words of Representative Claude Pepper, the Rules Committee chairman, to "allow the House the opportunity to consider a variety of policy options insuring [*sic*] that conflicting policies would not be reported back to the House" (Pepper 1984, 15693). This new usage drew no criticism during debate on the rule or during consideration of the amendments. In two cases, one of the amendments in order was adopted.

At this stage of its development and usage, the king-of-the-hill procedure was generally not characterized during debates in any way that was substantially different from any other form of restrictive rule. The form of the rule was evolving, however. In the first several instances of its use, the minority was allowed to go last. By the 98th Congress, the last slot was more typically reserved to allow the original text of the measure to be considered as the final amendment in order to ensure a direct vote in the event that one or more of the other amendments had already been adopted, although it seldom proved necessary to offer this amendment. In addition, the first six times the procedure was used, it was for the purpose of considering amendments in the nature of substitutes, mutually exclusive options for the measure as a whole. The seventh time it was applied, it was used to provide for the consideration of amendments to a smaller portion of the measure in order to guarantee direct votes by the House on multiple, mutually exclusive, options on a specific issue. While the minority was not always satisfied with the amending options left available to them under these rules, there was very little criticism directed at the king-of-the-hill procedure itself as unfair.

Even from this limited sample, then, it is hard not to conclude that at this stage, the king-of-the-hill rule was being used in the way the Rules Committee characterized it: as a way to guarantee debate and a direct vote on specified options, albeit within the construct of a restrictive rule that limited debate and amending options typically to complete alternatives.

Proliferation and Opposition

Over the course of the next five congresses (1985–1994), king-of-the-hill procedures became increasingly common. There were eight such rules in both the 99th and 100th Congresses, fifteen each in the 101st and 102nd Congresses, and thirteen in the 103rd Congress. By 1985, the pattern had generally been set for their use. King-of-the-hill rules were used for the consideration of budget resolutions (ten times) for reasons that have already been described. In addition, king-of-the-hill structures were routinely incorporated into special rules providing for consideration of defense authorization measures (fourteen times) and various other foreign relations/use of the military issues (nine times, including several on appropriations measures). These are the types of measures that have typically been viewed in strictly partisan terms. Although the theoretical possibility that king-of-the-hill rules could produce confusion would eventually be raised as an issue, the historical record does not seem to indicate that members of the House considered the procedure difficult to understand. Speaking in favor of the king-of-the-hill rule in 1994, Democratic Representative Barney Frank stated:

> People are for or against the king-of-the-hill rule, depending on which hill it is. The notion that the king-of-the-hill rule somehow distorts the House probably ought to be taken down when mentioned. That is, it unfairly denigrates the House, because the argument is that when Members vote for something, they cannot understand that if they later vote for something else, they will undo what they did.
>
> In other words, the notion is that the Members are so stupid that, having voted for something once, they will then vote for something else and not understand that they have undone it. Obviously, the king-of-the-hill rule fools no one and is intended to fool no one. It is a rational way to structure a lot of different preferences. (Frank 1994, 20479)

Between 1985 and 1994, each budget resolution was considered under the terms of a king-of-the-hill rule that made in order an average of 3.7 substitutes per year. Of the thirty-seven substitutes offered in this period, only one was adopted. In 1987, an amendment offered by the chairman of the Budget Committee as the first amendment of four was adopted. None of the three remaining alternatives that year received more than fifty-six votes. Looking at the entire ten-year period, in only five years did any losing substitute receive more than one hundred votes, and in no year did the order in which substitutes were offered play any role in the outcome. In fact, over the entire period, the procedure was clearly used as a means for allowing different groups in both parties to demonstrate their own budget priorities. Allowing this kind of broad position-taking was undoubtedly intended to have some election-oriented benefit for those offering the alternatives, but it does not seem clear that there was a singular intent underlying the motivation of the Rules Committee, since the outcome was never in any serious doubt.

Beginning in 1986, the idea of using a king-of-the-hill structure to consider mutually exclusive alternatives within a specific policy area rather than substitutes for an entire measure took hold for consideration of competing programs within defense authorization measures. In some cases, more than one special rule was used to provide for consideration of one of these bills, and in some years a special rule might provide for multiple king-of-the-hill structures for various issues, so that the number of king-of-the-hill structures varied from one (for 1989 and 1991) to ten (for 1988). In all, a total of thirty policy issues were subjected to king-of-the-hill structures.

In only one of these cases was there more than one alternative adopted, bringing the unique feature of king-of-the-hill rules into play. In 1988, one of the issues addressed in H.R. 4264, the defense authorization bill, was nuclear testing. Competing amendments were made in order, which would provide first for a sense of Congress provision supporting the efforts of the Reagan administration to negotiate effective nuclear testing regimes with the Soviet Union, and subsequently for an amendment reiterating previous enactments placing limits on U.S. nuclear explosive testing, a position opposed by the administration (Towell 1988, 1141). The first amendment was adopted by a vote of 399–0, and the second was subsequently adopted by a vote of 214–186, superseding the first. Despite the unprecedented nature of this result, there does not seem to have been any significant consternation afterward regarding the procedure that allowed this action to occur.

This was not to be the only case, however, in which a king-of-the-hill rule allowed an amendment to be adopted only to be subsequently superseded when a second amendment was also adopted. It happened on two additional occasions in 1988, both during consideration of omnibus drug policy legislation, once in 1989 concerning joint U.S./Japanese development of the FSX aircraft, once in 1992 on the Transportation Appropriations Act, and once in 1993 concerning U.S. troops in Somalia. In five of these six cases, including the nuclear testing provision described above, the superseded alternative got more votes than the one considered as finally agreed to. Therefore, it might be possible to argue that in these cases the structure of the king-of-the-hill procedure actually allowed the outcome to be manipulated in a way that could be described as thwarting a policy preference expressed by a majority of the members. However, when the particular issues and circumstances involved are examined, the extent to which the outcome can be said to have undone the will of the House comes into question.

For example, one of the issues subject to a king-of-the-hill process during the consideration of drug policy legislation was the imposition of criminal penalties for certain drug-related offenses. The rule provided first for the consideration of an amendment offered by Representative Charles Rangel, chair of the House Select Committee on Narcotics Abuse and Control, to impose mandatory life sentences. It was agreed to 410–1. It was superseded by an amendment offered by Representative George Gekas to allow the death penalty to be imposed. It too was approved, 299–111. While approval of the Gekas amendment undid approval of the Rangel amendment, this progression can, and probably should, be read as simply meaning that a significant number of representatives wanted to at least provide for mandatory life sentences, but preferred the option of allowing the death penalty. For most of the other cases as well, the policy choices expressed through the king-of-the-hill procedures can hypothetically be accounted for by an understanding other than advantaging the alternative favored by the majority party leadership to simply overrule the will of the House.

Although opposition was occasionally directed toward the use of king-of-the-hill procedures, in many cases there was substantial support from the minority. For example, king-of-the-hill was identified by the minority as preferable for consideration of legislation to provide aid to the Nicaraguan Contras. In 1985, H.Res. 136 provided for consideration of H.J.Res. 247, and allowed two competing amendments to be considered. The first was offered by Representative Lee Hamilton for the Democrats, and the second by Representative Michel for the Republicans. During consideration of the rule, Representative Lott stated that "at least we will have our chance to offer a substitute and be heard fairly in the debate" (Lott 1985, 8961). Although the Hamilton amendment prevailed in this instance, the fight over Contra aid continued in several measures, including supplemental and regular appropriations bills. When the issue of Contra aid was considered again in April 1986, on a supplemental appropriations bill under the regular amending procedure rather than a king-of-the-hill procedure, Representative Lott asked, "Whatever happened to the king-of-the-mountain approach that we had in last year's supplemental rule? So much for fairness, decency and civility" (Lott 1986a, 7535). Republicans subsequently attempted to sever the issue and use the discharge procedure to bring H.Res. 419, a king-of-the-hill rule, before the House to decide the issue on a freestanding Contra aid measure. Although that effort did not succeed, when the issue was next considered in June 1986, on the military construction appropriations bill, Representative Lott stated, "I think this is as fair a rule as we can expect. . . . I feel somewhat vindicated. Some of my colleagues over there were critical of the discharge petition we filed because we had a king-of-the-hill process. And yet that is what we have here today, and the last one that is left standing wins. . . . Nobody is going to love this rule. . . . I would hope that we would pass the rule and get on to the substance" (Lott 1986b, 15468). When the House did get to the substance of the matter, this time it approved the Republican alternative, 221–209, and subsequently defeated the Democratic alternative, 183–245, so that again being offered as the last alternative did not, in practice, confer an advantage to that alternative.

In other circumstances, minority support was more qualified. In the 103rd Congress, Representative Gerald Solomon, ranking Republican on the Rules Committee, speaking during debate on H.Res. 509, for consideration of H.R. 4590, legislation granting Most Favored Nation status to China, said:

> I do not support king of the hill procedures like this and I voted against it in the Rules Committee. However, as I just mentioned there was bipartisan cooperation on bringing these three bills to the floor with as much as four hours of debate on these controversial measures and therefore, as we have done in the past, like on the defense authorization bill, we will not press the king of the hill issue, because all sides were consulted . . . and the author of the bill agreed to the king of the hill procedure. (Solomon 1994a, 20476)

As king-of-the-hill rules grew more common, however, and they became used on a greater variety of policy issues, the minority became more frequently critical. In 1989, for example, during debate on H.Res. 111, the rule to provide for consideration of H.R. 2, legislation to amend the Fair Labor Standards Act, Representative Solomon, managing the rule for the Republicans, said, "This is a king-of-the-hill rule which, at quick glance, looks to be fair, but on which closer examination reveals its true purpose. In this case that purpose is to stack the deck against the administration's proposal" (Solomon 1989, 5135). Later that same year, during a special order speech, Representative Fred Upton, a member of the Republican whip organization, decried the use of a king-of-the-hill structure for the consideration of amendments to H.R. 3299, the Omnibus Budget Reconciliation Act of 1989, concerning repeal of catastrophic health care. Mr. Upton spoke of concern that members

> didn't realize that—under the king-of-the-hill procedure—even if the repeal got 400 votes, it could be defeated if the second amendment received as few as 216 votes. In other words, even if the repeal had overwhelming support, it would have been defeated by the second amendment if the second amendment had just enough votes to squeak by. If it lost, it would still win.
>
> I doubt that's the way they teach it in ninth grade civics classes. Most students of democratic processes are taught that victory goes to the legislation that gets the most votes. But not when you're playing king-of-the-hill.

This is especially important in light of today's votes. This wasn't simply a procedural gimmick. . . . The king-of-the-hill procedure was the trick that nearly confused enough Members to vote in a way that would have defeated their own intention to repeal catastrophic health care. (Upton 1989, 23292)

Despite the concern expressed by Mr. Upton, the vote on the second amendment had not been close, and the outcome was likely never in doubt. The first amendment passed by a margin of 360–66, while the second alternative failed by a vote of 156–269. His concerns, however, do indicate the growing frustration with restrictive rules generally, and an effort to raise the potential for either confusion or unfairness under a king-of-the-hill structure.

During the 103rd Congress, Representative Porter Goss, a Republican on the Rules Committee, stated his belief that rules like H.Res. 384, providing for the consideration of H.Con.Res. 218, the budget resolution for fiscal year 1995, prevented the House from truly working its will, because "king-of-the-hill tends to reduce Members' accountability by giving them free votes, while allowing the majority a last chance to undo anything that is done and still get their budget passed" (Goss 1994, 4347).

Later during the same Congress, while debating H.Res. 512, Representative Solomon also spoke of the potential for king-of-the-hill rules to produce results at odds with the policy preferences of the House:

Believe me, if the day ever comes when one of these Democrat king-of-the-hill rules results in a weaker amendment being reported to the House, there will be a bipartisan uproar like my colleagues have never heard before. The king will be seen to have no clothes, and naked power will be exposed in its rawest form. Mark my word on that; it is going to happen. (Solomon 1994b, 21535)

The increase in the use of restrictive rules generally caused the Republican minority to focus criticism on the loss of opportunities to present alternatives. It is not surprising, therefore, that by the 1990s the use of king-of-the-hill rules specifically became increasingly controversial as well, even though there does not seem to be any evidence that such rules consistently or inherently produced results that prevented the House from working its will.

Queen-of-the-Hill

When the Republicans became the majority party in the House in the 104th Congress, they made a point of ending the use of king-of-the-hill rules (*Roll Call*, Jan. 1, 1995, "Under New Rules Chairman, 'King of Hill' Will End Reign").

In the majority, the Republicans generally chose not to guarantee debate and a vote on specific policy alternatives during the consideration of legislation.

Even in the case of budget resolutions, for which they continued the practice of restricting amendments to a handful of complete substitutes, the regular amending process served. The specified substitutes could be offered and debated, but should any of them be agreed to the process would be over, and any additional amendments would be out of order. It hardly mattered, as amendments offered by the minority had rarely passed anyhow, and no minority substitutes had passed since that offered by Representative Latta in 1981. Few seem to have noticed that the practice of guaranteeing the consideration of alternative budgets had been abandoned, and the matter does not seem to have been raised during debate on any of the rules for consideration of budget resolutions during the later half of the 1990s.

For a time, the Republicans attempted to make occasional use of a close cousin of king-of-the-hill rules, termed queen-of-the-hill, under which the alternative that received the most votes would prevail, regardless of the order in which the alternatives were considered (as long as they received a majority of the votes). In the 104th Congress, this process was used three times. In the 105th Congress it was used twice, and in the 107th Congress it was used a single time. Even this meager number overrepresents its use, however, since the last two times it was used represent a response to successful discharge efforts in connection with campaign finance reform, so that the choice to use this kind of amendment structure came from members working to force the House to take action in conflict with the preferences of the majority leadership, rather than from the Rules Committee.

One thing that is notable about the use of queen-of-the-hill rules is that three of the six occasions on which they were used were for proposed constitutional amendments, a balanced budget requirement in the 104th Congress and congressional term limits in both the 104th and 105th Congresses. The first use of this variant, for a balanced budget amendment, was the only time at which more than one alternative was agreed to. The first substitute, offered on behalf of the Judiciary Committee to require a three-fifths supermajority to run a deficit, increase the debt limit, or increase taxes, was adopted, 253–173. After four additional substitutes were rejected, the final substitute, offered by Representative Dan Shaefer, to require a three-fifths supermajority to run a deficit or increase the debt limit, but a majority to increase taxes, was adopted, 293–139. For all of the other occasions on which queen-of-the-hill rules were used, one or none of the amendments made in order was agreed to.

The controversy that had built around the process ultimately outweighed its usefulness, and the Republicans chose to instead impose restrictions on the opportunities to consider amendments in other ways. For example, H.Res. 225 (104th Congress) simply specified those amendments that would be in order to be offered during the course of consideration. H.Res. 104 (104th Congress) did not specify the contents of amendments to be in order, but limited the period for amendment to seven hours. A more complex alternative is illustrated by

H.Res. 488 (104th Congress). This rule provided that if a specified amendment were adopted, the bill as amended would be considered as original text (that is, as if it were unamended text) for purposes of further amendment. In short, the Rules Committee did not lack for less controversial, and more efficient, ways of managing consideration of legislation, in the absence of king-of-the-hill rules.

Conclusion

Big changes in the rules are sometimes difficult to accomplish, but smaller innovations in practice happen from time to time because innovation is brought about, not by rethinking basic concepts, but by a desire to solve specific problems. King-of-the-hill represents only a small part of the attempt by the House Rules Committee to solve the problem of a messy and unruly amending process by using restrictive rules to structure it. King-of-the-hill was simply one new form of restrictive rule that created a novel amendment tree structure that would guarantee a sufficient number of members/groups a voice and a vote while still managing the time.

Republicans in the minority initially supported king-of-the-hill rules as more fair than other forms of restrictive rules, while still expressing concerns that their voice and preferred policy options were not being sufficiently heard when the rule limited them to offering only one or two alternatives. Over time, however, this dissatisfaction with all forms of restrictive rules, not just king-of-the-hill rules, led them to express an overall theme of unfair treatment based on a loss of debate and amending opportunities, and to raise the specter of confusion or perverse outcomes resulting from king-of-the-hill rules.

The conventional wisdom about king-of-the-hill rules is wrong. The conventional wisdom is based on hypothetical problems and concerns raised by the minority in their efforts to highlight what they perceived as unfair treatment. The conventional wisdom, however, is not borne out by an examination of the historical record. The majority did not always, or even consistently, place the alternative preferred by the majority party leadership as the last alternative. In most cases, the majority did not actually need to have specified the order in which alternatives were offered because the House so rarely voted to agree to more than one alternative that it just did not matter. Furthermore, the level of support for alternatives does not make it seem likely that members voted more frequently for multiple alternatives under a king-of-the-hill procedure than they would have under some other form of restrictive rule.

So if the conventional wisdom is wrong, what does the use of king-of-the-hill rules mean? King-of-the-hill rules were an innovation that gave the House a better alternative than other forms of restrictive rules to guarantee that previously identified alternate policy preferences could be debated, especially when there were more of them than the traditional amendment tree could accommodate. Over time, their use expanded because, unlike the traditional amendment tree, they could guarantee not only time for debating alternatives, but also that each alternative would be voted on directly. For example, there would not be a case in which agreeing to a second-degree amendment would prevent an up or down vote directly on the policy expressed in an underlying first-degree amendment. As a procedure, it served its intended purpose of managing time while guaranteeing a better opportunity than other forms of restrictive rules for considering alternative policy options.

Despite this guarantee, however, king-of-the-hill rules came to be perceived by the minority as just another form of restrictive rule, something that prevented them from determining the timing and form of debate of their preferred policy alternatives. Whether they were more or less unfair than other restrictive rules became irrelevant. The Republicans' main argument turned on the fact that they were not open rules. Had Democrats remained in the majority, they would undoubtedly have continued to use king-of-the-hill rules to manage debate, but because the Republicans had made an issue of their potential for confusion and perverse results, when they became the majority it became politically difficult to continue to use them on such a broad range of issues. After briefly experimenting with queen-of-the-hill rules, the Republicans chose to use other forms of special rules to manage time or amending opportunities.

By examining the historical record of the use of king-of-the-hill rules, it is possible to follow the entire life cycle of a procedural innovation, from its early, unsteady triumphs to its later controversy and demise. Over the course of that cycle it's possible to see how the procedure served as a tool for more efficient management of time in an era in which the House was vexed by inefficiency in the amending process, how it came to symbolize restriction and potential manipulation of procedural opportunities for the minority, and finally how that image overwhelmed actual practice to create enough controversy that it was discarded. The Rules Committee has continued to experiment with various forms of special rules to manage time or amending, but has not chosen to structure consideration in such a way that multiple policy options can be debated with both time and a vote guaranteed for all. The demise of king-of-the-hill rules should not be seen as an isolated phenomenon. Other changes in rules and practices have contributed to this becoming an evolutionary dead end.

For example, in the case of budget resolutions, since 1995 majorities from both parties have continued to make in order several alternative budgets in the form of amendments in the nature of a substitute, but without a guarantee that all of them will be debated and receive a direct vote as they would under a king-of-the-hill rule. These rules have included language that reminds members that "the adoption of an amendment in the nature of a substitute shall constitute the conclusion of consideration of the concurrent resolution for amendment."

Because no full substitute amendment to a budget resolution has been adopted in this time, however, no amendment has been prevented from being offered despite the lack of a guarantee. In effect, because the outcome has not been in doubt, the Rules Committee has been able to allow multiple alternatives to be offered and yet avoid the controversy that might come with a king-of-the-hill rule. Without the guarantee, however, these arrangements are just another form of restrictive rule that goes uncategorized.

In addition, a change in House rules in the 104th Congress effectively guaranteed the minority the right to offer a motion to recommit with "instructions to report back an amendment otherwise in order." With this mechanism in place, arguably it may have become less important for the majority to also provide a specific guarantee for a minority party alternative to be offered while a measure was being read for amendment. Certainly, the minority came to utilize this mechanism with greater frequency as a means for offering its preferred policy alternative.

With no class of restricted rules in use that attracts attention or criticism as a specific, isolated phenomenon, perhaps it should not be a surprise that nearly a decade after their last use in any form, king-of-the-hill rules are still thought of as a separate phenomenon and mentioned as a viable and potentially useful method for the consideration of legislation.

References

Bach, Stanley, and Steven S. Smith. 1988. *Measuring Uncertainty in the House of Representatives: Adaptation and Innovation in Special Rules.* Washington, DC: Brookings Institution.

Bauman, Robert. 1980. "Providing for Consideration of House Concurrent Resolution 307, First Concurrent Resolution on the Budget—Fiscal Year 1981." *Congressional Record*, House, April 23, vol. 126, part 7.

Bolling, Richard. 1980. "Providing for Consideration of House Concurrent Resolution 307, First Concurrent Resolution on the Budget—Fiscal Year 1981." *Congressional Record*, House, April 23, vol. 126, part 7.

———. 1981. "Providing for Consideration of House Concurrent Resolution 115, First Concurrent Resolution on the Budget—Fiscal Year 1982." *Congressional Record*, House, April 30, vol. 127, part 6.

Cox, Gary, and Mathew D. McCubbins. 1993. *Legislative Leviathan: Party Government in the House.* Berkeley and Los Angeles: University of California Press.

CQ Weekly Report. 1979. "Budget Making Is 'Devilishly Difficult Thing,' House Finds." May 12.

Derrick, Butler. 1984. "Providing for Consideration of House Concurrent Resolution 280, First Concurrent Resolution on the Budget—Fiscal Year 1985." *Congressional Record*, House, April 4, vol. 130, part 6.

Frank, Barney. 1994. "Providing for Consideration of H.J. Res. 373, Disapproving Most-Favored-Nation Treatment for China and for Consideration of H.R. 4590, United States–China Act of 1994." *Congressional Record*, House, August 9, vol. 140, part 14.

Frenzel, Bill. 1984. "Providing for Consideration of House Concurrent Resolution 280, First Concurrent Resolution on the Budget—Fiscal Year 1985." *Congressional Record*, House, April 4, vol. 130, part 6.

Goss, Porter. 1994. "Providing for Consideration of House Concurrent Resolution 218, Concurrent Resolution on the Budget—Fiscal Year 1995." *Congressional Record*, House, March 10, vol. 140, part 4.

Hook, Janet. 1987. "GOP Chafes under Restrictive House Rules." *CQ Weekly Report*, October 10.

Latta, Delbert. 1980. "Providing for Consideration of House Concurrent Resolution 307, First Concurrent Resolution on the Budget—Fiscal Year 1981." *Congressional Record*, House, April 23, vol. 126, part 7.

———. 1984. "Providing for Consideration of House Concurrent Resolution 280, First Concurrent Resolution on the Budget—Fiscal Year 1985." *Congressional Record*, House, April 4, vol. 130, part 6.

Lott, Trent. 1981. "Providing for Consideration of House Concurrent Resolution 115, First Concurrent Resolution on the Budget—Fiscal Year 1982." *Congressional Record*, House, April 30, vol. 127, part 6.

———. 1982. "Providing for Consideration of House Concurrent Resolution 345, First Concurrent Resolution on the Budget—Fiscal Year 1983." *Congressional Record*, House, vol. 128, part 8.

———. 1985. "Providing for Consideration of House Joint Resolution 239, Making Appropriations for Aid to Nicaragua." *Congressional Record*, House, April 23, vol. 131, part 7.

———. 1986a. "Waiving Certain Points of Order against Consideration of H.R. 4515, Urgent Supplemental Appropriations, Fiscal Year 1986, and Providing for Consideration of a Joint Resolution Relating to Central America." *Congressional Record*, House, April 15, vol. 132, part 6.

———. 1986b. "Military Construction Appropriations Act, 1987." *Congressional Record*, House, June 25, vol. 132, part 11.

Lynch, Megan Suzanne. 2011. "The Motion to Recommit in the House of Representatives: Effects and Recent Trends." *Congressional Research Service*. Washington, DC: Library of Congress.

Marshall, Bryan W. 2002. "Explaining the Role of Restrictive Rules in the Postreform House." *Legislative Studies Quarterly* 28:61–85.

Miller, Susan M., Kenneth W. Moffett, and L. Marvin Overby. 2010. "Standing Atop the Hill: King of the Hill and Queen of the Hill Sequencing Procedures in Recent Congresses." Paper presented at the annual meeting of the Midwest Political Science Association, April 22–25.

Ota, Alan K. 2011. "Battle to Balance Budget May Resurrect Vintage Floor Move." *CQ Today Online News*, May 2.

Pepper, Claude. 1984. "Providing for Consideration of House Resolution 519, Immigration Reform and Control Act of 1983." *Congressional Record*, House, June 11, vol. 130, part 11.

Perkins, Carl. 1981. "Providing for Consideration of House Concurrent Resolution 115, First Concurrent Resolution on the Budget—Fiscal Year 1982." *Congressional Record*, House, April 30, vol. 127, part 6.

Rohde, David W. 1991. *Parties and Leaders in the Postreform House*. Chicago: University of Chicago Press.

Schickler, Eric. 2001. *Disjointed Pluralism: Institutional Innovation and the Development of the U.S. Congress*. Princeton, NJ: Princeton University Press.

Sinclair, Barbara. 1995. "House Special Rules and the Institutional Design Controversy." In *Positive Theories of Legislative Organization*, edited by Kenneth A. Shepsle and Barry R. Weingast, 235–52. Ann Arbor: University of Michigan Press.

———. 2007. *Unorthodox Lawmaking: New Legislative Processes in the U.S. Congress*, 3rd ed. Washington, DC: CQ Press.

Smith, Steven S. 1989. *Call to Order: Floor Politics in the House and Senate.* Washington, DC: Brookings Institution.

Solomon, Gerald. 1989. "Providing for Consideration of H.R. 2, Fair Labor Standards Amendments of 1989." *Congressional Record*, House, March 22, vol. 135, part 4.

———. 1994a. "Providing for Consideration of H.J. Res. 373, Disapproving Most-Favored-Nation Treatment for China and for Consideration of H.R. 4590, United States-China Act of 1994." *Congressional Record*, House, August 9, vol. 140, part 14.

———. 1994b. "Providing for Consideration of H.R. 4907, Full Budget Disclosure Act of 1994." *Congressional Record*, House, August 11, vol. 140, part 15.

Tate, Dale. 1982. "Votes on Budget Alternatives Set in House; Senate Alters GOP Blueprint for Fiscal 1983." *CQ Weekly Report*, May 22.

Towell, Pat. 1988. "House Again Rebuffs Reagan Arms Policies." *CQ Weekly Report.*

Upton, Fred. 1989. "Need for Congressional Reform." *Congressional Record*, House, October 4, vol. 135, part 16.

U.S. Congress, House of Representatives, Committee on Rules. 1994. *Survey of Activities of the House Committee on Rules.* 103rd Cong., 2nd sess., H.Rept. 103-891. Washington, DC: Government Printing Office.

Walker, Robert. 1981. "Providing for Consideration of House Concurrent Resolution 115, First Concurrent Resolution on the Budget—Fiscal Year 1982." *Congressional Record*, House, April 30, vol. 127, part 6.

———. 1984. "Providing for Consideration of House Concurrent Resolution 280, First Concurrent Resolution on the Budget—Fiscal Year 1985." *Congressional Record*, House, April 4, vol. 130, part 6.

Weiss, Theodore. 1981. "Providing for Consideration of House Concurrent Resolution 115, First Concurrent Resolution on the Budget—Fiscal Year 1982." *Congressional Record*, House, April 30, vol. 127, part 6.

4

The Appropriations Process and Limitation Amendments

A Case Study on Party Politics and the House Floor*

Jessica Tollestrup

T HE INTERNAL RULES OF THE HOUSE AND SENATE generally encourage the separation of money and policy decisions. These rules are based on the principle
that the activities of government, and the funding of those activities, should be
chosen through distinct processes. In the area of appropriations,[1] this separation is promoted by long-standing rules that prohibit the inclusion of legislative
language in either the text of a general appropriations bill or as an amendment
thereto. These prohibitions are enforced on the floor during each chamber's
respective consideration of appropriations measures.

Despite the procedural and institutional separation that exists between substantive and fiscal decision-making during the consideration of appropriations
measures, policy may still be affected through funding *limitations* (Deschler
1977, vol. 8, ch. 26, §51.15), which are provisions that negatively restrict the
amount, purpose, or availability of appropriations funds without changing existing law. The effect of these provisions is to limit the actions for which funds may
be used through the capping or outright denial of funds for specific purposes.
Limitation provisions have routinely been included in the text of appropriations
measures reported from committee or inserted through amendments on the
floor by both chambers.

During the post-reform era in the House, the average number of limitation
amendments proposed on the House floor has increased considerably, from
less than three per appropriations bill in the 97th Congress to over thirteen

*The views expressed herein are those of the author and are not presented as those of the Congressional
Research Service or the Library of Congress. The author is grateful for the valuable comments provided by
Christopher Davis, James Saturno, and Jacob R. Straus on previous drafts of this chapter.

per appropriations bill in the 110th Congress. A variety of institutional factors have contributed to this increase, including a general rise in party polarization, switches in party control in the House, and the presence (or absence) of divided government. In addition, changes in House rules related to limitation amendments and, more broadly, alterations in institutional practices related to the way that both policy and money bills are considered on the House floor, have also had a significant effect on the number of limitations proposed each Congress.

This chapter examines limitation amendments in the context of the annual appropriations process as a case study on party politics and the House floor. The chapter first provides background on the development of the appropriations process in the House and the practice of including limitation provisions in appropriations measures. Next, reasons why members of Congress generally, and members of the majority or minority parties in particular, might support the inclusion of limitations to achieve both strategic and substantive ends are discussed. Then the chapter provides an overview of the House floor process, selected avenues for majority party influence, and ways that the minority party has used the amending process to counter this influence. Finally, this chapter examines trends in the offering and adoption of limitation amendments on the House floor between the 97th (1981–1982) and 112th Congresses (2011–2012), and the ways in which these trends have been influenced by internal procedural developments, as well as changes in institutional composition.

Money versus Policy and the Congressional Appropriations Process

In his study of the early congressional appropriations process, Stewart (1989) notes that "the parameters of budgetary regimes—such as committee structures and jurisdictions and rules of floor debate—help to limit the types of budgetary decisions that legislators are likely to make" (13). While a long-standing procedural and institutional separation exists in Congress between substantive and fiscal policymaking, this is complicated by the reality that decisions regarding the allocation of money directly impact substantive policy priorities (Hartman 1982). As a result of this tension, the House and Senate have developed procedures for influencing policy through the appropriations process designed to leave this separation intact.

The Development of the Appropriations Process in the House

The evolution of what would become the modern appropriations process began in 1794 with the enactment of two annual appropriations bills, which provided general funding for government and military activities (Fisher 2003). While the details of this process were initially slow to develop, Congress gradually began the practice of considering appropriations bills for more specific purposes over the first half of the nineteenth century (Schick 1984). During this period, the Senate Finance Committee and House Ways and Means Committee had jurisdiction over both appropriations and revenue. As the activities of federal government became more complex, however, and the number of annual appropriations bills increased, the workloads of these committees became difficult to manage (Fisher 1975). This problem was exacerbated during the Civil War, when the high level of spending necessary for the war effort required extensive coordination (Fisher 2003). In response, the House (in 1865) and Senate (in 1867) removed jurisdiction over appropriations from the Ways and Means and Finance Committees, and vested it with newly created Appropriations Committees.

After the Civil War concluded, tensions gradually developed between the Appropriations Committees and members who wanted greater expenditures for their own districts (Brady and Morgan 1987). In addition, many policy committees in Congress perceived the new arrangement as tending to encroach on their jurisdictions (Fisher 2003). Between 1877 and 1885, these areas of dissatisfaction led the House and Senate to gradually confer jurisdiction over appropriations, as well as the responsibility to report annual appropriations measures, on the individual policy committees (Stewart 1989). The consequent fragmentation of appropriations power, however, led to higher levels of government spending that could not be effectively controlled in the initial stages of the legislative process by the individual committees. In the House, the party leadership responded by attempting to impose fiscal discipline during floor consideration of appropriations measures, where the Speaker, through his unappealable power of recognition, could simply refuse to recognize members that intended to introduce such measures (Fisher 2003).

At the turn of the twentieth century, widespread dissatisfaction among House members with the Speaker's control over the floor agenda led to institutional changes that strengthened the prerogatives of both individual members and standing committees (Cooper and Brady 1981). Additionally, the enactment of the Budget and Accounting Act of 1921 consolidated the executive branch budget process and expanded its influence over spending decisions (Fisher 1975). In anticipation of this development, in 1920, the House again vested jurisdiction over appropriations with the Appropriations Committee, an action which the Senate mirrored in 1922 (Stewart 1989). The Legislative Reorganization Act of 1946 expanded the power of the Appropriations Committees by increasing staff allocations and further codifying committee jurisdictions to avoid disputes (Davidson 1990; Deering and Smith 1997).

The era preceding the 1970s was generally characterized by extensive committee autonomy over the legislative agenda and floor process in the House. During this period, however, the autonomy of the Appropriations Committee was somewhat constrained by the general expectation that it be responsive to the wishes and sentiments of fellow House members (Fenno 1973). In addition, the high level of involvement party leaders had in assignments to that particular committee allowed them to exert influence over the initial shape that appropriations legislation took as it was reported (Fenno 1966). Finally, while the Appropriations Committee chair could use procedural tools available to other committee chairs during the floor process to deter changes to the committee's legislative product, control over the legislative outcome was ultimately shared with the party leadership (Fenno 1966).

During the period of institutional reform in Congress that occurred in the 1970s, the Congressional Budget Act (CBA) of 1974 was enacted. The CBA formed a budget committee in each chamber to draft the congressional budget, created a nonpartisan Congressional Budget Office to provide budget analysis to Congress, and established a timetable for the completion of the budget before the beginning of the fiscal year (Palazzolo 1992). The purpose of these budgetary reforms was aligned with the larger institutional reforms that took place during this period, which tended to shift control over policy outcomes from the standing committees to the party leadership, which could coordinate the budget process to align the outcome with the majority caucus's priorities (Thurber 1992). This shift in power over appropriations from the committee to the party leadership was gradually realized through the 1980s. As party control consolidated due to the higher level of ideological cohesion within the parties, these changes rapidly led to the transference of policy debates into the fiscal realm, where resource allocation became influenced by partisan and ideological conflicts (Patashnik 2005).

Appropriations Limitations

While many changes have occurred in the congressional appropriations process since it began in 1794, the process itself has consistently been characterized by both a procedural and institutional separation between substantive and fiscal policymaking. This has stemmed from the principle that the process through which the activities of government are chosen should be distinct from the process through which those activities are later funded. Both chambers formally established rules prohibiting the inclusion of *legislation* in appropriations during the mid-1800s (Kravitz 1963; Schick 1984)—provisions that have the effect of either changing existing law or creating new law.[2] In the years since these rules were established, however, the practice of attaching funding limitations to appropriations measures has evolved—provisions that place a cap on the total funding for a project or activity, or define the purposes for which funds may not be used, without also affecting existing law.

The allowability of limitations under the precedents of the House and Senate is based upon the principle that, while Congress can create programs or legally authorize certain activities to take place when engaging in substantive policymaking, it is under no obligation to subsequently fund them (Deschler 1977, vol. 8, ch. 26, §64; Oleszek 2007). As a result, during the appropriations process, Congress may choose to fully fund a project or activity, provide a lesser level of funding than was originally contemplated, or provide no funds at all (Oleszek 2007).

In the time since limitations have come into use, various parliamentary rulings have attempted to establish and refine the distinction between proper limitations and legislative provisions. This can be distilled down to four basic principles. First, a proper limitation can only apply to the appropriations bill under consideration. Second, a proper limitation cannot operate beyond the fiscal year for which the appropriation is made. Third, a proper limitation cannot modify (either by expanding or narrowing) the existing powers or duties of federal agents or agencies. Fourth, a proper limitation cannot be subject to a contingency, such as withholding funds until some action is taken or avoided. If a provision in an appropriations bill, or one offered as an amendment thereto, violates any of these principles, it is regarded as legislative in nature and prohibited under House Rules (Deschler 1977, vol. 8, ch. 26, §64).

Despite the above restrictions on what a proper limitation can entail, however, such provisions still have significant potential to affect the actions federal government agencies undertake. Some of the first limitations offered by members of the House attempted to curtail the federal supervision of elections and the extension of revenue laws to the territories (Devine 1987). During the twentieth century, limitations have similarly been attempted to prevent federal government entities from engaging in actions of which Congress disapproves. For example, appropriations limitations were proposed to stop the closure of military installations under the Hoover Commission during the 1950s (Carper 1960). At the beginning of the 112th Congress (2011–2012) during House consideration of the appropriations measure, H.R. 1, limitations aimed at curtailing agency rulemaking in certain specified cases were added as floor amendments (Koss 2011).

Stewart's (1989) observation that the structure of budgetary decision-making is chosen based upon the outcomes it is likely to create is evidenced both by the evolution of the appropriations process and the rise of limitations. In many respects, both the historic growth and the contraction of Appropriations Committee strength parallel larger patterns of institutional development that occurred at the same time. In the House, during periods when the Speaker was particularly powerful and the institutional mood was in favor of centralization, there tended to be less power vested in the Appropriations Committee; when institutional power was more decentralized, the Appropriations Committee was stronger and more impervious to outside influences. Despite the institutional and procedural separation between money and policy decisions that exists within the House and Senate, the practice of influencing policy through the denial of funds has gradually evolved. With the increase in policy implications of fiscal decisions since the institutional reforms of the 1970s, the importance of the procedural tools that exist within the appropriations process for both the majority and minority party to achieve more substantive ends has been significantly amplified.

Policy Implementation and Party Politics

Historically, the use of limitation provisions to influence policy implementation has been motivated both by inter-branch rivalries and partisan struggles. The appointment power of the president in consultation with the Senate, as well as the ability that each possesses to retrospectively sanction noncompliant agencies, provides both Congress and the president with an inherent influence over bureaucratic behavior (Calvert, McCubbins, and Weingast 1989). The delegation of aspects of the decision-making process from Congress to the bureaucracy, however, requires a basic ceding of direct control over policy implementation (Lindblom 1968). Due to the nature of inter-branch rivalries, a lack of ideological alignment between Congress and the president can lead to less decision-making authority being delegated to the executive branch, as Congress attempts to exercise the maximum influence possible over agency structure and decision-making (MacDonald 2007). Limitations provide a powerful tool for Congress to influence policy implementation through the denial of funds for specific purposes, as well as an additional high-stakes method of forcing the president to cooperate with the intentions of Congress in agency structuring and decision-making (Sundquist 1983).

Limitations can also be used strategically to shape an appropriations measure in ways that impact its likelihood of eventual passage. Individual members can, theoretically, support limitation provisions in the hopes that their adoption will cause the eventual bill to either fail or be significantly revised during the veto bargaining process. Moreover, individual members who generally favor the policy that a limitation provision promotes might vote against its inclusion due to concern that it might weaken a program in the long-term (Melnick 1983). Members of Congress can also add limitations to appropriations bills because the policies they contain cannot pass as free-standing bills, and an appropriations measure is unlikely to be vetoed over the addition of such a provision (Oleszek 2007). While the inclusion of limitation provisions may sometimes trigger inter-branch conflict, at a minimum they provide the congressional negotiators with a better bargaining position (Oleszek 2007). An early example of such a negotiation occurred during the post–Civil War reconstruction, when a Democratic Congress attached appropriations limitations to restrict funding for the deployment of federal troops and marshals to polling places in the South, which was an important mechanism for enforcing the Force Act of 1870, a key aspect of the Republican and President Hayes's postwar agenda. After negotiations failed and Hayes vetoed four different appropriations bills, the ultimate result was the extraction of concessions from Hayes in other areas in exchange for the removal of the limitation provisions (Vazzano 1993).

The inclusion of limitation provisions in appropriations measures, through either the committee or floor process, can be used by a congressional majority to achieve certain strategic and substantive ends. For example, the majority party can insert limitations that are later enacted to influence executive branch policy implementation. In addition, the majority party can also use limitation provisions as leverage in veto negotiations in order to extract concessions from the president on other matters (MacDonald 2010).

The use of appropriations limitations can also be an aspect of majority party procedural strategy during periods of divided government—where the presidency and one or both houses of Congress are controlled by different parties. During such periods, funding provided through the appropriations process has been used to control opposition executives and resolve issues of significant disagreement (Stewart 1989; Sinclair 1997). Limitation provisions can help further a majority party's policy goals by cutting off funds for projects or activities with which it disagrees. Limitations can also motivate the president to negotiate with the opposition majority party in order to resolve areas of disagreement over particular projects or activities, because Congress might alternatively decline to provide funding. In contrast, during periods of divided government, the congressional majority (particularly in the House) has sometimes also chosen to pass controversial policy measures designed to highlight divisions within the president's party and damage his future electoral prospects (Rose 2001a, 2001b); the inclusion of funding limitations during the appropriations process can serve similar ends.

The majority party leadership has also historically used limitation provisions as a means of expeditiously addressing concerns related to substantive policy when the policy committees were unable to do so. For example, in the 104th Congress (1995–1996), despite the increase in the ideological cohesion of the majority party (Aldrich and Rohde 1997), there remained significant disagreements between factions within the Republican majority as to how the party's policy goals should be pursued (Marshall, Prins, and Rohde 2003). Such disagreements sometimes made it difficult for the policy committees to cooperate with the leadership in fast-tracking the Speaker's legislative priorities (Aldrich and Rohde 1997). In some of these instances, majority leadership instead chose to utilize appropriations limitations, attached during the committee and floor processes, as one tool to combat policy gridlock (Marshall, Prins, and Rohde 2003).

Members of the minority party can also seek to include limitations in appropriations measures to accomplish different types of goals. As is the case with the majority party, minority party members might also have an interest in influencing executive branch policy implementation through the successful inclusion of appropriations limitations, particularly if the president is from a different party.

In addition, the minority might similarly seek to use limitation provisions as wedge issues in order to embarrass the majority party and force majority party members to take votes on high-profile, controversial topics. Finally, during divided government, the successful insertion of limitations that reflect the position of the minority party might also serve to strengthen the president's veto bargaining position.

Appropriations limitations have historically been used by both majority and minority party members of Congress when engaging in inter-branch or partisan conflict. While such provisions can serve a variety of ends for either party, the nature of the political context is particularly important in determining both their overall utility and how they might be used in a given situation. Limitations are particularly useful to the majority party during divided government, because they can aid in veto negotiations, assure executive branch compliance, and highlight divisions within the president's party. While limitations might be more useful to minority party members when attempting to achieve certain policy goals during periods of unified government, limitations can also be useful during divided government to bolster the president's leverage in veto bargaining. Despite the potential value of appropriations limitations for members of the minority party, however, the extent to which opportunities to successfully propose and insert such provisions are available is significantly influenced by both the procedural context and the institutional composition that exists at the time.

Party Politics and the House Floor

As has been previously noted, the insertion of limitation provisions in the House, either in committee or on the floor, can assist both the majority and minority parties in the accomplishment of substantive or strategic goals. The opportunities available to the majority versus the minority, however, vary considerably. Institutionally, the House is structured to give the majority party certain advantages in the legislative process, in terms of both agenda setting and controlling the floor. The minority party, however, often retains the ability to influence policy and achieve certain strategic ends during the amending phase of floor proceedings, particularly when regular appropriations bills are being considered.

In the House, after regular appropriations measures are reported by the Appropriations Committee, they are generally brought to the floor one of two different ways. First, under House Rules, such a measure can be brought directly to the floor as "privileged business" and called up for consideration by the Appropriations Committee chair after it has met certain layover requirements (House Rule XIII, clause 5). For at least the last two decades, however, most appropriations measures have instead been brought to the floor pursuant to a special order of business, or *special rule*. Special rules are simple resolutions reported by the

House Rules Committee, and approved by a majority vote in the House, that set the terms of consideration for a specific legislative measure. Such terms of consideration can include the length of time a legislative measure will be considered, the amount and type of debate that will be allowed, and any amendments that might be eligible for consideration. In addition, special rules can provide waivers for any parts of the bill, or any amendments, that might violate House Rules (Davis 2011). Historically, both ways of bringing appropriations bills have generally had an open amendment process, which generally allows amendments that comply with House rules to be offered.

Once an appropriations measure is brought to the House floor, it is considered in the *Committee of the Whole* pursuant to clause 3 of House Rule XVIII. The Committee of the Whole is a committee composed of all House members that meets on the House floor for the purposes of considering certain types of legislation. After a period of general debate, the appropriations bill is read for amendment under the *five-minute rule,* unless otherwise specified in the special rule or by unanimous consent. Members may offer their amendments when the relevant paragraph of the appropriations bill is under consideration. Any member offering an amendment is allotted five minutes to debate the amendment, with five additional minutes being allotted to another member who wishes to speak against the amendment. After debate on an amendment is concluded, the amendment is voted upon, either at that time or at a time designated by the chair pursuant to clause 6(g) of House Rule XVIII. A member may request a roll call vote with the support of an additional twenty-four members.

Once the Committee of the Whole is ready to recommend action to the House, it dissolves itself back into the House of Representatives through a *motion to rise and report,* or automatically pursuant to the special rule. The House then typically votes on at least three different matters. First, the House votes whether to approve or disapprove the committee's actions. Second, the House votes on a motion to recommit (with or without instructions) that is offered by minority party, which provides the minority one final chance to offer changes to the bill. Finally, the House votes on the disposition of the measure itself (Heniff and Rybicki 2006).

In the House, the majority party exercises control over the floor process through three key procedural tools. First, the chair of the committee reporting a measure (always a member of the majority party) is able to select the legislative vehicle that will be marked up and reported and, as such, has significant influence over its content. Second, the majority party is able to choose which measures will be scheduled for floor consideration. Third, through control over the Committee on Rules, the majority party is virtually always able to bring legislation to the floor of the House under the procedural circumstances it prefers.

Scholars have long theorized that the extent to which the majority party leadership in the House controls legislative outcomes using procedural tools, such as the three discussed above, is dependent upon a variety of internal and external factors. For example, Cooper and Brady (1981) condition the "style" of majority party leadership upon the external electoral environment. When majority party strength is high, power is concentrated in the hands of its party leaders; when party strength is low, power is dispersed and leaders hold more "maintenance-oriented" roles. Sinclair's (1983, 1986, 1995) principal-agent approach similarly posits that the amount of power that the party leadership possesses is dependent upon the amount of agreement on collective aims that exists within the caucus at that time. Party members must collectively navigate tradeoffs between the delegation of power to the leadership in order to facilitate collective action, and the equal distribution of power and resources resulting in higher autonomy for individuals to pursue their legislative goals.

The conditional party government perspective developed by Rohde (1991) and Aldrich (1995) asserts that the ability of the majority party leadership to exercise control over the legislative agenda and its membership's voting decisions is conditioned by the amount that the majority and minority parties are ideologically polarized, as well as the level of ideological cohesion present within the majority party caucus. When polarization and cohesion are low, the majority caucus is often unable to agree to legislative goals and, as a result, power is centered in the committees, where small groups of legislators and the committee chairs control the policymaking agenda with a high degree of autonomy. When polarization and cohesion are high, a high degree of agreement as to policy aims exists within the majority caucus, and the majority party leadership is consequently empowered by its membership to pursue those aims.

All of the theoretical perspectives discussed above agree that institutional change in the House over the past century has vacillated between centralization and decentralization of institutional power. The decreasing homogeneity within the congressional parties at the turn of the twentieth century led the members to alter the rules of the House in support of decentralized power. The consequent era of "committee governance" between 1920 and 1970 was ended because the composition of the majority party became cohesive enough to initiate changes that refocused power in the hands of the caucus and leadership. The continued consolidation of party leadership authority through the 1990s and early twenty-first century has continued this trend of centralization, as institutional arrangements conducive to the exercise of party leadership power have been further entrenched.

While the majority party leadership in the House is able to exercise control over the floor process through the selection of the legislative vehicle, scheduling power, and special rules, the minority has the opportunity to respond through the offering of amendments. The amendment process on the House floor can help the minority achieve the substantive goal of changing legislation so that it more closely aligns with its own partisan perspective. In addition, offering amendments can help a minority achieve strategic goals, by forcing the majority party to take votes on issues that are outside of its agenda, that are internally divisive, or that make individual majority party members go "on the record" in ways that might be electorally unpopular.

The success of the minority party in offering amendments in a given context is highly dependent on the extent to which the majority party controls the floor process. If the majority selects a vehicle with a narrow subject, many amendments the minority wishes to offer may be out of order due to the germaneness restrictions that exist in House Rule XVI, clause 7. Similarly, if the majority declines to bring bills to the floor that are related to the minority's agenda, germaneness restrictions on amending may prevent the minority's amendments from being in order. Perhaps most importantly, if the majority chooses to use a *restrictive* special rule that limits the amendments the minority can offer, or a *closed* rule that does not allow amendments at all, the minority may have little or no opportunity to offer amendments. If the majority chooses to utilize such rules in a widespread manner for the consideration of policy legislation, offering amendments to appropriations measures may be one of the only opportunities the minority has to advocate its own policy ideas.

In light of the general issues with amending that have been discussed above, limitation amendments to appropriations measures provide the minority party and individual members an opportunity to circumvent many of the difficulties that might be caused by the exercise of majority control over the floor process. Due to the broad subject matter of most annual appropriations measures and the allowability of limitation provisions, amendments on a variety of topics are typically in order. Additionally, as discussed, annual appropriations bills are traditionally brought to the floor under *open* rules that allow the minority considerable latitude in offering amendments. In the past, this amending process has often been further structured through unanimous consent agreements (Davis 2008). Such agreements, which are only binding if no member objects at the time they are propounded, further protect the procedural prerogatives of minority party members.

Theoretically, in the absence of strict majority party control over the appropriations floor process, minority party members can use limitation amendments to achieve both substantive and strategic objectives. However, the frequency with which the minority is given the opportunity to use this procedural tool is at least somewhat conditioned by the extent to which the majority party leadership has been empowered by the homogeneity within its caucus to exercise procedural control over the floor process. In addition, other contextual conditions discussed in the previous section, such as divided government and the level of desire within either party to influence executive branch policy implementation or veto negotiations, likewise affect the extent to which limitation amendments are offered by either party. Finally, the successful insertion of limitation amendments offered by the majority or minority party is dependant upon the level of cohesion within the majority party caucus, and the related ability of the minority to offer such amendments to exploit divisions that might exist within that caucus.

Limitation Amendments: 97th–110th Congresses

Figure 4.1 illustrates the average number of limitation amendments offered and adopted during initial consideration of regular appropriations measures on the House floor between the 97th and 110th Congresses (1981–2010). Figure 4.2 illustrates the proportion of limitation amendments offered by members of the majority party versus those offered by the minority party during the same period. Figure 4.3 illustrates the adoption rate of the limitation amendments offered by members of the majority and minority parties. Overall, when comparing the 97th Congress to the 110th Congress, the average number of limitation amendments offered has increased considerably, while the adoption rate of such amendments has significantly declined. Similarly, while there has been considerable variance in whether the majority or minority party offered more limitation amendments each Congress, the adoption rate of those limitations for both parties has declined during the period under study. Some possible reasons for these trends are discussed in the remainder of this section.

97th–103rd Congresses (1981–1994)

The institutional reform that occurred in the 1970s substantially altered many of the institutional norms and practices that had predominated in the House since the 1920s, by restricting committee chair power over the policy agenda, increasing party leadership control over the policy process, and vesting many institutional bases of power in the majority party caucus (Rohde 1991). These reforms, however, had the effect of pulling the House in two distinct organizational directions. While some of these reforms gave greater authority to the subcommittees and provided for greater equality among House members via the collectivization of power, others served to centralize decision-making by

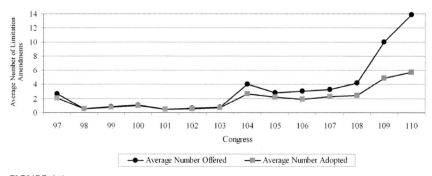

FIGURE 4.1
Average Number of Limitation Amendments Per Appropriations Measure: 97th–110th Congresses

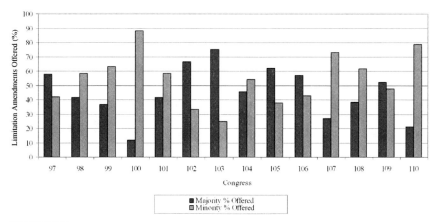

FIGURE 4.2
Percent of Limitation Amendments Offered by Majority versus Minority Party Members: 97th–110th Congresses

empowering the party leadership (Oppenheimer 1980). During the following decade, the difficulties these reforms created in coordinating majority party action can be observed in the evolution of the floor process.

One significant procedural change that occurred in 1971, at the beginning of the 92nd Congress (1971–1972), affected the consideration of amendments in the Committee of the Whole. At this time, House rules were changed to allow for recorded votes on amendments, if requested by a member, as long as twenty other members supported that request (*House Manual* 1972, 314–15). When combined with the implementation of electronic voting in 1972, which significantly reduced the amount of time required to vote, this change had an immediate and

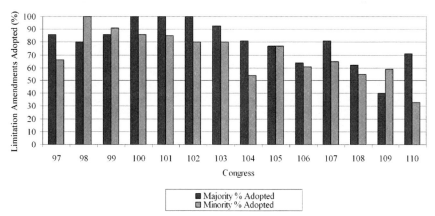

FIGURE 4.3
Percent of Limitation Amendments Adopted by Majority versus Minority Party Members: 97th–110th Congresses

numerically positive effect on the number of floor amendments (Smith 1989). This high volume of amendments, however, created coordination challenges for the majority party leadership while raising the amount of uncertainty and time devoted to the floor process (Smith 1989). The majority party responded to this issue by again changing House rules in the 96th Congress (1979–1980) to raise the threshold for recorded votes on floor amendments to twenty-five members (plus the member that requested it), and by the 98th Congress (1983–1984) it had increased the use of restrictive rules to over three-quarters of the time. The effect of these changes was a steep decrease in the number of floor amendments successfully offered after the 97th Congress (1981–1982) (Bach and Smith 1988).

The 1970s growth in floor amendments can be at least partially attributed to the rise in the number of limitation amendments being proposed on the floor (Sachs 1984). During this time, however, the use of special rules to structure the amending process for appropriations bills had not yet developed, and appropriations bills were primarily brought to the floor as privileged. In addition, even after the rule changes in the 96th Congress that raised the threshold for requesting a recorded vote, a total of sixty-four limitation amendments were offered on the House floor during the 97th Congress. To address this specific issue, the majority chose again to change House rules at the beginning of the 98th Congress (1983–1984) with the addition of clause 2(d) to Rule XXI, which specifically restricted the ability of members to offer limitation amendments to general appropriations bills.[3] This was accomplished by making the consideration of limitation amendments only in order after the bill was completely read for amendment. At that time, a member could offer a limitation amendment, but the consideration of that or any other limitation amendment could be precluded by a successful motion to rise and report. This motion could be offered by any member, and would have precedence over the consideration of amendments. If the motion were successful, the Committee of the Whole would rise and report, thus truncating consideration of any further amendments.

In his evaluation of the potential impact of House Rule XXI changes, Bach (1983) predicted that it would result in an overall decrease in limitation amendments and would ultimately facilitate closer cooperation between the leadership and committee chairs in order to coordinate successful motions to rise. This prediction was correct. In the 98th Congress the number of limitation amendments offered on the floor dropped to a total or thirteen, remaining at a similarly low level through the 103rd Congress (1993–1994). Between the 98th and 103rd Congresses, the average number of limitation amendments offered during the initial House consideration of each regular appropriations act was one or less, which was a drop of over one-half when compared to the 97th Congress. The adoption rate of these limitations was quite high—over 80 percent for both parties in each Congress during this period. An additional change that occurred between the 97th and 98th Congresses was that members of the minority began proposing more amendments than the majority, a trend that lasted through the 101st Congress. It abruptly reversed for the 102nd and 103rd Congresses, with the majority again proposing the bulk of the limitations, although the total number still remained quite small.

The low number of limitations that were offered on the floor during the period between the 98th and 103rd Congresses suggests that the House rule changes in the 98th Congress were highly effective. The majority party now had the ability to fend off minority limitation amendments that were not aligned with their agenda or were strategically disadvantageous. In addition, the relatively low number of limitation amendments offered by members of the majority during this period—despite the fact that the House and presidency were controlled by opposite parties until the 103rd Congress—is probably due to a combination of two factors. First, the majority party leadership may have been able to influence the committees to insert limitation provisions into the appropriations bills during the committee phase of the legislative process, thereby decreasing the need to utilize the floor process for such purposes. In addition, the Appropriations Committee would have been able to utilize the ability to offer the motion to rise and report to prevent limitations for both majority and minority members from being offered.

While the total number of amendments offered during this period by minority members was quite low, many of the limitation amendments that were offered by members of the minority party involved contentious policy issues. For example, during consideration of the District of Columbia appropriations bills during the 99th Congress, amendments were offered to prohibit funds from being spent on abortion. Similar amendments were offered during the 98th Congress to the Treasury, United States Postal Service, and Executive Branch appropriations bills to prohibit funds from being used to administer any federal employee health plan that covered abortion. Also during this period, a number of amendments were offered to prohibit funds for government contractors that did not have a certified drug-free workplace. Despite the low number of such amendments that were offered during this period, minority members were nevertheless able to use limitation amendments to pursue their own policy goals and, in some instances, force members of the majority to publicly support or oppose those goals.

104th Congress (1995–1996)

While party leadership power over the committees continued to grow during the Democratic majority in the 1980s, the change to a Republican majority in the 104th Congress accelerated this trend. The new majority had a higher level of interparty cohesion than the previous Democratic majority, which led to a greater degree of agreement as to common policy goals that should be pursued and enabled the further consolidation of majority leadership power (Dodd and Oppenheimer 2009). The House eliminated three policy committees, reduced the seats available on the other panels by 12 percent, and cut committee staff allocations by one-third (Aldrich and Rohde 1997). In the case of the Appropriations Committee, the Speaker took the unprecedented step of bypassing more senior members on the panel in the selection of the chair (Aldrich and Rohde 1997). The Speaker further undermined the committees by bringing a majority of bills to the floor under open rules (Davidson 1995), although restrictive and closed rules were still utilized to maintain control over the proceedings in many instances (Aldrich and Rohde 2009). In the case of appropriations bills, the practice of bringing the bills to the floor through an open special rule, rather than as privileged, further structuring consideration through unanimous consent agreements, began (Davis 2008).

Changes specific to the consideration of limitation amendments also occurred, with the revision of clause 2(d) of Rule XXI. The new rule restricted the ability to make a preferential motion to rise and report to the majority leader or a designee.[4] This effectively gave the majority leadership greater discretion over what limitation amendments would be allowed, and removed the ability of the appropriations subcommittee chairs to block unfriendly limitation amendments (Bach 2003).

The consequences of these procedural and compositional changes in the House at the beginning of the 104th Congress were considerable. The total number of limitation amendments that were offered during the 104th Congress was 105, over five times greater than the number in the 103rd Congress. In addition, members of the minority party offered fifty-seven of those amendments, up from five minority limitation amendments in the 103rd Congress. However, the cohesion of the majority party caucus resulted in an adoption rate for the minority limitation amendments of just over one-half. The increase in the number of majority party limitation amendments when compared to the previous Congress is also striking. The majority party offered more than three times as many limitation amendments during the 104th Congress than had been offered during the 103rd Congress, and these amendments had an adoption rate of over 80 percent.

The change in majority party, the emergence of divided government, and new House rules were all contributing factors to the higher proportion of limitation amendments offered by members of the majority and minority compared to the previous congresses. The 104th Congress not only began a six-year period of divided government, but the Republicans were in the majority for the first time since the 83rd Congress (1953–1954). Due to that significant lapse in years, the Republicans faced some initial challenges organizing and pursuing their agenda via the policy committees (Marshall, Prins, and Rohde 2003). In addition, while negotiating any of these policy priorities with an opposition executive would be challenging within the regular policy context, the high degree of party polarization provided incentives to both the majority and minority parties to force the other to take votes that might be politically embarrassing or would send a message to various constituency groups. While the appropriations process could be used to achieve many of the above goals, the House rules change restricting the preferential motion to rise and report gave members of both parties a more expansive opportunity to use limitation amendments toward these ends.

105th–110th Congresses (1997–2008)

After the 104th Congress, the consolidation of majority leadership power continued, as the ideological homogeneity and voting cohesion within the majority party caucus continued to increase (Aldrich and Rohde 2009). The use of restrictive and closed special rules was gradually increased to structure floor consideration and block minority amendments so that by the 107th Congress, fewer than half of all bills were brought to the floor under open rules (Aldrich and Rohde 2009). For regular appropriations bills, however, the practice of considering these measures under open rules was largely maintained, and further consideration was structured through unanimous consent agreements (Davis 2008).

During the 105th and 106th Congresses (1997–2000), when the House and presidency were controlled by opposite parties, the proportion of limitations being offered on the floor by members of the majority party was higher than that of the minority party. However, the adoption rate of the majority party limitations began to decline considerably, and was just above 60 percent for the 106th Congress (1999–2000). During the 107th through 109th Congresses (2001–2007), when government was unified, the proportion of limitation amendments offered by the majority initially declined to less than 30 percent of all such amendments offered that Congress. That number, however, began to again increase in the 108th and 109th Congresses, even as the adoption rate for majority limitation amendments declined to around 40 percent for the 109th Congress.

The increase in limitation amendments offered by members of the majority, along with the lower adoption rate overall, can be partially accounted for by the fact that many were aimed at forbidding funds for appropriations "earmarks" contained in the pending measure or the committee report (Pear 2006; Tollestrup 2010). Such provisions, through which funds are suggested or set aside for local projects at the request of individual members or the president, were the target of over 20 percent of the limitations offered during the 109th Congress. Limitation amendments to forbid funds for such purposes, however, were almost always defeated as members opted instead to protect their prerogative to request such funds.

With the reemergence of unified government beginning in the 107th Congress, the previous trend of the majority proposing more limitation amendments than the minority was reversed. The aggregate number of minority limitations also grew—from twenty-seven in the 105th Congress to ninety-five in the 109th Congress. At the same time, however, the adoption rate of these amendments declined, from 78 percent in the 105th Congress to 59 percent in the 109th Congress. The rise in the number of limitation amendments offered by members of the minority relative to the majority during this period can be at least partially explained by the dynamics of unified government. The minority party no longer had an ally in the president, and offering limitation amendments to appropriations measures was a significant way for the minority's agenda to get a vote, and possibly be enacted. In addition, because bills were brought to the floor under restrictive or closed rules over half of the time, appropriations measures were one of the few significant avenues that were widely available for offering floor amendments. Despite the fact that the opportunity to offer limitation amendments remained available for the minority party during the consideration of appropriations measures, however, the growing ideological cohesion within the majority party, which resulted in greater voting discipline, made such amendments less likely to be adopted.

At the beginning of the 110th Congress, despite the switch in the House majority (from the Republicans to the Democrats) and return to divided government, the same institutional trends toward leadership control over the legislative process continued. In addition, the leadership initially allowed appropriations bills to come to the floor largely under open rules. As in the previous Congress, however, members of the minority continued to offer a large number of limitation amendments aimed at blocking funding for earmarks (Ruyle 2009; Tollestrup 2010). While these amendments were rarely adopted, their volume significantly prolonged the initial consideration of appropriations measures on the House floor, and prompted the majority to begin utilizing special rules to restrict the amending opportunities available to the minority (Higa and Clarke 2007; Ota 2007).

During this same Congress, majority party members were responsible for less than 20 percent of the limitations that were offered on the floor, although they were adopted over 70 percent of the time. The relatively low number of majority-sponsored limitations during this period of divided government is somewhat surprising, but is possibly explained by the insertion of majority party limitations during the committee phase of the legislative process. In addition, it is also possible that the majority party chose to utilize different tools to attack the opposition president, such as the passage of free-standing legislation. This potential explanation is supported by the majority party's decision to delay floor consideration of nine out of the twelve regular appropriations bills for fiscal year 2009 until after the conclusion of the 2008 national election.

111th–112th Congresses (2009–2011)

The return to unified government in the 111th Congress saw a continuation of the trend toward majority control over floor consideration of appropriations measures, where limiting the opportunities available for floor amendments to appropriations measures through restrictive rules became even more frequent (Krawzak and Conlon 2009). While members of the majority party argued that such rules were necessary to avoid delays in the appropriations process, members of the minority countered that the majority was simply attempting to avoid embarrassing votes on amendments involving issues of controversy (Clarke 2009). The fiscal year 2010 appropriations process was completed in mid-December, over two months after the start of the fiscal year, with half the measures being combined into an omnibus for final passage. Only two of the regular appropriations bills for fiscal year 2011, however, were considered on the House floor before the 2010 national election was concluded, and attempts to complete the process in the weeks before the 112th Congress began were unsuccessful.

The 112th Congress ushered in a new era of divided government, with control of the House switching from the Democratic to the Republican Party. In order to complete the fiscal year 2011 appropriations, the majority leadership in the House opted to bring all twelve of the regular appropriations bills to the House floor in one legislative vehicle (H.R. 1) under an open rule, which allowed the consideration of any amendments otherwise in order that had been preprinted in the *Congressional Record* (H.Res. 92). The amendments that could be offered were further limited by a unanimous consent agreement that was propounded three days after consideration of H.R. 1 began. In total, 583 amendments were filed, of which 162 were considered on the floor (Weyl 2011). Many of these amendments were limitation amendments offered by members of the majority, which sought to cut government spending across the board or forbid funds for certain specified activities (Young and Goldfarb 2011). The ability to offer such amendments on the floor gave members of both parties the opportunity to go on the record on issues of import to their constituents, by targeting policy areas such as funding for the 2010 health care overhaul and environmental rulemaking (Koss 2011; Young and Goldfarb 2011).

During negotiations with the Senate majority party and president over the final appropriations package, some of the limitation provisions were used by the House majority party leadership to extract greater concessions in funding cuts (Friel 2011; Young 2011). In addition, the House majority leadership was ultimately able to negotiate the inclusion of the remaining limitation provisions, with the intention of influencing policy implementation across a wide range of areas (Ethridge and Smith 2011; Friel 2011).

Conclusion

The use of limitation amendments as a procedural tool by members of the majority and minority parties since the 97th Congress has been significantly influenced by changes in institutional composition, as well as the recent emergence of the new issue of earmarks. As the ideological polarization between the two parties and the internal ideological cohesion of the members of each party have risen, the number of limitations offered on the floor during consideration of regular appropriations measures has also increased. This was particularly the case during the 104th Congress, when the increased cohesion and polarization, combined with divided government, created incentives for members of the majority and minority parties to propose exponentially more limitation amendments than had been offered during the previous Congress.

The proportion of amendments offered by the majority tended to be higher than that of the minority during the remaining periods of divided government during the 105th and 106th Congresses, while the reverse was true during the period of unified government during the 107th and 108th Congresses. While the reemergence of divided government during the 109th Congress did not have the same effect of increasing the number of majority limitations as in the 104th Congress, this can be largely attributed to the emergence of the new issue of earmarks, for which limitation amendments were used disproportionately by certain members of the majority party in attempts to block funding. Most recently, in the 112th Congress, limitations have continued to be an important tool for the majority party to take votes on issues of importance to their constituents, provide leverage in spending negotiations, and exert control over policy implementation.

Changes in the rules of the House have also had significant effects on the number of limitations offered as amendments on the House floor during this period. The change in rules during the 98th Congress, which specifically restricted the ability of members to offer limitation amendments to general appropriations bills, was a likely contributing factor to the low number of limitations successfully offered on the floor through the 103rd Congress. When the ability to make the motion to rise and report was transferred through a subsequent rules change to the majority leadership in the 104th Congress, the procedural opportunity to offer limitations was also significantly increased, and it resulted in a greater number of limitations being offered by members of both the majority and minority parties. In addition, changes in procedural practices related to how appropriations bills are considered and the extent to which amending opportunities are available elsewhere have also affected the number of limitations that are offered.

In conclusion, the use of limitation amendments in the House during the past thirty years has been motivated by both inter-branch rivalries and partisan struggles. Changes in institutional composition, combined with internal procedural developments, have significantly influenced the extent to which members of the majority and minority parties have chosen to utilize this procedural tool. While the future evolution of internal party politics and legislative procedure in the House is difficult to predict, the procedural avenues provided by the appropriations process for members to achieve more substantive ends are likely to remain significant.

Notes

1. The modern congressional budget process currently distinguishes between two types of spending: *direct* and *discretionary*. Direct spending programs are typically established in permanent law, and they specify an obligation on the part of the federal government to spend funds for certain purposes. These obligations are either funded by a permanent appropriation, or through the annual appropriations process. Discretionary spending, which currently comprises around 40 percent of all government spending, provides funding for federal government activities, such as national defense, education, and homeland security, as well as general government operations. This type of spending is controlled through an annual appropriations process. There are three types of appropriations bills that Congress passes to allocate discretionary funds: *regular appropriations bills, continuing resolutions*, and *supplemental appropriations bills*. Regular appropriations bills are enacted annually and are divided into a series of sections that generally comprise an individual budgetary account. These measures provide detailed directions to the departments and agencies contained within the bill on the distribution of funding among the various activities or programs funded within an account. When there is a delay in enacting a regular appropriations bill before the beginning of the upcoming fiscal year, continuing resolutions are utilized to maintain temporary funding for agencies and programs until the regular bills are enacted. Finally, supplemental appropriations bills provide funding for unforeseen needs, or increase funding for programs for which appropriations have previously been provided (Streeter 2010).

2. In the House, prohibitions on legislation in appropriations are currently found in Rule XXI and clause 5(a) of Rule XXII. In the Senate, such prohibitions are currently found in Rule XVI.

3. In the House, "general appropriations bills" are the regular appropriations acts (or any combination thereof) and any supplemental appropriations acts that cover more than one agency. Continuing resolutions are not considered to be general appropriations bills (Brown and Johnson 2003, chapter 4, p. 75, §3).

4. This clause was further amended in the 105th Congress to make the motion to rise and report preferential to any motion to amend once the bill had been read for amendment (*House Manual*, §1043).

References

Aldrich, John H. 1995. *Why Parties? The Origin and Transformation of Political Parties in America.* Chicago: University of Chicago Press.

Aldrich, John H., and David W. Rohde. 1997. "The Transition to Republican Rule in the House: Implications for Theories of Congressional Politics." *Political Science Quarterly* 112:541–67.

———. 2009. "Congressional Committees in a Continuing Partisan Era." In *Congress Reconsidered*, 9th ed., edited by Lawrence C. Dodd and Bruce I. Oppenheimer, 217–40. Washington, DC: CQ Press.

Bach, Stanley. 1983. "The Status of Limitation Amendments under the Rules of the House of Representatives for the 98th Congress." *Congressional Research Service*. Washington, DC: Library of Congress.

———. 2003. *The Amending Process in Congress*. New York: Novinka Books.

Bach, Stanley, and Steven S. Smith. 1988. *Managing Uncertainty in the House of Representatives: Adaptation and Innovation in Special Rules*. Washington, DC: Brookings Institution.

Brady, David, and Mark A. Morgan. 1987. "Reforming the Structure of the House Appropriations Process: The Effects of the 1885 and 1919–20 Reforms on Money Decisions." In *Congress: Structure and Policy*, edited by Mathew D. McCubbins and Terry Sullivan, 207–34. New York: Cambridge University Press.

Brown, W[illia]m Holmes, and Charles W. Johnson. 2003. *House Practice: A Guide to the Rules, Precedents, and Procedures of the House*. Washington, DC: Government Printing Office.

Calvert, Randall L., Mathew D. McCubbins, and Barry R. Weingast. 1989. "A Theory of Political Control and Agency Discretion." *American Journal of Political Science* 33:588–611.

Carper, Edith T. 1960. *The Defense Appropriations Rider*. Vol. 59. Tuscaloosa: University of Alabama Press.

Clarke, David. 2009. "Time-Consuming Tactics Dim Chances for Remaining 2010 Spending Bills." *CQ Today Print Edition*, October 14.

Cooper, Joseph, and David W. Brady. 1981. "Institutional Context and Leadership Style: The House from Cannon to Rayburn." *American Political Science Review* 75:411–25.

Davidson, Roger H. 1990. "The Legislative Reorganization Act of 1946." *Legislative Studies Quarterly* 15:357–73.

———. 1995. "Congressional Committees in the New Reform Era: From Combat to Contract." In *Remaking Congress: Change and Stability in the 1990s*, edited by James A. Thurber and Roger H. Davidson, 28–52. Washington, DC: Congressional Quarterly.

Davis, Christopher M. 2008. "Considering Regular Appropriations Bills on the House Floor: Current Practice regarding Comprehensive Unanimous Consent Agreements." *Congressional Research Service*. Washington, DC: Library of Congress.

———. 2011. "How Legislation Is Brought to the House Floor: A Snapshot of Recent Parliamentary Practice." *Congressional Research Service*. Washington, DC: Library of Congress.

Deering, Christopher J., and Steven S. Smith. 1997. *Committees in Congress*. 3rd ed. Washington, DC: CQ Press.

Deschler, Lewis. 1991. *Deschler's Precedents of the U.S. House of Representatives*. 94th Cong., 1st sess., H.Doc. 94-661, vol. 8. Washington, DC: Government Printing Office.

Devine, Neal E. 1987. "Regulation of Government Agencies through Limitation Riders." *Duke Law Journal* 1987:456–500.

Dodd, Lawrence C., and Bruce I. Oppenheimer. 2009. "The Politics of the Contemporary House: from Gingrich to Pelosi." In *Congress Reconsidered*, 9th ed., edited by Lawrence C. Dodd and Bruce I. Oppenheimer, 23–52. Washington, DC: CQ Press.

Ethridge, Emily, and Lauren Smith. 2011. "Democrats Fend Off Riders In Labor, HHS, Education." *CQ Weekly*, April 18.

Fenno, Richard. 1966. *The Power of the Purse: Appropriations Politics in Congress*. Boston: Little, Brown and Company.

———. 1973. *Congressmen in Committees*. Boston: Little, Brown and Company.

Fisher, Louis. 1975. *Presidential Spending Power*. Princeton, NJ: Princeton University Press.

———. 2003. *The House Appropriations Process, 1789–1993*. New York: Novinka Books.

Friel, Brian. 2011. "An Array of Policy Riders Makes Final Cut, but Sweeping Changes Avoided." *CQ Today Online News*, April 12.

Froman, Lewis A., Jr., and Randall B. Ripley. 1965. "Conditions for Party Leadership: The Case of the House Democrats." *American Political Science Review* 59:52–63.

Goldfarb, Sam, and Brian Friel. 2011. "House and Senate Leaders Prepare for a Showdown over Government Shutdown." *CQ Today Online News*, February 17.

Hartman, Robert W. 1982. "Congress and Budget-Making." *Political Science Quarterly* 97:381–402.

Heniff, Bill, Jr., and Elizabeth Rybicki. 2006. "Debate, Motions, and Other Actions in the Committee of the Whole." *Congressional Research Service*. Washington, DC: Library of Congress.

Higa, Liriel, and David Clarke. 2007. "Spending Bills Stalled amid Stalemate in Earmark Dispute." *CQ Today Online News*, June 14.

Hinds, Asher C. 1907. *Hinds' Precedents of the House of Representatives of the United States*. Washington, DC: Government Printing Office.

Koss, Geoff. 2011. "Republicans Prepare a Flood of Amendments against EPA." *CQ Online News*, February 15.

Kravitz, Walter. 1963. "A Brief History of the Appropriations Committees and Procedure in Congress before 1867." *Legislative Reference Service*. Washington, DC: Library of Congress.

Krawzak, Paul M., and Chuck Conlon. 2009. "Republicans Chafe under Proposed Limit on Amendments to Homeland Bill." *CQ Today Online News*, June 24.

Lindblom, Charles E. 1968. *The Policy-Making Process*. Englewood Cliffs, NJ: Prentice-Hall.

MacDonald, Jason A. 2007. "Agency Design and Postlegislative Influence over the Bureaucracy." *Political Research Quarterly* 60:643–95.

———. 2010. "Limitation Riders and Congressional Influence over Bureaucratic Policy Decisions." *American Political Science Review* 104:766–82.

Marshall, Bryan W., Brandon C. Prins, and David W. Rohde. 2003. "Majority Party Leadership, Strategic Choice, and Committee Power: Appropriations in the House, 1995–98." In *Congress on Display, Congress at Work*, edited by William T. Bianco, 69–100. Ann Arbor: University of Michigan Press.

Melnick, R. Shep. 1983. *Regulation and the Courts: The Case of the Clean Air Act*. Washington, DC: Brookings Institution Press.

Oleszek, Walter J. 2007. *Congressional Procedures and the Policy Process*. 6th ed. Washington, DC: CQ Press.

Oppenheimer, Bruce I. 1980. "Policy Effects of the U.S. House Reform: Decentralization and the Capacity to Resolve Energy Issues." *Legislative Studies Quarterly* 5:5–30.

Ota, Alan K. 2007. "Democrats Prepare for Martial Law; Republicans Say It Feels Like It Already." *CQ Today Online News*, August 1.

Pear, Robert. 2006. "Fiscal Conservatives Heighten Fight Over Pet Projects." *New York Times*, May 25.

Palazzolo, Daniel J. 1992. *The Speaker and the Budget: Leadership in the Post Reform House of Representatives*. Pittsburgh, PA: University of Pittsburgh Press.

Patashnik, Eric. 2005. "Budgets and Fiscal Policy." In *The Legislative Branch*, edited by Paul J. Quirk and Sarah A. Binder, 382–406. New York: Oxford University Press.

Rohde, David W. 1991. *Parties and Leaders in the Postreform House*. Chicago: University of Chicago Press.

Rose, Melody. 2001a. "Losing Control: The Intraparty Consequences of Divided Government." *Presidential Studies Quarterly* 31:679–98.

———. 2001b. "Divided Government and the Rise of Social Regulation." *Policy Studies Journal* 29:611–26.

"Rules of the House of Representatives." 1973. In *House Manual, Ninety-Third Congress*, edited by Louis Deschler, H.Doc. No. 384, 92nd Cong., 2nd sess. Washington, DC: Government Printing Office.

———. 2009. In *House Manual, One Hundred Eleventh Congress*, edited by John V. Sullivan, H.Doc. 110-162, 110th Cong., 2nd sess. Washington, DC: Government Printing Office.

Ruyle, Megan. 2009. "Flake Threatens New Assault on Earmarks." *The Hill*, July 15.

Sachs, Richard C. 1984. "Limitation Amendments to Appropriation Bills: The Implementation of the House Rule XXI(2)(d) in the Ninety-Eighth Congress." *Congressional Research Service*. Washington, DC: Library of Congress.

Schick, Allen. 1984. "Legislation, Appropriations, and Budgets: The Development of Spending Decision-Making in Congress." *Congressional Research Service*. Washington, DC: Library of Congress.

Sinclair, Barbara. 1983. *Majority Leadership in the U.S. House*. Baltimore: The Johns Hopkins University Press.

———. 1986. "The Role of Committees in Agenda Setting in the U.S. Congress." *Legislative Studies Quarterly* 11:35–45.

———. 1995. *Legislators, Leaders, and Lawmaking: The U.S. House of Representatives in the Postreform Era*. Baltimore: The Johns Hopkins University Press.

———. 1997. *Unorthodox Lawmaking: New Legislative Processes in the U.S. Congress*. Washington, DC: CQ Press.

Smith, Steven S. 1989. *Call to Order: Floor Politics in the House and Senate*. Washington, DC: Brookings Institution.

Stewart, Charles H., III. 1989. *Budget Reform Politics: The Design of the Appropriations Process in the House of Representatives, 1865–1921*. New York: Cambridge University Press.

Streeter, Sandy. 2010. "The Congressional Appropriations Process: An Introduction." *Congressional Research Service*. Washington, DC: Library of Congress.

Sundquist, James L. 1983. "The Legislative Veto: A Bounced Check." *Brookings Review* 2:13–16.

Thurber, James A. 1992. "New Rules for an Old Game: Zero-Sum Budgeting in the Postreform Congress." In *The Postreform Congress*, edited by Roger H. Davidson, 257–78. New York: St. Martin's Press.

Tollestrup, Jessica. 2010. "Limitation Riders in the 97th through 110th Congresses: A Test of Procedural Cartel and Conditional Party Government Theories." Paper presented at the annual meeting of the Midwest Political Science Association, Chicago, Illinois, April 22–25.

Vazzano, Frank P. 1993. "President Hayes, Congress, and the Appropriations Riders Vetoes." *Congress and the Presidency* 20:25–37.

Weyl, Ben. 2011. "House Passes GOP Spending Plan." *CQ Today Online News*, February 19.

Young, Kerry. 2011. "Policy Riders Remain on Table in Spending Talks." *CQ Today Online News*, March 29.

Young, Kerry, and Sam Goldfarb. 2011. "House Leaders Let the Right Make Its Case on Fiscal 2011 Spending." *CQ Today Online News*, February 15.

5

Minority Party Strategies and the Evolution of the Motion to Recommit in the U.S. House

Jennifer Hayes Clark

M AJORITY RULE AND MINORITY RIGHTS are fundamental values of representative democracy. One of the critical issues that motivates the design of institutions and the formation of constitutions is how to achieve a system that empowers the majority to carry out the public will while maintaining rights for the minority. Over two centuries ago, Thomas Jefferson recognized the vital role of institutional rules and procedures in guaranteeing the minority the opportunity to meaningfully participate in the legislative process when he said:

> As it is always in the power of the majority, by their numbers, to stop any improper measures proposed on the part of their opponents, the only weapons by which the minority can defend themselves against similar attempts from those in power are the forms and rules of proceeding. (Sullivan 2011, 126)

Questions regarding the role of the minority party in majoritarian institutions persist in contemporary politics with frequent charges by the minority party that the majority party is abusing the rules to suppress opposition to their agenda. Objections to the Democratic majority's proposed rules changes, such as those alluded to by Representative Lincoln Diaz-Balart at the beginning of the 111th Congress (2009–2011), set the stage for a variety of procedural and policy battles that would play out over the course of the Democrats' unified control of government. For example, Representative Diaz-Balart said:

> For 100 years, the motion to recommit has really been sacrosanct in this House, and the essence of representative democracy is, yes, rule by the majority with respect to the rights of the minority. Today, history will record that in this rules package by

the majority, the severe limitation of the right of the minority to offer an alternative in legislation, this severe limitation of the motion to recommit, is a sad, unfortunate, and wholly unnecessary step that takes a very strong, a very significant step toward unaccountability. (Diaz-Balart 2009, H15)

From the vantage point of Representative Diaz-Balart, a member of the minority party, the rules package pushed by Speaker Nancy Pelosi and congressional Democrats severely threatened the ability of opponents to voice their opposition and to offer policy alternatives through use of a motion to recommit with instructions reported "promptly." This would prove critical as the 111th Congress took on an impressive agenda spanning comprehensive health care reform, energy policy, and financial reform.

Although it may seem obvious that the majority party would dominate the policymaking process in a system predicated on majority rule, it has not always been the case that congressional rules and procedures were stacked in favor of the majority party. Indeed, the rules and procedures established during the 1st Congress (1789–1791) gave equal authority to the parties (Binder 1997). Many argue that subsequent changes to the rules, particularly in the U.S. House of Representatives, have stacked the deck in favor of the majority party. Partisan theories of legislative organization, for example, contend that majority party dominance is achieved and maintained not exclusively through cohesive voting majorities but also through the strategic structuring of legislative rules as tools of the majority party (Cox and McCubbins 1993, 2005). Despite this belief of majority party dominance in the U.S. House, some tools for the minority party also exist in the legislative rules.

This chapter examines the motion to recommit, which has often been described as one of the fundamental rights afforded to the minority party in the U.S. House. Krehbiel and Meirowitz (2002) argue that the motion to recommit serves as an ex post veto power that affords the minority party significant policymaking influence. In this chapter, I reexamine the motion to recommit and its ability to confer significant legislative influence to the minority party. Through historical analysis and empirical modeling, I cast doubt upon the notion that the motion to recommit confers real policy gains to the minority party. These findings contribute to one of the long-standing debates of congressional research concerning the role of political parties in legislative decision-making.

Party, Procedure, and the Motion to Recommit

Article I, section 5 of the Constitution states that each chamber shall determine its own rules of legislative proceedings. Shortly following the seating of each new Congress, members come together to determine the rules and procedures that govern the legislative process. The adoption of legislative rules at the beginning of the session is anything but pro forma though. According to former House Republican Leader Bob Michel, "Procedure hasn't simply become more important than substance—it has, through some strange alchemy, become the substance of our deliberations. Who rules House procedures, rules the House—and to a great degree, rules the kind and scope of political debate in this country" (Oleszek 2007). Stated more bluntly, Representative John Dingell maintained that "if you let me write procedure and I let you write substance, I'll screw you every time." The rules of the legislative game determine whose legislation receives consideration on the House floor, who can offer amendments to legislation, and who has veto authority. In theory, representative institutions should embrace equal participation among all members. In practice, institutional rules and norms confer unequal weight, empowering some at the expense of others, thereby determining who wields influence over legislative outcomes.

Partisan theorists argue that majorities structure the rules in ways to enhance their power and achieve their most preferred policy outcomes. Cox and McCubbins (1993) argue that the majority party acts as a cartel usurping power to craft rules that facilitate moving policy toward the majority party's ideal position (and away from the median voter in the chamber). Cox and McCubbins's partisan cartel theory holds that the majority party successfully advances its policy objectives not simply through cohesive majorities but also through the strategic structuring of legislative rules and procedures that provides the majority party control over the legislative agenda.

The majority party leadership has various mechanisms, including regular party caucus meetings, party whips, and representation of diverse actors in leadership positions, to communicate party interests to rank-and-file members and to extract information about legislative preferences, thereby reducing uncertainty about legislative outcomes. Leadership can then utilize this information to craft bills that will pass the full chamber (*positive agenda control*) or block legislation that internally divides the party from consideration on the floor (*negative agenda control*). Additionally, leaders may employ standard carrot-on-a-stick methods to promote party discipline through its institutional prerogatives to determine the composition and makeup of congressional committees, the scheduling of legislation on the floor, and its privilege to steer distributive benefits to members' legislative districts (Carroll and Kim 2010). Cox and McCubbins (2005, 47–48) argue that centrist members may be induced to support majority party policies through distributive benefits (e.g., pork-barrel projects for their districts). Centrists may withstand policy losses if provided real distributive benefits by their party leaders.

A second theory, known as the conditional party government theory, was developed by Aldrich and Rohde (1998, 2001). The conditional party government theory argues that the costs and benefits accrued by rank-and-file members delegating authority to the leadership vary according to the ideological homogeneity within the party and differentiation/polarization between the parties. Delegating authority to leadership is less costly to members when their party is internally cohesive and polarized from the other party. This is an important distinction of the U.S. Congress, where party discipline—even in the current polarized era—is much lower than party discipline in other legislatures around the world, such as the U.K. House of Commons (Spirling and McLean 2007). In the United States, legislators have strong incentives to cultivate a personal vote (given the electoral rules) and therefore, in some instances, the costs of voting with the party outweigh the benefits, particularly when it conflicts with the preferences of the constituency on a highly salient issue. Thus, the costs and benefits of delegating authority to the party leadership are clearly affected by the ideological character of the membership of the party in Congress (Rohde 1991).

Critics of the partisan theory have contended that the decisions of legislators are primarily driven by their ideological preferences and that the inclusion of partisanship in the model does not contribute anything significant to the explanation (Krehbiel 1993, 1998). The informational theory of congressional organization contends that legislative institutions are created to facilitate the gathering of information to reduce the level of uncertainty faced by legislators when formulating policy. Since the U.S. House is a majoritarian institution and the rules are subject to change by a simple majority of the membership, stacking the deck to favor some interests over others may prove especially difficult. Krehbiel (1993, 1998) contends that the preferences of legislators alone are sufficient to explain legislative behavior and the inclusion of party in the model does not significantly improve its predictive power. From Krehbiel's perspective, the median voter in the chamber ultimately controls policy and, therefore, his model predicts centrist legislative outcomes.

Scholars have argued that partisan influence in legislative politics may take various forms, including blocking unfavorable legislative proposals and amendments, arm-twisting to ensure that members vote for the party's proposal, rewarding party discipline with the appointment of influential or beneficial committee assignments, etc. The partisan cartel theory focuses in large part on the negative agenda control powers of political parties (i.e., the ability of the majority party to keep proposals that it dislikes off the floor and to prevent its policy proposals from losing on the floor). It is in the best interest of the majority party to use its pre-floor procedural powers to prevent legislation that would be less favorable than the status quo from coming to the floor, receiving a roll call, and possibly being passed.

To the extent that the rules and procedures enable a coalition to amend, debate, or obstruct the majority's agenda, they impede the ability of the majority to achieve its most preferred policy outcomes. The motion to recommit, as established by House Rule 19, permits opponents of a measure to offer an alternative for consideration prior to the previous question. Krehbiel and Meirowitz (2002) argue that the motion to recommit affords the minority an unrestricted opportunity to make a final take-it-or-leave-it proposal, which greatly undermines the ability of the majority party to control the legislative agenda. Thus, they argue that this lends support to their nonpartisan theory of legislative politics in which the median voter in the chamber prevails.

Before considering the partisan consequences of the motion to recommit, it is important to elaborate on some details of how this motion works. The motion to recommit may be offered in various forms. The first type of motion to recommit is commonly referred to as a "straight" motion to recommit. The straight motion to recommit is a motion offered without instructions and allows for no debate. If the motion is adopted by the chamber, the underlying bill is returned to committee. There is no promise that the bill will receive further consideration by the House; therefore, opponents of a measure may use the motion to recommit without instructions to effectively dispose of legislation by bottling it up in committee in hopes that it will not be returned to the floor for further consideration.

Opponents of a measure may also offer the motion to recommit with "forthwith" instructions. A motion to recommit "forthwith" contains amendatory language that is considered on the House floor without being referred back to committee. A successful motion to recommit with instructions to report back "forthwith" allows any amendatory language included in the motion to be adopted immediately without the measure leaving the House floor. Finally, the motion to recommit with "non-forthwith" instructions returns the measure back to committee with no real assurance that the committee will ever act on the bill. In some instances, the motion to recommit will instruct the committee to "promptly" act and report back to the House; however, this has no true effect in urging the committee to act. This last form of the motion to recommit may include amendatory language, instruct further research or hearings on a matter, or urge action on the part of the committee; however, these actions are simply advisory and do not in fact require the committee to take any action on the measure. Rules changes during the 111th Congress only provide for a motion to recommit a bill or joint resolution to include instructions "forthwith."[1]

The motion to recommit has been hailed as an important right of the House minority party, which lacks the institutional tools available to its counterpart in the U.S. Senate (Binder 1997; Wawro and Schickler 2006). Unlike the filibuster or other tools available for the minority to obstruct the majority party's policy agenda, Krehbiel and Meirowitz (2002) argue that the motion to recommit affords members of the minority party the opportunity to positively shape the legislative agenda through offering policy alternatives to legislation currently under consideration. Before touting the motion to recommit as the great equalizer between the parties in the House, a few points concerning how the motion has worked in practice, the limitations placed upon the minority party's amendatory powers, and its place in the broader policymaking context must be considered.

Although this procedural right has existed since the 1st Congress and may be traced back to the British Parliament, the motion to recommit has operated differently over time. This institutional prerogative recently has been touted by members of the majority party as evidence of their commitment to procedural fairness. In rebuffing claims of abusive majority party tactics at the beginning of the 108th Congress (2003–2004), Representative David Dreier, who served as chairman of the Rules Committee, stated the following:

> If my colleagues look at the reforms that we have maintained we initiated once we became a majority and frankly built upon, they do, in fact, increase the accountability and the deliberative nature of this Congress. We have items that are included in this measure which guarantee the minority the right to offer a motion to recommit on legislation. (Dreier 2003, 18)

In an essay on the motion to recommit, Donald Wolfensberger (2003) characterizes the motion to recommit as "a convenient last bastion of institutional fairness in an otherwise unfair process" (28). A historical view of the motion to recommit casts doubt on the perspective of the motion to recommit as a legislative prerogative that affords the minority meaningful influence in the policymaking process. Although the procedural right has existed in the codified rules since the inception of Congress, in the earlier congresses the motion was frequently used to further majority party interests, thereby limiting its use as a tool for the minority party. In the earlier years, the motion to recommit was frequently used by supporters to correct technical errors in the bill's language. The relevant language concerning the motion to recommit did not make any explicit reference to the opposition or minority party. Only during the 1909 rules changes did reformers include language that explicitly referenced the opposition or minority party. Consequently, the Speaker was given great discretion in determining who could offer the motion to recommit and frequently ruled that the motion to recommit was intended to provide an opportunity for supporters of a bill to clean up the language before final adoption. On the matter concerning a motion to recommit a legislative, executive, and judicial appropriations bill during the 62nd Congress (1911–1913), House Speaker Joseph Cannon clarified the intent of the motion:

> The object of this provision was, as the Chair has always understood, that the motion should be made by one friendly to the bill, for the purpose of giving one more chance to perfect it, as perchance there might be some error that the House desired to correct. (Cannon 1936, 383)

Others have likewise interpreted the motion to recommit as a tool for the majority party to make small technical changes before legislation is adopted. Representative John Dalzell describes the motion in the following way: "We all know that the motion to recommit, under existing practice, has been used not to secure recommittal, but to prevent recommittal. The custom has grown up to have a member of the majority party move to recommit and then to have his colleagues vote the motion down" (Dalzell 1909, 31).

Thus, early interpretations of the motion to recommit undermined the opposition's authority to participate meaningfully by advancing its own policy alternatives into the discussion. In fact, this interpretation of the motion to recommit also facilitated the majority party's efforts in controlling the legislative agenda. However, Wolfensberger (2003) points out that from 1880 to 1909 Speakers were much more inclined to recognize members of the minority party than members of their own party to offer the motion to recommit. Nonetheless, the lack of clear language concerning who should be recognized to offer the motion to recommit in the event of multiple authors of motions served to empower the Speaker. Consequently, between 1880 and 1909, the minority party's rights were far from guaranteed and rested upon the Speaker's goodwill.

The rules changes of 1909 clarified the intent of the motion to recommit as a tool of the opposition. Specifically, the House amended what is now Rule 19, clause 2(a) to include language stating that the Speaker give preference to "a Member, Delegate, or Resident Commissioner who is opposed to the measure" to offer the motion to recommit. This rule change seemingly benefited the minority party by taking the guesswork out of determining who should be recognized to offer the motion to recommit. By 1932, House precedents interpreted this rule as granting preferential recognition to a member of the minority party opposed to the underlying measure. The new recommit rule stated that

after the previous question shall have been ordered on the passage of a bill or joint resolution, one motion to recommit shall be in order, and the Speaker shall give preference in recognition to a member who is opposed to the bill or joint resolution.[2]

Moreover, the rule prohibited the Rules Committee from reporting "any rule or order that would prevent the motion to recommit from being made as provided in paragraph 4 of Rule XVI." These changes in the language concerning the motion to recommit seemingly strengthen the prerogatives of the minority party to offer policy alternatives. However, there are still reasons to doubt that these changes have substantially increased involvement of the minority party in legislative decision-making.

Following the 1909 rules changes, one of the first major hits to minority party rights occurred in 1934 when Speaker Henry Rainey determined that the Rules

Committee had the ability to issue special rules that prohibit all amendments and limit (but not completely prohibit) amendatory language offered by the motion to recommit. The justification in limiting motions to recommit with amendatory language was that the 1909 rule only pertained to the straight motion to recommit. Speaker Rainey argued that only a straight motion to recommit was guaranteed to the opposition. According to Wolfensberger (1991), this limitation set the stage for the majority party to begin issuing special rules to curb the ability of the minority to offer motions to recommit with instructions. The issuance of restrictive rules by the Rules Committee dates back to 1883 (Nelson 1994). However, restrictive rules did not become commonplace until the mid-1970s (Bach and Smith 1988; Sinclair 1994, 1997). The rise in closed and semi-closed rules, which place restriction on amending, by the Rules Committee was accompanied by other tactics, including the "king-of-the-hill," to restrict the ability of the minority party to offer a motion to recommit with instructions. These restrictions were in addition to those already in place, such as the requirement of germaneness and stipulations of PAYGO (Lynch 2008).

With the Republicans' takeover of the House during the 1994 midterm election, the new leadership pushed a broad package of reforms as part of the Contract with America, including changes in the rules and procedures of Congress. Included in their proposed changes was a section titled "Affirming the Minority's Right on Motions to Recommit." In short, the new Republican majority altered the standing rules of the House to ban special rules that prevent a motion to recommit. This came after several decades of being in the minority party and complaining of perceived abuses in legislative procedures. Since the 104th Congress, the minority party has frequently exercised its prerogative to offer the motion to recommit. Figure 5.1 shows contemporary trends in the motion to recommit (104th–110th Congresses). These data were compiled using the Library of Congress THOMAS database. During the 110th Congress, 120 motions to recommit were offered, with 72 including "forthwith" instructions and 47 "non-forthwith" instructions. Over the course of this period, few "straight" motions to recommit have been offered.

Of the various types of motions, the motion to recommit with "forthwith" instructions is the most common. In the 109th to the 110th Congresses, there was a sharp increase in members offering the motion with "forthwith" instructions as well as the passage of "forthwith" instructions. There was also a substantial increase in motions to recommit with "non-forthwith" instructions in the 109th and 110th Congresses. However, none of these motions passed during this time period. During the 110th Congress (2007–2008), the minority party offered motions to recommit that spanned the legislative agenda from the Lobbying Transparency Act to the D.C. Voting Rights bill. In more recent cases, the majority party has charged that the minority party is simply using its institutional prerogative for political gain. In a recent essay, Norman Ornstein (2010) argued

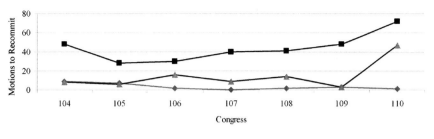

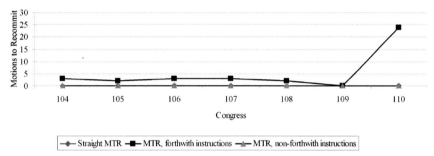

FIGURE 5.1
Incidences of the Motion to Recommit, 104th–110th Congresses: Total Number of Motions to Recommit by Type

that "the motion to recommit with instructions has for more than a decade become a hollow vehicle and a farce. . . . The minority has eschewed the chance to use the motion to recommit to offer constructive amendments to bills or to show a minority alternative vision, and instead has used the gotcha route." One recent example cited is the American COMPETES reauthorization, in which the bipartisan legislation focused on increasing our investment in science research and training. The motion to recommit offered by the minority required that any federal employee who had viewed or downloaded pornography be fired.

Despite the charge that the motion to recommit has become nothing more than a farce, the increasing use of this tool by the minority party (whether for political or policy gains) deserves some explanation. Thus, in the next section, I expand upon the theories of legislative politics discussed earlier and investigate whether one theory better describes the politics surrounding the motion to recommit in the U.S. House. In particular, under what conditions do motions to recommit pass the House in the face of majority party opposition? Understanding the factors that shape voting outcomes on motions to recommit will enhance our knowledge about the role of parties in legislative decision-making and the institutions that enhance or diminish the ability of the minority party to participate in the policymaking process.

The Motion to Recommit and Partisan Theories of Legislative Politics

The previous sections demonstrate the theoretical foundations of the motion to recommit and trace its evolution over the course of congressional history. In this section, I consider the partisan consequences of the motion to recommit. Does the motion to recommit undermine majority party control over the legislative agenda and provide an opportunity for the minority party to exert influence over legislative outcomes? In particular, I test competing theories of legislative organization—partisan and preference-based theories—to understand how and under what conditions the opponents of a measure can effectively offer a motion to recommit. The party cartel theory developed by Cox and McCubbins (1993, 2005) predicts that the majority party should never suffer a loss in the form of a motion to recommit. Indeed, they argue that the majority party should either defeat the motion through its superior numeric size (and voting cohesion among members) or through tight control of the legislative agenda, in which no unfavorable legislation is able to reach the House floor for consideration.

The conditional party government theory offered by Aldrich and Rohde (2001) predicts that party leaders are strongest and best able to promote the party agenda when the two parties are polarized from each other yet internally cohesive. Under these conditions, the costs for legislators to delegate power to their leadership are much less. Thus, the conditional party government theory suggests that the majority party will be most effective in staving off defeat via a motion to recommit when the majority party is more internally cohesive (high intraparty cohesion) and the two parties are more ideologically polarized (high interparty polarization). The nonpartisan theory espoused by Krehbiel and Meirowitz (2002) predicts that a large number of motions to recommit will be offered regularly and that these motions will pass.

To test these competing theories, I compiled a dataset of all motions to recommit offered during the 61st Congress (1909–1911) through the 110th Congress (2007–2008). Upon identifying whether a motion to recommit was offered, I then coded whether the motion had amendatory language and whether it contained a forthwith or non-forthwith instruction, whether the motion passed or failed, and whether the motion passed with a majority of the majority party in opposition to the motion (a majority party "roll"). The nonpartisan theory suggests that motions to recommit will frequently (if not always) pass the House. The party cartel theory predicts a low passage rate of motions to recommit, as they undermine the majority party policy priorities. Finally, the conditional party government theory suggests that the majority party will be more successful when it is internally homogeneous and ideologically distant from the minority party.

The average majority party roll rate on motions to recommit is about 2 percent. The low rate of majority party rolls on motions to recommit provides some limited support for the partisan theories. However, to provide a stronger test of the competing theories, I employ multivariate analysis of motion to recommit outcomes. Under what conditions do recommittal motions pass the House in the face of majority party opposition?

I employed a number of independent variables that should influence majority party roll rates on the motion to recommit. To assess the conditional party government theory, I construct measures of the internal homogeneity of the majority party, which is simply the standard deviation of first dimensional DW-NOMINATE scores for legislators (Poole and Rosenthal 1997). DW-NOMINATE scores were obtained using a scaling procedure on all competitive roll call votes (i.e., at least 5 percent voting in the minority) developed by Keith Poole and Howard Rosenthal. Roughly, these scores provide us with a measure of legislators' ideological positions relative to those of other members. Conditional party government theory suggests that majority party rolls on the motion to recommit increases with majority party ideological heterogeneity. Thus, as the majority party becomes more ideologically heterogeneous, the minority party may be better equipped to convince some members of the majority to join its recommittal efforts at the expense of their party.

The conditional party government theory predicts that as the two parties become more differentiated ideologically (i.e., greater polarization) the majority party roll rate on motions to recommit should decline. Ideological polarization between the parties is measured as the absolute difference between the median party members' first dimensional DW-NOMINATE scores. These measures have been employed frequently in the literature to measure ideology of individual members (Poole and Rosenthal 1997) as well as ideological dispersion within and between parties (Aldrich and Rohde 2001).

Drawing upon the earlier analysis of Roberts (2005), the model includes a dummy variable controlling for recorded voting in the Committee of the Whole during the 92nd Congress (1971–1972). Roberts (2005) argues that the adoption of electronic voting technology produced an increase in the ability of the minority party to achieve a recorded vote on amendments. Likewise, the model also controls for the frequency of restrictions placed on amendatory instructions by House Democrats (Wolfensberger 1991). These restrictions are expected to have a negative impact on the number of rolls during a given Congress. Finally, I also include dummy variables for motions that concern social issues and appropriations issues.

The dependent variable for this analysis is a count (number of rolls per Congress); thus it was important that I control for the number of opportunities for the event to occur (King 1989). The number of rolls is potentially important theoretically, as Cox and McCubbins (2005) argue that one of the most important procedural powers of the majority party is to control the legislative agenda by keeping items that divide the party off the floor, thereby keeping the status quo intact. Majority party roll rates have been used extensively in legislative research (Cox and McCubbins 2005; Gailmard and Jenkins 2007). However, Krehbiel (2007) notes a number of limitations of the measure and its ability to effectively measure "party influence." In cases where the majority party experiences deep divisions, it is unlikely that the majority leadership would place legislation on the calendar for consideration. Consequently, I included the natural log of the number of measures being voted upon to control for differential opportunities that the majority party will face a roll across different legislative sessions.

Table 5.1 presents the multivariate analysis of the number of majority party rolls on recommittal motions per legislative session. The results of the analysis lend strong statistical support for the theory of conditional party government. Majority party heterogeneity is positively associated with the majority party rolls on recommittal motions. In instances where the majority party has greater ideological diversity, motions to recommit are much more likely to actually pass despite majority party opposition to them. Interparty polarization is also statistically significant in the model and in the predicted negative direction. Thus, the majority party is much less likely to face a roll on a recommittal motion when its ideological distance is farther from the other party. This makes intuitive sense, as the minority party is less able to convince members of the majority party to join their coalition to pass the motion when the two parties are highly polarized.

The variable controlling for the size of the majority party is also statistically significant. Larger majorities are less likely to suffer rolls on motions to recommit. This again is intuitive, as a small minority would need to convince a greater number of members in the majority party to join them in passing the motion to recommit. The interactive variable (majority party size × heterogeneity) did not reach the conventional levels of statistical significance. The results of the model also suggest that the majority party is more likely to face a

TABLE 5.1
Generalized Event Count Model of the Motion to Recommit

Predictor	Estimated Coefficient
Majority Party Polarization (DW-NOM)	−1.79*
Majority Party Cohesiveness (DW-NOM)	24.23*
Size of the Majority Party	−3.11*
Majority Size x Heterogeneity	5.01
Ln (Final Passage Votes)	0.01
Restrictions on Instructions	0.12*
Social Policy	1.58*
Appropriations Issue	−2.31
Electronic Voting	1.76
Constant	−1.05
Log—Likelihood	−67.12

*$p < 0.05$

roll on the motion to recommit on social issues. However, there is no statistically significant difference in the roll rates of appropriation bills. The baseline prediction of majority party rolls is about 1.1 with all variables held constant. These results lend support for partisan theories and suggest a conditional relationship of party strength and recommittal rolls for the majority party. These results cast doubt upon the predictions of the Krehbiel and Meirowitz (2002) model. These empirical results further highlight the contingent nature of minority party influence over legislative outcomes.

Conclusion

In 1809, Jefferson asserted that codified rules and procedures were vital in protecting the rights of the minority. Although institutional prerogatives granted to the minority may be a necessary condition for meaningful participation and influence in the legislative process, this research suggests that the rules alone are not sufficient for ensuring members of the minority party a seat at the decision-making table. The contingent nature of minority party rights in legislative decision-making has been relatively unexplored in congressional scholarship, despite the fact that the American political system is founded upon the values of majority rule and minority rights.

The motion to recommit is one of the few institutional prerogatives afforded to the minority party in the U.S. House of Representatives. Although some have argued that this right firmly establishes a mechanism for the minority party to meaningfully participate in the policymaking process, norms and customs governing its practice demonstrate how the majority party may suppress minority party influence in the legislative process even in the face of codified rules that seemingly empower the minority party.

The Republican Party's outrage concerning the changes adopted by congressional Democrats at the beginning of the 111th Congress seems to suggest that they perceive the motion to recommit as a valuable right. Systematic analysis of recommittal motions shows that the minority party is rarely successful in fundamentally shaping legislative outcomes. However, there may be other ways, besides policy outcomes, that these motions provide benefits to the minority. As Wolfensberger suggests, the value of the motion to recommit may come in the form of position-taking (Mayhew 1974). Members of the minority party may utilize their institutional prerogatives to put forth a different vision, which they may draw upon come Election Day. On the flip side, it may also be used as a means to force majority party members to take positions that may eventually be used against them in elections. Finally, the mere suggestion of changing the rules may also be used by the minority to cast the majority party as a tyrannical faction seeking a power grab to run roughshod over the opposition.

Notes

1. *Rules of the House of Representatives*, Rule 19, Clause 2(b)(2).
2. *Rules of the House of Representatives*, Rule 19, Clause 2(2)(a).

References

Aldrich, John H., and David Rohde. 1998. "Theories of Party in the Legislature and the Transition to Republican Rule in the House." *Political Science Quarterly* 112:112–35.

———. 2001. "The Logic of Conditional Party Government: Revisiting the Electoral Connection." In *Congress Reconsidered*, 7th ed., edited by Lawrence Dodd and Bruce Oppenheimer, 269–92. Washington, DC: CQ Press.

Bach, Stanley, and Steven S. Smith. 1998 *Managing Uncertainty in the House of Representatives: Adaptation and Innovation in Special Rules*. Washington, DC: Brookings Institution.

Binder, Sarah. 1997. *Minority Rights, Majority Rule*. New York: Cambridge University Press.

Cannon, Clarence, ed. 1936. "The Motion to Refer as Related to the Previous Question." In *Cannon's Precedents*, vol. 8, sec. 2762, 393–94. Washington, DC: Government Printing Office.

Carroll, Royce, and Henry A. Kim. 2010. "Party Government and the 'Cohesive Power of Public Plunder.'" *American Journal of Political Science* 54:34–44.

Cox, Gary W., and Mathew D. McCubbins. 1993. *Legislative Leviathan: Party Government in the House*. Berkeley and Los Angeles: University of California Press.

———. 2005. *Setting the Agenda: Responsible Party Government in the U.S. House of Representatives*. New York: Cambridge University Press.

Dalzell, John. 1909. "Rules." *Congressional Record*, House of Representatives, March 15, vol. 44, part 1: 31.

Deschler, Lewis. 1976. *Deschler's Precedents of the United States House of Representatives*. 94th Cong., 2nd sess. H.Doc. 94-661. Washington, DC: Government Printing Office.

Diaz-Balart, Lincoln. 2009. "Rules of the House." *Congressional Record*, House of Representatives, January 6, vol. 155, daily edition: H15.

Drier, David. 2003. "Rules of the House." *Congressional Record*, House of Representatives, January 7, vol. 149, part 1: 18.

Gailmard, Sean, and Jeffery A. Jenkins. 2007. "Negative Agenda Control in the Senate and House: Fingerprints of Majority Party Power." *Journal of Politics* 69:689–700.

King, Gary. 1989. "Variance Specification in Event Count Models: From Restrictive Assumptions to a Generalized Estimator." *American Journal of Political Science* 33:762–84.

Krehbiel, Keith. 1993. "Where Is the Party?" *British Journal of Political Science* 23:235–66.

———. 1998. *Pivotal Politics: A Theory of U.S. Lawmaking*. Chicago: University of Chicago Press.

———. 2007. "Partisan Roll Rates in a Nonpartisan Legislature." *Journal of Law, Economics, and Organization* 23:1–23.

Krehbiel, Keith, and Adam Meirowitz. 2002. "Minority Rights and Majority Power: Theoretical Consequences of the Motion to Recommit." *Legislative Studies Quarterly* 27:191–218.

Lynch, Megan S. 2008. "The Motion to Recommit in the House of Representatives: Effects, Recent Trends, and Options for Change." *Congressional Research Service*. Washington, DC: Library of Congress.

Mayhew, David. 1974. *Congress: The Electoral Connection*. New Haven, CT: Yale University Press.

Nelson, Garrison. 1994. *Committees in the U.S. Congress, 1947–1992. Volume II: Committee Histories and Member Assignments*. Washington, DC: CQ Press.

Oleszek, Walter J. 2007. *Congressional Procedures and the Policy Process*. Washington, DC: CQ Press.

Ornstein, Norman. 2010. "The Motion to Recommit, Hijacked by Politics." *Roll Call,* May 18.

Poole, Keith T., and Howard Rosenthal. 1997. *Congress: A Political-Economic History of Roll Call Voting.* New York: Oxford University Press.

Roberts, Jason M. 2005. "Minority Rights and Majority Power: Conditional Party Government and the Motion to Recommit in the House." *Legislative Studies Quarterly* 30:219–34.

Rohde, David. 1991. *Parties and Leaders in the Post-Reform House.* Chicago: University of Chicago Press.

Sinclair, Barbara. 1994. "House Special Rules and the Institutional Design Controversy." *Legislative Studies Quarterly* 19:477–94.

——. 1997. *Unorthodox Lawmaking: New Legislative Processes in the U.S. Congress.* Washington, DC: CQ Press.

Spirling, Arthur, and Iain McLean. 2007. "UK OC OK? Interpreting Optimal Classification Scores for the United Kingdom House of Commons." *Political Analysis* 15:1–12.

Sullivan, John V., ed. 2011. "Jefferson's Manual of Parliamentary Practice." In *Constitution, Jefferson's Manual, and Rules of the House of Representatives of the United States, One Hundred Twelfth Congress.* 111th Cong., 2nd sess., H.Doc. 111-157: 126.

Wawro, Gregory, and Eric Schickler. 2006. *Filibuster: Obstruction and Lawmaking in the U.S. Senate.* Princeton, NJ: Princeton University Press.

Wolfensberger, Donald. 1991. "Motion to Recommit in the House: The Rape of a Minority Right." U.S. Congress, House Subcommittee on Rules of the House, *Roundtable Discussion on the Motion to Recommit.* 102nd Cong., 2nd sess. Washington, DC: Government Printing Office.

——. 2003. "The Motion to Recommit in the House: The Creation, Evisceration, and Restoration of a Minority Right." Paper presented at the History of Congress Conference, University of California, San Diego.

6

Let's Vote

*The Rise and Impact of Roll Call Votes in the Age of Electronic Voting**

Jacob R. Straus

T HE HOUSE OF REPRESENTATIVES regularly uses one of two methods for voting on legislation, amendments, and procedural matters: voice votes and recorded (i.e., roll call) votes. Voice votes are most common and decide a question when no member of the House asks for a recorded vote.[1] Historically, recorded votes were used sparingly, in part because of the time commitment necessary. If a recorded vote was requested, approximately forty-five minutes were often required for a clerk to orally call the membership roll (Sinclair 1995, 69).

Beginning in 1886, some members expressed concern that roll call votes could be used by the minority party to slow down the legislative productivity of the House. Not only were roll call votes being used more often for final passage of legislation, but the minority could also request recorded votes on procedural questions. To address the time spent on floor voting, several proposals were introduced in the House to potentially automate the voting process.

While none of these early legislative proposals ever advanced beyond a hearing, the concept behind the proposals—speeding up an aspect of legislative floor action—opened a debate about tension between members of the majority and minority parties and strategies attached to voting in Congress. Connelly (2010) suggests that minority parties have long debated their role in government. The minority must decide whether to cooperate or be in opposition to the majority and whether to compromise with or confront the majority (18). Nowhere is this truer than in the House of Representatives, where the elected leaders of

*This chapter reflects the views of the author and does not necessarily reflect the views of the Congressional Research Service or the Library of Congress. The author would like to thank Christopher Davis, Courtney Dell, Matthew Glassman, and Jessica Gerrity for their comments on earlier drafts.

the chamber represent the majority party and historically have had the ability to control chamber activities and the scheduling of legislation (Cooper and Brady 1981; Krehbiel and Wiseman 2001).

Because of the majority's control of the legislative agenda, the voting process in the House matters. Electronic voting, for the first time, allowed the majority party to more quickly move through votes, thus providing opportunities to schedule additional bills and resolutions for floor debate.

Using electronic voting as a lens, this chapter explores early proposals for automated voting beginning in the nineteenth century to understand how rules structure outcomes in Congress. After framing the historic rationale for automating the voting process, the chapter discusses the passage and creation of the modern electronic voting system. The chapter then examines the connection between electronic voting (an operational change) on procedural activity, the impact of technology in the House, and issues of transparency that are raised through electronic voting. Finally, the chapter briefly examines patterns of roll call voting both before and after electronic voting and discusses the effects electronic voting has had on the House of Representatives.

History and Adoption of Electronic Voting

The first legislative proposals to create an automated voting system in the House of Representatives were introduced in 1886. As early as 1869, however, Thomas Edison had filed a patent for an "Electrographic Vote-Recorder" (Edison 1869; Thomas Edison Papers 2011). In 1890, Edison and his colleague Dewitt Roberts demonstrated the machine to Congress. As Edison recalled in an interview with *Harpers New Monthly Magazine*:

> We got hold of the right man to get the machine adopted, and I enthusiastically set forth its merits to him. Just imagine my feelings when, in a horrified tone, he exclaimed: "Young man, that won't do at all! That is just what we do not want. Your invention would destroy the only hope the minority have of influencing legislation. It would deliver them over, bound hand and foot, to the majority. The present system gives them a weapon which is invaluable, and as the ruling majority always know that it may some day become a minority, they will be as much averse to any change as their opponents." (Lathrop 1890, 431–32)

Early Legislative Proposals

In 1886, the first two legislative proposals to create an automated voting system were introduced. The first, introduced by Representative Lewis Beach, directed the Committee on Rules to "inquire into the feasibility of a plan for registering votes" (Beach 1886). The second, introduced by Representative Benjamin Le Fevre, would have amended the rules of the House to allow for the "electrical recording of the yeas and nays" (Le Fevre 1886). Neither proposal received further consideration.

While Representatives Beach and Le Fevre did not get their proposals adopted, they established the basic legislative strategies that would be used for future automated voting proposals. Between 1886 and 1969, twenty-one representatives introduced a total of fifty-one proposals to install some type of automatic, electrical, or mechanical voting system in the House of Representatives. Like the proposals introduced by Representatives Beech and Le Fevre, subsequent proposals either directed the House to study the feasibility of automated voting or ordered the chamber to adopt automated voting technology.

After 1886, another proposal to use automated voting technology in the House was not introduced for twenty-eight years. In the 63rd Congress (1913–1914), Representative Allan Walsh introduced H.Res. 513, which would have created an electrical and mechanical system of voting for the House of Representatives (Committee on Accounts 1914). A special subcommittee of the Committee on Accounts held hearings on H.Res. 513 and discussed what an automated voting system might look like. The report described a system in which each member would have his own voting box with a unique key. Votes would be transmitted electrically and recorded mechanically by a machine installed on the clerk's desk, with votes displayed on boards throughout the chamber and in the cloakrooms (Committee on Accounts 1914, 4–6).[2] No further action was taken on H.Res. 513.

In the 64th Congress (1915–1916), a similar proposal (H.Res. 223) was introduced by Representative William Howard. Hearings were held by the Committee on Accounts in which testimony was heard from outside experts, including representatives of a company then installing an electrical voting system in the Wisconsin legislature (Committee on Accounts 1916a; Holst 1919, 53). H.Res. 223 was favorably reported by the Committee on Accounts, but was not acted upon by the House (Committee on Accounts 1916b).

During hearings on H.Res. 513 and H.Res. 223, three major themes on the potential impact of automated voting emerged: the length of time needed to conduct a vote, the accuracy of automated roll call systems, and the cost of developing and implementing a vote-recording system. Each would be major points of debate for all automated voting proposals introduced between 1913 and 1970.

Time Needed to Vote

During testimony on H.Res. 513, Representative Walsh stated that "taking 45 minutes as the average time consumed in a roll call, the time consumed in the

Sixty-second Congress in roll calls was 275 hours, or 55 legislative days" (Walsh 1914, 9). Members of the Committee on Accounts, however, were concerned that shortening votes could "flood the country with legislation" and disrupt then-used delaying tactics, resulting in "filibuster by means of roll calls" (Committee on Accounts 1914, 9). Although the Committee on Accounts eventually recommended the adoption of an automated voting system, there was still considerable division over the system's desirability. The committee's majority found that an electrical and mechanical system could help members save time and avoid the practice of reading each name twice for every roll call vote and quorum call. Conversely, the minority opposed the concept of an electronic system and the potential loss of floor time on legislation prior to casting a vote (Committee on Accounts 1916b, 2).

In 1923, the time savings potentially associated with automated voting was again highlighted in a Committee on Accounts report on H.Res. 497, introduced by Representative Melville Kelly. H.Res. 497 would have provided "for the purchase and installation of an electromechanical voting system in the House of Representatives."[3] In the committee report, it was noted that similar resolutions were favorably reported by the committee in the 63rd and 64th Congresses and "it was also shown that a great saving in times could be affected [*sic*] in the calling of the roll in the House by the use of one of these voting machines" (Committee on Accounts 1923, 1).

Representative Charles Bennett, a longtime proponent of automated voting, strongly believed that automated voting would not only save the House time by reducing the amount required for a vote, but could force members to be present in the chamber and engaged in debate more frequently. Representative Bennett recounted the a story of a member who would go home between votes, knowing that he could make it back to the Capitol in time for the next vote, since it often took more than forty-five minutes to call the roll (Bennett 1952, 59). Automated voting proposals aimed to end this type of practice and allow the House to conduct more roll call votes using less time.

Accuracy of Automated Roll Call Votes

Hearings on automated voting proposals also discussed members' concerns about voting mistakes using an electrical and mechanical system. In 1914, during hearings on H.Res. 513, Representative Walsh testified that the voting system he envisioned would automatically cut off after a prescribed time to end a vote. In instances where a member missed a vote, Representative Walsh's proposal left the decision on whether the member would be allowed to vote up to the Speaker of the House (Committee on Accounts 1914, 10–11). When Representative Howard introduced H.Res. 223 in 1916, the resolution allowed for vote changes either through the mechanical system or through a more traditional paper method.

Cost of Developing and Implementing a Vote-Recording System

The cost of developing and implementing an automated voting system permeated the debate on early proposals. In addressing cost, Representative Walsh testified that his proposed voting system was estimated to cost no more than $25,000 (Committee on Accounts 1914, 12). In the 64th Congress, however, the report recommending adoption of Representative Howard's resolution estimated that an automated voting system would cost approximately $125,000 (Committee on Accounts 1916a, 4). By the 91st Congress (1969–1970), the cost of an electronic voting system was estimated between $80,000 and $600,000, with $500,000 considered adequate to install a comprehensive system (Committee on House Administration 1969, 7).

Adopting Electronic Voting

Interest in an automated voting system continued to grow in the House, with fifty-one bills and resolutions introduced between 1886 and 1970. In 1970, Congress undertook a comprehensive reorganization for the first time since the Legislative Reorganization Act of 1946 (Davidson, Oleszek, and Lee 2008, 351). The Legislative Reorganization Act of 1970 (P.L. 91-510) took many provisions from previously introduced legislation and provided for electronic voting in the House generally and on recorded votes on floor amendments in the Committee of the Whole (Dodd and Oppenheimer 1977; Schickler 2005, 52).

Prior to 1970, it was relatively easy for a committee chair to defeat floor amendments, because votes on amendments were generally not recorded. Because votes were not recorded, constituents often did not know how individual representatives had voted. In the absence of constituent pressure, committee chairs were well positioned to defend bills against floor assaults. By providing the public with information on how individual members voted on amendments, the Reorganization Act fueled floor amending activity and thereby weakened the position of the chairs (Schickler 2005, 52).

Proposals

On January 6, 1969, the Democratic Caucus adopted a resolution asking Speaker of the House John McCormack to "take such steps as may be necessary to improve the vote recording procedures in the House of Representatives" (House Democratic Caucus Records 1969). In response to the Democratic Caucus's request, Speaker McCormack asked the Committee on House Administration to examine automated voting.

In response to the Speaker's request, the Committee on House Administration established a special subcommittee on electrical and mechanical office equipment. In April 1969, the subcommittee held a hearing to focus on electrical and mechanical voting (Committee on House Administration 1969, 7).[4] No specific legislative action resulted from the committee hearing, however, but the hearing served as a preview for the debate over electronic voting in 1970.

Electronic Voting Provisions in the Legislative Reorganization Act of 1970

The Legislative Reorganization Act of 1970, as introduced and reported in the House, did not initially include provisions to create an electronic voting system in the House (House Committee on Rules 1970). On July 27, 1970, Representative Robert McClory offered a floor amendment to authorize the development of an electronic voting system and to amend then House Rule 15 to allow the system to be used to conduct votes and quorum calls in the House. The amendment was agreed to by voice vote.

Work on the electronic voting system began almost immediately after President Richard Nixon signed the Legislative Reorganization Act of 1970 into law on October 26, 1970. While use of the electronic voting system was to begin on January 3, 1973, Speaker Carl B. Albert announced that the voting system was not yet operational and that "members will be given sufficient notice as to when the electronic voting system will be activated" (Albert 1973). The electronic voting system was used for the first time on January 23, 1973, for a quorum call.

Electronic Voting and House Operations

The adoption of the Legislative Reorganization Act of 1970 marked the beginning of a period of change in the House. While the act prescribed numerous changes to almost all aspects of House operations and functions, electronic voting signaled the modernization of chamber operations and a shift in attitude toward incorporating technology in day-to-day operations. The impact of electronic voting in the House has been significant. Electronic voting has had consequences for House operations, technology and modernization, and transparency.

Operational Change

In institutions, rules often structure outcomes. For the House, the majority party has almost complete control over setting the rules at the beginning of each Congress and setting the terms of debate on individual pieces of legislation brought to the floor. In fact, the Committee on Rules is one of the only House committees that has an overwhelming membership imbalance in favor of the majority, regardless of the majority's size, and therefore has been characterized as "an essential arm of the majority party leadership" (Dion and Huber 1996, 26).

Rules, precedents, and norms are designed by the majority in an effort to control the chamber. Ostrom (2005) describes these as "institutional statements" that provide guidance to members and "prescribe, permit, or advise action or outcomes for participants in an action situation" (138). For the House of Representatives, rules are generally adopted at the beginning of each Congress. Introduced by the majority, the rules package is largely based on the rules from the previous Congress, with some modifications. In addition to the rules, the House parliamentarian has compiled numerous volumes of precedents to guide the Speaker in making decisions on the House floor. The rules and precedents, together with the institutional norms of the House, constitute the "institutional statements" of the chamber.

The power of the "institutional statements" should not be underestimated. Agenda setting is one of the spoils of majority party status. In 1970, Democrats—then in the midst of a forty-year period of majority status in the House—saw numerous advantages to allowing electronic voting and making the operational and structural changes necessary to accommodate more frequent and shorter votes. Since its implementation, electronic voting has provided opportunities for both the majority and minority to request additional roll call votes without the consequence of losing floor debate time. While rules changes generally favor those making the rules, the procedural changes made for the electronic voting system has empowered both the majority and minority.

Technology and Modernization

In general, the House is slow to change and modernize, especially with the adoption of technology. As the story of the adoption of electronic voting illustrates, the process of adopting technology on a chamber-wide level often takes years. The debate over the placement of television cameras in the House chamber and the possible ramifications of providing live access to House proceedings also developed over a number of years (Garay 1984; Frantzich and Sullivan 1996; Wolfensberger 2000, 103–21). To maintain control over the images and content of House proceedings, rules were adopted to limit potential embarrassment to members and ensure that only official business was covered (Frantzich 1982, 99). While the television networks did not initially appreciate the restrictions, the public was able to receive real-time access to House floor debates through C-SPAN and other outlets.

Additionally, the House has, at times, been reluctant to allow for the adoption of technology for individual member use. In the late 1960s, the House charged the Committee on House Administration with creating and maintaining lists of approved technology that could be purchased using official funds.[5] More recently, the House has grappled with members' desires to use social media to contact their constituents (Straus et al. 2010).

In many ways, the successful adoption of electronic voting paved the way for the House to more easily adopt additional technology. While there are no direct links between the adoption of electronic voting and other technological upgrades, the relative ease of designing and implementing electronic voting likely provided members with more confidence in technology. Today, the House uses technology for many aspects of its operation, including sending dear colleague letters (Straus 2009), communicating with constituents (Straus et al. 2010), and creating public information portals and websites (Adler, Gent, and Overmeyer 1998).

Transparency

Transparency has been a buzzword in recent congresses. In both the 111th and the 112th Congresses numerous bills were introduced to "open" Congress and make congressional records more accessible to the general public.[6] These bills continue the tradition of past House rule changes and administrative actions that have required committee reports, financial statements, and bills and amendments be placed online in a timely fashion. Congressional action of this nature was sought by some because many of the general federal open government provisions did not apply to Congress.

Electronic voting is another tool Congress has at its disposal that increases transparency. The electronic voting system allows the real-time display of votes during a roll call. Where once party leadership had to manually count how a member was voting, today, voting display boards throughout the House chamber show the aggregate number of "yeas" and "nays," while other boards list each member and how he or she has voted.

The historic debate on the advantages and disadvantages of electronic voting in many ways hinged on transparency. Throughout the early debate in the 1914 and 1916 Congresses, members were concerned about the transparency of their votes and the consequences of public and lobbyist access to voting information prior to publication in the *Congressional Record*. Members were also concerned about lobbying by other members during votes, whether votes could be changed once they were cast but before voting time expired, and if changes would be published in the *Record*.

Electronic voting has also allowed the House the flexibility to conduct as many roll call votes as are requested by the membership. While in the past roll call votes took a significant amount of time, today they can generally be dispensed with in no more than fifteen minutes.[7] This change is significant for transparency. Since 1973, the number of opportunities to put members on the record for non-final-passage votes has increased. Current House rules allow for the recording of votes on amendments in the Committee of the Whole and for a member to request recorded votes on a variety of motions during regular debate. While the overall time for votes may be less than before electronic voting, the total number of roll call votes has increased (see figure 6.1).

Roll Call Voting Studies

The adoption of electronic voting was not, by itself, a catalyst for roll call voting studies. What electronic voting provides is an enhanced opportunity to analyze roll call votes and the institutional impact of voting. This type of analysis stands in contrast with traditional roll call voting studies, which tend to evaluate individual member votes, analyze the roll call voting patterns of groups of legislators, or examine voting on a specific policy area.

Poole and Rosenthal (1997) devised a widely used systematic statistical approach to analyzing roll call votes. In their NOMINATE and DW-NOMINATE scores, Poole and Rosenthal built on previous roll call studies of member voting along party lines (Weisberg 1978; Poole and Rosenthal 1985) to create a systematic and reliable statistic for measuring individual voting behavior.

Using NOMINATE and DW-NOMINATE, many roll call voting studies began focusing on how individual members voted vis-à-vis their party leadership. The study of party unity votes allowed the development of measures examining individual members' loyalty to the party agenda. As a result of the increased scrutiny of individual and party voting patterns, analytics were created to allow the measurement of disagreement between legislator and party on any given vote (Rohde 1991, 8). This measure has increased understanding of the dynamics between individual members and party leadership positions, with majority/minority status, unity of the opposition party, and electoral outcomes identified as strong predictors of party influence in Congress (Lebo, McGlynn, and Koger 2007). Additionally, party unity votes have been used to show that majority party members who vote with the party leadership are more likely to be successful in the House (Hasecke and Mycoff 2007).

In addition to studies on party loyalty, roll call voting studies have generally focused on individuals or groups of legislators. These studies have examined roll call votes for a specific demographic—such as women, blacks, or Hispanics (Schwindt-Bayer and Corbella 2004; Hogan 2008; Rocca, Sanchez, Nikora 2009; Frederick 2010), specific policies (Dunlap and Gale 1974; Gross 1979; Xie 2006), presidential positions on legislation (Covington 1987; King and Riddlesperger 2006; Conley and Yon 2007), constituency connections (McDonagh 1989; Wolman and Marckini 2000; Clinton 2006; Ansolabehere and Jones 2010), and elections (Deckard 1976; Kuklinski 1977; Thomas 1985; Wright 2007; Hirano 2008). Such studies add to the overall understanding of how individual members choose to vote in the House, but none examine broader institutional implications of vote choice by members.

As these roll call studies show, the focus is generally on the individual member, not the institution. Very few studies focus on the institutional implications of roll call voting. Riker (1986), for one, discusses institutional effects through an example of how not voting during a roll call can aid a party in defeating legislation. Riker argues that a single Virginia state senator's refusal to vote on the Equal Rights Amendment to the U.S. Constitution caused the amendment to be defeated (Riker 1986, 103–5).

The power of a single vote and the implications of strategic voting by a party or group of members should not be underestimated. For example, in the 112th Congress (2011–2012), during debate on the fiscal year 2012 budget, the Republican leadership brought competing budget plans to the floor. One, sponsored by Budget Committee chair Paul Ryan, was backed by the Republican Party leadership, and the other was compiled by the conservative Republican Study Committee (RSC). In an effort to force the House to adopt the more conservative budget plan, minority leader Steny Hoyer organized a group of about 120 Democrats to vote "present" on the RSC budget (Sonmez 2011). By organizing votes of "present" instead of "no," Mr. Hoyer reduced the number of votes necessary to adopt a proposal and nearly succeeded in forcing passage of the more conservative measure.

Studying overall roll call voting patterns, instead of focusing on how individual members vote, allows us to understand how electronic voting has changed the way roll call votes are used on the floor. Since the first electronic vote was cast in 1973, asking for and conducting roll call votes has become easier. What was once a long and sometimes tedious procedure has become routine. What once required the parties to maintain running tallies of member votes is now fully automated, with electronic boards throughout the chamber displaying both running vote totals and the votes of individual members.

Impact of Electronic Voting

Adoption of electronic voting in 1970, and the first use of the system in 1973, gave the House the ability to quickly and accurately record votes. As a consequence the total number of roll call votes per Congress has increased. Increases in the number of roll call votes, however, began prior to the adoption of electronic voting. Between the 80th Congress (1947–1948) and the 92nd Congress (1971–1972), the number of roll call votes rose, but only slightly. Following the passage of the Legislative Reorganization Act of 1970, the number of roll call votes began to rise more rapidly, peaking in the 95th Congress (1977–1978) before stabilizing at about nine hundred roll call votes per Congress. In recent years, the number of roll call votes has begun a dramatic increase to more than eighteen hundred roll call votes in the 110th Congress (2008–2009).

Between 1946, when the last major rules changes were implemented with the passage of the Legislative Reorganization Act of 1946, and 1972, the average number of roll call votes per Congress was 286, with the most roll call votes (949) taken in the 92nd Congress and the fewest (147) taken in the 83rd Congress (1953–1954). Following the passage of the Legislative Reorganization Act of 1970 and the implementation of electronic voting in 1973, the average number of roll call votes has increased to 1,169 per Congress, with the most votes (1,865) taken in the 110th Congress and the fewest (812) taken in the 97th Congress (1981–1982). Figure 6.1 shows the total number of roll call votes taken in each Congress between the 80th Congress and the 111th Congress (2009–2010).

As shown in figure 6.1, the number of roll call votes per Congress began increasing prior to the adoption of electronic voting. Beginning in the 89th Congress (1965–1966), the number of roll call votes began to climb from an average of 195 votes per Congress between the 80th and the 88th Congresses (1967–1968) to 394 roll call votes in the 90th Congress (1967–1968). The decision to adopt electronic voting likely occurred partly in response to the increasing number of roll call votes and the increase in floor time being spent on voting. Once electronic voting was adopted, however, the number of votes continued to increase because of the ease of conducting a vote under the new system.

Rules Changes

Since 1970, two major rules changes have been adopted by the House that affect the number of roll call votes taken during a given Congress. The first,

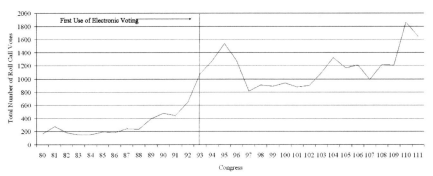

FIGURE 6.1
Total Roll Call Votes in the House of Representatives (80th–111th Congresses). (Poole and Rosenthal, "Democrat and Republican Party Voting Splits Congresses 35–111" [updated January 9, 2011], http://www.voteview.com/partycount.htm)

adopted as a provision of the Legislative Reorganization Act of 1970, allowed recorded votes in the Committee of the Whole. The second, adopted in the 93rd Congress (1973–1974), allowed the Speaker (or chair of the Committee of the Whole) to cluster votes and to reduce voting time after the first fifteen-minute vote. Both of these changes provided increased opportunities to obtain a recorded vote in the House.

Record Voting in the Committee of the Whole

As part of the Legislative Reorganization Act of 1970, House rules were amended to accommodate the use of electronic voting. Prior to the act, House rules only permitted unrecorded votes in the Committee of the Whole by voice, division, or tellers. For voice votes, the chair determines which position prevails by the number of members answering "yea" or "nay" verbally (Kravitz 2001, 275). For both division and teller votes, the number of members on either side of a question, but not their names, were recorded and reported in the *Congressional Record* (Kravitz 2001, 86–87 and 258).

The act amended the rules for voting in the Committee of the Whole and, for the first time, authorized the recording of votes and the publishing of individual voting positions. Subsequently, post-1970 roll call vote totals include votes on amendments in the Committee of the Whole in addition to regular procedural and final passage votes. As figure 6.1 shows, the number of roll call votes began to increase in the 92nd Congress, corresponding with the first full Congress operating under the Legislative Reorganization Act's amended voting provisions. The increase in roll call votes in the 92nd Congress, therefore, is a function of both the ease of voting electronically, compared to a manual roll call, and the increase in opportunities to request a vote on amendments in the Committee of the Whole.

Clustered and Reduced-Time Votes

Prior to the Legislative Reorganization Act of 1970, all roll call votes were conducted in roughly the same length of time—approximately forty-five minutes. With the first use of the electronic voting system, House rules were amended to reduce the amount of time required to conduct a recorded vote. In the 93rd Congress, the House agreed to H.Res. 998, which allowed votes to be clustered on motions to suspend the rules. Further rules changes were made in subsequent congresses, including providing the Speaker with "discretionary authority to postpone recorded votes on the final passage of bills, the adoption of resolutions and conference reports to a time certain within two legislative days" (Deschler and Brown 1976, 396) and authorizing the presiding officer to cluster votes on the previous question motion and the adoption of resolutions reported by the Rules Committee (396–99).

House rules were also amended to authorize a reduction in voting time for clustered votes—"sequential recorded votes in the House on a series of measures or amendments that the House finished debating at an earlier time or on a previous day" (Kravitz 2001, 43). Instead of requiring that all clustered votes be conducted in no less than fifteen minutes, the new rules allow the presiding officer to "reduce the voting time on passage of a bill to five minutes, following a 15-minute vote" (Deschler and Brown 1976, 449). The postponement and clustering of votes provided the majority leadership a powerful tool that, combined with electronic voting, has resulted in an overall reduction of time for subsequent votes and allowed additional roll call votes without halting debate. Clustering and then shortening vote times has allowed individual members, including the party leadership, to use voting as a tactic to require other members to state a position on the record.

Prior to electronic voting, if a member, during a vote, wanted to know how other members were voting, he or she had three options. She could ask her party's leadership to check its tallies, she could ask other members, or she could stay on the floor for the entire vote and observe other members answering the call of the roll. With the implementation of electronic voting, this strategy changed. Because of the electronic display boards, members can now see how others have voted in real time and make decisions with more complete information.

Additionally, shortened vote times allow the chamber to function more effectively. Committee hearings and other business can be conducted away from the floor without the constant need to return to vote. By clustering votes and reducing voting time, it is easier for the party leadership to keep members on the floor when they know a series of votes will occur. In the 112th Congress, House rules were further amended to allow certain votes in a series to be reduced to two minutes. This should further allow the House leadership to schedule votes and reduce the time the chamber is required to spend voting on resolutions, bills, and motions.

Major Membership Transitions

Part of the recent increase in the number of roll call votes appears to be membership-centric, mostly surrounding majority party transitions. As figure 6.1 shows, following the adoption of electronic voting, there were three peaks in the number of roll call votes per Congress. The first occurred following the 1974 elections—and continued through the 95th Congress—when a large class of freshmen Democrats were elected, bolstering the ranks of the Democratic majority. The other two peaks occurred with the transition in majority party—from

Democratic to Republican in the 104th Congress (1995–1996) and from Republican to Democratic in the 110th Congress.

Watergate Democrats

The increase in roll call votes in the 94th and 95th Congresses can be explained in a number of ways. First, the increase in the number of roll call votes could be a continuation of the upward trend in requesting roll call votes that began in the 89th Congress. This explanation suggests that as requesting roll call votes became easier and more politically viable, the membership availed itself of the opportunity and continued to request more votes. Second, the large class of freshmen that entered in the post-Watergate election desired to place themselves on the public record as often as possible. This could have been to demonstrate that they were different from their older counterparts or to ensure that they established political track records early in their careers in an effort to maintain their positions in Congress.

Finally, the increase in roll call votes in the early 1970s could be a reflection of newness of the electronic voting system. While it is true that the number of roll call votes per Congress was increasing prior to the adoption of electronic voting, once electronic voting became available, and voting became faster and easier, members wanted to vote more often. In fact, the number of roll call votes in the 95th Congress was not eclipsed until the 110th Congress, a period of twenty years.

Republican Revolution

Following the Republican takeover of the House in the 104th Congress, the number of roll call votes increased to levels not seen since shortly after the electronic voting system's introduction. The increase in roll call votes in the 104th Congress was likely a function of the Republican leadership's desire to take multiple votes on campaign agenda items (e.g., the Contract with America) and to put members on the record supporting or opposing these items (Cheney and Cheney 1996; Fenno 1997; Killian 1998).

For example, in January 1995, the House debated its version of a bill to fulfill a Contract with America pledge to prohibit unfunded mandates by the federal government. During the course of the debate on H.R. 5, the Unfunded Mandate Reform Act of 1995, the House utilized an open rule and took forty votes on amendments and motions related to the bill, both in the Committee of the Whole and in the House. In addition, several quorum calls and votes on motions to adjourn and motions to rise were also recorded during the course of debate. The idea of taking more than forty roll call votes during debate on a single piece of legislation would have been unthinkable prior to electronic voting, as the time needed would have caused the House to cease additional work.

Partly because of electronic voting, the new Republican majority was able to use the electronic voting system to its advantage and allow votes on numerous amendments, without concerns about allotting additional time to voting. Allowing numerous amendments and votes serves two purposes. First, by allowing an open rule (per the terms of H.Res. 38, which set the rules for debate on H.R. 5), the new Republican majority demonstrated that they were willing to allow an open amendment process, even for important agenda items. Second, conducting roll call votes for so many amendments put members on the public record. Conducting many votes early in the Congress also allowed the majority leadership to see where members stood on Contract with America items generally, and on issues raised through the amendment process specifically.

Democratic Takeover

Similarly, the number of roll call votes increased when the House transitioned from a Republican to Democratic majority in the 110th Congress. While the Democratic Party did have a legislative plan for the first hundred days, it was not a unifying document like the Contract with America. They did, however, have an extensive agenda of leadership-sponsored measures. Many of these, including H.R. 547, the Advanced Fuels Infrastructure Research and Development Act, had multiple roll call votes on amendments in the Committee of the Whole and final passage. While there were not nearly as many roll call votes as on H.R. 5 in the 104th Congress, having multiple recorded votes, especially on amendments in the Committee of the Whole, would have been untenable prior to the amendments to House rules made to accommodate the electronic voting system.

Creating a Public Voting Record

Since the implementation of electronic voting, there has been more floor time for members to request roll call votes. While members have always been able to request recorded votes (Galloway 1958, 457), the time needed to fulfill that request often caused the chamber to hesitate prior to granting the roll call vote. Members request roll call votes for any number of reasons. These include establishing visibility and forcing their political opponents (most often members of the opposing party) to vote on measures not popular among their supporters. Each of these is a legitimate reason for requesting a roll call vote and each has its own unique set of consequences.

Visibility

Cain, Ferejohn, and Fiorina (1987) discuss the importance of visibility for members of Congress, calling it the "cornerstone of an effective district strategy"

(27). Visibility, however, is just one of many factors members must consider when performing their official functions. To ensure reelection, members must connect with their constituents and prove their legislative and representative worth (Mayhew 1975; Fenno 1978). Additionally, members must remember that they are operating within the "public sphere" and that their actions can have consequences beyond a specific roll call vote (Mayhew 2000).

Roll call votes can impact elections. How a member votes is a direct reflection of his or her strategy for representing the district. Erickson and Wright (2000) remind us that constituency service and accurately reflecting the district's interests is essential for member reelection. In fact, while no member represents his or her district exactly the same way as another member, a "member who ignores constituents is likely to be given the boot by the voters" (149). By being an active participant in the roll call voting process, members can ensure their visibility. Electronic voting allows members to be more visible than ever. Instead of a few hundred votes a year, members now take well over a thousand and have ample opportunity to establish voting track records.

Cornering a Political Opponent

In some cases, members may request a roll call vote in an effort to put a political opponent on the record. More often than not, this happens for measures that are politically unpopular for the opposition party. In making these requests, members are using the electronic voting system to potentially score political points or stop legislation they are strongly opposed to. Sometimes called killer amendments, these measures are often designed to "kill" the underlying piece of legislation, if they are adopted (Davidson, Oleszek, and Lee 2010, 279). Jenkins and Munger (2003) provide a historic example of a killer amendment. In the 42nd Congress (1871–1873), a bill was introduced to reimburse the College of William and Mary for property destroyed during the Civil War. After a heated debate, Representative John Shanks offered an amendment that would have required the college to allow open and equal enrollment for all in order to receive the funds (505–6). As a result of the amendment, which was adopted by the House, the underlying bill was defeated.

Interestingly, prior research has indicated that killer amendments are not an effective legislative strategy for killing the underlying bill, with the underlying bill failing only on rare occasions (Wilkerson 1999). If introducing and forcing votes on killer amendments are not effective, then why do they occur? While the ultimate answer to this question is beyond the scope of this chapter, electronic voting plays a central role in the decision to introduce and request a roll call vote on a killer amendment. Since roll call votes were allowed in the Committee of the Whole, forcing a vote on a killer amendment can require members to go on the record in support or opposition of a controversial matter. Regardless of whether members believe they are voting strategically (Enelow 1981), the vote can be analyzed out of context for political reasons and provide important campaign material.

Strategic Voting

The adoption of electronic voting changed the strategy of voting in the House of Representatives. Prior to 1973, when members came to the floor to cast roll call votes, they were required to cast their votes in public (i.e., orally respond to the clerk reading the roll). Because of the public nature of voting, members might choose to vote early in the process, or they might choose to wait until the second call of the roll to determine how other members were voting. Either choice could require the individual member or the party whip to closely observe voting activity on the floor in an effort to pick the optimal voting time.

Since the adoption of electronic voting, the act of voting has become private. When members vote today, they take their voting card, insert it into a voting station, and press a button that corresponds with their vote choice (Clerk of the House 2011). Once they vote, however, their choice immediately becomes public on display boards located throughout the Hall of the House. The electronic display boards stay illuminated for the duration of the vote, and other members can very easily see how their colleagues have voted. In the current scenario, when a member votes could be strategically important. McCrone (1977) examined roll call votes to identify member voting strategies. In his analysis, McCrone identifies four strategies by combining the content of a specific vote and the general support for the measure in an effort to predict how a member will vote (McCrone 1977, 178–80).

What McCrone does not identify, however, is the timing of a member's vote. This is significant because electronic voting provides the opportunity for members to clearly see how others voted and allows members to adjust their votes, without a change being recorded in the *Congressional Record*. For each vote, each member must decide the best time to vote (i.e., early or late) and whether to change a vote once it has been cast. Further examination of the timing of votes is virtually impossible in the modern House. Because there is no way to know exactly when or in what order a member votes, strategy associated with vote timing is restricted to arguments on public position-taking (Caldeira and Zorn 2004) or party influence on individual roll calls (Synder and Groseclose 2001).

Open Government and Media Scrutiny

In many ways, the adoption of electronic voting by the House marked a period of transition to a more open government. While the merits of open government are outside the scope of this chapter, more information exists on member behavior and position-taking today then ever before because of electronic voting and the expansion of recorded votes.

While electronic voting has had far-reaching consequences for chamber operations, it has also had broad consequences for media examination of member activity. The rise of CNN, Fox News, MSNBC, and non-TV news outlets has led to media analysis of member activity in ways that were inconceivable in the era before cable TV and Internet news services. Electronic voting and the associated increase in the number of roll call votes have provided members with the ability to put themselves on the record and to demonstrate to their constituents that they are listening to their preferences and acting on them in Congress. Reporting roll call voting positions is undoubtedly a piece of a member's reelection strategy (Mayhew 1975). It can, however, also provide opponent campaign material. The labyrinth of possible roll call votes in the House continues to leave many congressional observers confused about how a member voted on everything but final passage.

The use of electronic voting in the House has also made it easier for interest groups to follow and grade members (Jackson and Kingdon 1992; Poole and Rosenthal 1997; Groseclose, Levitt, and Snyder 1999). The most famous of these scores are produced by the Americans for Democratic Action (ADA) and the American Conservative Union (ACU), but almost all interest groups create some kind of "score" that shows how closely member votes align with the group's position. These scores are invaluable for group members, who can use them when contacting their representatives or when deciding whether to support the incumbent in future elections.

Studies on congressional behavior and member activities are almost sure to use Poole and Rosenthal's (1997) DW-NOMINATE scores. These studies have, and can continue to be, invaluable to students of Congress. As we move forward with using roll call votes as a proxy for congressional and legislative behavior, it continues to be important to remember how the current system for recording roll call votes developed and the implications for analysis as more and more votes are recorded in the House of Representatives.

Conclusion

The adoption of electronic voting by the House of Representatives changed more than just the way members vote. Rules changes adopted alongside the adoption of electronic voting provided the majority leadership with powerful tools with which to influence legislative outcomes. Electronic voting served as a significant tool for implementing other institutional changes, including cluster voting, the further adoption of technology, and increased transparency in the voting process. Additionally, electronic voting has allowed more recorded votes using less floor time, thus putting members on the record more often.

Roll call votes can be a useful tool to examine certain aspects of legislative behavior. Scholars who choose to use roll call voting as the basis of their studies, however, must consider how electronic voting has changed member behavior. Prior to 1973, members were at the mercy of party leadership, the media, and their own observations when determining how other members were voting. Today, all a member has to do is look up at the display boards and see what color dot appears next to their colleague's name. The increase in information available in real time to members has undoubtedly changed voting strategies.

Electronic voting has also impacted the organization of party leadership (see chapter 2), the design of special rules for legislative floor consideration (see chapter 3), voting on amendments to appropriations bills (see chapter 4), the ability of the minority to request votes on the motion to recommit (see chapter 5), and strategies employed by caucuses on the House floor (see chapter 7). While elements of each of these themes were present prior to electronic voting, electronic voting has streamlined the gathering and processing of information for all members.

Notes

1. Under House rules, some questions require a recorded vote. For example, House Rule 20, clause 10 provides that the Speaker order the "yeas and nays" for questions "on passage of a bill or joint resolution, or on adoption of a conference report, making general appropriations, or increasing Federal income tax rates, or on final adoption of a concurrent resolution on the budget or conference report thereon."

2. The buttons on the voting box would indicate "yea," "nay," "present," and "paired." When a button was depressed, the appropriate light would come on next to the member's name in the appropriate column.

3. H.Res. 497 (67th Congress) was introduced on January 29, 1923. See also "Public Bills, Resolutions, and Memorials," *Congressional Record*, vol. 64, part 3 (January 29, 1923), 2678.

4. In the 86th Congress (1959–1960), the Committee on House Administration renamed the Subcommittee on Office Equipment as the Special Subcommittee on Electrical and Mechanical Office Equipment. The Subcommittee on Office Equipment had been created during the 84th Congress (1955–1956).

5. Between 1955 and 1968, the Committee on House Administration had a Special Subcommittee on Electrical and Mechanical Office Equipment. This subcommittee was in charge of approving office equipment, among other items, available for purchase by member and committee offices. For more information, see U.S. Congress, House of Representatives, *Guide to the Records of the United States House of Representatives at the National Archives: 1789–1989*, 100th Cong., 2nd sess., H.Doc. 100-245 (Washington, DC: Government Printing Office, 1989).

6. For examples of legislation to promote congressional transparency, see H.R. 4983 (111th Congress) and H.R. 2340 (112th Congress), introduced by Representative Mike Quigley.

7. Pursuant to House Rule 20, clause 2 (a), the minimum time for a recorded vote or quorum call is fifteen minutes, except as authorized under Rule 20, clause 8 or clause 9, or Rule 18, clause 6(f), where the Speaker may reduce to five minutes the minimum time for electronic voting under certain conditions. Under a rules change adopted by the 112th Congress, the chair of the Committee of the Whole may reduce to two minutes the voting time on questions following a fifteen-minute vote.

References

Adler, E. Scott, Chariti E. Gent, and Cary B. Overmeyer. 1998. "The Home Style Homepage: Legislator Use of the World Wide Web for Constituency Contact." *Legislative Studies Quarterly* 23:585–95.

Albert, Carl. 1973. "Announcement by the Speaker Concerning Electronic Voting." *Congressional Record* 119:27.

Anderson, William D., Janet M. Box-Steffensmeir, and Valeria Sinclair-Chapman. 2003. "The Keys to Legislative Success in the U.S. House of Representatives." *Legislative Studies Quarterly* 28:357–86.

Ansolabehere, Stephen, and Philip Edward Jones. 2010. "'Constituents' Response to Congressional Roll-Call Voting." *American Journal of Political Science* 54:583–97.

Bach, Stanley, and Steven S. Smith. 1988. *Managing Uncertainty in the House of Representatives: Adaption and Innovation in Special Rules.* Washington, DC: Brookings Institution Press.

Beach, Lewis. 1886. U.S. Congress, House of Representatives. *Plan to Register Votes, etc.* 49th Cong., 1st sess., Mis.Doc. 98, Serial Set 2415.

Bennett, Charles E. 1952. "Yeas and Nays Waste Time: Today We're in an Era of Pushbuttons, but Congress Is Still in the Horse-and-Buggy Age with Its Voting Procedure." *U.S.A.: The Magazine of American Affairs* 1:59–63.

Cain, Bruce, John Ferejohn, and Morris Fiorina. 1987. *The Personal Vote: Constituency Service and Electoral Independence.* Cambridge, MA: Harvard University Press.

Caldeira, Gregroy A., and Christopher Zorn. 2004. "Strategic Timing, Position-Taking, and Impeachment in the House of Representatives." *Legislative Studies Quarterly* 57:517–27.

Cheney, Richard B., and Lynne V. Cheney. 1996. *Kings of the Hill: How Nine Powerful Men Changed the Course of American History.* New York: Touchstone Books.

Clerk of the House of Representatives. U.S. Congress. 2011. "Electronic Voting Machine." *Art & History.* http://artandhistory.house.gov/art_artifacts/virtual_tours/house_chamber/voting.aspx.

Clinton, Joshua D. 2006. "Representation in Congress: Constituents and Roll Calls in the 106th House." *Journal of Politics* 68:397–409.

Committee on Accounts. U.S. Congress. House of Representatives. 1914. *Electrical and Mechanical System of Voting.* Hearing on H.Res. 513. 63rd Cong., 2nd sess. July 31. Washington, DC: Government Printing Office.

———. 1916a. *Electrical and Mechanical System of Voting.* Hearing on H.Res. 223. 64th Cong., 1st sess. May 15. Washington, DC: Government Printing Office.

———. 1916b. *Electrical and Mechanical System of Voting.* 64th Cong., 1st sess. H.Rept. 940. Washington, DC: Government Printing Office.

———. 1923. *Providing for the Purchase and Installation of an Electromechanical Voting Machine in the House of Representatives.* 67th Cong., 4th sess. H.Rept. 1739. Washington, DC: Government Printing Office.

Committee on House Administration, Special Subcommittee on Electrical and Mechanical Office Equipment. U.S. Congress. House of Representatives. 1969. *Computer System-Vote Recording Procedures.* Unpublished hearing. 91st Cong., 1st sess. April 1.

Committee on Rules. U.S. Congress, House of Representatives. 1970. *Legislative Reorganization Act of 1970.* 91st Cong., 2nd sess. H.Rep. 91-1215. Washington, DC: Government Printing Office.

Conley, Richard S., and Richard M. Yon. 2007. "The 'Hidden Hand' and White House Roll-Call Predictions: Legislative Liaison in the Eisenhower White House, 83d–84th Congresses." *Presidential Studies Quarterly* 37:291–312.

Connelly, William F., Jr. 2010. *James Madison Rules America: The Constitutional Origins of Congressional Partisanship.* Lanham, MD: Rowman and Littlefield.

Cooper, Joseph, and David W. Brady. 1981. "Institutional Context and Leadership Style: The House from Cannon to Rayburn." *American Political Science Review* 72:411–25.

Covington, Cary R. 1987. "'Staying Private': Gaining Congressional Support for Unpublicized Presidential Preferences on Roll Call Votes." *Journal of Politics* 49:737–56.

———. 1995. "A 'Presidency-Augmented' Model of Presidential Success on House Roll Call Votes." *American Journal of Political Science* 39:1001–25.

Davidson, Roger H., Walter J. Oleszek, and Frances E. Lee. 2008. *Congress and Its Members*. 11th ed. Washington, DC: CQ Press.

———. 2010. *Congress and Its Members*. 12th ed. Washington, DC: CQ Press.

Deckard, Barbara Sinclair. 1976. "Electoral Marginality and Party Loyalty in House Roll Call Voting." *American Journal of Political Science* 20:469–82.

Deschler, Lewis, and William Holmes Brown. 1976. *Deschler-Brown Precedents of the United States House of Representatives*, vol. 14. Washington, DC: Government Printing Office.

Dion, Douglas, and John D. Huber. 1996. "Procedural Choice and the House Committee on Rules." *Journal of Politics* 58:25–53.

Dodd, Lawrence C., and Bruce I. Oppenheimer. 1977. "The House in Transition." In *Congress Reconsidered*, edited by Lawrence C. Dodd and Bruce I. Oppenheimer, 21–53. New York: Praeger Publishers.

Dunlap, Riley E., and Richard P. Gale. 1974. "Party Membership and Environmental Politics: A Legislative Roll-Call Analysis." *Social Science Quarterly* 55:670–90.

Edison, Thomas. 1869. "Improvement in Electrographic Vote-Recorder," U.S. Patent 90,646, June 1. http://edison.rutgers.edu/patents/00090646.PDF. Accessed May 20, 2011.

Enelow, James M. 1981. "Saving Amendments, Killer Amendments, and an Expected Utility Theory of Sophisticated Voting." *Journal of Politics* 43:1062–89.

Erickson, Robert S., and Gerald C. Wright. 2000. "Representation of Constituency Ideology in Congress." In *Continuity and Change in House Elections*, edited by David W. Brady, John F. Cogan, and Morris P. Fiornia, 149–77. Stanford, CA: Stanford University Press.

Fenno, Richard F. 1978. *Homestyle: House Members in Their Districts*. New York: Scott, Foresman.

———. 1997. *Learning to Govern: An Institutional View of the 104th Congress*. Washington, DC: Brookings Institution Press.

Frantzich, Stephen. 1982. "Communications and Congress." *Proceedings of the Academy of Political Science* 34:88–101.

Frantzich, Stephen, and John Sullivan. 1996. *The C-SPAN Revolution*. Norman: University of Oklahoma Press.

Frederick, Brian. 2010. "Gender and Patterns of Roll Call Voting in the U.S. Senate." *Congress & the Presidency* 37:103–24.

Galloway, George B. 1958. "Precedents Established in the First Congress." *Western Political Quarterly* 11:454–68.

Garay, Ronald. 1984. *Congressional Television: A Legislative History*. Westport, CT: Greenwood Press.

Groseclose, Tim, Steven D. Levitt, and James M. Snyder, Jr. 1999. "Comparing Interest Group Scores across Time and Chamber: Adjusted ADA Scores for the U.S. Congress." *American Political Science Review* 93:33–50.

Gross, Donald A. 1979. "Measuring Legislators' Policy Positions: Roll Call Votes and Preferences among Pieces of Legislation." *American Politics Quarterly* 7:417–38.

Hasecke, Edward B., and Jason D. Mycoff. 2007. "Party Loyalty and Legislative Success: Are Loyal Majority Party Members More Successful in the U.S. House of Representatives?" *Political Research Quarterly* 60:607–17.

Hirano, Shigeo. 2008. "Third Parties, Elections, and Roll-Call Votes: The Populist Party and the Late Nineteenth-Century U.S. Congress." *Legislative Studies Quarterly* 33:131–60.

Hogan, Robert E. 2008. "Sex and the Statehouse: The Effects of Gender on Legislative Roll-Call Voting." *Social Science Quarterly* 89:955–68.

Holst, Christian A. 1919. *The Wisconsin Capitol: Official Guide and History.* 2nd ed. Madison, WI: Office of the State Chief Engineer.

House Democratic Caucus Records. 1969. Container 2, folder 5. Manuscript Division. Library of Congress.

Jackson, John E., and John W. Kingdon. 1992. "Ideology, Interest Group Scores, and Legislative Votes." *American Journal of Political Science* 36:805–23.

Jenkins, Jeffery A., and Michael C. Munger. 2003. "Investigating the Incidence of Killer Amendments in Congress." *Journal of Politics* 65:498–517.

Killian, Linda. 1998. *The Freshmen: What Happened to the Republican Revolution?* Boulder, CO: Westview Press.

King, James D., and James W. Riddlesperger. 2006. "Roll Call Votes on Cabinet Confirmations." *Congress & the Presidency* 33:1–19.

Kravitz, Walter. 2001. *American Congressional Dictionary.* Washington, DC: CQ Press.

Krehbiel, Keith, and Alan Wiseman. 2001. "Joseph G. Cannon: Majoritarian from Illinois." *Legislative Studies Quarterly* 26:357–89.

Kuklinksi, James H. 1977. "District Competitiveness and Legislative Roll-Call Behavior: A Reassessment of the Marginality Hypothesis." *American Journal of Political Science* 21:627–38.

Lathrop, George Parsons. 1890. "Talks with Edison." *Harper's New Monthly Magazine* 80:425–35. http://edison.rutgers.edu/NamesSearch/SingleDoc.php3?DocId=SC90012A. Accessed June 21, 2011.

Lebo, Matthew J., Adam J. McGlynn, and Gregory Koger. 2007. "Strategic Party Government: Party Influence in Congress, 1789–2000." *American Journal of Political Science* 51:464–81.

Le Fevre, Benjamin. 1886. *U.S. Congress, House of Representatives, Electrical Recording of Yeas and Nays.* 49th Cong., 1st sess., Mis.Doc. 315, Serial Set 2418.

Mayhew, David, R. 1975. *Congress: The Electoral Connection.* New Haven, CT: Yale University Press.

———. 2000. *America's Congress: Actions in the Public Sphere, James Madison through Newt Gingrich.* New Haven, CT: Yale University Press.

McCrone, Donald J. 1977. "Identifying Voting Strategies from Roll Call Votes: A Method and an Application." *Legislative Studies Quarterly* 2:177–91.

McDonagh, Eileen L. 1989. "Issues and Constituencies in the Progressive Era: House Roll Call Voting on the Nineteenth Amendment, 1913–1919." *Journal of Politics* 51:119–37.

Ostrom, Elinor. 2005. *Understanding Institutional Diversity.* Princeton, NJ: Princeton University Press.

Poole, Keith T., and Howard Rosenthal. 1985. "A Spatial Model for Legislative Roll Call Analysis." *American Journal of Political Science* 29:357–84.

———. 1997. *Congress: A Political-Economic History of Roll Call Voting.* New York: Oxford University Press.

———. 1999. "The Dynamics of Interest Group Evaluation of Congress." *Public Choice* 97:323–61.

Riker, William H. 1986. *The Art of Political Manipulation.* New Haven, CT: Yale University Press.

Rocca, Michael S., Gabriel R. Sanchez, and Ron Nikora. 2009. "The Role of Personal Attributes in African American Roll-Call Voting Behavior in Congress." *Political Research Quarterly* 62:408–14.

Rohde, David W. 1991. *Parties and Leaders in the Postreform House.* Chicago: University of Chicago Press.

Schickler, Eric. 2005. "Institutional Development of Congress." In *The Legislative Branch*, edited by Paul J. Quirk and Sarah A. Binder, 35–62. New York: Oxford University Press.

Schwindt-Bayer, Leslie A., and Renato Corbella. 2004. "Gender Turnover and Roll-Call Voting in the U.S. House of Representatives." *Legislative Studies Quarterly* 29:215–29.

Seroka, Jim, and Andrew D. McNitt. 1984. "Energy and Environment Roll Call Voting in the U.S. Congress in 1975 and 1979." *Policy Studies Review* 3:406–16.

Sinclair, Barbara. 1995. *Legislators, Leaders, and Lawmaking: The U.S. House of Representatives in the Postreform Era.* Baltimore, MD: Johns Hopkins University Press.

Snyder, James M., Jr., and Tim Groseclose. 2001. "Estimating Party Influence on Roll Call Voting: Regression Coefficients versus Classification Success." *American Political Science Review* 95:689–98.

Sonmez, Felicia. 2011. "In Surprise Move, House Democrats vote 'Present' on Conservative Budget, Forcing Republicans' Hand." *Washington Post,* April 15. http://www.washingtonpost .com/blogs/2chambers/post/in-surprise-move-house-democrats-vote-present-on-conservative -budget-forcing-republicans-hand/2011/04/15/AFAgKbjD_blog.html. Accessed June 16, 2011.

Straus, Jacob R. 2009. "Dear Colleague Letters in the House of Representatives: The Impact of Internal House Communications." Paper presented at the annual meeting of the Midwest Political Science Association, Chicago, Illinois, April 2–5.

Straus, Jacob R., Colleen Shogan, Matthew Eric Glassman, and Susan Navarro Smelcer. 2010. "Communicating in 140 Characters or Less: Members Use of Twitter in the 111th Congress." Paper presented at the annual meeting of the Midwest Political Science Association, Chicago, IL, April 22–25.

Thomas, Martin. 1985. "Electoral Proximity and Senatorial Roll Call Voting." *American Journal of Political Science* 29:96–112.

Thomas Edison Papers. 2011. "Vote Recorder." The Edison Papers, Rutgers University. http:// edison.rutgers.edu/vote.htm. Accessed on June 21, 2011.

Walsh, Allan. 1914. "Testimony before the House of Representatives Committee on Accounts." *Electrical and Mechanical System of Voting.* 63rd Cong., 2nd sess., July 31. Washington, DC: Government Printing Office.

Weisberg, Herbert F. 1978. "Evaluating Theories of Congressional Roll-Call Voting." *American Journal of Political Science* 22:554–77.

Wilkerson, John D. 1999. "'Killer' Amendments in Congress." *American Political Science Review* 93:535–52.

Wolfensberger, Donald R. 2000. *Congress and the People: Deliberative Democracy on Trial.* Washington, DC: Woodrow Wilson Center Press.

Wolman, Harold, and Lisa Marckini. 2000. "The Effect of Place on Legislative Roll-Call Voting: The Case of Central-City Representation in the U.S. House." *Social Science Quarterly* 81:763–81.

Wright, Gerald C. 2007. "Do Term Limits Affect Legislative Roll Call Voting? Representation, Polarization, and Participation." *State Politics & Policy* 7:256–80.

Xie, Tao. 2006. "Congressional Roll Call Voting on China Trade Policy." *American Politics Research* 34:732–58.

7

The Caucus Process as a
Catalyst for Democracy

Honorable Major R. Owens

CAUCUSES ARE THE SMALLEST AND MOST NATURAL CELL of the governance process, where the micro-germs of democracy originate and deserve greater scrutiny. My recently published book *The Peacock Elite: A Case Study of the Congressional Black Caucus* (Owens 2011) is one example of focusing on this overlooked catalytic element of decision-making. The question that needs the most thorough exploration is this: How can the enormous waste of brainpower and leadership resources within legislative bodies be eradicated? Or, stated in a more positive form, how can greater creativity and more robust participation in the complex process of legislating be nurtured among the chosen representatives closest to the citizens?

In 1971, the use of the term "caucus" was the least alarming language for a group of blacks organizing within the club atmosphere of the House of Representatives. There were already caucuses of many kinds and it was assumed that the new entity would follow the same pattern.

It is important to note that caucuses are not authorized in the Constitution, nor are they incorporated into law—not even the largest and most powerful caucuses, such as the Democratic Caucus and the Republican Conference. Only House rules, which are authorized by a majority vote of the incoming Congress every two years, establish governance procedure for caucuses. Each party caucus may impose additional rules and regulations upon its members, so long as they are not in conflict with House rules. Party groups such as the Democratic Caucus and the Republican Conference have elaborate sets of by-laws and the ultimate power to promulgate rules for all party members.

Under the purview of the powerful Democratic Steering Committee many different types of caucuses have been established. These include regional groups based on geography and population (e.g., the New York delegation, Rust Belt states), ideology (e.g., Democratic Budget Group), and issues (e.g., human rights, farming, steel, Social Security, fisheries, the environment). Additionally, other caucuses have been developed among those with common interests. These groups include the Congressional Hispanic Caucus, the Congressional Asian Caucus, the Women's Caucus, the Blue Dogs, the Progressive Caucus, the Congressional Arts Caucus, the Congressional Diabetes Caucus, and the Congressional Gaming Caucus. It is among these groups that the Congressional Black Caucus finds its home.

The study of the Congressional Black Caucus (CBC), a caucus uniquely structured for longevity and endurance, provides an opportunity to explore a caucus's structure and substance at the same time. For comparative purposes, I use the Blue Dog Coalition (BDC) in my analysis. The BDC is a House group of equal sophistication on the opposite end of the Democratic ideological spectrum from the CBC. Additionally, the continued success of the CBC and BDC has recently inspired the creation of a stronger Progressive Caucus and a new Tea Party Caucus. At this point, as new political challenges rapidly arise, an in-depth examination of the caucus process as a catalyst for democracy is an appropriate and productive enterprise.

Creating the Congressional Black Caucus

When we consider that Congressman Adam Clayton Powell was not allowed to eat in the House of Representatives dining room until after 1965, it should not be hard to imagine the hostile environment the first black members of the House encountered in Washington between 1865—the year that President Abraham Lincoln was assassinated—and 1901, when the last ex-slave congressman, George White, saw his term expire while he stood alone on the floor of the House Chamber. Would George White and his colleagues—who numbered as many as eight in the 44th Congress (1875–1877)—have survived if they had been united in a caucus? At that time, organizing such a simple mechanism would have been a difficult task since there were so few black members and the players were constantly changing. The environment in Washington, however, was so volatile that greater unity and cohesion among this tiny group would have likely had no measurable impact.

A brief review of the fluctuating numbers of black members of Congress from 1870 to 1901 tells part of the story. The first black member of the House, John W. Menard from Louisiana, was elected in 1868. Menard defeated a white opponent 5,107 votes to 2,833 votes, but was denied his seat. Consequently, not until 1870 was the first black sworn in, with the second seated in 1871. Subsequently, the 42nd Congress (1871–1873) convened with five blacks, the 43rd Congress

TABLE 7.1
Founding Members of the
Congressional Black Caucus, 1971

Name	State
Shirley Chisholm	New York
William Clay	Missouri
George Collins	Illinois
John Conyers	Michigan
Ronald Dellums	California
Charles Diggs	Michigan
Walter Fauntroy	Washington
Augustus Hawkins	California
Ralph Metcalfe	Illinois
Parren Mitchell	Maryland
Robert Nix	Pennsylvania
Charles Rangel	New York
Louis Stokes	Ohio

(1873–1875) with seven, and the 44th Congress with the then historic high of eight blacks. By the 47th Congress (1881–1883) the number had dropped to two, and by the 50th Congress (1887–1889) there was only one. The number of black members remained one until 1901, when George White left the House. Between 1901 and April 15, 1929, when Oscar De Priest was sworn in to the 71st Congress (1929–1931) from Illinois, there were no black members of Congress.

Election of blacks to the House began to increase again in the 1940s. In 1943, William F. Dawson was elected and in 1945 Adam Clayton Powell Jr. was sworn in as the first elected black congressman from the East. In 1969, a then record high of nine House members and Senator Edward W. Brooke were sworn in. Among them was the first black woman representative, Shirley Chisholm. Blacks had been in Congress for 101 years (1870–1971) before they decided that they had enough members of Congress (thirteen) to form the Congressional Black Caucus. In 1971, the Congressional Black Caucus was formally organized. Table 7.1 lists the thirteen original members of the Congressional Black Caucus.

The Congressional Black Caucus in the House of Representatives

A productive, consistently performing legislature can become a force for accountability and an appropriate check on the executive branch of government. This check-and-balance mechanism has been investigated since Julius Caesar. Strong rulers (executives) can only be checked by the parliament or by the gallows. In a lecture at the John W. Kluge Center at the Library of Congress, Gerhard Casper, president emeritus of Stanford University, related the thesis of

German scholar Max Weber, who, long before Hitler or Stalin, concluded that legislators might be the only effective remedies for autocracy.

According to Casper, Weber was a caustic critic of the charismatic Chancellor Bismarck, who used his tremendous political prestige to intimidate the parliament.

> The level of parliament depends on whether it does not merely discuss great issues, but decisively influences them; in other words its quality depends on whether or not what happens there matters, or whether parliament is nothing but the unwillingly tolerated rubber stamp of a ruling bureaucracy. (Casper 2007)

In order to influence decision-making each legislator needs resources—office, staff, phone—as well as physical and financial security. Although few would admit that their budgets are large enough to keep pace with the demands being made upon them, the members of the U.S. Congress have, during the twentieth century, slowly increased their fiscal support to reasonable levels. When all expenses are combined—covering travel, mail, office leases, staff, communications equipment, and services—each member receives directly or in-kind an allocation of no less than $2 million. The member salaries, which have now passed $170,000 per year, are also reasonable.

It is possible that the CBC has emerged as a role model with evolutionary promise that should be replicated because of its potential power to check unbridled imperial legislative rule. A caucus of forty people will dare to pose questions and make demands that no lone member would attempt. Speakers, majority leaders, whips, and committee chairs possess reward, punishment, and control privileges that are perfected to guarantee loyalty, obedience, and a minimum of independence from members. Congress, prior to Watergate and Vietnam, was dominated by strong-willed men with dictatorial impulses that were blatantly displayed. Resistance, slow but steady, was the mood of the post-Watergate incoming representatives. The "old bulls" of both parties yielded to pressure and allowed greater appearances of democracy. In the 1990s, Minority Leader Richard Gephardt went further and encouraged maximum interaction and democratic decision-making in order to rebuild a unified Democratic Party Caucus with solidarity and a joint strategy for winning.

In the dispensation of rewards and incentives among equals (every congressman has approximately the same size constituency), the leadership usually insists upon one-on-one negotiation. One of the earliest and probably most significant of the CBC deviations from tradition was the insistence as a group that leadership appointments to committees be made not in consultation with each individual, but in negotiation with the group. This simple objective of the early CBC founders had powerful ramifications: they wanted to ensure that their members were appointed to all of the major committees of the House. Not by accident, and certainly over the objections of entrenched dictatorial and sometimes openly bigoted chairmen, the following critical appointments were achieved: Charles Rangel to the Committee on Ways and Means; Louis Stokes to the Appropriations Committee; Julian Dixon to the Committee on Intelligence; William Clay as chair of the Committee on Postal Services; Shirley Chisholm to the Committee on Education and Labor (after protesting an appointment to the Agriculture Committee); Gus Hawkins as chair of the Committee on House Administration; Parren Mitchell to the Committee on Energy and Commerce; Ron Dellums to the Committee on Armed Services.

By the 110th Congress (2007–2008), the rewards for the wisdom of this early strategy became abundantly clear. As the victorious Democrats launched their new majority, twenty members of the CBC held positions as chairs of committees or subcommittees. Table 7.2 lists members of the CBC who served as chair of a committee or subcommittee when the Democrats assumed majority control of the House in the 110th Congress. All members, with the exception of Representative James E. Clyburn, who served as the House majority whip, served as chair of their committee or subcommittee.

In contrast to the CBC, the Blue Dog Coalition (BDC) has chosen not to build committee leaders but instead to support a clear set of conservative vested interests that benefit a limited clientele. Nevertheless, it has a record of effectiveness. First and foremost on its list is the perpetuation of farm subsidies. An informative comparison of the BDC and the CBC is offered in the text of *The Peacock Elite* (Owens 2011).

The amended by-laws (in January 2007) of the BDC, however, have catapulted the organization into the sphere of a secret society. With their membership numbers limited, the BDC now requires that each aspiring new member have a sponsor, write an essay, and pass muster in an interview before a panel of five current members (Kaplan 2007).

Borrowing from the frequently utilized and very practical procedure of House-Senate conferees, table 7.3 provides a side-by-side comparison of the BDC and the CBC.

In viewing table 7.3, it becomes clear that the purpose and mission of the Blue Dogs has finite and clearly defined boundaries. On the other hand the sweep of the CBC mission assumes responsibility as the federal advocate for 13 percent of the nation's population. The range of possible CBC social and political involvements becomes almost infinite. And while the BDC maintains close ties with a fiscally strong complex, the CBC faces demands for assistance from an expanding constituency, which brings no resources with it.

The overall success of the BDC in delivering to its constituency is illustrated by table 7.4. It sponsored the Farm Security and Rural Investment Act at the same time that the Reauthorization of the Personal Responsibilities Act was sponsored by the CBC.

TABLE 7.2
Congressional Black Caucus Members Serving as
Committee or Subcommittee Chairs, 110th Congress

Name	Committee
Corrine Brown	Subcommittee on Railroads, Pipelines, and Hazardous Materials [Committee on Transportation and Infrastructure]
Donna M. Christian-Christensen	Subcommittee on Insular Affairs [Committee on Natural Resources]
William Lacy Clay	Subcommittee on Information Policy, Census, and National Archives [Committee on Oversight and Government Reform]
James E. Clyburn	House Majority Whip
John Conyers Jr.	Committee on the Judiciary
Elijah Cummings	Subcommittee on Coast Guard and Maritime Transportation [Committee on Transportation and Infrastructure]
Danny K. Davis	Subcommittee on Federal Workforce, Postal Service, and District of Columbia [Committee on Oversight and Government Reform]
Alcee L. Hastings	Committee on Security and Cooperation in Europe (Helsinki Commission)
Sheila Jackson-Lee	Subcommittee on Transportation Security and Infrastructure Protection [Committee on Homeland Security]
Eddie Bernice Johnson	Subcommittee on Water Resources and Environment [Committee on Transportation and Infrastructure]
John Lewis	Subcommittee on Oversight [Committee on Ways and Means]
Eleanor Holmes Norton	Subcommittee on Economic Development, Public Buildings, and Emergency Management [Committee on Transportation and Infrastructure]
Donald M. Payne	Subcommittee on Africa and Global Health [Committee on Foreign Affairs]
Charles B. Rangel	Committee on Ways and Means
Bobby L. Rush	Subcommittee on Commerce, Trade, and Consumer Protection [Committee on Energy and Commerce]
Robert C. "Bobby" Scott	Subcommittee on Crime, Terrorism, and Homeland Security [Committee on the Judiciary]
Bennie G. Thompson	Committee on Homeland Security
Edolphus Towns	Subcommittee on Government Management, Organization, and Procurement [Committee on Oversight and Government Reform]
Maxine Waters	Subcommittee on Housing and Community Opportunity [Committee on Financial Services]
Melvin L. Watt	Subcommittee on Oversight and Investigations [Committee on Financial Services]

TABLE 7.3
Side-by-Side Comparison of the Blue Dog Coalition
and the Congressional Black Caucus

Item	Blue Dog Coalition	Congressional Black Caucus
Basic Purpose and Mission	Serves as primary guardians and protectors of the agricultural-industrial complex. Responsible for the siphoning of federal funds to the base constituents by any available legal means. Relentlessly combative against social program expenditures.	Founded to improve service to each district represented and via committee assignment expertise to provide assistance to blacks not yet represented by sympathetic members. Established to speak with one voice on the major issues and problems confronting the African American community and to deliver federal resources to the most needy in America.
Primary Legislative Objective	The management of the authorizations and appropriations of the Farm Subsidy Act and other matters under the jurisdiction of the Department of Agriculture.	The presentation of a comprehensive budget reflecting the needs of black America with subsequent follow-up in the appropriations process, as well as the assumption of leadership on civic and civil rights issues and also national security policies such as the war in Iraq.
Bureaucratic Affiliations (Sympathizers)	Patron of the Department of Agriculture. In a symbiotic relationship, the department serves as a secretariat to the coalition.	No concrete or shadow affiliate relationship with any department or bureau of the government.
Position on Military-Industrial Complex Spending	Strong supporter of open-ended military spending in return for reciprocal support for big-spending agricultural projects.	Strong opposition to wasteful spending by the military-industrial complex, which siphons funds from other discretionary programs.
Preemptive Actions on Competing Expenditures	Fanatically opposed to social program expenditures, especially Temporary Aid to Needy Families (TANF). Also opposed to expanding federal assistance to education.	Strong supporters of education aid and social program funding that is necessary to guarantee that all three hundred million Americans are enabled to function as assets in support of national goals and agendas.

(continued)

TABLE 7.3
(*continued*)

Item	Blue Dog Coalition	Congressional Black Caucus
Composition of Present Membership	Mostly from southern and Midwestern rural districts; four black members.	Members elected from voting rights districts plus a few from majority white districts, but to date all are black.
Relationship to Democratic Congressional Campaign Committee (DCCC)	In response to Rahm Emanuel's contempt, the group rallied and raised $50 million for the 2006 election.	Treated with contempt by Rahm Emanuel for its inability to raise significant amounts through the CBC-PAC.

In the arithmetic of American legislative democracy there is a set of magic numbers seldom noticed or understood. In the House of Representatives with 435 members, the majority is 218—the amount necessary to prevail on any vote. This means that when the logic of the democratic process flows smoothly, the power is really in the hands of 110 members, the minimal majority of the dominant party. Most votes of great importance are conducted along party position lines, which means that each party's caucus is involved in the adoption of such positions. If a vote is demanded in the party caucus during deliberations, then half plus one can determine the party position. In the 109th Congress (2005–2006) there were 202 Democratic Party members, which theoretically meant that 102 members could decide Democratic Party positions. Forty of these 102 votes were in the hands of the members of the Congressional Black Caucus. While it remains true that one member among 435 is of minor significance, this special arithmetic of party decision-making, when utilized by a party caucus, greatly magnifies the power of each caucus member.

For three decades the CBC matured and expanded to the point at which, despite its small numbers, its unity and consistency achieved significant clout. One

TABLE 7.4
Blue Dog Coalition Success in Farm Subsidies

Title of Bill	The Farm Security and Rural Investment Act of 2002	Reauthorization of Personal Responsibilities Act
Length of Bill	Six years	Five years
Annual Appropriation	$100 billion	$16.5 billion
Number of Beneficiaries	Six million	Fifteen million
Maximum Allowed Per Beneficiary	$360,000 per quota	$6,000 for family of four (average among the states)
Number of Years for Eligibility	Indefinite	Five years

critical example occurred at a Democratic Caucus meeting about President Bill Clinton and the allegations that he had sex with Monica Lewinsky. Assembled for a meeting a few days after President Clinton had conceded that he had sexual relations with Ms. Lewinsky, there were many signals among Democrats that a motion would be offered in the caucus to demand that the president resign. In fact, Senator Joe Lieberman had already publicly stated that Clinton should resign. In that Democratic Caucus meeting room, a congressman who had also publicly stated that the president should resign seemed poised to offer the motion that, regardless of outcome, would have greatly weakened Clinton's position during a period when public opinion was still in formation.

To block the disaster of a motion and debate, Representative Maxine Waters, speaking out of turn and without the aid of any microphone, shouted the consensus of her colleagues: "The members of the Congressional Black Caucus are unanimously opposed to any motion requesting the president to resign—and we greatly resent the offering of such a motion at this time." The motion was never made and there is a graphic historical record of the long weekend with ministers praying at the White House. As the clouds lifted on Monday, public opinion polls slowly emerged to give President Clinton a 60 percent approval rating.

The bold attack of Representative Waters, acting against the backdrop of her knowledge of the power of forty votes in a situation that required 102 for passage, will probably never be noted by major historians. But such micro-maneuvers remain vitally significant despite the historians' omissions. Certainly it was the kind of maneuver that caught the attention of the most brilliant of all the Republicans, Newt Gingrich. As he had ascended to power in the House, Gingrich had placed the destruction of the CBC as a major priority.

In 1995, after failing to strip the CBC of its legislative organization status by restructuring the rules, the newly installed Speaker Gingrich declared that the CBC Alternative Budget would not be allowed on the floor of the House unless it complied with a requirement that all budget bills show a balance projection by the year 2002. In response, Representatives Donald Payne and Major Owens proposed a CBC alternative that balanced the budget by increasing corporate taxes and making deep cuts in defense spending. They proposed no cuts in Medicare or Medicaid and increased spending on several safety net programs. Although they never passed, the annual CBC budget statements were respected for their thoroughness, for the spotlight thrown on the worst expenditures, and for their power in pricking the conscience of their fellow Democrats.

From its inception, despite some serious blunders, the CBC has established an impressive record of triumphs. These have included the following:

- In 1983, despite the loud veto threats of the powerful and popular President Ronald Reagan, CBC members negotiated with Republican conservatives and southern whites to win passage of the law declaring the third Monday in January a legal holiday honoring Martin Luther King. After it passed the House with a vote of 338–90 and later passed the Senate with a 78–22 vote, the president set aside his veto threat and H.R. 3706 (P.L. 98-144) was signed into law.

- Again, in 1985, the CBC directly negotiated with the Republicans and won passage of a bill imposing sanctions on apartheid South Africa. When President Reagan vetoed the bill, the Senate voted to override the veto with a 78–21 vote. The House veto override vote was 313–83.
- On September 14, 1994, President Clinton ordered U.S. forces to escort the democratically elected president of Haiti, Jean Bertrand Aristide, back to his country. Direct negotiations and skirmishes between the CBC Task Force on Haiti and the White House achieved this liberation despite the fact that the polls showed that two-thirds of the public was against such positive action. Not only floor speeches and press conferences but also direct civil disobedience involving the arrest of nine members of the CBC were used to pressure a reluctant White House into action.

Although the three examples cited above involved direct initiatives by the CBC, this was not the usual pattern of operation. Most triumphs were achieved through steadfast bargaining. For example, with the help of enlightened and fair members on the Education and Appropriations Committees, federal funding for 113 historically black colleges and universities was moved from $0 in 1987 to an accumulated total of more than $5 billion by 2010. Additionally, with the direct intervention of Speaker Tip O'Neal, the CBC was able to shield eight safety net programs from the first set of President Reagan's across-the-board budget cuts. The overall list of cooperative and collaborative responses to the CBC spark plug role is impressive, including the renewal of an expanded Voting Rights Act with almost unanimous consent on both sides of the aisle.

Even with all of its success, the CBC has had several lamentable lapses. The CBC failed to keep the thrust of Lyndon Johnson's Economic Opportunity Act alive. On the issue that it ranked as its number one priority, education, the CBC failed to maintain the intense focus necessary to achieve the breakthroughs needed by the nation's most neglected children. Another priority, summer youth employment, was allowed to slip away. Drastic cuts in federal public housing subsidies by Reagan were never challenged. The CBC never mounted an appropriate fight to end the greed of farm subsidies, and probably the greatest blunder was the failure to lead forcefully against the Clinton-Gingrich destruction of the Personal Responsibilities Act program for aid to families with dependent children.

Although the CBC can rightfully claim a medal for its role in saving the federally mandated E-Rate from destruction by the communications industry, and along with the American Library Association guaranteed access to the Internet for students and library users all over the nation, the CBC was unable to negotiate reasonable terms to support more community access to the publicly owned airwaves. This is a failure that has long-range negative consequences as the poor residents in our swelling urban centers struggle to gain a broadcast voice in decision-making.

Conclusion

Around negotiating tables, in hearings, and on the floor and in platforms that shape public opinion there is a great amount of work remaining before the CBC can realize its original objective. Group members seek to operate more effectively to serve their districts while they are also pledged to follow in the footsteps of Martin Luther King and apply their political skills in service to the total black community and nation. Congress as an institution must encourage the fulfillment of this mission.

Among American institutions (private or government) systematically wasting the most leadership talent, the U.S. House of Representatives would find itself at the top of the list. In both parties the "command and control" ethic preserved fervently by the old bulls dutifully guarding tradition guarantees the ongoing loss of vital human energy and brainpower. A greater number of more formally organized caucus groups is not the total answer to this long-term human resources disaster. It would, however, constitute a much-needed significant step forward.

References

Casper, Gerhard. 2007. "Caesarism in Democratic Politics—Reflections on Max Weber." Lecture presented at the John W. Kluge Center at the Library of Congress, Washington, DC, March 22.

Kaplan, Jonathan E. 2007. "Rushing the Blue Dogs." *The Hill,* May 30, 6.

Owens, Major. 2011. *The Peacock Elite: A Case Study of the Congressional Black Caucus.* Jonesboro, AR: GrantHouse Publishers.

Section III

SENATE

8

The Death of Deliberation

Party and Procedure in the Modern United States Senate

James Wallner

DURING THE SUMMER OF 2008, the United States Senate considered the Lieberman-Warner Climate Security Act of 2008 (S. 3036), a measure that sought to address global climate change by reducing emissions of carbon dioxide and other greenhouse gases. Reflecting the climate change concern of millions of Americans, Senate Majority Leader Harry Reid stated on the Senate floor that "global warming is easily the gravest long-term challenge that our country faces and the world faces. It is the most critical issue of our time" (Reid 2008c, S10187). Indeed, both Republicans and Democrats demanded action to address this issue. Majority Leader Reid recognized this, arguing that "the American people have a right to expect their legislature, their Congress to address this issue" (Reid 2008a, 11323).

Yet, despite the gravity of the situation and a popular demand for action, Senator Reid used his prerogative as Senate majority leader to block amendments and end debate on the Climate Security Act less than five minutes after bringing the measure to the Senate floor for consideration. Senator Reid utilized a once rare, but increasingly common, parliamentary procedure known as "filling the amendment tree" to block other senators from offering amendments to the measure and file cloture. Such a move effectively ended debate on an issue that the majority leader, his party, and many Americans considered "the most critical issue of our time."

While the Democratic leadership used procedure to block amendments to S. 3036, the Republican leadership also utilized the procedural tools at its disposal to slow down consideration of the legislation. In response to an unrelated matter concerning the confirmation of district and appellate court judges,

Minority Leader Mitch McConnell objected to waiving the often routine requirement that legislation be read by the Senate's clerks prior to its consideration. As a result, consideration of the Climate Security Act stalled as the clerks spent an entire calendar day reading the measure into the *Congressional Record*.

Similarly, in 1990, the Senate considered legislation regulating emissions of harmful pollutants into the atmosphere. During the debate on the Clean Air Amendments Act of 1990, the Democrats controlled both houses of Congress and President George H. W. Bush occupied the White House. However, the Senate's consideration of this legislation differed significantly from its work on the Climate Security Act of 2008. During consideration of the Clean Air Amendments Act, 181 amendments were offered, of which 131 were disposed of. Democrats sponsored only sixty. The outcome for this measure was also much different from that of the Climate Security Act 2008, which was pulled from the floor amid partisan rancor less than a week after debate began without there having been voting on a single amendment. The Clear Air Amendments Act of 1990 ultimately passed the Senate 89–11 and was signed into law by President Bush (P.L. 101-549).

The juxtaposition of the Senate's deliberation on the Clean Air Amendments Act in 1990 with its consideration of the Climate Security Act in 2008 underscores a narrative popular in the academic literature on Congress—the Senate has gradually evolved from a collegial body governed by tradition and mutual respect to a majoritarian institution in which excessive partisanship and ideological polarization has led to perpetual gridlock. The literature largely argues that this transformation accelerated in the last two decades of the twentieth century. As such, a common refrain at the beginning of the twenty-first century is that the Senate is broken and that institutional reform is needed to restore its ability to pass legislation. While the literature correctly points out that Senate decision-making has changed considerably over the last thirty years, its emphasis on cooperation and conflict as mutually exclusive patterns of parliamentary behavior obscures current procedural practice in the institution and fails to account for the Senate's legislative productivity despite its increasingly partisan and ideologically polarized environment.

Perhaps no one was able to intuitively grasp the nuanced nature of the legislative process in the Senate better than the late Senator Edward M. Kennedy, who recognized the inherent fluidity of Senate decision-making as a result of his nearly five decades of service. Senator Kennedy once said, "The Senate is a chemical place. Something happens when Senators are all in the room, debating an issue, especially when everyone understands that we are going to stay in and not adjourn until we get things done" (Kennedy 2009, 458). Kennedy's comment highlights the seemingly unpredictable nature of the legislative process in the Senate. Yet where Kennedy grasped the true nature of decision-making in the modern Senate, most scholarly treatments fall short.

Accustomed to the formal, centralized, and predictably majoritarian House of Representatives, many political scientists have had difficulty forming an accurate understanding of the informal, decentralized, and less predictable nature of the Senate. The limited number of observations and absence of predictable parliamentary procedures complicate scholarly efforts to form generalized models with which to measure statistically significant behavior in the Senate. As a result, the academic literature on congressional decision-making has largely neglected the Senate and focused instead on the House. Moreover, the scholarship that has addressed the Senate has failed to fully grasp the nuanced nature of the institution's decision-making process as it currently operates. Such misunderstanding results from approaching the Senate from the perspective of what is currently known about the House or because works focused exclusively on the Senate have largely been published prior to recent important developments in its formal and informal institutional features. In addition, the most recent scholarship that seeks to explain the impact of partisanship and ideological polarization on Senate decision-making either overstates the problem or misinterprets its consequences. Specifically, the literature does not account for why obstructionism is not as persistent a feature of the legislative process as one would expect, given the ease with which any individual member can effectively halt the Senate's activity. As a result, it fails to describe the decision-making process in the modern Senate particularly well.

A Broken Senate?

A common observation of the Senate today is that it is paralyzed by excessive levels of legislative gridlock (Binder 2003; Ornstein and Mann 2006; Ornstein 2008; Theriault 2008; Lee 2009). Yet one observation too often overlooked in the literature is that the Senate is capable of resolving the differences of its membership on measures of significant import without descending into an endless debate characterized by ideological partisanship and irreconcilable gridlock. As a consequence, scholarly accounts of Senate decision-making all too often seek to explain why gridlock happens (Binder 1997; Krehbiel 1998; Binder 2003; Theriault 2008; Lee 2009). The more important question, and the one that forms the basis of this chapter, is why gridlock does not happen.

At first, this realization may seem contrary to what reason would suggest. The Senate is currently composed of ideologically polarized members. Also, party leaders undoubtedly exercise more influence in the decision-making process by virtue of more cohesive political parties. Furthermore, the overall number of public laws passed by Congress over the past twenty-five years has declined.

Presumably, gridlock in the Senate is to blame for such legislative inefficiency. Yet the inescapable fact remains that senators are capable of resolving their differences on measures of significant import without descending into an endless debate characterized by excessive partisanship and ideological polarization. While partisan competition in the Senate has presumably been elevated in recent years as a result of polarization, the legislative process in the institution has not been characterized by irreconcilable gridlock. The Senate continues to formulate policy and pass legislation on controversial and noncontroversial issues alike.

Such an observation raises several important questions. Why is gridlock not a persistent feature of Senate decision-making in this environment? What explains the Senate's ability to pass legislation despite the opposition of procedurally empowered and ideologically polarized partisan minorities? Why do individual senators and the minority party leadership consistently refrain from utilizing all of the tools available to them under Senate rules to obstruct the agenda of the majority party? Any understanding of decision-making in the modern Senate must account for why obstructionism is not a persistent feature of the legislative process despite these concerns.

This chapter argues that understanding the unique nature of decision-making in the modern Senate is ultimately dependent on popular opinion and the impact of the Senate's institutional development on the policy process since the early 1990s. Since that time, the Senate has grown more accountable to an electorate that has become more interested in its deliberations. Yet it is important to note that strengthening the relationship between the Senate and the American people was not, in and of itself, sufficient to precipitate the development of strong institutional parties. Rather, it was the increased accountability that resulted from this new relationship that allowed the electorate's polarization to be *quickly* and *directly* reflected inside the Senate for the first time in its history. Such a process inevitably changed the character of the institution. The practical effect of the external ideological polarization was that the Senate became more internally partisan and confrontational (Sinclair 2002, 246).

Viewing Senate decision-making from this perspective suggests a new way to conceptualize party leadership in the Senate. Such an approach can be observed in the changing nature of the legislative process in the institution. To this end, this chapter develops three generalized patterns of decision-making that can be observed in the Senate and tested empirically. In an effort to understand how the prevalence of these patterns, and thus the nature of the party leadership's involvement in the legislative process, has changed over the last two decades, this chapter examines the decision-making process for major legislation in the 102nd and 110th Congresses.

The Senate and Party Leadership

The centralization of influence inside the Senate was both a result of the changing relationship between its members and their constituencies and a necessary condition for popular opinion to be translated into public policy. Specifically, influence was centralized under the leadership of the two political parties in response to the new demands placed upon the Senate by increasingly interested and polarized constituencies. The standing committees and their chairmen gradually ceded influence to their party leadership as the Senate floor emerged as an acceptable arena for legislative decision-making in the second half of the twentieth century (Sinclair 1989, 114–15; Smith 1989, 6–8, 11, 97).

The privileged institutional position of committees in the 1950s initially gave way to the more active participation of individual members in the 1960s and 1970s. However, the Senate gradually became more centralized in the 1970s and 1980s as the number of "decision-making units" that once served to structure member participation declined significantly from numerous standing committees to ultimately just the Senate floor. This institutional arrangement eventually led to the emergence of the party leadership as the primary arbiter of influence in the Senate in the late 1980s and 1990s (Sinclair 1989, 5, 71–72, 85; Smith 1989, 3, 95).

The open environment of the Senate floor led minority party Senators, and majority party members who were out of step with their colleagues on various issues, to more fully exploit their procedural rights in an effort to achieve their goals. Senators quickly recognized the increased importance of the floor as an arena for decision-making and increasingly utilized the filibuster to obstruct legislation. In addition to the traditional use of the filibuster to block measures, members also began to aggressively use the threat of protracted debate to positively affect the content and outcome of legislation, as well as to force action on unrelated matters. As such, filibusters rapidly increased in both scope and frequency during the second half of the twentieth century (Smith 1997). The prominence of the party leadership in Senate decision-making increased in such an environment. In the absence of any credible alternative, the majority leader, and to a lesser extent the minority leader, emerged as the one institutional actor who could successfully manage the floor, negotiate agreements between interested parties, and ensure that the Senate completed its business (Gamm and Smith 2002a, 213).

One individual perhaps had the greatest role in precipitating the emergence of modern party leadership in the Senate. During Lyndon Johnson's tenure as majority leader (1951–1961), the structural balance of power slowly began to shift from the committees and their chairmen to the party leadership. Before Lyndon Johnson, "party leadership" in the Senate was a derisive term. These positions had little influence and were ultimately of little consequence. Johnson gave party leadership in the Senate real influence for the first time and, by extension, created the means by which political parties could be truly effective. Out of this process emerged a Senate transformed from a sleepy nineteenth-century body focused on deliberation to an active institution focused on legislative decision-making at the end of the twentieth century.

Yet Senator Johnson did not completely alter the structural balance of power between committees and the party leadership. Even after many of his innovations, committees and committee chairmen remained highly autonomous and powerful actors that provided substantive policy leadership in the Senate. Indeed, the centralized position of party leadership under Johnson precluded a sustained effort to directly and proactively shape policy because the majority leader's primary task was to broker compromise among highly fractious partisan blocs and facilitate the consideration of legislation in the Senate. As such, party leadership in the mid-twentieth century was more concerned with the procedural aspects of the policy process (Smith 1993, 259).

Despite the many important contributions made by Senator Johnson to the development of party leadership in the Senate, the centralized role of party leaders in the policy process would not emerge as a persistent feature of the Senate until the 1980s and 1990s under the leadership of Senators Robert Byrd and George Mitchell in the Democratic Party and Howard Baker and Bob Dole in the Republican Party. During this period, the majority and minority leaders became increasingly involved in substantive decision-making. In addition to facilitating procedural decision-making, the party leadership played a more central role in developing and managing the party's agenda inside the Senate. The leaders also assumed a larger role in the development and implementation of each party's communications strategy outside the Senate (Smith 1993; Gamm and Smith 2002b, 287–89; Riddick 1981).

Despite the emergence of strong party leadership at the end of the twentieth century, individual senators, and the minority party collectively, continue to possess considerable procedural rights with which to obstruct the majority party as it seeks to pass its agenda. Indeed, this simple fact largely informs conventional wisdom, journalistic reports, and most of the current scholarship on the Senate. Such observations typically hold that a more ideologically polarized electorate produces a more partisan and ideologically polarized Senate membership. As a result, senators are more likely to utilize their procedural rights to pursue more partisan and ideologically polarized goals. The majority party is likely to avail itself of all of its procedural tools to enact a more partisan and ideologically polarized agenda. In response, the minority party will likely seek to obstruct the majority for perceived policy and electoral gain. This obstructionism leads to gridlock precisely because the Senate is unable to overcome the instability inherent in its institutional structure and pass legislation in such a polarized environment (Theriault 2008, 3–4, 55). The dramatic increase in the number of cloture motions filed and invoked over the last twenty-five years and the rapid rise in the practice of "filling the amendment tree" to block the consideration of unwanted amendments seemingly support this argument.

A Different Interpretation

There is something to be said for analytical clarity gained by viewing decision-making in the modern Senate as characterized by excessive levels of legislative gridlock. The Senate today is certainly composed of more ideologically polarized members who generally reflect their ideologically polarized constituents. Party leaders, therefore, undoubtedly exercise more influence in the decision-making process by virtue of leading more ideologically polarized and cohesive political parties. Furthermore, the overall number of public laws passed by Congress over the past twenty-five years has declined. In addition, the percentage of all bills passed by the Senate has declined from the 97th Congress (1981–1982), when Republicans regained control of the Senate for the first time in over twenty years, to the 110th Congress (2007–2008), as illustrated in figure 8.1. Presumably gridlock in the Senate is to blame for such legislative inefficiency. As previously argued, such decline is often attributed to the increased prominence of partisanship and polarization.

Yet this hardly seems sufficient to justify the indictment that the institution is "broken" or that it is paralyzed by gridlock. The inescapable fact remains that partisan competition in the Senate has been relatively constrained in recent years. Indeed, the Senate continues to formulate policy and pass legislation on controversial and uncontroversial issues alike. For example, 786 bills passed the

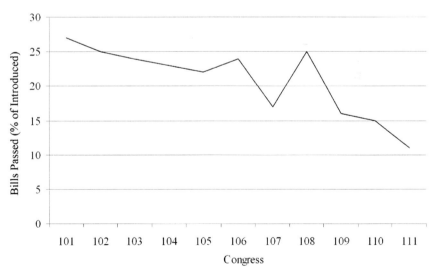

FIGURE 8.1
Senate Bills Passed

Senate during the 97th Congress. In the 110th Congress, 556 bills passed the Senate. In the 111th Congress, 454 bills passed the Senate. These included such highly controversial legislation as health care reform and financial regulatory reform (Wallner 2010). Moreover, the number of measures passed by the Senate in the 104th, 105th, and 108th Congresses indicate that the institution can be productive despite the increasing partisanship and polarization characteristic of its larger environment. These congresses also signify that such productivity can occur in periods of divided government (104th and 105th Congresses) and in periods of unified government (108th Congress).

A closer examination demonstrates that the decline in the percentage of bills passed by the Senate reflects a decline in the number of bills actually considered on the Senate floor. This is illustrated in figure 8.2.

Thus, the data presented in figures 8.1 and 8.2 support the conclusion that the Senate passes fewer bills precisely because it is considering fewer of them on the floor. Interestingly, the percentage of bills considered that actually pass the Senate has *increased* over the last two decades, as illustrated in figure 8.3.

Figure 8.3 indicates that a bill is far more likely to pass the Senate if it receives consideration on the floor. It also demonstrates that an overwhelming percentage of bills considered on the Senate floor pass when compare to the percentage of those that are defeated. Figure 8.4 illustrates this relationship between bill passage and floor consideration. The difference in the number of bills considered on the floor and the number of bills that the Senate passes actually *narrows* over the course of the period observed.

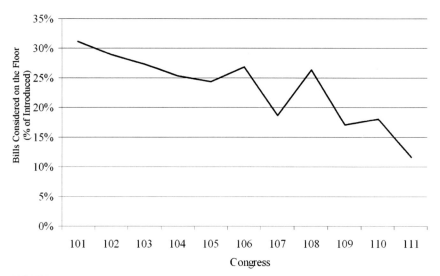

FIGURE 8.2
Percentage of Introduced Bills Considered on the Senate Floor

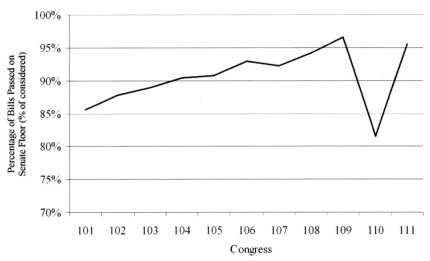

FIGURE 8.3
Percentage of Bills Passed on Senate Floor

The argument that the combination of polarized parties with the Senate's permissive procedures leads to persistent gridlock is not persuasive if partisan minorities are not using the tools at their disposal to obstruct the majority on the most significant and controversial issues. For example, the fact that the Senate Republican minority chose to cooperate procedurally on health care reform

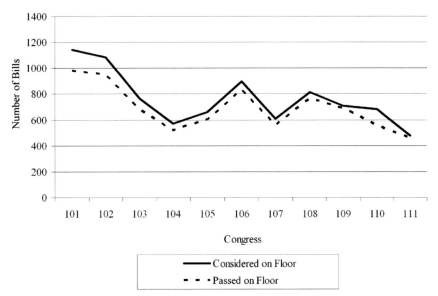

FIGURE 8.4
Legislation: Floor Consideration and Passage

in the 111th Congress presumably implies that they also chose not to obstruct more uncontroversial legislation. What explains such productivity despite the opposition of procedurally empowered and ideologically polarized partisan minorities? Significant external and internal developments in Senate decision-making in the second half of the twentieth century have not been accompanied by similar changes in the institution's formal rules and procedures designed to limit minority rights. Why do individual senators and the minority party leadership consistently refrain from using Senate rules to obstruct the agenda of the majority party if doing so is perceived to bring them policy and electoral gain?

A New Theory of Senate Decision-Making

The premise of this chapter is that the majority *and* minority party leaders serve a moderating function in the Senate by acting within certain bounds to ameliorate the conflict and instability inherent in the institution and its broader environment. The permissive procedural environment of the Senate ensures that the minority leader shares responsibility for managing the institution's ever increasing workload with the majority leader. Such cooperation is possible because the goals of the majority and minority parties, while not identical, are not necessarily always mutually exclusive.

While counterintuitive, such cooperation stems from the fact that party leaders have flexibility in fulfilling their responsibilities (Sinclair 1995; Green 2010). In addition, members of Congress have conflicting and/or weak preferences, as well as incomplete information about what their leaders do (Sinclair 1995). Members and leaders occupy an environment in which obstruction can negatively impact both the majority and minority parties. However, the threshold for obstruction is low because of Senate rules. As a result of the combination of these considerations, party leaders possess the ability and have incentives to pursue the structured consent pattern of decision-making in an effort to resolve conflict in the Senate.

Such behavior by leaders arises from the fact that congressional parties and their members are motivated by multiple and conflicting electoral, policy, and power goals. When the goals of a party's membership conflict with one another, it is typically the responsibility of the party leadership to choose among the competing goals and fashion a unified party position on a particular course of action (Smith 2007, 4, 12). The ability to effectively and consistently choose among the competing courses of action represents the foundation of party leaders' power in the modern Senate. Powerful party leaders are able to convince or compel their partisan colleagues to support the decisions even though they may periodically conflict with a member's own parochial goals. It is important to note that an individual senator need not actively support a course of action. As previously stated, each individual member possesses the ability to act autonomously to achieve his or her goals. A senator, therefore, can be said to acquiesce to a course of action that contradicts with his or her goal by choosing not to utilize the procedural prerogatives at his or her disposal.

Leaders typically possess significant influence over the decision-making process by virtue of their leadership positions alone, largely regardless of their party's particular level of ideological cohesion. Leaders often utilize this increased influence in an attempt to "restructure" and "reconstitute" their party's position on policy and legislative strategies. In contrast to both the institutional context and principal-agent theories, party leaders may utilize their influence to *moderate*, rather than exacerbate, the procedural choices of their partisan colleagues (Truman 1959; Lee 2009).

Patterns of Senate Decision-Making

Conventional wisdom and current scholarship suggest that the Senate functions largely according to one of two general patterns of decision-making: *collegial* or *majoritarian* (Smith 1989, 3–5).[1] Yet an examination of the Senate in recent years demonstrates that the institution increasingly functions according to a third general pattern of decision-making: *structured consent*. The collegial, majoritarian, and structured consent patterns of decision-making each represent a point on a continuum of Senate decision-making rather than concrete procedural road maps. This chapter seeks to explain these three general patterns and define the criteria for each. It argues that major legislation is increasingly considered under conditions of structured consent.

To test this hypothesis, major legislation, as defined by *Congressional Quarterly (CQ)*, considered in the 102nd Congress (1991–1992) and 110th Congress (2007–2008) is examined to determine whether the bills were agreed to under collegial, majoritarian, or structured consent decision-making.[2]

The 102nd and the 110th Congresses were chosen because of their similarities—each had unified Democratic control of Congress and Republican control of the White House. In addition, examining two congresses sixteen years apart allows observations on dramatic changes to decision-making over the last two decades. Finally, the analysis concludes with a comparison of the predominant pattern of decision-making in each Congress in an effort to better distinguish between the three patterns and articulate the conditions under which structured consent operates.

In the collegial pattern of decision-making, conflict is muted. In the majoritarian pattern of decision-making, conflict is significant. In the structured consent pattern of decision-making, conflict is limited, and thus successfully managed. Furthermore, collegial, majoritarian, and structured consent patterns of decision-making feature procedural characteristics that are unique to each. Table 8.1 shows the characteristics of these three patterns of decision-making.

TABLE 8.1
Patterns of Senate Decision-Making: Characteristics

Characteristics	Collegial	Majoritarian	Structured Consent
Overall	Open	Closed	Structured (either open or closed)
Senator Participation	No significant barriers	Significant barriers	Moderate barriers
Participants	Interested members (any number)	Majority party leadership	Majority and minority party leadership
Process	Decentralized	Centralized	Centralized
Constraints on Debate and Amendments	Limited	Significant	Moderate
Place of Primary Action	Senate floor	Off the Senate floor, in majority party conference	Off the Senate floor, in both party conferences and negotiations between both party leaders
Amendments Allowed	Large number from both parties	None/only from majority party	Limited number from both parties; preselected and identified in unanimous consent agreements
Cloture Motions	None	Used to speed consideration of obstructed measures	Requirements set by unanimous consent/ necessary in some cases
Vote Outcomes	Bipartisan	Partisan	Partisan for amendments and bipartisan for final passage
Resolving House-Senate Differences	Conference committee	Amendment exchange	Conference committee or amendment exchange

Collegial Decision-Making

The collegial pattern of decision-making arose out of the reforms of the 1970s. Specifically, a large number of members began to take part in the legislative process on the Senate floor (Smith 1989, 3, 11). It is important to note that the Senate rules are not always followed in collegial decision-making. In fact, Senate rules are rarely followed in any pattern of decision-making. Rather, the important aspect of collegial decision-making is that it is an inclusive process in which there are few constraints on member participation and conflict is muted. It is a committee-based process in which legislation is placed on the Senate calendar only after it has been considered by the relevant committee of jurisdiction. Efforts to move to legislation by the majority leader are usually uncontroversial and measures are often laid before the Senate by unanimous consent. In some cases, cloture on the motion to proceed is filed. However, vote outcomes on these motions are usually bipartisan, if not unanimous.

Once legislation is made pending, the collegial pattern is largely characterized by an open decision-making process on the Senate floor. There are no significant barriers to the participation of interested members other than their own time and resources. The total number of members directly involved in the process is a function of the salience of the issue under consideration. An issue with high salience will lead to greater member involvement; an issue with low salience will lead to a lesser amount of member involvement.

The decision-making process itself is relatively decentralized and there are few constraints on interested members when participating in the debate and amendment process. As a result, action occurs predominantly on the Senate floor as legislation is openly debated and amended. Majority and minority amendments are allowed and cloture is rarely used to limit debate. A large percentage of the amendments filed are offered and most of those are disposed of by voice vote or unanimous consent. Recorded votes on amendments are rare, but exhibit largely bipartisan patterns when they occur. While a majority of one party may vote against a majority of the other party on some amendments, the overall number of such instances is relatively low. Majority and minority party success rates on amendments offered are also high. Vote outcomes on the final passage of legislation are bipartisan. Finally, conference committees are typically used to resolve differences between the House and Senate.

As a result of its relatively open and deliberative process, the collegial pattern of decision-making is incapable of resolving significant conflict between members while simultaneously maintaining its legislative productivity. This is due to the fact that its procedural features cannot efficiently accommodate proposals that significantly divide the Senate membership. It is not difficult to imagine a highly contentious measure dragging on for months as members freely engage in procedural combat under the collegial pattern of decision-making.

Majoritarian Decision-Making

At the other end of the spectrum is majoritarian decision-making. In contrast to collegial, the majoritarian pattern of decision-making is an exclusive process in which there are significant constraints on member participation and conflict is unbounded. Majoritarian decision-making typically circumvents the committee process and legislation developed within the majority party under the direction of the party leadership is placed directly on the Senate calendar.[3] As a result, subsequent efforts to move to the legislation by the majority leader are highly controversial. Cloture on the motion to proceed to such legislation is very common and vote outcomes on such motions are highly partisan.

Majoritarian decision-making is characterized by a closed process on the Senate floor. There are significant barriers to participation, even for interested members willing to expend the necessary time and resources to be involved. As its name implies, majoritarian decision-making is a partisan process in which the minority party is essentially blocked from any meaningful participation. The majority party leadership is the only meaningful participant and it exercises centralized, partisan control over the debate and amendment process. As a result, action occurs predominantly off the Senate floor within the majority party. Decisions made there are merely ratified on the Senate floor. At that stage, the majority leader usually seeks to control the number and nature of the amendments offered by threatening to fill the amendment tree and file cloture. If any amendments are allowed, they are typically majority party amendments. A low percentage of amendments filed are offered and recorded votes, typically motions to table, are usually necessary to dispose of minority amendments. Vote outcomes on amendments are largely partisan in nature and the success rate of majority amendments is high while the success rate for minority amendments is low.

Cloture is periodically used preemptively by the majority leader to speed consideration of legislation throughout the process regardless of the time spent on the floor. Vote outcomes on the final passage of legislation are highly partisan. Finally, differences between the House and Senate are typically resolved by a process of amendment exchange between the two chambers.

The majoritarian pattern of decision-making is dependent on a party conference cohesive enough to repeatedly produce the procedural supermajorities necessary to pass legislation over minority party objections. In this process, the majority party obstructs the minority's ability to freely debate measures and offer amendments pursuant to the Senate rules. Such majoritarian obstructionism may simply result from the anticipation of expected obstruction by the minority party. It could also represent a genuine effort to push the majority's agenda unchanged through the Senate in a timely manner. The restrictive process could also be utilized to defend carefully negotiated legislation from killer amendments or to protect majority party members from having to take tough votes. Regardless of the motivations, majoritarian decision-making is unlikely to be successfully sustained for a significant period of time. This is due to the fact that its procedural features cannot accommodate the inevitable demands of individual members from both parties to debate and amend legislation on the Senate floor.

Structured Consent Decision-Making

Located between the collegial and majoritarian patterns of decision-making is structured consent. Similar to majoritarian decision-making, structured consent is a semi-exclusive process in which there are moderate constraints on member participation. It differs from the majoritarian pattern in that conflict between the majority and minority parties is bounded. Structured consent usually circumvents the committee process and legislation developed within the majority party under the direction of the party leadership is placed directly on the Senate calendar. However, the majority leader often works with the minority leader to schedule legislation for floor consideration. Subsequent efforts to move legislation by the majority leader may not be controversial. Cloture on the motion to proceed for such legislation remains common, as some minority party members may refuse to grant unanimous consent to make the legislation pending in protest of the closed process in which it was originally developed. As a result, vote outcomes on cloture on the motion to proceed may be either partisan or bipartisan.

In contrast to both the collegial and majoritarian patterns, the structured consent pattern of decision-making is characterized by a prearranged floor process (either open or closed). There are moderate barriers to the participation of highly interested members who are willing to devote the time and resources necessary to be involved. Decision-making in conditions of structured consent takes the form of a centralized bipartisan process in which the majority *and* minority party leadership serve as the only meaningful participants on a consistent basis and across all issues. While a small number of highly interested members may participate at times, the majority and minority party leaders largely determine the nature of floor consideration by negotiating comprehensive unanimous consent agreements to structure debate and amendment activity. As a result, action occurs predominantly off the Senate floor in negotiations between the two leaders and within each party under the direction of its leadership.

Relatively few amendments are allowed to be offered to legislation under conditions of structured consent. The majority and minority leaders negotiate to determine the amendments that are allowed on each side. Once a list is agreed upon, each leader works to get the consent of their rank-and-file members. Because the majority leader is unlikely to approve minority amendments that are opposed by a significant number of his party, but could potentially be successful when offered, minority amendments typically fail while majority amendments usually succeed. The majority leader has more leverage to enforce such an agreement in negotiations with the minority leader, as constant obstruction by the minority could lead the majority leader to threaten to adopt a majoritarian pattern of decision-making and shut the minority out of the decision-making process entirely. Recorded votes are used to dispose of amendments and pre-arranged sixty-vote thresholds are common when disposing of controversial issues.

Cloture is not always necessary to end debate in structured consent, as the majority and minority leaders usually agree to set its requirements by unanimous consent, thus avoiding lengthy procedural delays. However, a structured consent pattern of decision-making can also be followed in tandem with the cloture process. Vote outcomes on amendments are largely partisan in nature. Vote outcomes on the final passage of legislation are largely bipartisan. Finally, conference committees and amendment exchanges can be used to resolve differences between the House and Senate.

The structured consent pattern of decision-making is dependent on relatively cohesive parties, as well as majority and minority leaders that are capable of mollifying their most ideological members without upsetting their negotiations. Moreover, majority and minority party goals must not be mutually exclusive. For example, a minority leader concerned with messaging and improving his party's position in the next election may not be concerned with whether or not its amendments are successful. In turn, a majority leader primarily concerned with translating his party's agenda into law may not be as concerned with the minority's messaging amendments so long as they do not jeopardize that agenda. When these conditions are not present, or when the majority party is more united than the minority party, structured consent can easily turn into a majoritarian process.

Measuring Decision-Making: A Note on Procedure

As a result of its small size and the importance of inherited rules, the Senate has proved less amenable than the House to more quantitative or abstract analysis. Moreover, limiting an examination to a single quantifiable aspect of decision-making, such as voting, member preferences, or political parties, invariably fails to grasp the complexity of the Senate's legislative process. Conclusions reached by such approaches can distort, albeit unintentionally, our understanding of the modern Senate by privileging one aspect of its decision-making over another. In contrast, analyzing decision-making from a procedural perspective incorporates these aspects and yields important insights about the complex and multifaceted nature of the legislative process at the beginning of the twenty-first century.

C. Lawrence Evans and Walter J. Oleszek (2000) argue that because procedure shapes policy, the nature of Congress as a representative body can be understood by looking at the direction in which its procedures have evolved. While the precise motivations for individual member activity cannot be known with a great degree of certainty, several assumptions about Senate decision-making can be made by consulting the procedural record. To this end, various procedural activities commonly observed in collegial, majoritarian, and structured consent patterns of decision-making can be measured by examining the manner in which legislation is considered in the Senate. Steven Smith (2010) has correctly observed that Senate procedures resemble a "geologic record" (10). He argues that "they are the formal record of more complicated interaction between the majority and minority parties, much of which does not get recorded" (Smith 2010, 11). As such, the path a measure takes to the Senate floor, the nature of debate limitations and amendment activity once on the floor, as well as the partisan nature of roll call voting can be used to measure the presence of each pattern of decision-making.

All legislation introduced in the Senate is referred to specific committees according to defined areas of jurisdiction. Senate Rule 14, however, provides individual members with the ability to place measures directly on the Senate calendar without first receiving committee consideration. Yet Rule 14 simply allows measures to be placed on the calendar for *potential* consideration. According to Senate precedents and traditions, scheduling measures for *actual* consideration is the prerogative of the majority leader. As such, a measure remains on the calendar if the majority leader refuses to schedule it for floor consideration, even if it was placed there pursuant to Rule 14. Rule 14 thus represents a powerful tool with which the majority leader can bypass committee consideration and advance his party's agenda.

According to Senate rules, there are very few limits to the total number of amendments members are allowed to file when considering legislation on the floor. The ability to offer amendments on the floor is particularly useful for senators in the minority party, especially if the majority-controlled committees resist reporting minority-sponsored measures. As a result, minority party senators have a potentially powerful way to achieve their individual policy and political goals by virtue of offering amendments.

While there is no general restriction on an individual senator's ability to offer amendments on the Senate floor, structured consent is marked by an informally negotiated decision-making process that seeks to limit a member's procedural prerogatives by unanimous consent. Today, party leaders increasingly utilize unanimous consent agreements as "structured consent" agreements. Far from merely setting dates for a future vote and scheduling speeches, these consent agreements are much more comprehensive. Typically, unanimous consent agreements stipulate how much time can be used to debate a bill and divide time between the majority and the minority. They also serve to limit what amendments will be allowed and state when they can be offered. These structured requests may also limit other prerogatives of individual members. As a result of their utility, comprehensive unanimous consent agreements are now used to manage the decision-making process on the Senate floor to an unprecedented degree. What had been a very permissive procedural environment has gradually become more restrictive, and at no other time in its history has the outcome of the Senate's work been less in doubt.

It is important not to overstate the power of unanimous consent agreements. Such agreements still require the consent of every single member. Yet the two party leaders' centralized positions allow them to more easily secure the needed support because they usually know what members need in return for their "consent." It is also common for party leaders to secure favors to ensure that they receive future consent from reluctant members.

Finally, pursuant to Rule 22 three-fifths of senators duly chosen and sworn are required to end debate on a measure over the objection of individual members and proceed to a vote. As a result, any member can force the majority leader to file cloture on a bill. Such an objection increasingly takes the form of a senatorial "hold" and poses relatively few costs to the member raising the objection.

As a result of these rules and practices, individual senators have considerable power with which to affect the legislative process. As such, constraints on member interest and participation associated with each pattern of decision-making can be identified by measuring the number of amendments filed, the percentage of amendments filed that are offered to legislation, the nature of unanimous consent agreements, and the number of cloture motions filed on a bill. While such an approach is admittedly limited, it does not seem probable that ideologically polarized members will simply refuse to consistently participate in the decision-making process. If the number of amendments filed and the percentage of those offered are low in the current environment, for example, then it is a safe assumption that something caused such behavior other than waning member interest.

Furthermore, the use of highly detailed unanimous consent agreements to manage the decision-making process on the Senate floor depends upon some level of coordination. Such coordination can be exerted by exogenous or endogenous institutions. Since it has already been argued that the changing nature of the Senate's exogenous environment has helped make the modern Senate a more confrontational institution, it seems safe to assume that endogenous developments such as the unanimous consent agreement serve to facilitate decision-making.

Keith Krehbiel wrote that "in the absence of binding agreements, endogenous conditions may be the next best thing when, as UCAs, they permit leaders to construct situations in which the socially desired behavior is rational by individual cost-benefit standards" (1986, 22). With this observation, Krehbiel implicitly acknowledges the central tenet of this chapter: that the majority and minority party leaders utilize procedures to structure the decision-making process in a way that facilitates the legislative productivity of the Senate. Krehbiel argues that the particular procedural characteristics of Senate decision-making serve to create "opportunities, indeed invitations, for leaders to construct situations in which potential defectors' extreme temptations to object are tempered by the prospect of severe costs" (22).

Ainsworth and Flathman take a similar approach and argue that "convincing members to restrict their own freedoms is a fundamental element of leadership in the U.S. Senate" (1995, 177). According to this analysis, party leaders will attempt to "counter senators' increasing individualism with strategic ploys of their own" (188). Exacerbating these tendencies is the inescapable fact that only the leadership of the two political parties occupies the centralized institutional position necessary to *repeatedly* influence member behavior and induce senatorial constraint throughout each party and across all issue areas at the beginning of the twenty-first century.

Decision-Making in the 102nd Congress

Based on the categories in table 8.1, the collegial pattern of decision-making was, at least for key votes, the most prevalent in the 102nd Congress. *CQ* rated actions on twenty-six different bills as key votes in 1991 and 1992. Of these bills, 81 percent were considered under procedural conditions of collegial decision-making. Only 8 percent could be identified as majoritarian and 11 percent as structured consent.

Collegial Decision-Making

Of the twenty-one measures considered under conditions of collegial decision-making, seventeen were placed on the Senate calendar after receiving committee consideration. Four items bypassed the committee process and were placed directly on the Senate calendar. Of those, two had previously been considered by the relevant committee of jurisdiction. The Civil Rights Act of 1991 (S. 1745) was placed on the calendar after the Labor and Human Resources Committee reported a companion measure (S. 611) by unanimous consent. Additionally, the Senate placed the House-passed Soviet Nuclear Threat Reduction Act of 1991 (H.R. 3807) on the calendar and considered it by unanimous consent out of procedural convenience even though the Foreign Relations Committee had previously reported a companion measure (S. 1987).

Pursuant to the characteristics of collegial decision-making, seventeen measures were laid before the Senate by unanimous consent. In addition, objections to proceeding to the remaining four measures were minor and cloture on the motion to proceed to each passed. In each instance, an overwhelming majority supported ending debate on the motion to proceed.

Because consensus was reached to move to these twenty-one measures, few constraints on the debate and amendment process were placed on their consideration. In all but one case, over 75 percent of filed amendments were offered. More importantly, in all but six cases, over 75 percent of the amendments offered were agreed to. In twenty out of twenty-one cases of collegial decision-making, more than 50 percent of the amendments offered were agreed to. The percentage of amendments offered and agreed to dropped below 50 percent on only one measure—only 33 percent of the amendments offered to the Family and Medical Leave Act of 1991 (S. 5) were agreed to. However, this low rate should not be interpreted as evidence of significant disagreement between members, as only three amendments were filed to S. 5 and all were offered.

Further illustrating the inclusive nature of the collegial pattern of decision-making, the number of majority and minority amendments offered to each measure was relatively even. In nine cases the minority party offered more amendments than the majority party. Success rates for majority and minority amendments were also consistently even, falling between 67 percent and 100 percent. For example, during the consideration of S. 5, while only one minority amendment was agreed to, all three minority amendments filed were offered. Additionally, during consideration of the Neighborhood Schools Improvement Act (S. 2), 43 percent of the minority party amendments offered were agreed to, compared to 67 percent for the majority. Finally, 50 percent of the minority amendments offered to the Unemployment Compensation Amendments of 1992 (H.R. 5260) were agreed to.

Amendments to the measures considered under conditions of collegial decision-making were generally disposed of by voice vote. While recorded votes were taken on some amendments, these votes only represent a small portion of the total amendments considered.

Unanimous consent agreements were utilized on all but three of the measures considered under conditions of collegial decision-making. These consent agreements were largely used to set the debate and amendment process. For example, the unanimous consent agreement for the Freedom for Russia and Emerging Eurasian Democracies and Open Markets Support Act (S. 2532) illustrates the scheduling function included in many collegial decision-making agreements.

Mr. FORD: Mr. President, I ask unanimous consent that when the Senate completes its business today, it stand in recess until 8:30 a.m., Thursday, July 2; that following the prayer, the Journal of proceedings be deemed approved to date, and the time for the two leaders be reserved for their use later in the day; that there then be a period for morning business, not to extend beyond 10:30 a.m., with Senators permitted to speak therein for up to 5 minutes each; that immediately after the Chair's announcement, Senator NUNN be recognized to speak for up to 30 minutes; that Senators McCAIN, GORTON, and PRYOR be recognized for up to 10 minutes each; with Senator SIMPSON, or his designee, recognized for up to 10 minutes; with the time from 9:30 a.m. to 10 a.m., under the control of the majority leader or his designee, Senator LIEBERMAN; that Senator GRASSLEY be recognized for up to 20 minutes; that at 10:30 a.m., the Senate resume consideration of S. 2532, the Freedom Support Act; that once the bill is resumed, Senator LIEBERMAN be recognized to offer an amendment relating to business centers; that upon disposition of the first Lieberman amendment, Senator LIEBERMAN be recognized again to offer an amendment relating to science foundation; that no second degree amendments be in order to either of the Lieberman amendments; and that upon disposition of the second Lieberman amendment, Senator BRADLEY be recognized to offer an amendment relating to educational exchanges. (Ford 1992, S9473)

Unanimous consent agreements were also utilized to limit the number of amendments offered. However, these instances were relatively rare in the 102nd Congress. Instead, the restrictive consent agreements typically included all of the amendments members wanted to offer. For example, such agreements were utilized during the consideration of the Foreign Operations, Export Financing, and Related Programs Appropriations Act (H.R. 5368) and the Cancer Registries Amendment Act (H.R. 2507). In both cases, the number of amendments allowed to be offered (42 for H.R. 5368 and 12 for H.R. 2507) exceeded the number of amendments ultimately offered to each measure (28 for H.R. 5368 and 7 for H.R. 2507).

The cloture process was used to end debate on only one out of the twenty-one bills considered under collegial decision-making. Yet a majority of both parties voted to end debate and invoke cloture on the Biden-Thurmond Violent Crime Control Act of 1991 (S. 1241) after ten days of floor consideration during which 101 amendments were considered and 92 were agreed to. Fifty-six of the amendments were offered by the minority party and forty-six were offered by the majority party. Fifty-seven members participated in the amendment process and the success rate for majority and minority amendments was 93 percent and 86 percent, respectively.

On final passage, eight out of the twenty-one measures passed by voice vote. Of the thirteen remaining bills that passed by recorded vote, a majority of both parties supported passage on twelve. Only on the United States–China Act of 1991 (H.R. 2212) did a majority of one party vote against a majority of the other party on final passage. Yet it is important to note that the minority party was not blocked from participating in floor consideration of H.R. 2212. A companion measure (S. 1367) was previously laid before the Senate by unanimous consent after being reported by the Finance Committee. During consideration of S. 1367, 86 percent of the amendments filed were offered and 100 percent of these were agreed to. Cloture was not needed to end debate on either the motion to proceed or the bill itself.

Finally, a conference committee was used to resolve differences between the House and Senate versions in nineteen out of the twenty-one cases of collegial decision-making. Only S. 1745 and H.R. 3807 failed to go to conference. However, the House simply passed the Senate bill in both cases.

Majoritarian Decision-Making

In contrast to the prevalence of collegial decision-making, only 8 percent of the measures identified by *CQ* were considered under a majoritarian pattern of decision-making. In all of these cases, the legislation failed to receive substantive floor consideration during the 102nd Congress. A majority of one party voted against a majority of the other party on cloture on the motion to proceed to the consideration of both the National Energy Security Act of 1991 (S. 1220) and the Appropriations Category Reform Act of 1992 (S. 2399). As a result, it is unclear whether the pattern would have held if the Senate had chosen to move to their consideration instead.

Structured Consent Decision-Making

Structured consent was utilized for 11 percent of the bills *CQ* identified as receiving a key vote during the 102nd Congress. During the consideration of these three measures, opportunities to debate and amend each bill were not fully utilized by either party. In none of these cases was cloture, on either the motion to proceed or the underlying measure itself, necessary to make the legislation pending or to end debate. For example, consideration of the Authorization for Use of Military Force against Iraq Resolution (S. J. Res. 2) needed only one day on the Senate floor and no amendments were filed or offered. The lack of debate and amendment activity, however, cannot be interpreted as evidence of wide-spread support for the resolution in the Senate, as only 18 percent of Democrats supported the resolution compared to 95 percent of Republicans.

Similarly, a majority of one party opposed a majority of the other party during consideration of the Unemployment Insurance Reform Act of 1991 (S. 1722). Yet despite the partisan nature of the opposition, S. 1722 passed after only two days of floor consideration. Also, a majority of Democrats opposed a majority of Republicans during consideration of the Congressional Campaign Spending Limit and Election Reform Act of 1991 (S. 3). S. 3 was on the Senate floor for seven days and 100 percent of the thirty-two amendments filed were offered to the legislation. While only 44 percent of these were agreed to, twenty-one of the amendments offered were minority party amendments. The success rate for minority party amendments was 19 percent compared to 91 percent for the majority, and a majority of both parties opposed each other on 95 percent of the recorded votes on the amendments considered. Yet, despite this procedural combat, S. 3 passed 56–42.

A House-Senate conference committee was used to resolve the differences in two cases. S. J. Res. 2 was incorporated into H.J.Res. 77, which the Senate then passed and sent to the president to be signed into law.

Decision-Making in the 110th Congress

In contrast to the 102nd Congress, the structured consent pattern of decision-making was the most prevalent in the 110th Congress based on the categories in table 8.1. *CQ* rated actions on twenty different bills as key votes in 2007 and 2008. Of these bills, 60 percent can be identified as being considered under procedural conditions of structured consent. Only 20 percent each could be identified as collegial or majoritarian.

Structured Consent Decision-Making

Out of the twelve measures considered under conditions of structured consent, eleven were placed on the Senate calendar by the Rule 14 process, thus bypassing committee review. Only three of these measures received any committee consideration prior to being placed directly on the calendar: the Water Resources Development Act (H.R. 1495) had a companion measure (S. 1248) that was reported by the Environment and Public Works Committee; a companion measure (S. 2302) to the Food, Conservation, and Energy Act (H.R. 2419) was reported by the Agriculture, Nutrition, and Forestry Committee; and the Energy and Natural Resources Committee reported a companion measure (S. 1321) that ultimately became the Energy Independence and Security Act (H.R. 6) as passed by the Senate. In each of these three cases, Rule 14 was utilized to make the legislative process more efficient by proceeding directly to the House-passed measure and amending it with the legislation reported by a relevant Senate committee.

Seven of the twelve measures considered under conditions of structured consent were laid before the Senate only after cloture on the motion to proceed was successfully invoked. In four of these cases, at least eighty members voted for cloture. For example, during consideration of the Medicare Improvements for Patients and Providers Act (H.R. 6331) and the Comprehensive Immigration Reform Act (S. 1348), sixty-nine members voted to invoke cloture. Cloture on the motion to proceed to another comprehensive immigration bill, S. 1639, was the only measure on which less than two-thirds of the Senate (67) did not vote to invoke cloture. However, in this instance, sixty-four members voted to end debate and proceed to the measure's consideration, four more than the three-fifths (60) required under Senate rules.

As illustrated by these numbers, a broad consensus existed to move to each measure either by unanimous consent or by invoking cloture on the motion to proceed. Yet despite this consensus, constraints were placed on the debate and amendment process during floor consideration. While these constraints were subtle, examining the amendment data for the eleven measures considered under conditions of structured consent on which amendments were filed is illustrative.

For four these bills, more than 50 percent of the amendments filed were allowed to be offered. For example, during consideration of the Preserving United States Attorney Independence Act (S. 214) and the Protect America Act (S. 1927), 100 percent of the amendments filed were offered. However, fewer than three amendments were filed on each of these measures. Similarly, during the consideration of the FISA Amendments Act (H.R. 6304) and the Emergency Economic Stabilization Act (H.R. 1424), 60 percent and 75 percent of the amendments filed were offered. Again, however, only a small number of amendments were filed. In the remaining seven cases, less than 50 percent of the amendments filed were eventually offered. In six cases, less than 25 percent of the amendments filed were offered, and more than thirty amendments were filed on five of these measures.

As with the number of amendments filed that were eventually offered, the number of amendments ultimately agreed to was disproportionate to those offered. More than 50 percent of the amendments offered were agreed to in five cases. Yet out of these five cases more than 50 percent of the amendments filed were actually offered only during the consideration of two measures: S. 1927 and H.R. 1424. In the remaining three cases, less than 25 percent of the amendments filed were offered. This suggests that despite the relatively high rates of amendment success on these measures, the decision-making process was far from inclusive due to the low rates of filed amendments actually being offered.

This semi-exclusive process can be further illustrated by examining the six remaining measures to which amendments were offered. During consideration of S. 214, S. 1639, and H.R. 6304, none of the amendments offered were agreed to. Less than 30 percent of the amendments offered were agreed to during the consideration of the Fair Minimum Wage Act (H.R. 2), H.R. 1495, and H.R. 2419.

In contrast to the collegial pattern of decision-making, a relatively uneven number of majority and minority members offered amendments to the eleven measures considered under conditions of structured consent. Members from one party were responsible for at least 60 percent of amendments to measures that had more than four amendments filed. For those measures on which a significant number of amendments were filed, both parties were relatively even on only two: S. 1348 and H.R. 2419. In both cases, a bipartisan coalition supported the underlying legislation. Minority amendments outnumbered majority amendments on only three measures.

Success rates for majority and minority amendments were also relatively uneven. In only three cases did the majority and minority success rates each exceed 50 percent. In the cases in which both majority and minority amendments were offered, the majority success rate was higher than the minority's on five measures. The minority success rate exceeded the majority's only on the Housing and Economic Recovery Act (H.R. 3221). Neither majority nor minority amendments were successful during the consideration of two measures.

Amendments to the measures considered under conditions of structured consent were mostly disposed of by recorded vote. Those disposed of by voice vote or unanimous consent exceeded those disposed of by recorded vote on only H.R. 6 and H.R. 3221. On H.R. 2 and H.R. 2419, more than twenty amendments were withdrawn. In each case, however, cloture was invoked and non-germane amendments currently pending were subsequently and automatically withdrawn.

A majority of one party opposed a majority of the other party on more than 50 percent of the recorded votes in seven cases. During the consideration of S. 214 and H.R. 6304, a majority voted against a majority on 100 percent of the recorded amendment votes. During consideration of S. 1348, S. 1639, and H.R. 6, a majority voted against a majority on more than 80 percent of the recorded amendment votes. During the consideration of H.R. 2419, a majority of each party opposed each other on 75 percent of the recorded amendment votes. Finally, a majority of each party voted against each other less than 50 percent of the time in only three cases. During the consideration of H.R. 1495 and H.R. 3221, a majority of each party voted against each other on 43 percent and 38 percent of the recorded amendment votes, respectively. During the consideration of H.R. 1424, a majority never voted against a majority.

Comprehensive unanimous consent agreements were used to manage the decision-making process for the twelve measures considered under conditions of structured consent. These agreements were used to structure debate and set vote times for amendments and final passage in all but one case. More importantly, unanimous consent agreements were utilized to limit amendment activity in ten cases. Unanimous consent agreements were not used to limit amendment activity during the consideration of H.R. 6331 because no amendments were offered to the legislation. Three amendments were offered to S. 1639, but the process governing decision-making in this instance was procedurally unique and consent was not needed to manage amendment activity during its consideration.[4] The following example illustrates how comprehensive unanimous consent agreements were utilized to structure the entire decision-making process on the Senate floor during the 110th Congress:

> Mr. REID: Mr. President, I ask unanimous consent that on Wednesday, October 1, following the debate with respect to H.R. 7081, the Senate proceed to the consideration of Calendar No. 610, H.R. 1424; that once the bill is reported, the Dodd, et al., amendment, which is at the desk, be considered; except that this agreement is only valid if both leaders are in concurrence with the provisions of the Dodd, et al., amendment and have so notified the Chair, and that there be general debate on the amendment for 90 minutes, with the time equally divided and controlled between the leaders or their designees; that upon the use or yielding back of this time, the amendment be set aside, and the Senate then consider the only other amendment in order to the bill, a Sanders amendment re: tax on high-income individuals; that there be 60 minutes of debate with respect to that amendment, with the time equally divided and controlled in the usual form; that upon the use or yielding back of all time with respect to the bill and amendments, the measure be set aside

to recur upon disposition of H.R. 7081; that with respect to the disposition of the amendments to H.R. 1424, the first vote occur with respect to the Sanders amendment; that upon disposition of that amendment, the Senate would then consider the Dodd, et al., amendment, that upon disposition of that amendment, the bill, as amended, if amended, be read a third time and the Senate proceed to vote on passage of the bill; that upon passage, with the above occurring without further intervening action or debate, the Dodd, et al., amendment and the bill be subject to a 60-vote threshold. (Reid 2008c, S10187–88)

Additionally, the unanimous consent agreement for H.R. 6304 illustrates how comprehensive unanimous consent agreements were utilized to structure debate and limit amendment activity even in a highly partisan environment. In this case, a majority of each party opposed one another on every amendment vote and final passage. Yet, despite this partisan conflict, a unanimous consent agreement was used to structure the decision-making process:

Mr. REID: Mr. President, I ask unanimous consent that on Tuesday, July 8, at a time to be determined by the majority leader, following consultation with Senator McCONNELL, all post cloture time be yielded back and the motion to proceed to Calendar No. 827, H.R. 6304, be agreed to, the motion to reconsider be laid upon the table, and the Senate then proceed to the consideration of the bill; that once the bill is reported, the only amendments in order be the following: Dodd-Feingold-Leahy amendment to strike immunity; a Specter amendment which is relevant; a Bingaman amendment re: staying court cases against telecom companies; that no other amendments be in order; that debate time on the Bingaman amendment be limited to 60 minutes, equally divided and controlled in the usual form, and 2 hours each with respect to the Dodd and Specter amendments, equally divided and controlled, with 10 minutes of the Dodd time under the control of Senator LEAHY; that upon the use or yielding back of all time, the Senate proceed to vote on the pending amendments; there be 2 minutes of debate equally divided and controlled in the usual form prior to each vote; that after the first vote in the sequence, succeeding votes be limited to 10 minutes each; that upon the disposition of all amendments, the bill, as amended, if amended, be read a third time and the Senate then proceed to vote on a motion to invoke cloture on the bill, with the mandatory quorum waived; that prior to the cloture vote, there be 60 minutes plus the time specified below for debate time, equally divided and controlled between the two leaders or their designees, with 10 minutes under the control of Senator LEAHY, with an additional 30 minutes under the control of Senator FEINGOLD, with an additional 15 minutes under the control of Senator DODD; further, that if cloture is invoked on H.R. 6304, then all post cloture time be yielded back, and without further intervening action or debate, the Senate proceed to vote on passage of the bill, as amended, if amended; further, that it be in order to file the cloture motion on the bill at any time prior to the cloture vote, with the mandatory quorum waived, notwithstanding rule XXII, if applicable, and that if applicable, post cloture time be charged during this agreement. (Reid 2008b, 14027)

The cloture process was utilized to end debate on six of the twelve measures considered under conditions of the structured consent. Cloture was successfully invoked in four cases. Cloture was not successfully invoked during the consideration of S. 1348 and S. 1639. In the remaining six cases, cloture was not needed to end debate and proceed to a vote on final passage.

Nine out of the ten measures that reached final passage received a recorded vote; H.R. 6331 passed by unanimous consent. Of these nine measures, a majority of each party voted in support of the legislation in six cases. A majority of one party opposed a majority of the other party on final passage of S. 1927, H.R. 6304, and H.R. 6.

Finally, a conference committee was used to resolve differences between the House and Senate versions of legislation that passed under conditions of structured consent in only two cases. A process of amendment exchange between the two chambers was utilized in three cases. The House simply passed the Senate bill or the Senate passed the House bill in the five remaining cases.

Majoritarian and Collegial Decision-Making

In contrast to the prevalence of structured consent, only 20 percent of the measures identified by *CQ* in the 110th Congress were considered under either a majoritarian or collegial pattern of decision-making. The procedural characteristics of these patterns are consistent with those in the 102nd Congress. However, what is striking is that the majoritarian pattern of decision-making was successfully followed beyond the motion to invoke cloture on the motion to proceed in two cases. The Economic Stimulus Act (H.R. 5140) eventually passed the Senate despite the majority leader filling the tree and using cloture to end debate. Additionally, the Senate proceeded to the consideration of the Lieberman-Warner Climate Security Act (S. 3036) and processed amendments to it. However, cloture could not be invoked on the bill itself and it thus failed to receive a final vote.

The increased success of the majoritarian pattern of decision-making would seem to suggest that either the majority party was more cohesive in the 110th Congress, and thus better able to sustain such a restrictive decision-making process internally, or that the minority party was more fractured, and thus less able to uniformly oppose majoritarian obstructionism.

Decision-Making Transformed: From Collegial to Structured Consent

In the 102nd Congress, Senate decision-making was overwhelmingly characterized by a collegial pattern of decision-making. There were no significant barriers to the participation of interested members and the total number of members involved in the decision-making process was usually quite large. As such, decision-making was relatively decentralized and there were few constraints on members in the debate and amendment process. Moreover, action occurred predominately on the Senate floor. Both majority and minority members participated in the process and a high percentage of amendments filed by members of both parties were ultimately offered to the legislation under consideration. Furthermore, the percentage of amendments offered that were ultimately agreed to was high for all measures. As a result, the success rates for majority and minority amendments were relatively even and most amendments offered were disposed of by voice vote. In those cases in which a recorded vote was necessary, a majority of one party voted against a majority of the other party most of the time. However, these votes represented only a small fraction of the total amendments disposed of during the 102nd Congress.

For most measures examined, cloture was not needed to end debate. In the few instances in which the cloture process was utilized on the motion to proceed, a majority of both parties supported the efforts to end debate. A majority of both parties also generally supported final passage. In all but two cases, conference committees were used to negotiate differences between the House and Senate. In each of these cases, the House simply passed the Senate-passed legislation.

The dominance of the collegial pattern of decision-making in the 102nd Congress can be attributed to the lingering effects of several Senate norms that create an institutional culture of restrained individualism. Specifically, the Senate was characterized by a high degree of courtesy, reciprocity, and institutional patriotism during the first half of the twentieth century. In such a permissive procedural environment, these norms alone were largely responsible for ensuring that the Senate remained a functional yet deliberative body (Matthews 1960, 97–101).

However, these norms were increasingly being eroded by the changing nature of the Senate's external environment and the subsequent response of its members. The new environment created incentives for senators to be involved in a broader array of issues. New procedural mechanisms—like the hold process—gave individual members the ability to be more active in the Senate's deliberations, regardless of their seniority or committee assignments. Furthermore, the increasingly crowded Senate agenda and the corresponding growth of interest groups seeking representation in the policy process created more opportunities for members to become legislatively active.

As the norms that previously restrained member behavior eroded, obstructionism increased. The typical senator was increasingly likely to avail himself of extending debate and other procedural tools to protect his interests. This transformation created significant problems for the institution and led to the creation of the "Sixty-Vote Senate" (Sinclair 1989, 88; Sinclair 2002, 260). The growth of obstructionism has left a partisan and confrontational environment in its wake. It is now more difficult for the Senate to complete work on the legislation it must pass each year. This results from broader member participation and is exacerbated by narrower partisan majorities and a crowded agenda, as well as the willingness of individual senators to pursue their own agendas at the expense of the institution's collective interests. Yet the Senate continues to function despite these difficulties.

In an effort to compensate for the erosion of Senate norms, increasingly influential majority and minority leaders gradually began to work together to ensure that the Senate continued to pass legislation dealing with controversial and uncontroversial issues alike. Over the course of the 1990s and the first decade of the twenty-first century, the party leaders would eventually supplant the old norms and customs of the Senate as the predominant force making the institution work. As a result, Senate decision-making changed dramatically by the 110th Congress.

In contrast to the 102nd Congress, Senate decision-making in the 110th was largely characterized by conditions of structured consent. There were moderate barriers to the participation of interested members and the debate and amendment process was semi-exclusive. While both majority and minority members continued to participate in the amendment process, a much lower percentage of the amendments filed were eventually offered to legislation on the Senate floor. Furthermore, the percentage of amendments offered that were ultimately agreed to was also low for most measures. The success rates for majority and minority amendments were relatively uneven and most amendments were disposed of by recorded vote. On these votes, a majority of each party voted against each other most of the time.

Finally, cloture was necessary to end debate on most measures. Curiously, a majority of both parties supported final passage in all but a few cases. A process of amendment exchange between the House and Senate was increasingly utilized to resolve differences between the two chambers. However, conference committees and House passage of Senate-passed legislation were also common.

Conclusion

This chapter has examined recent developments in Senate decision-making. Specifically, it has argued that the institution's growing accountability to the American people led to informal reforms internally. These reforms effectively altered the structural balance of power in the Senate between committees and the party leadership. In addition, they led to procedural and cultural innovations that sought to better translate the public's will into institutional action. Commensurate with its growing accountability, influence inside the Senate has been centralized in the party leadership.

Deliberation, and the open decision-making process on which it depends, is no longer characteristic of the legislative floor process. Instead of deliberation, scripted speeches and prearranged colloquies fill floor time while the party leadership works out the legislative details and resolves controversies out of public view. Yet developments external to the Senate would quickly lead to gridlock if not counterbalanced by the internal changes. Such changes have admittedly made the Senate, its committees, and the floor operate more efficiently than at any time in the past, despite the partisanship and ideological polarization characteristic of the current environment.

Yet the question remains: Is the transformation of the Senate into a more centralized, restrictive, and partisan institution a negative development if such a change is needed to maintain its legislative productivity? Like all democratic institutions, the Senate certainly needs to adapt to changing circumstances in order to maintain its legitimacy and relevance in the political system. In light of the significant changes in Senate decision-making described in this chapter, can we then embrace the modern Senate as an example of how Congress can adapt to a changing environment in order to maintain its legitimacy and relevance without undertaking major internal reform of its formal rules?

The progressive scholars of the 1950s and 1960s would probably argue that the Senate remains inefficient despite these changes and that it is still unable to pass public policy to address society's most pressing problems. However, was such an activist institution what the framers of the Constitution envisioned when creating the Senate? While a single theoretical view of the Senate was lacking at the Constitutional Convention, the framers did broadly share in the belief that they were creating a deliberative institution designed to bring a different perspective to Congress. The framers created a Senate with two fundamental yet contradictory roles: producing legislation and checking popular opinion through the deliberative process. The framers and original leaders of the Senate conceived of deliberation as a means to educate Senators and the public on the great choices before the institution. While passing legislation was certainly important, it was not the *most* important function of the Senate. Indeed, the framers gave as much consideration to the necessity of deliberating on intemperate measures as to the need to quickly pass legislation.

It is in this sense that the modern Senate may be viewed as broken. While the Senate continues to produce important legislation at relatively consistent rates despite a rapidly changing environment and increasing workload, it has done so largely at the expense of the institution's deliberative function. Reasoned deliberation has nearly disappeared in the modern Senate as decision-making has gradually migrated from committee hearings and the Senate floor to informal and ad hoc meetings of interested members typically held under the auspices of the party leadership and out of public view. This death of public deliberation has ultimately undermined our representative democracy. Despite the fact that more groups are participating in the federal policy process than ever before, they are expressing their viewpoints within an echo chamber absent thoughtful deliberation. As a result, the American people are increasingly disillusioned with the Congress and cynical about its accomplishments (or perceived lack thereof).

Contrary to conventional wisdom, an increasingly partisan and ideologically polarized Senate in which deliberation takes place in public may not have an inherently negative influence on American politics in the twenty-first century. Politics organized around two opposing sets of principles is not a bad thing in and of itself. Indeed, the current state of politics in the United States and public disapproval with the political process in general seemingly calls for an ideologically driven yet deliberative Senate. However, such a Senate may not be possible in the current environment. The modern Senate is increasingly accountable to the American people to a degree not envisioned by the framers of the Constitution. A Senate directly accountable to popular opinion may not be able to quickly and efficiently translate such deeply and closely divided opinion into legislation without sacrificing its deliberative nature. As a consequence, we may be forced to choose between an efficient Senate and the death of deliberation.

Notes

1. Smith identifies three patterns of decision-making in the Senate: decentralized, centralized, and collegial. Specifically, Smith defines collegial decision-making as "broad participation within one or few organizational units" (Smith 1989, 4).

2. *CQ* (2008a) selects key votes for the Senate on major issues considered in each Congress according to the following criteria: "a matter of major controversy; a matter of presidential or political power; a matter of potentially great impact on the nation and lives of Americans." For the purposes of this chapter, any measure receiving a key vote was analyzed. Measures with more than one key vote were counted only once. Nominations were excluded. In addition, legislation was only analyzed at the stage of initial consideration in the Senate.

3. In its literal sense, majoritarian decision-making could apply to any organized majority in the Senate, including geographical and ideological. However, in this chapter, "majoritarian" decision-making will refer to partisan majorities. For a theoretical perspective that relies on nonpartisan majorities, see Krehbiel (1998).

4. Prior to the consideration of S. 1639, members from both parties that supported the bill negotiated a single amendment containing the text of thirteen Democratic and thirteen Republican amendments and one manager's amendment. Parliamentary procedures were utilized to block other amendments from being offered. This comprehensive amendment was subsequently divided into three separate parts, which would be considered individually. These three divisions were subsequently voted on and serve as the three amendments to S. 1639.

References

Ainsworth, Scott, and Marcus Flathman. 1995. "Unanimous Consent Agreements as Leadership Tools." *Legislative Studies Quarterly* 20:177–95.

Binder, Sarah A. 1997. *Minority Rights, Majority Rule: Partisanship and the Development of Congress.* New York: Cambridge University Press.

——. 2003. *Stalemate: Causes and Consequences of Legislative Gridlock.* Washington, DC: Brookings Institution Press.

Binder, Sarah A., and Steven S. Smith. 1997. *Politics or Principle? Filibustering in the United States Senate.* Washington, DC: Brookings Institution Press.

Congressional Quarterly Weekly Report. 1991. "Senate Votes." 49:3806.

——. 1992. "Senate Votes." 50:3914.

——. 2008a. "How CQ Picks Key Votes." December 15, 3342.

——. 2008b. "Key Senate Votes." 66:67.

——. 2008c. "Senate Votes." 66:3353.

Evans, C. Lawrence, and Walter J. Oleszek. 2000. "The Procedural Context of Senate Deliberation." In *Esteemed Colleagues: Civility and Deliberation in the U.S. Senate,* edited by Bert A. Loomis, 78–104. Washington, DC: Brookings Institution.

Ford, Wendall. 1992. "Orders for Tomorrow." *Congressional Record,* Senate, July 1, vol. 138, part 12.

Gamm, Gerald, and Steven Smith. 2002a. "Emergence of Senate Party Leadership." In *U.S. Senate Exceptionalism,* edited by Bruce I. Oppenheimer, 212–38. Columbus: Ohio State University Press.

——. 2002b. "Policy Leadership in the Development of the Modern Senate." In *Party, Process, and Political Change in Congress: New Perspectives on the History of Congress,* edited by David Brady and Mathew D. McCubbins, 287–311. Palo Alto, CA: Stanford University Press.

Green, Matthew N. 2010. *The Speaker of the House: A Study of Leadership.* New Haven, CT: Yale University Press.

Kennedy, Edward M. 2009. *True Compass: A Memoir.* New York: Hachette Book Group.

Krehbiel, Keith. 1986. "Unanimous Consent Agreements: Going Along in the Senate." *Journal of Politics* 48:541–64.

——. 1998. *Pivotal Politics: A Theory of U.S. Lawmaking.* Chicago: University of Chicago Press.

Lee, Frances E. 2009. *Beyond Ideology: Politics, Principles, and Partisanship in the U.S. Senate.* Chicago: University of Chicago Press.

Mann, Thomas E., and Norman Ornstein. 2006. *The Broken Branch: How Congress Is Failing America and How to Get It Back on Track.* New York: Oxford University Press.

Matthews, Donald R. 1960. *U.S. Senators and Their World.* New York: Vintage Books.

Ornstein, Norman. 2008. "Our Broken Senate." *The American,* March/April. http://www.american .com/archive/2008/march-april-magazine-contents/our-broken-senate/article_print. Accessed August 3, 2011.

Reid, Harry. 2008a. "Climate Security Act." *Congressional Record,* Senate, June 4, vol. 154, part 8.

——. 2008b. "Unanimous-Consent Agreement—H.R. 6331 and H.R. 2642." *Congressional Record,* Senate, June 26, vol. 154, part 10.

——. 2008c. "Unanimous Consent Agreement—H.R. 7081." *Congressional Record,* Senate, September 30, vol. 154, daily edition.

Riddick, Floyd M. 1981. *Majority and Minority Leaders of the Senate: History and Development of the Offices of the Floor Leaders.* Washington, DC: Government Printing Office.

Sinclair, Barbara. 1989. *The Transformation of the U.S. Senate.* Baltimore, MD: Johns Hopkins University Press.

——. 1995. *Legislators, Leaders, and Lawmaking: The U.S. House of Representatives in the Postreform Era.* Baltimore, MD: Johns Hopkins University Press.

——. 2002. "The '60-Vote Senate': Strategies, Process, and Outcomes." In *U.S. Senate Exceptionalism,* edited by Bruce I. Oppenheimer, 241–61. Columbus: Ohio State University Press.

Smith, Steven S. 1989. *Call to Order: Floor Politics in the House and Senate.* Washington, DC: Brookings Institution Press.

———. 1993. "Forces of Change in Senate Party Leadership and Organizations." In *Congress Reconsidered*, 5th edition, edited by Lawrence C. Dodd and Bruce I. Oppenheimer, 259–90. Washington, DC: CQ Press.

———. 1997. "The Politics and Principle of the Senate Filibuster." *Extensions* 5:15–19.

———. 2007. *Party Influence in Congress.* New York: Cambridge University Press.

———. 2010. "The Senate Syndrome." *Issues in Governance Studies* (June):1–30.

Theriault, Sean. A. 2008. *Party Polarization in Congress.* New York: Cambridge University Press.

Truman, David. B. 1959. *The Congressional Party: A Case Study.* New York: John Wiley & Sons.

Wallner, James I. 2010. "The Death of Deliberation: Popular Opinion, Party, and Policy in the Modern United States Senate." Paper presented at the annual meeting of the Midwest Political Science Association, Chicago, Illinois, April 22–25.

9

Beyond Motions to Table

Exploring the Procedural Toolkit of the Majority Party in the United States Senate

Aaron S. King, Francis J. Orlando, and David W. Rohde

IN FEBRUARY 2010, SENATOR EVAN BAYH announced that he was not seeking reelection. In a press release summarizing the reasons for his retirement he stated:

> After all these years, my passion for service to my fellow citizens is undiminished, but my desire to do so by serving in Congress has waned. For some time, I have had a growing conviction that Congress is not operating as it should. There is too much partisanship and not enough progress. . . . I love working for the people of Indiana, I love helping our citizens make the most of their lives, but I do not love Congress. . . . My decision should not be interpreted for more than it is: a very difficult, deeply personal one. I am an executive at heart. I value my independence. I am not motivated by strident partisanship or ideology. These traits may be useful in many walks of life, but they are not highly valued in Congress. (Bayh 2010)

Senator Bayh's statement shows a member fed up with the overly partisan nature of his chamber. His entire statement is laced with undertones of what is widely considered to be an individualistic Senate turned upside down. According to Senator Bayh, partisan concerns have taken over the Senate and changed its nature. We may be surprised to see such polarization in the Senate, but we are certainly not surprised when we hear the House described as strongly partisan. A long line of research has shown the role that parties play in the House to be of the utmost importance (Rohde 1991; Cox and McCubbins 1993). But even throughout this time period, Senate partisanship was thought to be muted by rules and folkways on the floor of the upper chamber. This is not without reason, as the Senate has several characteristics that make it more difficult for strong majority party leaders to have their say. Senate rules allow for an open amendment processes, in contrast with House special rules that curtail efforts to alter bills. The Senate has no germaneness requirement to keep the focus of debate on the substance of the underlying bill. Finally, there is no easy way to cut off debate in the Senate, unlike the simple majority previous question technique that House leaders regularly employ. Faced with these obstacles, it is no wonder that there is widespread belief that the Senate is a place with few touches of partisanship, a place where the individual senator still rules.

What we observe however, is quite different. Sitting senators are now deciding to forego their careers in the Senate because they dislike the partisan atmosphere. Some members are working to undermine the long-standing Senate cloture rule in order to help the majority pass its agenda. Senate Majority Leader Harry Reid is continuously butting heads with Minority Leader Mitch McConnell not only over the substance of issues, but also over the ways in which they are debated. One need only recall the reconciliation debate related to the health care bill in the 111th Congress (2009–2010) for reference. In addition, congressional scholars are uncovering tools that the majority party is using in order to stack the deck in its favor.

Our goal is to examine these tools in greater depth. We believe that tools used in the House are well documented, but partisan techniques in the upper chamber have been understudied. This chapter seeks to add to the growing momentum to redress this imbalance. We employ a new dataset in order to explore and analyze questions that have received little attention before now. Why does the majority need these tools in the Senate? Is there one preferred tool of the majority party? Are these tools used consistently across time and setting? We examine motions to table amendments, budgetary points of order, and cloture in detail throughout the chapter.

Past Research

While the Senate shares an equal constitutional role in lawmaking with the House, the treatment researchers have given the two chambers is far from equivalent. There is a variety of reasons for this lack of parity. First, it is simply easier for researchers looking for partisan effects to find them in the House due to the aforementioned structural differences between the chambers. Second, there are consistently more votes and more members in the House, leading to larger datasets for researchers to study. Finally, until now, there has not been a Senate roll call database rich enough to compare with House data. Despite these factors, research on partisanship in the Senate has been growing slowly but steadily over the past fifteen years.

Binder and Smith (1998) found that decisions on institutional change in the Senate are driven by partisan and political considerations, not concern for protecting the institutional role of the chamber. Others have focused on party leadership in the Senate. Campbell, Cox, and McCubbins (2002) utilized a far-reaching dataset and found that roll rates for the minority are much higher than for the majority throughout the Senate's history. Still others have studied the tactics that majority party leaders use to rein in the individual freedoms that senators enjoy (Evans and Lapinski 2005). Frances Lee (2008) examined the major role that the president plays in exacerbating partisanship in the Senate, showing that parties are farther apart on items on the president's agenda. Research found that the stock prices of Democratic and Republican firms fluctuated with the changing of hands of the majority after the Jim Jeffords switch in 2001 (Monroe and Den Hartog 2005). Sinclair (2005) provided a detailed account of the transformation from an individualistic to a more partisan institution that has taken place in the Senate since the 1950s. While the Senate still prides itself on the leverage that individual members can exert, the growth of partisanship in the upper chamber is undeniable. This mixture of individuality and partisan polarization drives both procedure and outcomes in the Senate.

Indeed, research on partisan organization in the Senate has been growing exponentially in the last few years. Stimulated by a conference on the subject, the edited volume *Why Not Parties?* deals specifically with party effects in the Senate (Monroe et al. 2008). The volume contains articles on party loyalty, the tradeoff between constituency concerns and party pressure, roll call analysis, the whip system, minority party strength, and a number of other topics. One of the more noted weapons the majority can use is the motion to table, specifically the motion to table amendments (Oleszek 2004; Gold 2008). Marshall, Prins, and Rohde (1997, 1999) showed that motions to table were a favorite way to stop members of the minority from altering bills on the floor. They specifically studied the way in which appropriations bills are shielded from amendment by motions to table. They also concluded that majority committee members had changed goals, from protecting bipartisan agreements to protecting the will of the majority party. Den Hartog and Monroe (2008) delved deeper into the study of tabling motions. They argued that motions to table were a cost-effective way for the majority party to manipulate the agenda.

Beth and colleagues (2009) take an in-depth look at the diverse tactics that the majority leadership has at its disposal. We believe that these tools may be useful in shifting outcomes away from the floor median and toward the party median. They find that there is no silver bullet that the majority can use, but that there are a variety of techniques that comprise a toolkit for the majority party. The techniques used by leadership on a specific piece of legislation depend on the setting in which the bill takes place. The usefulness of a tool is conditional on the type of environment it would be used in. Some key considerations deal with the size of the majority party and the amount of time the leadership is willing to spend on an issue. In this chapter we systematically examine the usage of the various tools over time and in varying contexts.

Theory

Before delving into an empirical analysis of the varying techniques used by the majority, it is important to work through the logic of partisan agenda control. In order to understand the steps that the majority party would undertake to try to control the agenda and shape policy, we need to ask a fundamental question: What are the main goals of a congressional party? This question has received considerably more attention in the House, but the question is equally relevant for Senate parties. In our view, majority party members would like to protect themselves from being damaged by the minority in a few specific ways. First, the majority would like to prevent its legislation from being altered by the minority. Second, the majority would like to stop the passage of legislation it does not prefer. Third, the majority would like to protect itself from politically embarrassing situations. All of these things must be accomplished while not damaging individual members' electoral aspirations.

Achieving these diverse goals would be simple if party members were perfectly internally cohesive and served in electorally safe districts. However, this is not true for all party members. Party leaders must work hard to set the agenda and realize preferred policy outcomes, as some members will have incentives to vote against their party's position. Unlike proportional representation systems that are common in Europe, where slate systems encourage party loyalty, single-member districts with nomination through primaries may lead to cross-pressures between party and constituency. On the one hand, leaders can provide positive incentives for members to vote for the party against the wishes of their constituents by offering carrots such as substantial campaign funds, plum committee positions, and opportunities to climb the leadership ladder of the chamber. These incentives serve to counterbalance the negative consequences that could accrue from taking a stance at odds with a sizable chunk of one's constituents. The party might also provide disincentives for failing to support the agenda by threatening to take away chairmanships, encouraging primary challengers, and halting the upward mobility of members who decide to shirk their partisan duties. Finally, members may face a form of peer pressure to vote with the members of their caucus. The amount of time spent interacting with one's own party is great, and it makes some sense to believe that vote choice is influenced by the stances taken by the legislators that the member spends the most time with.

While these pressures indubitably shift votes at the margin and help to produce non-majoritarian outcomes in the Senate, there are still drawbacks to pressuring members. Controversial votes on policy leave a paper trail that can be exploited by the opposing party in general election campaigns. Compiling an overly partisan voting record in a moderate district or state may lead to lower probabilities of reelection (Canes-Wrone et al. 2002). Where contentious votes are present, the majority leadership is therefore faced with the unenviable choice between endangering its members at the expense of preferred policy or vice versa. It is almost never in the best interest of the majority to put its members in a tough spot, so it follows that the only way for the majority to have its cake and eat it too is to limit the occurrence of potentially controversial votes.

The ways in which the party-friendly House achieves agenda control is well documented (Cox and McCubbins 1993; Aldrich 1994). Bills that a majority of the majority prefer, but would not pass, are held off the floor by gate-keeping chairmen and a compliant Rules Committee. Likewise, bills that a majority of the majority dislikes, but would pass, are held off the floor in a similar manner. This means that only those bills that are supported by the majority leadership are likely to reach the floor, and this alone serves to decrease the cross-pressures that House members face.

But even if only majority-approved bills reach the floor, they still face the possibility of damaging amendments. Minority members could introduce amendments that would cause members to go on record and take a position. Here once again though, House members can get around this problem by preventing undesirable amendments from being offered. The majority-controlled Rules Committee could write a closed or restrictive rule for consideration of the bill. As is the case with most other votes in the House, a simple majority is required to put these restrictive rules in place. Once the rule passes, the underlying bill almost always passes with ease. In creating a dichotomous choice between the status quo and a majority-sponsored proposal, voting for the majority-sponsored bill becomes much more palatable. Despite the fact that other alternatives would be preferred to the majority-sponsored bill, the cohesive special rule vote opens the door to outcomes that are undesirable to the median voter. This begs the question: Where is the constituent pressure?

While we certainly do not take the American public as fools, they simply are not knowledgeable enough about the congressional process to understand the partisan maneuvering discussed above. Members are able to justify voting for the bill against the status quo to their constituents. Additionally, members may be able to side against their party on the final passage vote when the party has enough votes to win comfortably. Finally, members can explain yes votes on restrictive rules in a myriad of ways, which either appeases or confuses the vast majority of constituents (Farquharson 1969; Fenno 1978). So in the House, we see that the majority party is able to accomplish many of its goals without taxing its members with difficult votes.

But what about the Senate? Here, we are less likely to see safe members representing homogenous districts. The job of the majority leadership, therefore, is often even more difficult as it attempts to push policy in a relatively costless fashion. Additionally, the Senate does not have a rules committee that can keep bills off the floor or restrict amendments, nor does it have a germaneness requirement for amendments, meaning the minority can easily introduce amendments that can put pressure on majority members. In the parlance of cartel theory, the majority party in the Senate should have less negative agenda power relative to its counterpart in the House (Cox and McCubbins 1993, 2005). However, as mentioned above, the Senate majority does have some tools at its disposal to curtail minority amending activity and protect its caucus members.

In order to further their goals, majority members can move to block minority amendments when they are offered by attempting to table them. This strategy helps to keep amendments that would move policy away from the majority party's preferred policy off the agenda. In addition, tabling can help to keep killer amendments off the agenda. These killer amendments can make a bill so unsatisfactory that it will not pass the Senate. This could then lead to an embarrassing legislative defeat (Jenkins and Munger 2003). If these amendments could be so damaging to the desires of the majority party, why bother restricting amendments when the majority could just as easily vote them down? First, debate on the subject may take a long time, time that is valuable for other legislative purposes. More importantly, voting on the substantive content of the amendment may force members to go on record opposing either their party or their constituents. Voting against the party may lead to failure of the agenda and less favorable treatment in the caucus, while voting against perceived constituent wishes may lead to the immediate threat of removal from office at the next election. While party leaders want their agenda passed (and therefore need some standard of cohesiveness), they also would prefer to keep their members out of electoral peril. After all, a loyal member of the party has limited use if he or she will just be ushered out of office when his or her term is up.

Motions to Table Amendments

One way the majority can restrict amendments is by tabling them. A motion to table is a privileged motion that is voted on immediately (and without debate) and cannot be filibustered. Therefore, once a motion to table is before the chamber, there is no way for the minority to protect their amendment except by defeating the motion. In addition, tabling motions need only a simple majority to pass. This means that the majority can achieve the goal of restricting amendments in a cost-efficient manner.

Motions to table amendments hold great promise. While an unpopular vote on the substance of an amendment is fodder for an opposing campaign, a procedural vote is less well understood. Just as a vote on the rules of debate in the House is difficult for constituents to comprehend, a vote to table an amendment diminishes the potential campaign harm. Incumbents can explain away votes on tabling motions for technical reasons and this obfuscation may limit the degree to which he or she is held accountable. Decreasing the risk of voting with the party frees up members to pass the caucus's agreed-upon agenda.

Budgetary Points of Order

As we will demonstrate, however, motions to table are not the only way to stop amendments. Motions to table amendments offer many attractive properties, but there is another tool that may be more efficient where it applies. While motions to table amendments (MTTs) may still be applicable, when dealing with the budget and appropriations, it may be more efficient to raise budgetary points of order. A budgetary point of order may be raised any time a bill, conference report, or amendment would violate a provision of any of the budgetary rules governing debate of the bill (Saturno 2004, 2008, 2011). Once a budgetary point of order is raised and upheld by the chair, a motion to waive the budget act must be adopted or the underlying bill or amendment falls.

While some members will preemptively attempt to waive the budget act with respect to their own amendments, this is extremely rare. More commonly, we observe the following pattern. An amendment is offered, often by a member of the minority. A member of the majority then raises a point of order against the amendment on the grounds that it violates a provision of the Congressional Budget Act of 1974, Gramm-Rudman requirements, PAYGO requirements, or the rules laid out in that year's budget act. Points of order can be raised for a variety of reasons, including violating germaneness requirements, exceeding budget authority, not properly offsetting expenses, or causing long-term budget deficits. Once this point of order is raised, and the Senate parliamentarian upholds the point of order, the amendment falls unless the provision cited in the point of order is waived. Almost always, the member who attempts to waive the budget rules is the member that sponsored the original amendment. As such, this often ends up being a member of the minority.

The use of budgetary points of order meshes with the theory behind agenda control in the Senate discussed earlier. Raising a point of order is a relatively costless, but efficient, way for the majority to restrict the ability of the minority to amend bills. This technique serves as an important way to keep the preferred policy of the majority intact, which is one of the goals of the majority party. In addition, this technique can keep language that would endanger final passage out of the bill. For example, a Democratic majority could invoke the germaneness requirement against amendments that dealt with abortion on budget or reconciliation bills in order to avoid an embarrassing derailing of the bill. Although the germaneness requirement accounts for just a few of the many budget-waiving votes, it is a valid and often efficient use of a budgetary point of order. Furthermore, raising a point of order on an amendment accomplishes the same thing as an MTT—it precludes a vote on the actual substance of the bill. In fact, it provides an even more plausible explanation for members to give to constituents than an MTT by allowing members to equate the vote with preserving the budget's integrity.

The final major advantage of raising budgetary points of order is the fact that it takes a supermajority, or sixty votes, for the minority to overcome them and to proceed to consideration of the amendment. While it originally took only a simple majority to waive a point of order, this requirement was raised to three-fifths in the Gramm-Rudman-Hollings Budget Act of 1985. This creates a significant contrast to the simple majority it takes for the minority to circumvent a tabling motion. The benefits here are twofold. First, and most obviously, it is much easier for the majority to control the agenda with forty-one votes as opposed to the majority needed on tabling motions. Second, the fact that the majority only needs forty-one votes to prevail means that a member has some leeway in supporting the budget waiver if he or she feels that support could be detrimental to his or her reelection efforts.

Cloture

There is yet another technique that the majority may use that does not involve stopping amendments on the floor. While many casual observers of the Senate believe that cloture serves the solitary purpose of stopping the filibuster, we believe, as Beth and colleagues (2009) do, that they are more broadly a part of the majority toolkit. Cloture is often invoked in order to prohibit a plausible filibuster threat. Cloture by-products include saving time, decreasing the overall number of amendments offered, and forcing amendments that are offered to be germane. In addition, cloture can be used for both negative and positive agenda control. This is something that we cannot say for MTTs. Once cloture is invoked, only those amendments already filed are in order. This stops the minority from proposing amendments ad nauseam or attempting to derail bills by attaching non-germane amendments. MTTs and budget-waiving votes are not needed as frequently if the overall number of amendments is restricted. One does not need to table an amendment that is not on the floor, nor must a point of order be raised against an amendment that does not exist. A drawback to cloture is that it requires a supermajority of three-fifths to be invoked. Cloture, however, can be successful when members want to eventually pass the bill. Although the process of cloture takes time, it can ultimately be a time-saving measure because it limits debate on frivolous amendments.

Analysis

To examine the toolset available to the majority party, we utilize data from a newly collected database that is designed to mirror the Political Institutions and Public Choice (PIPC) House Database (Rohde 2010). Issue and vote types are coded similarly in the two databases to enable easy comparisons between the chambers and make access easy for researchers already accustomed to the House database. The data cover the Senate from the 91st to the 110th Congress (1969–2008). We hope to expand the scope of the database in the future, but we already have a rich dataset with over sixteen thousand votes across a variety of issues and vote types.

We first examine the partisanship of these different measures. In examining figure 9.1, it is apparent that there are asymmetries between Senate voting behavior on amendments that change policy and procedural votes dealing with amendments. First, we examine party unity votes. These votes occur when a majority of one party opposes a majority of the other. When looking at MTTs, party unity votes occur 68 percent of the time, while only occurring on 50 percent of amendment votes. There was only one Congress examined, the 109th Congress (2005–2006), where we found a higher proportion of amendments meeting the party unity criteria than on MTTs.

The differences are even starker when we examine budget-waiving votes. Over 86 percent of these votes pit one party against the other, with only one of the eighty-seven Congressional Budget Act (CBA) waivers not counting as a party unity vote. We observe a similar pattern on a variety of other partisan statistics. Well over one-third of the budget-waving votes place 90 percent of the majority against 90 percent of the minority. This is contrasted with the fact that standard amendments reached this threshold at a mere 10 percent level until the 103rd Congress (1993–1994). Finally, when we examine the average party difference in support of a roll call, we see the same strong relationships. This measure is calculated by taking the absolute value of the difference between the proportions of each party supporting the vote, with higher values indicating a more partisan vote. While standard amendment votes achieve an average party difference score of 0.39 over our dataset, motions to table amendments register a score of 0.48. Once again, motions to waive the CBA mark an average party difference of 0.72.

Clearly, there is a major difference between votes that will alter the content of the bill and procedural votes dealing with whether an amendment will receive an up or down vote. The parties tend to oppose each other more vigorously on these votes in ways that fit with our theory of procedural politics in the Senate. While in the Senate it is difficult to restrict amending activity with the broad stroke of a special rule (which would need a unanimous consent agreement), MTTs and budgetary points of order offer a piecemeal approach that can shield the majority from taking stands on potentially dangerous or embarrassing amendments. These votes feature a stronger partisan pattern than standard amendment votes. The ability of senators to obfuscate the meaning of votes on procedural matters may free them to vote in a partisan manner, which could then hurt them on votes that the public better understands. As Carson and colleagues (2010) argue, it is extreme partisanship that costs members of Congress at the ballot box. Acting in a more partisan manner on difficult to understand votes may mitigate some of the electoral costs that senators face in being loyal to their party.

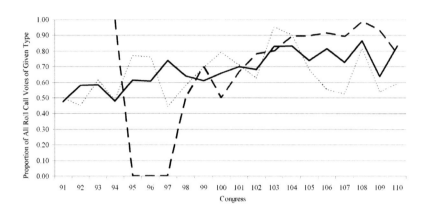

Figure 1a—Party Unity Votes

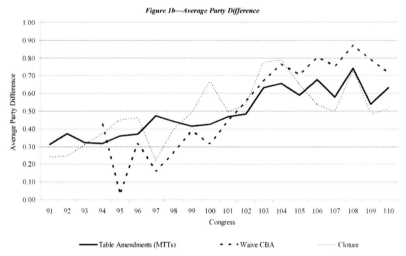

Figure 1b—Average Party Difference

Table Amendments (MTTs)   • • • Waive CBA   ⋯⋯⋯ Cloture

FIGURE 9.1
Partisanship of Motions in the U.S. Senate, 91st–110th Congresses

In contrast to the procedures just mentioned, a vote on cloture can affect an entire bill, not just a single amendment. But although there are fundamental differences between the amendment-specific MTT and budgetary point of order votes and cloture, we observe a similar pattern in partisanship. Votes on cloture are consistently more partisan than regular amendment or final passage votes. Around two in three cloture votes pit one party against the other, while a quarter of all votes to limit debate on a topic feature 90 percent of the majority against 90 percent of their colleagues in the minority. We see that cloture votes also feature a higher average party difference than MTTs, though not quite as high as what is observed on motions to waive the Congressional Budget Act. It seems certain that these procedural tools are handled in a more partisan manner than other passage and amendment votes, but we still need evidence that the majority is using these tools for its benefit to argue that they are the corollary to the methods used in the House.

The next step in this analysis is to examine the usage of the various tools by the majority party. It is one thing to establish that the votes are overly partisan in nature, but we need evidence that the majority is disproportionately using these tools. As shown in figure 9.2, we find that the majority is disproportionately using these tools to stop the minority from offering amendments. While the majority and minority offer votes on amendments in equal parts throughout our dataset, the majority is responsible for 84 percent of all tabling motions. Furthermore, whereas majority-sponsored amendments pass at a rate of 58 percent, the motions to table offered by members of the majority pass at a rate of 82 percent. While the majority and minority offer amendments at roughly a one-to-one ratio, the majority is much more aggressive and successful in tabling amendments. The majority offered a tabling motion against a minority amendment fifteen hundred more times than a member of the minority attempted to table a member of the majority in our dataset. While this tool is available to both parties, it makes sense that the majority would make use of it in greater numbers because of its numerical advantage. While the minority may attempt to move a motion to table, there is little chance of its success in persuading members of the majority to vote along with it on what seems to be a partisan procedural vote.

We observe a similar pattern with budgetary points of order. As shown in figure 9.3, the majority disproportionately raises points of order that are nearly

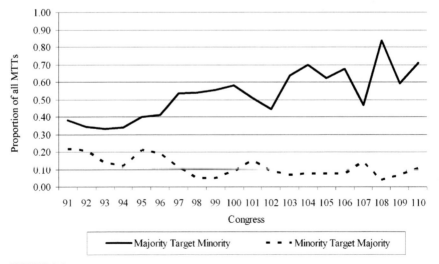

FIGURE 9.2
Motions to Table Amendments Across the Aisle, 91st–110th Congresses

FIGURE 9.3
Motions to Waive Budget Points of Order Across the Aisle, 91st–110th Congresses

impossible to overcome at a sixty-vote threshold. This forces the minority to attempt to waive the CBA at a high rate. Over our dataset, the minority attempted to waive the budget act 374 times, but they were only successful in eleven cases, or just under 3 percent. The majority needed only to attempt to waive CBA requirements 184 times, and found a much higher rate of success. Fifty-four of these waivers passed, amounting to a little under one-third of all cases. It is clear that in the case of MTTs and CBA waivers, the majority is using these tools at a higher rate than the proportion of their chamber would indicate. We theorize that the reason members of the majority feel the need to block more amendments is because they hold greater control over the bill-writing process than their counterparts in the minority. They have some procedural advantages, including the right of first recognition and the subsequent ability to schedule bills for debate on the floor. This means that the bills that reach the floor are already more favorable to the majority party. Although we find that the majority and minority offer amendments at equal rates, the majority has more of an incentive to keep the bill intact throughout the process.

Still, the fact that the majority is using these methods more is not absolute evidence that it is using procedure to stop the minority. Surely, if the majority were using MTTs and budgetary points of order to stop its own members in equal proportion to those of the minority, then the partisanship of these tools would rightly be called into question. However, we do not find that this is the case. Nearly two-thirds of all MTTs are targeting minority-sponsored amendments, and this proportion has been increasing over time. Furthermore, these MTTs are passing at a rate of 85 percent. That is a substantially higher percentage than what we observe from motions to table targeting majority amendments, which register at just under 62 percent. We observe the same pattern on budgetary points of order. Such budget waivers that attempt to allow minority amendments are much more frequent than the other way around. Those waivers also tend to fail at a much higher rate than those waivers designed to allow majority amendments. Majority-sponsored amendments receive a budget waiver around 16 percent of the time. While this percentage is still relatively low, it is eight times as large as the 2 percent success rate of the minority.

Beyond the data presented above, there still may be questions dealing with the partisan nature of these procedures. Although beyond the scope of this work, there is ample evidence to provide an explicit partisan element to MTTs, budget waivers, and cloture votes. Some may argue that these procedures are merely significant because of numbers or ideology, but as shown in other research, this is not the case. When ideology, committee membership, partisanship, and party leadership are included in the same analysis, the effects of party and leadership have the most substantial impact, highlighting a link to partisan theories of congressional organization. This is true of both motions to table and budgetary points of order, with the effects of the party growing stronger and committees growing weaker as we move into the polarized era (Theriault 2008). Some may still argue that these differences are symptomatic of the nature of procedural votes vis-à-vis amendments. For example, budgetary points of order deal primarily with issues of the budget, which have a history of being more contentious. However, when we examine MTTs and budget-waiving votes that have direct amendment corollaries, we find vast evidence of switching in a partisan manner (King et al. 2010). If senators were treating votes in a similar manner across the board, then they would not feel the need to switch positions on votes covering the same substance. Butler (2010) finds a similar relationship with cloture votes. It is apparent that these votes produce a partisan procedural advantage, but we must still explore the changing context with which these tools are used.

Procedural Tool Usage over Time

Our dataset starts in the 91st Congress (1969–1970) and ends in the 110th Congress (2007–2008). During that time, there has been great change in the way that the Senate does business. Although not as widespread as movement in the House, we noted that there is evidence that the Senate has become a more partisan body over this period, moving from a chamber where committee status and personal relationships mattered to one where partisan affiliation was of greater importance. Has the change in atmosphere led to a change in the procedures used by the Senate majority party? Evidence indicates that the answer is undoubtedly yes. Just as the rise of restrictive special rules stands as evidence of a hyper-partisan House, so too does the increased emphasis on budgetary points of order and cloture mark the Senate's evolution.

We can begin to see this shift by tracking the usage of motions to table amendments over time, as shown in figure 9.4. The ability to table amendments in the Senate has been around since the earliest congresses and was used relatively frequently at the beginning of our dataset. Usage increased throughout the 1970s and 1980s, reaching a high point in the 99th Congress (1985–1986), where 36 percent of all roll calls taken were dealing with motions to table amendments. This proportion exceeded the frequency with which amendments were being voted on. Indeed, starting with the 99th Congress, four of six Senates recorded more votes on motions to table amendments than they recorded votes on amendments to actually change the language of a bill. It seemed as though the MTT was the weapon of choice used by the majority on an issue. The rise of this procedure can be explained by an increased need to protect bills from amendments. While this became a popular tool for committee members to restrict amendments from others on the floor in a less partisan era (Marshall et al. 1999), it evolved with the chamber to be used by party leaders to stop counter-partisans from altering a bill that the party endorsed.

Despite the success that this procedure brought to the majority party, usage began to decline after the 104th Congress (1995–1996). Since then, the proportion of all roll calls devoted to motions to table amendments has decreased in each subsequent Senate, from 0.35 to 0.07 in the 110th Congress. This is the

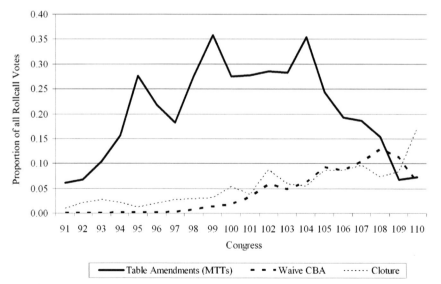

FIGURE 9.4
Usage of Select Procedural Tools in the U.S. Senate

lowest rate since the 91st Congress. If we can explain the rise of this procedural tool by invoking a spike in Senate partisanship, then it becomes more difficult to explain the decline when the chamber becomes even more partisan. One explanation may be that there are simply fewer amendments to table. However, when we look at the number of amendments offered, we find that they are being offered in high proportion throughout the dataset, and that the decline in MTTs does not correspond with a similar decrease in amending activity. In addition, the number of amendments originating from the minority seems to be increasing relative to those sponsored by the majority. This seems to rule out the argument that the nature of amendments being offered is more amenable to the majority party. Unless the minority party decided to stop offering amendments that the majority deemed harmful (which seems unlikely in an era of confrontational minority parties), then there must be other ways in which the majority is controlling the flow of amendments.

We have already shown the partisan nature of budgetary points of order, and now we can examine their relationship to the decrease in MTTs. Since the framework to raise budgetary points of order was not created until the 1974 Congressional Budget Act (CBA), use of this tactic was nonexistent during the early stages of our dataset. However, even after this tool was conceived, usage was sporadic and seemingly limited to idiosyncratic cases on narrow budgetary issues. Although a waiver vote did not necessarily follow a budgetary point of order in each occasion, the correlation was high. Between the 94th and 98th Congresses (1975–1984), there were only eleven budget-waiving votes. Furthermore, it seems as though this tool had not been politicized in this era the way the motion to table had been. Only three of the first eleven waivers were party-unity votes at the 50 percent threshold. This stands in strict contrast with what was to come. From the 99th Congress on, the budgetary point of order became more widespread and more partisan in makeup, slowly rising in usage through the 1990s and early 2000s. By the 108th Congress (2003–2004), there were eighty-seven budget-waiving votes, and all but one of them met the party-unity standard. In the 109th Congress, there were twenty-six fewer MTT votes than votes to waive the CBA. In the present Congress, motions to waive the budget act have become politicized and popular, but how did this change occur?

There is a variety of reasons that budgetary points of order gained prevalence as a majority tool to complement and, to some extent, replace MTTs. First, budgetary points of order are generally only useful on issues that affect the budget or deficit. The proportion of votes that deal with the budget have increased since the 1974 CBA, with the advent of the reconciliation procedure and the subsequent increase in use of this method to pass policy without needing to deal with possible filibusters. As the proportion of votes taken on the budget and under the auspices of reconciliation, the opportunity to use budgetary points of order increased. Still, there were several budget resolutions and a few reconciliations that passed with little emphasis on budget-waiving votes through the 99th Congress.

Why does the upward trend begin then? During the Gramm-Rudman debates of the mid-1980s, the threshold to defeat a budgetary point of order was raised from fifty votes to sixty votes (Gold 2008). Before this change, it was just as easy for a target to avoid having their motion being tabled as it was for them to overcome a budgetary point of order. In fact, initiating a budgetary point of order could be seen as more costly to a member wanting to restrict an amendment. They would need to raise the point of order and receive a satisfactory ruling from the Senate parliamentarian. A motion to table needed no grounding in budget law and could be initiated at any point. The advantages of using budgetary points of order were few, making the motion to table a more attractive option. The change to the sixty-vote threshold, however, altered this calculus. It would become much more difficult for a minority amendment to raise the sixty votes needed to overturn a point of order, rather than the fifty votes needed to fend off a motion to table an amendment and secure a straight up or down vote. An institutional change meant to further prohibit deficit spending fundamentally changed the nature of procedural tactics in the Senate. Today, budgetary points of order are raised when they can be, with MTTs still being used in those instances where the CBA or budget resolution does not apply.

Still, even if we add the number of MTTs and budget-waiving votes together, there is a decrease both proportionally and in raw numbers of votes to restrict amendments from reaching the floor. Another tool that is growing in popularity is cloture. While cloture appears to be a defensive mechanism, the advantages outlined above mean that it has a number of positive agenda-setting features for the majority. If amendments must be germane after cloture is filed, then many amendments that the majority would need to table are blocked from the agenda. If amendments need to be pre-filed before cloture is invoked, then the minority is less able to alter bills at the last minute or continue to stall the process.

Still, cloture is difficult to achieve, with sixty votes required (for the majority of our dataset) to shut off debate on a bill and move forward. The frequency of cloture votes, however, is conditional upon the maneuverings of the minority. Because of this, cloture votes carry a major reactive component. If the minority's objective becomes less about altering legislation on the floor and more about stopping the majority from carrying out its agenda, then the majority will be forced to invoke cloture more often or give up its legislative goals. Most researchers and observers agree that the distance between the majority and minority has increased over time. If this is so, we should see an increase in cloture motions, and we certainly do. The 91st Congress featured only six votes on cloture. Since that low-water mark, cloture has steadily increased in number and as a proportion of overall votes. By the 110th Congress, of 657 votes taken in the Senate, 112 were on cloture. Cloture votes were more numerous than budget-waiving votes and motions to table amendments combined in the last Congress of our dataset.

What is the cause for this increase in the Senate? As mentioned above, the minority party's decision to aggressively stall the Senate agenda plays a large role. But we must also realize that the minority may have also been reacting to having a large number of its amendments stopped via MTTs and budgetary points of order. Whatever the reason for this change, one main by-product is a decrease in amendments troublesome to the majority leaking through to the floor. The dramatic increase of cloture motions correlates well with a lack of pinpointed amendment restriction. We can gain a better understanding of the times when each of these methods is appropriate by analyzing when most of these techniques are used.

We analyze the usage of MTTs and budget waivers on bills on which cloture has been invoked. We only analyze cloture votes that deal with the entire bill and record what types of votes occurred on those bills before and after cloture was invoked. We see that 57 percent of all MTT votes take place before cloture is invoked on a bill. If we only look at the 104th Congress and on, where cloture began its meteoric rise and MTTs began their steep decline, we see that 77 percent of tabling motions on amendments occur before cloture is invoked on a bill. Budget-waiving votes suffer a similar fate, with around 80 percent of budget-waiving votes occurring before the amendment restricting cloture takes effect. To be sure, the number of amendments that reach the floor after cloture also decreases, but the proportion is much smaller than for MTTs. Since the 104th Congress, before cloture is invoked, there are roughly two votes on amendments for every one motion to table an amendment. However, after cloture is invoked, this ratio increases. At that point, there is one tabling motion for just over every three substantive amendments. This is strong evidence that cloture motions are forestalling the need to use tabling motions.

In order to better understand the root causes of the decline of tabling motions, we split the agenda of each congress into three parts: one dealing with roll calls on budget resolutions and reconciliations, one dealing with roll calls on appropriations, and a third category dealing with votes on everything else. We show a summary of each of these categories in table 9.1 and include the percentage of roll calls within each category over our entire dataset, where the votes are coded as positive amending activity, motions to table amendments, budget waivers, and cloture motions. When we examine the budget category over time, we find that motions to table have become nearly extinct. This subset of votes is particularly interesting because here we have a situation that most closely approximates the House. Filibustering is prohibited, as are non-germane amendments by rule. This is the place where we should see the lowest need to table amendments, and indeed, this is the case. There have been only five MTTs in the last four

TABLE 9.1
Procedural Tools in the Senate by Vote Category

Vote Category	Total Votes	Percent of Roll Call Votes on . . .			
		% on Motions to Table (MTTs) Amendments	*% on Positive Amending*	*% Budget Waivers*	*% on Cloture*
Appropriations	3242	24.7	37.4	4.9	2.5
Budget	1230	20.2	52.0	14.1	0.0
Other	11797	19.0	38.3	2.1	5.9
Total	**16269**	**20.2**	**39.2**	**3.6**	**4.8**

Note: Row percentages will not add up to 1 as there are many other types of votes other than the four represented here. This just shows the various tools we have discussed throughout the chapter.

congresses combined, and budget-waiving votes have outnumbered MTTs in five of the last six congresses. Although budget waivers have picked up some of the slack from the departing MTTs, the amount of partisan agenda control cannot be completely accounted for by budgetary points of order. Appropriations votes display a less clear pattern, but there is a general upward trend in cloture votes coupled with a decrease in MTT votes. When we examine non-budget and non-appropriations roll calls, we see the true ascendancy of cloture votes. The decline of MTTs is stark and the budget-waiving votes remain modest, but for this subset, cloture votes made up over 22 percent of the non-budgetary votes.

Conclusion

We have argued that the majority party has a number of tools at its disposal. Members treat certain procedural votes as different from pure policy votes. We take this as a sign that senators are more willing to vote with their party on procedural votes than on substantive votes, and they are more likely to worry about being taken to task by constituents for their stance on policy, not technical, votes. The several different pieces of analysis that we provide leave little doubt that MTTs, budget waivers, and cloture are tools of the majority party.

It has been somewhat more difficult to pin down what has been replacing the vanishing motions to table. We had anticipated that there might be a single culprit in this procedural politics whodunit. As it turns out, there does not appear to be just one factor. However, we did examine two other techniques in some depth and have determined that they appear to be playing some role in a reduction in the use of MTTs. We analyzed budgetary points of order and discovered the procedural similarity they share with motions to table. A pattern of vote switching exists on budget-waiving votes that mimics what is observed with MTTs. Members are switching positions when faced with actual substantive votes, which shows that a vote on budget procedure is much different from a pure policy vote on an amendment. This seems like a more efficient way of killing amendments, where budget rules apply, considering the fact that three-fifths of the Senate must vote to proceed to the actual amendment. When we analyzed success rates of budget waivers, we saw that the majority status of the member moving to waive budget provisions was most important. Minority members attempting to waive budget provisions were far less successful ceteris paribus. This is evidence in support of the majority party colluding to control the agenda.

We also examined the role cloture votes play in assisting the majority. The use of cloture has seen a strong increase over the past thirty years, and votes on cloture are consistently partisan. Furthermore, the increase in cloture votes leads directly to fewer tabling votes because there is less need to table unwanted amendments after cloture is invoked. While the number of amendments decreases, the number of non-germane and ad hoc amendments that are prime candidates for tabling and budgetary points of order shrink toward zero. While some amendments will still be tabled, fewer amendments that the majority feels must be tabled to protect its agenda and members will be offered.

We chose to focus on these three techniques, but we believe that there are a number of tools that the majority can use that we did not consider here. For example, filling the amendment tree, a process where the majority leader offers so many amendments that the minority is blocked out, is becoming more widespread in the Senate—with dozens of examples in each of the last few congresses. The majority also has the ability to offer amendments to amendments. This fighting fire with fire in the House was studied by Weingast (1992). Unanimous consent agreements (UCAs) that require sixty votes to pass amendments are also becoming more in vogue. These UCAs pass because they allow straight up or down votes on amendments that would otherwise be tabled. The majority has less to worry about here, as it is difficult for the minority to reach the three-fifths required to amend the bill, and some majority members may be freed up to vote with his or her constituency without fear of damaging the party's agenda. These are just a few examples of tools that the majority can use in order to stop the minority from altering the agenda, or forcing majority members into a corner.

It is also important to note that the focus here has been on recorded votes. Our data focus only on activity that reaches a formal vote, and because of this we necessarily miss part of the story. We acknowledge that a great deal of policymaking in the Senate occurs without a vote being taken, but we defend using only recorded votes as a place to start learning about Senate tools. Indeed, finding significant effects of party on the most visible and arguably most consequential issues is substantial. Finally, the tools we are focusing on go hand in hand with recorded votes. While an analysis of filling the amendment tree would require a scouring of the *Congressional Record*, it is perfectly appropriate to focus on recorded votes when conducting an analysis of tabling motions, CBA waivers, and cloture votes.

Unlike the House, there is no special rule in the Senate that can accomplish everything the majority wants via a simple majority vote. There may not be a silver procedural bullet, but there is a toolkit. Just as a carpenter does not use a hammer to turn a screw, the majority leader cannot raise a budgetary point of order on an amendment that fails to deal with the budget. In the Senate, the tools used are conditional upon the setting and what works best to achieve party goals. The majority's tool choice is made in response to the strategies used by the minority. After all, there is no pressing need to invoke cloture if filibuster threats are not credible, nor is there a need to table amendments that are not dangerous. As the minority party works harder to derail the entirety of the majority leadership agenda, the leadership has to respond with the tools that are best suited to protect it. Using the parlance of game theory, the equilibrium strategy of the majority party is the best response to what the minority party undertakes in the first move of the game.

Our study of the Senate deals with an era where partisanship in the Senate has seen great growth. Motions to table have been used since the beginning of that time period, and our data show that the relationship has changed slightly. For the first half of our database, committee and ideological factors seemed to play a larger role in determining the success of an MTT than partisan concerns. This phenomenon points to the fact that committee members are protecting bills from amending on the floor. For the second half of the database, we see that partisan concerns take a greater role, shoving distributive and other concerns to the background. One plausible interpretation of this shift is that as the Senate became more partisan and leadership gained a stronger hand, members used agenda-control tools left over from a more committee-centric era.

While MTTs worked well, as more power was placed in the hands of the majority leadership, new techniques were introduced. Even though the CBA became law in 1974, we fail to see it being used often for partisan gain through the early 1990s. While the majority may be making a concerted effort to raise more points of order, it is also increasing the opportunities to raise them. There has been a marked increase in the amount of material passed via reconciliation over this timeframe. From welfare reform to tax cuts and health care, Senate majorities are using reconciliation to circumvent the possibility of minority obstructionism. By using budget reconciliation more frequently, the majority increases the amount of time that budgetary points of order are in effect.

We see a similar pattern when dealing with cloture. Cloture was originally used as a means to stop filibusters, but as Senate leadership has grown stronger, cloture is now used preemptively when there is a threat of a filibuster to help control the floor. On bills with little budgetary impact, where reconciliation is not an option, cloture is an excellent way to influence the debate on a bill. However, this technique can only be used when the majority can garner sixty votes. If the majority is unable to proceed using reconciliation, or by using cloture, then there are a number of techniques still available. Perhaps it involves crafting unanimous consent agreements that allow amendments that must pass at supermajoritarian margins, or perhaps it involves offering amendments to amendments. As we noted, recently a frequently used technique has been utilizing the right of first recognition of the majority leader to fill the amendment tree on a bill, thus denying minority amendments. Still, using a technique like filling the amendment tree could anger one's own members and lead to a revolt if overused. As much as the majority party in the Senate would like to restrict the flow of unwanted amendments, it is inevitable that some will slip through. In these cases, it still has the tested and true option of tabling.

In retrospect, it is not surprising that in such a complex institution as the Senate there would be multiple devices used by the majority. Unlike in the House, tools are chosen on a case-by-case basis. The effectiveness of the tool appears to be related to the context of the bill, time constraints, and the ideological makeup of the chamber. In the future, we plan on giving more attention to concepts like cloture and filling the amendment tree. We also want to see if partisan techniques work differently on major legislation or on bills where the president has taken a stand. Finally, this chapter has borrowed partisan theories developed in the House and attempted to test some of their implications in the Senate. We find that partisan theories appear to explain an increasing amount of the behavior of senators. It may have taken a while for the discipline to cast its eye on the Senate, but now that we have the data, we must give this chamber as much attention as has been given to the House over the past thirty years.

References

Aldrich, John H. 1994. "A Model of a Legislature with Two Parties and a Committee System." *Legislative Studies Quarterly* 19:313–39.

Bayh, Evan. 2010. "Sen. Evan Bayh Won't Run Again: 'Congress Is Not Operating As It Should' Transcript." *Lynn Sweet: The Scoop from Washington*, February 15. http://blogs.suntimes.com/sweet/2010/02/sen_evan_bayh_wont_run_again_c.html.

Beth, Richard S., Valerie Heitshusen, Bill Heniff, and Elizabeth Rybicki. 2009. "Leadership Tools for Managing the U.S. Senate." Paper presented at the annual meeting of the American Political Science Association, Toronto, Canada, September 3–6.

Binder, Sarah A., and Steven S. Smith. 1998. "Political Goals and Procedural Choice in the Senate." *Journal of Politics* 60:398–416.

Butler, Daniel M. 2010. "Testing Arnold's Theory of Responsibility: Evidence from Vote Switching between Cloture and the Underlying Motion." Paper presented at the annual meeting of the Midwest Political Science Association, Chicago, Illinois, April 22–25.

Campbell, Andrea, Gary W. Cox, and Mathew D. McCubbins. 2002. "Agenda Power in the U.S. Senate, 1877 to 1986." In *Party, Process, and Political Change in Congress: New Perspectives on the History of Congress*, vol. 1, edited by David W. Brady and Mathew D. McCubbins, 146–65. Palo Alto, CA: Stanford University Press.

Canes-Wrone, Brandice, David W. Brady, and John F. Cogan. 2002. "Out of Step, Out of Office: Electoral Accountability and House Members' Voting." *American Political Science Review* 96:127–40.

Carson, Jamie, Gregory Koger, Matthew Lebo, and Everett Young. 2010. "The Electoral Costs of Party Loyalty in Congress." *American Journal of Political Science* 54:598–616.

Cox, Gary W., and Mathew D. McCubbins. 1993. *Legislative Leviathan: Party Government in the House.* Berkeley and Los Angeles: University of California Press.

———. 2005. *Setting the Agenda: Responsible Party Government in the U.S. House of Representatives.* New York: Cambridge University Press.

Den Hartog, Chris, and Nathan W. Monroe. 2008. "Agenda Influence and Tabling Motions in the U.S. Senate." In *Why Not Parties?*, edited by Nathan W. Monroe, Jason M. Roberts, and David W. Rohde, 142–58. Chicago: University of Chicago Press.

Evans, C. Lawrence, and Daniel Lapinski. 2005. "Obstruction and Leadership in the U.S. Senate." In *Congress Reconsidered*, 8th ed., edited by Lawrence C. Dodd and Bruce I. Oppenheimer, 227–48. Washington, DC: CQ Press.

Farquharson, Robin. 1969. *Theory of Voting.* New Haven, CT: Yale University Press.

Fenno, Richard F. 1978. *Homestyle: House Members in Their Districts.* Boston: Little, Brown and Company.

Gold, Martin B. 2008. *Senate Procedure and Practice.* 2nd ed. New York: Rowman & Littlefield.

Jenkins, Jeffrey A., and Michael C. Munger. 2003. "Investigating the Incidence of Killer Amendments in Congress." *Journal of Politics* 65:498–517.

King, Aaron S., Frank J. Orlando, and David W. Rohde. 2010. "Beyond Motions to Table: Exploring the Procedural Toolkit of the Majority Party in the United States Senate." Paper presented at the annual meeting of the Midwest Political Science Association, Chicago, Illinois, April 22–25.

Lee, Frances. 2008. "Dividers, Not Uniters: Presidential Leadership and Senate Partisanship, 1981–2004." *Journal of Politics* 70:914–28.

Marshall, Bryan W., Brandon C. Prins, and David W. Rohde. 1997. "Theories of Legislative Organization: An Empirical Study of Committee Outliers in the Senate." Paper presented at the annual meeting of the Midwest Political Science Association, Chicago, Illinois, April 10–12.

———. 1999. "Fighting Fire with Water: Partisan Procedural Strategies and the Senate Appropriations Committee." *Congress and the Presidency* 26:113–32.

Monroe, Nathan W., and Chris Den Hartog. 2005. "The Value of Majority Status: The Effect of Jeffords's Switch on Asset Prices of Republican and Democratic Firms." *Legislative Studies Quarterly* 33:62–84.

Monroe, Nathan W., Jason M. Roberts, and David W. Rohde, eds. 2008. *Why Not Parties?* Chicago: University of Chicago Press.

Oleszek, Walter J. 2004. *Congressional Procedures and the Policy Process.* Washington, DC: CQ Press.

Rohde. David W. 1991. *Parties and Leaders in the Postreform House.* Chicago: University of Chicago Press.

———. 2010. *Political Institutions and Public Choice Roll Call Database.* Durham, NC: Duke University Press.

Saturno, James V. 2004. "The Congressional Budget Process: A Brief Overview." *Congressional Research Service.* Washington, DC: Library of Congress.

———. 2008. "Points of Order in the Congressional Budget Process." *Congressional Research Service.* Washington, DC: Library of Congress.

———. 2011. "Points of Order in the Congressional Budget Process." *Congressional Research Service.* Washington, DC: Library of Congress.

Sinclair, Barbara. 2005. "New World of U.S. Senators." In *Congress Reconsidered*, 8th ed., edited by Lawrence C. Dodd and Bruce I. Oppenheimer, 1–22. Washington, DC: CQ Press.

Theriault, Sean M. 2008. *Party Polarization in the Congress.* New York: Cambridge University Press.

Weingast, Barry R. 1992. "Fighting Fire with Fire: Amending Activity and Institutional Change in the Postreform Congress." In *The Postreform Congress*, edited by Roger H. Davidson, 142–68. New York: St. Martin's Press.

10

Defense Authorization

*The Senate's Last Best Hope**

Colleen J. Shogan

T HIS EXAMINATION BEGINS WITH a simple observation and a puzzle. While the United States Senate is widely considered an institution crippled by gridlock, obstruction, and increased partisan battles (Koger 2010), for the past forty-nine years, it has never failed to pass a National Defense Authorization Act (NDAA). Even though filibusters have grown increasingly frequent, the Senate has found ways, often creatively, to avoid a legislative impasse on NDAA. The subject of national defense is not, however, without controversy. Through Vietnam, the Cold War, two wars in Iraq, the global war on terrorism, Iran Contra, waterboarding, Tailhook, and numerous defense acquisition scandals, the NDAA has persevered.

The NDAA's endurance is noteworthy because other authorization processes have not fared nearly as well. Given increased polarization in both houses of Congress, the continuous campaign cycle, and higher levels of media scrutiny coupled with the twenty-four-hour news cycle, the frequency of authorizations has diminished in recent years (Price 2011). For example, as of the 112th Congress (2011–2012), the reauthorization of surface transportation funding is several years late, there is no concerted movement toward a Water Resources Development Act (WRDA) reauthorization, No Child Left Behind is almost five years beyond its anticipated renewal, and movement toward a farm bill appears slow.

Despite all odds, the NDAA persists—even when the specter of the repeal of "Don't Ask, Don't Tell" (DADT) almost derailed the fiscal year (FY) 2011 bill. Passing on the House and Senate floors by unanimous consent, procedurally

---

*The views expressed herein are those of the author and are not presented as those of the Congressional Research Service or the Library of Congress.

requiring all 100 senators and 435 representatives to agree without a vote on the contents of a condensed version of the bill, the dogged and sheer determination of NDAA shone brightly. If the controversy over DADT could not kill NDAA, it may very well be the case that this cat has a few lives left.

The mere fact that the NDAA has passed the Senate for forty-nine straight years is remarkable. But it begs an answer to the puzzling question: Why? It turns out that the easy answer is only a small part of the explanation. National defense is surely a bipartisan, perhaps even nonpartisan, issue. Yet the same can be said for other issues, such as education, surface transportation, and federal aviation reform—and major authorizing legislation in these areas has been scant in recent years.

It turns out the answer to the "why" question is complicated. A number of unique circumstances come together to produce an annual defense bill. Based upon over twenty interviews with former and current Senate staff and defense analysts, I argue that a complex mixture of committee traditions, rules, processes, a robust hearing schedule, bipartisanship, professional staff relationships, floor strategy, and widely shared belief in the overall mission contribute to the outcome.[1] All of these elements are critical and work simultaneously with each other. If one piece of the puzzle fails in the future, the passage of NDAA may be jeopardized. The greatest danger is that even a single failure to produce a bill one year could have a devastating effect on the Senate's subsequent commitment to NDAA passage.

In this chapter, after a brief discussion of the historical origins of the NDAA, I describe the process that Senate Armed Services Committee staffers undertake each year to produce an NDAA ready for the president's signature. The process itself is worthy of a detailed explanation since it provides an illuminating glimpse into the inner workings of one of the most powerful committees in Congress. The reasons for NDAA's continued success are provided, along with analysis when opinions diverge among congressional staff. This model of repeated legislative success is put to the test with a discussion of the fiscal year 2011 NDAA, which almost broke the forty-nine-year streak when the Senate failed to consider the bill using its regular legislative floor process. The conclusion offers some terse thoughts about what we can learn from the success of the NDAA, and postulates whether some of the lessons might be applicable to congressional policy venues besides defense.

History of the NDAA

After a failure of the Armed Services Committees in both the House and Senate to work in conjunction with the Department of Defense and the Army and Air Force on the location of anti-aircraft missiles and radars in the 1950s, a section authored by Senator Richard Russell was added to the fiscal year 1960 Military Construction Authorization Act. This provision required authorization for the procurement of major weapons systems and provided the legislative inception for the modern National Defense Authorization Act (Towell 2011, 79–80). The NDAA now mirrors the Defense Appropriations bill and authorizes the funds provided for nearly all appropriated defense accounts and the construction of military projects. It is a comprehensive annual policy bill that creates public law and amends relevant sections of the *United States Code.*

The effect of the Russell amendment was that the defense budget would no longer only be subject to scrutiny from the Defense Appropriations subcommittees in both houses of Congress. Instead, the policy committees—Armed Services—would be required to authorize such appropriations. Dawson (1962) argues that the Russell amendment was a strategic attempt by Congress to enhance its power in defense and national security policy relative to the president as commander-in-chief. It was not, in fact, a pure power play made by members of the Armed Services Committees to dethrone their colleagues on Appropriations, who previously held sole jurisdiction over the defense budget. Rather, House members and Senators on both the Appropriations and Armed Services Committees supported the Russell amendment (Dawson 1962, 42–43).

Why look to the Armed Services Committees to scrutinize the defense budget, when the appropriators possess the authority to alter how defense dollars are allocated? Even by 1960, the scope of the defense budget had grown to the point that it had become impossible for one subcommittee of the House and Senate Appropriations Committees to examine all aspects of the president's defense budget proposal. With so few resources at its disposal in comparison to the Department of Defense and service branches, Congress had no choice but to expand the scope of decision-making and knowledge by granting greater powers to the authorizing committees of jurisdiction in both houses. The Russell amendment introduced "one more means of leverage" in the process (Dawson 1962, 44). Instead of intermittent authorization bills, the Armed Services Committees shifted to an annual schedule that increased the likelihood of congressional relevance vis-à-vis the executive in defense policymaking.

There was a concerted effort to make clear that this new authorization process would not supplant the work of the Appropriations Committees. The Senate report that accompanied the Military Construction Authorization bill for fiscal year 1960 explicitly concluded that the Armed Services Committee should conduct an annual review of aircraft and missile procurement programs, and "a thorough examination of this area of activity may serve to reduce the enormous cost of defense and should assist the Committee on Appropriations in their consideration of the mammoth defense budget" (Senate Committee on Armed Services 1959, 16). It is worth mentioning that the House Armed Services Committee was not particularly supportive of the Russell amendment language. In particular, House committee chairman Carl Vinson worried that an annual process would require a level of detailed work his committee staff was not readily capable of producing. He also believed that "military men should make military decisions," thus questioning whether congressional relevance in defense policymaking should be intensified (Dawson 1962, 52). Nonetheless, the Senate Armed Services Committee held its ground, and the Russell amendment survived the conference. An explicit reference to an "annual process" was deleted, but it might be said in this respect that the Senate lost the battle yet won the war since the NDAA process soon became an annual affair. Testimony to the fact that all politics is local, the addition of "naval vessels" to the Russell amendment language sweetened the pot for Vinson (Dawson 1962, 53).

The strength of the NDAA is not that it sets a budgetary ceiling for appropriations. In fact, the Government Accountability Office (GAO) has argued that the Russell amendment does not restrain the actions of the appropriations process in Congress. According to GAO, "An authorization act is basically a directive to Congress itself, which Congress is free to follow or alter (up or down) in the subsequent appropriation act." In other words, if Congress passes a defense appropriations bill that exceeds the ceiling placed in the defense authorization bill, "there are no practical consequences" of that action (Towell 2011, 83).

But the reality of the situation is much more complicated than this legal pronouncement. The sheer longevity of the NDAA has made it a force to be reckoned with on Capitol Hill. Although there have been disputes between defense appropriators and authorizers over the years, the battles have been fairly fought and never settled on legal grounds akin to GAO's analysis. Instead, the institutionalized passage of the NDAA, along with the litany of oversight hearings that the Armed Services Committees conduct en route to the bill's markup and floor consideration, make the authorizing process an expected and integral part of annual defense policymaking in Congress.[2]

The formal relationship between the appropriators and the authorizers is almost irrelevant, particularly if the history of the Russell amendment is taken into consideration. After all, the legislative language that created the modern NDAA process did not originate from a battle between congressional committees. Rather, it arose from a desire to find an effective way to exercise appropriate congressional oversight concerning the executive branch's defense priorities, policies, and expenditures. In this sense, there is no doubt that the Russell amendment and the emergent annual NDAA process achieved their purpose.

The Process of the NDAA in the Senate

Political scientists have not written widely about defense policymaking in Congress. There has been some focused interest among scholars scrutinizing the connection between the concentration of defense industries in districts and states to committee membership on Armed Services (Goss 1972; Rundquist et al. 1997; Carsey and Rundquist 1999). Besides distributional examinations, recent work on the Senate Armed Services and Foreign Relations Committees concluded that the environments of Senate committees are so distinct, scholars must engage in "fine-grained analysis" to understand how such institutions work (Fowler and Law 2008a). An exhaustive literature concerning how Congress produces defense policy or fulfills its oversight authorities in defense does not exist. In fact, scholarly attention paid to Congress's role in defense usually emphasizes the declining abdication of authority by the legislative branch (Fisher 2000; Fowler and Law 2008b) rather than its exercise.

This examination takes a different approach by focusing on the yearly process undertaken by the Senate Armed Services Committee (known as SASC) in its production of the NDAA. Before determining why the defense authorization bill passes the Senate with unfailing regularity every year, it is important to understand SASC's process for considering the legislation.

For this information, I rely chiefly on interviews with over twenty current and former Senate Armed Services Committee staffers, personal office military legislative assistants (MLAs), and defense experts.[3] Some interviews were conducted on an individual basis, and others took place in a small-group setting. Interviews usually lasted approximately thirty minutes; sometimes the conversations extended over an hour. All personal office staff interviewed worked for a senator who serves or served on the Armed Services Committee. Staffers working for the majority and minority on SASC were interviewed, as well as MLAs representing senators from both parties.[4] Interviewees were solicited via word of mouth; many times, one interview led to a contact with another staffer, thus resulting in a subsequent conversation.

All current and former staff interviewed agreed that the particular process undertaken each year by SASC helped encourage the outcome of a final bill for floor consideration. Although the issues change widely from year to year, the legislative steps remain consistent, predictable, and methodical.

The submission of the president's budget (PB) request is the initiating event. Usually on the first Monday in February, as required by the Congressional Budget Act of 1974, the president submits a budget request to Congress detailing the estimated cost of defense for the following fiscal year. At that point in time, SASC staffers receive the PB and begin to familiarize themselves with the details, which indicate the president's preferences for the allocation of defense dollars and resources. The Pentagon routinely sends briefers to Capitol Hill that week, which help both SASC and personal office MLAs understand the broad, overarching budgetary message and some specifics, usually associated with major changes or decisions, contained in the PB. These meetings take place in a bipartisan fashion; both Republican and Democratic staffers attend the same briefings and receive the same message from the executive branch, regardless of which party controls the presidency or the Senate at the time.

Soon after the PB submission, sometimes only days after receipt of the PB, SASC begins a series of hearings on the budget request and other major related issues. These hearings are an important part of the process. The first hearing features the secretary of defense and the chairman of the joint chiefs of staff, who answer overall questions concerning the budget's priorities and challenges that may present themselves in the coming year. This hearing is followed by a number of more focused hearings with the combatant commanders (such as U.S. Special Operations Command and U.S. Central Command), the service chiefs (such as commandant of the U.S. Marine Corps), and the civilian department secretaries (such as the secretary of the U.S. Air Force) as witnesses. In each instance, issues concerning the president's budget request are raised, as well as other concerns that might require legislative language in the upcoming fiscal year defense authorization bill. Other full committee hearings, often focused on intelligence or current U.S. military operations abroad, also take place in February and March. The full committee's hearing schedule is packed in the months of February, March, and April to guarantee that all components of the military have a chance to testify and that all senators have had a chance to ask questions. The pace is rapid, with at least one major hearing and often several hearings scheduled each week.

Given the high level of substance and the expansive territory each hearing must cover, the amount of preparation is considerable, both for professional committee staff and the MLAs from the personal offices. Due to the current size of the committee, one round of questioning is common, and if time runs out, senators may submit additional questions to the witnesses as QFRs (questions for the record), generating a subsequent written response. The motivation behind the large number of hearings, conducted each year without fail, is to build a public record with respect to the policy or budgetary issues that may be addressed by the annual defense authorization bill. Staffers use the hearings to flag important issues and to receive civilian and military leadership positions on those issues that will likely receive considerable discussion and debate during consideration of the NDAA. As the bill is subsequently drafted during the spring months, the hearing record serves as a repository of information for staff.

In March, after the bulk of the full committee annual hearings are completed, the subcommittee hearing season begins. Six subcommittees hold hearings concurrently with additional full committee hearings. As one might expect, the subcommittee hearings are more specialized, focused on their specific jurisdictional responsibilities, and allow further probing of issues raised at the full committee. The chair and ranking member of the subcommittee are routinely provided by professional committee staff a hearing schedule that combines both the particular interests of the senators running the committee and the policy needs that require further scrutiny and debate. Most subcommittees conduct at least four hearings. With three subcommittee assignments, as well as participation at the full committee level, senators usually find membership on Armed Services a significant time commitment. Of course, all senators do not attend every subcommittee or full committee hearing. However, since SASC uses the hearings as a way to build the record for the annual defense authorization bill, senators who want to influence the bill in numerous areas usually find a way to attend as many hearings as possible.

Hearings continue in SASC throughout the year on a variety of topics relevant to the military and national security. The highest concentration of subcommittee and committee hearings begins to conclude in mid-May. This is in preparation for the markup of the defense authorization bill, which is usually (although not always) the only legislation produced by SASC in a given year.[5]

During this time, all senators have the opportunity to make requests to the chair or ranking member concerning the contents of the bill. Senators usually construct a list of requests to the committee for inclusion. Most requests ask for adjustments to programs that have already been recommended for funding in the president's budget. For example, a senator may ask for increased funding for a particular National Guard program. Or a senator may request more funding for a specific research and development program in the Navy. SASC staffers compile and evaluate these requests, relying heavily upon the Pentagon and the unfunded requirements lists compiled by each of the service chiefs and occasionally by a combatant commander. These requests are commonly known as "earmarks." However, in the mind of SASC staffers, they are actually requests for funding defense programs at different levels than what is contained in the president's budget. The majority staff's recommendations with regard to these requests are not revealed until the draft bill (known as the chairman's mark) is presented to the Armed Services Committee at the beginning of markup.

As the hearings are being conducted in the spring, SASC staffers work to produce a draft bill. Much of the work is done collaboratively, with both majority and minority committee staffers influencing the draft. Once the draft has been completed and receives the approval of the chair, a weeklong defense authorization markup (session in which a congressional committee debates, writes, and amends a proposed bill) is scheduled, usually near the end of May or early June. Several days before the markup, committee staffers provide briefing binders, with draft language, for senators on the committee and their MLAs. Staffers from both sides of the aisle receive the briefing books at the same time. Previously, the briefing books were not allowed to leave the committee hearing room. MLAs who wanted to review the books in preparation for markup remained in the hearing room; no photocopying was allowed and electronic transmission was not permitted. For the fiscal year 2012 NDAA, a slight procedural change allowed MLAs to remove the briefing book from the Armed Services Committee room and take it to the senator's office for examination. A strict embargo of the information contained in the books still applied, and no electronic transmission of the books occurred.

In the days leading up to markup (usually a weekend), MLAs work with committee staffers to plan amendments their bosses intend to offer. More often than not, SASC staffers try to find ways in which senators on the committee can have their amendments accepted without debate or votes during markup. Compromises are often formulated prior to markup to ensure that fewer disagreements during the actual formal procedure require time and attention.

Markup of specific portions of defense authorization begins at the subcommittee level on a Tuesday. All six subcommittee markups are usually conducted on Tuesday or early Wednesday. On Wednesday afternoon, the full committee markup commences and lasts until the committee has finished marking up the bill. Usually, markup finishes by Friday of the same week. During the full committee markup, issues are raised for debate, and, if necessary, votes are taken if such issues were not resolved at the subcommittee level. Often, these more controversial issues were identified through the hearings that occurred earlier in the year. If there is a disagreement about a provision in the bill, the chair may set the issue aside and instruct staff to work with senators with differing perspectives to reach agreement. During closed markup, brief "adjournments" are common. Staff and senators are given the appropriate time to construct an acceptable compromise. If such agreement cannot be reached, formal committee votes are taken to decide what will and will not be included in the full committee's bill and report. The goal is to produce a committee bill in which a considerable majority of senators on SASC can support to move the bill out of markup and onto the floor for full Senate consideration.

Usually, at some point in the summer or early fall, two weeks of floor time are reserved in the Senate for consideration of the defense authorization bill. Since both parties perceive the defense authorization bill as "must-pass" legislation, floor action on the bill can be hectic. Senators view the NDAA as a good opportunity to attach legislative language, sometimes unrelated to defense, to a bill that is likely to become law.

Committee staffers from both sides of the aisle work with senators (often who do not serve on SASC) to consider amendments for which agreement can be achieved and included as part of what is called a "manager's package" of uncontroversial amendments. Compromising with senators who wish to amend the bill on the floor is strategic in that it gives senators a stake in the bill and thus helps secure votes for cloture (ending debate) and final passage (interview with Senate staffer, January 3, 2011). A set of amendments from both sides of the aisle, which may require floor votes, is usually agreed to by unanimous consent prior to cloture. Once cloture is invoked on the bill itself, amendments must be germane. In typical practice, the manager's package moves forward through unanimous consent prior to cloture, and then a vote for final passage is scheduled. However, in recent years, floor consideration of NDAA has been compromised due to attempts to include controversial non-defense-related language (such as hate crimes legislation), political considerations prior to an election, and the inability to reach unanimous consent on a manager's package. Despite these considerable challenges, SASC staffers have implemented calculated, strategic maneuvers to ensure passage of the bill.

After both houses of Congress have considered and passed the bill on the floor, conference begins. Issues in which the House and Senate disagreed are divided into subcommittee jurisdiction and assigned to professional committee staffers who take the lead in the staff negotiations, with the House and Senate each explaining their positions. The vast majority of differences are resolved at the staff level. In recent years, the Senate has been able to present a united front in conference, with both Senate majority and minority staffers supporting the Senate position.[6] Due to this approach, the Senate has had a better record prevailing in conference negotiations vis-à-vis the House. One former SASC staffer commented that the Senate typically prevailed over the House in conference due to its presentation of a unified front (interview with Arnold Punaro, March 10, 2011).

When staff cannot agree to a final position, the committees' majority and minority staff directors try to reach a compromise. If they cannot agree, House members and senators join the conference and discuss the issues at hand. Usually, there are only a handful of issues that require compromise. With members of Congress, the goal is finding the middle ground in conference so the process can move forward (interview with Senate staffer, February 1, 2011). Votes on the final conference report in both houses are the final step in the process before sending the bill to the president for his signature.

An Analysis of the Senate Consideration of NDAA: Why Does It Work?

The previous section described, in some detail, the process in which the Senate considers the NDAA each year. But it begs the question: Why does it work? After all, there are not different rules governing passage of defense authorization than any other bill considered in the Senate. Interviews with current and former Senate defense staffers indicate that there are particular qualities, practices, and characteristics that increase the likelihood of NDAA passage on an annual basis. These variables influencing the outcome are distinct and often work in tandem with each other to reach the desired outcome. Four reasons explaining the NDAA's repeated successes were mentioned repeatedly throughout the staff interviews: bipartisanship, routine committee processes, staff interactions, and closed markups.

Bipartisanship

Staff most frequently cited the role of bipartisanship as an explanation for the continued passage of NDAA. Bipartisanship plays a key role in several ways. First, the subject matter itself—national defense—is an issue that lends itself to bipartisanship. There is a deep sense among staff that they are working on a bill that helps those serving in the military and that without the bill, the lives of service members would be more difficult. There is a resounding echo of patriotism among those who work on the NDAA, both professional committee staff and MLAs. One staffer remarked, "At the end of the day, we're doing it for the troops" (interview with Senate staffer, February 1, 2011). Another staffer commented, "What produces bipartisanship is the subject matter we deal with. We have partisan issues that divide us from time to time, but the men and women in uniform are important and we need to support them. That core remains bipartisan" (interview with Senate staffer, January 4, 2011). A veteran defense reporter and current congressional defense analyst concluded that many academics underestimate the motivations of elected members of Congress and their staffs. He explained, "If I had to identify one single, fundamental error people make in understanding the Hill it is that a tremendous amount of things go on here because someone really believes in this stuff" (interview with Pat Towell, June 8, 2011).

The inherent bipartisan belief in a shared mission is distinctive. A current committee staffer contrasted SASC to other Senate committees: "The reason other committees aren't successful is that they can't work on a bipartisan basis. There's so much to be said for motivation. When you're motivated by the men and women of the military, that's a powerful incentive. It's different than producing a farm bill or another major piece of legislation" (interview with Senate staffer, January 6, 2011). In a time in which partisanship and cynicism are abundant on Capitol Hill, the pure belief in the importance of the policy issue is distinctive.

Beside the fact that both parties consider national security a priority, defense policymaking often cuts across partisan lines. More often than not, defense-related constituencies do not align on a partisan basis. Rather, there are often parochial interests, such as the continued production of a weapons system or the closing of a military base, that converge geographically or along shared industries. "To the extent there is a parochial thread to pull," commented one staffer, "then Democrats and Republicans will work together" (interview with Senate staffer, January 3, 2011). Another staffer concurred: "You can't just run roughshod over the minority because there are coalitions on the issue forming. Most times, they are not partisan coalitions" (interview with Senate staffer, March 23, 2011).

The bipartisan culture of the Senate Armed Services Committee developed incrementally over time. The chairs and ranking members of the committee historically set the precedent of a bipartisan approach and tone (interview with Fred Downey, December 13, 2010). Senators Sam Nunn, John Stennis, John Tower, Barry Goldwater, Richard Russell, John Warner, and Carl Levin encouraged staff to work in a bipartisan fashion, and they set the example in how they dealt with senators from the minority party. Strong chairmen who believed that partisanship stopped at the water's edge contributed to the development and growth of the bipartisan SASC culture. Bipartisanship on the committee is easily detected during markup of the bill. A former MLA described the process: "We resolved issues amicably in markup. It didn't matter what side of the aisle you were on. Senators took off their jackets and did their job. I always felt you could have a soldier in the room and he would have been proud of that process" (interview with Bradford Foley, February 11, 2011).

Bipartisanship has policy effects, as well. For amendments to be accepted during markup or on the floor, compromises must take place that may require the majority to incorporate the views of the minority. One MLA recalled, "I've had one amendment whittled down. We had to take their [the minority's] views. In my experience with SASC, the minority has a voice" (interview with Senate staffer, February 4, 2011). Not infrequently, these policy compromises could be reached because senators were not that far apart on the issue in the first place. A current Senate staffer stated, "We're like the rudder on the *Queen Mary* in the Senate. We try not to go to extremes. We keep on a constant path, with some divergence to the left and right" (interview with Senate staffer, February 10, 2011).

Finally, bipartisanship guides the "building-block" approach to the creation of the bill. When the professional staff work together to write the chairman's mark, they adopt a bipartisan approach, largely including provisions agreeable to both sides in the mark, and cautiously and infrequently including some that are not. Controversial language is debated during the full committee markup, and the most controversial provisions receive votes.

In other committees, a number of controversial issues are often included in the chairman's mark. Senators must rely on the amending process in markup to remove such measures. This can force senators to make an "up or down" decision on the mark, sometimes without being able to vote on all controversial provisions. Such an approach can prove efficient, but may restrict the choices of senators (interview with Senate staffer, February 1, 2011). In contrast, SASC's "building-block" methodology starts with the premise of bipartisanship and agreement, and then proceeds from that starting point to add provisions after debate.

Routine Committee Processes

Another distinctive feature of the NDAA is that SASC uses a routine process each year in preparing the bill. Every year, the same hearings are held with the secretary of defense, the joint chiefs, the combatant commanders, and service civilian and military leaders. Markup always takes place in late spring, and it employs a similar schedule. There are no surprises in the process of producing the bill, which helps staff know what to expect. After new staffers complete the process once or twice, they understand how to participate fully in future bills. While the issues change, the process does not. A Senate staffer explained, "SASC has standard annual hearings as part of the process. I thought that was restrictive at first, but now I realize it's really helpful. It drives the process. Every year, you know what's going to happen. We begin with an end in mind—and that's getting the bill done" (interview with Senate staffer, February 1, 2011). Another staffer stated, "The hearing process seems more rigorous than other committees. It helps shake out positions. . . . The routinization of the process is important" (interview with Senate staffer, February 4, 2011).

Furthermore, the hearings are not simply an exercise in showmanship. Of course, senators use hearings to take public positions and demonstrate to their home constituencies that they care about the military bases in their state or the weapons systems manufactured there. But in addition to any electoral posturing, the hearings in SASC that take place from February through May are used to create a public record in preparation for the drafting of NDAA. A former SASC staffer commented, "Staff use the hearings to figure out what the big problems are" (interview with Greg Kiley, March 8, 2011). For example, in the fiscal year 2011 bill, SASC held committee hearings on metrics for the Joint Strike Fighter, which resulted in bill language that created a matrix to evaluate the program's progress (interview with Senate staffer, March 23, 2011). One committee staffer described how the hearings directly affect the composition of the bill: "We use transcripts from the hearings to help us develop the bill. Testimony sometimes can bring issues to light, like low-performing schools for children in military families" (interview with Senate staffer, December 29, 2010). The hearings serve a policy purpose for the bill; they set the stage for the drafting, identify key issues that must be included, and give signals to the public about what the committee plans to address in the upcoming NDAA. In summation, one staffer commented, "The entire committee is structured around the completion of one major task— the NDAA. How does it get done? Routinization and laser-like focus" (interview with Senate staffer, January 20, 2011).

Staff Interactions

Distinct from other aspects of bipartisanship evident in the Senate's consideration of the NDAA is the role of staff. Both committee staff and the MLAs from Senate personal offices believe that the unique, collegial relationships that exist between Senate staffers who work on defense authorization issues contribute considerably to the routine passage of the bill.

Why does this bipartisan collegiality exist? Part of the reason is that regardless of party affiliation, the staffers who work on the NDAA believe that their work is critically important to maintaining a strong national defense. They also agree that those who serve in the military deserve strong legislative support from Congress. Besides common goals, Senate Armed Services Committee staff also share office space. Party affiliation determines seating within the suite, but everyone has the same door key to one shared office space (interview with Senate staffers, December 29, 2010, and January 6, 2011). This type of office structure facilitates a productive bipartisan working environment. This unusual arrangement developed over time, but in large part was due to former chairman Richard Russell. Years earlier, he decided that instead of moving Armed Services Committee staff to the newly constructed Senate office building across the street, the committee would remain in its original location, even if the space was smaller. Since there was no room for separate partisan staffs in the office suite, the tradition of sitting together in a bipartisan fashion took root (interview with Senate staffer, January 4, 2011).

Partially due to the friendly relations between staff of different parties, the longevity of committee staff is considerable. Over time, working relations based upon mutual trust can develop since turnover is minimal. When a majority staffer tells his minority counterpart that he will include a particular provision in the chairman's mark of the bill, there is no doubt that the majority staffer will keep his word. If party control in the Senate flips the following year, reciprocal courtesy is standard operating procedure.

In addition to the seating arrangements, committee staffers conduct routine business in a bipartisan fashion. For example, staffers travel together on trips. This increases comity among staff and lessens the likelihood of open disagreements. Furthermore, when the Pentagon provides briefings to committee staff, both the majority and minority often attend the same meeting. This enables both sides of the aisle to hear the same information and responses. The sheer amount of time spent with each other also enables a strong working relationship. A former MLA recalled, "Staff is together so much of the time; I think that's important. Starting in February, you're together with these people all the time. Other committees in the Senate—that just wasn't the case. You got a perspective with SASC that you didn't get with other committees. It was a team effort in SASC" (interview with Bradford Foley, February 11, 2011).

Collegiality was similarly exercised on the MLA level. A bipartisan group of MLAs often met after work to discuss issues of importance and plan trips together. MLAs also trust committee staff from both parties to work with them in crafting the NDAA. One MLA remarked, "SASC is very transparent. They [committee staff] may not agree with you all the time, but they will tell you what's going on. On other committees, they don't want you to talk to the other side's professional staff. But I always talk to minority professional staff in addition to the majority. You don't cross a line, but there's a sense of open communication" (interview with Senate staffer, February 1, 2011). The trusting relationships between MLAs and committee staff help to facilitate substantive hearings in the early part of the process and, even more important, a smooth and efficient committee markup later in the year. Often, committee staff cannot accept the amendments submitted by MLAs for markup as prepared, but commit to working with them to craft compromise language that can be included in the bill as it moves out of committee. That commitment to working with personal office staff routinely on a bipartisan basis helps prevent the bill from stalling and keeps it moving toward Senate floor consideration.

Closed Markup

A key difference in the operations of the Senate Armed Services Committee's markup process compared to that of the House is the practice of conducting a closed markup of the NDAA. Only senators and staff holding an appropriate security clearance can attend. It is important to clarify that the decisions made in markup are not classified, but the discussions and the debate concerning such decisions can involve classified information.

In the days before the markup, SASC staffers provide detailed briefing books to senators on the committee and their MLAs. The information contained in the briefing books is under a strict embargo. MLAs must analyze the information in the mark and then report back to their bosses about proposed amendments or specific provisions of interest in the draft. The advantage of keeping the draft embargoed is that when markup begins, only a small number of staff and the senators on the committee actually know about the contents and the possible points of contention or debate. During the markup process, lobbyists and reporters are kept at a distance. Usually, the chair and the ranking member stress to staff at the beginning of the full committee markup the importance of confidentiality during the committee's deliberations. Leaks to the press or interest groups are taboo and considered unprofessional.

The closed nature of the markup enables the committee to move from unclassified to classified deliberations with rapidity and ease. If classified information, or occasionally industry proprietary information, is pertinent to a particular provision of the bill that is being considered during markup, the committee can discuss such details since all staffers who work the markup have the necessary security clearances. The decisions made during the markup, however, are not classified and are available to the public after completion.

Most committee staffers and MLAs agree that the closed markup in SASC results in a more efficient and candid policymaking process. Without reporters or lobbyists in the room, senators are free to debate difficult decisions and make deals without the pressures to posture or conform to narrow ideological or parochial views. If a provision is discussed in markup, it usually means that the committee staffers were unable to resolve differences on that provision prior to the mark. Or it could mean that the chair's preference on a provision differs from that of others on the committee. Consequently, it is then up to the senators, along with the assistance of the committee staff and MLAs, to come up with a compromise solution or a way forward. When dealing with weapons systems and military procurement, these decisions often have parochial and political consequences for senators on the committee. The closed markup allows senators with those concerns to sometimes craft a deal with others on the committee that would have been politically impossible if lobbyists or reporters had been present. Compromise often requires some degree of anonymity, and certainly the closed markup in SASC is testimony to that reality.

In the past several years, several senators on SASC have tried to change the closed markup process for the NDAA. They argue that an open process would be beneficial, pointing to the fact that the House Armed Services Committee does not close its markup of the NDAA. One staffer commented, "If it were open, the earmarkers would have to defend their requests in a public way. Some of the pork might be less. When we debate issues such as the future of a big weapons system, you couldn't be so parochial about it during an open session" (interview with Senate staffer, February 4, 2011).

Although a minority of senators supports moving from a closed to open markup, each year the proponents of an open process gain more traction. The most recent NDAA markup in the Senate broke from tradition. At the Readiness and Management Support subcommittee markup for the fiscal year 2012 NDAA, the portion of the legislation relevant to that subcommittee was considered in open session, although all other subcommittees and the full committee continued their procedures in closed session. One committee staffer theorized that moving to an open process in full committee is probably inevitable (interview with Senate staffer, December 29, 2010). Others are highly skeptical about the benefits of an open process. While increased transparency is certainly valued, many believe an open process would undermine vigorous and frank debate, and also frustrate compromise and bipartisanship. Furthermore, an open markup could have unintended consequences, such as pushing crucial decisions back to the proverbial smoke-filled room. A former SASC staff director explained, "Senate Armed Services has never had an open markup, and I'm proud of that. The Department of Defense is still standing. Why should we do it in the open? It would wreck the seriousness of the purpose. Staff needs to give candid views to senators, and you can't do that in open session. Governing in the sunshine shouldn't be applied to everything. In the House, open markup forces cutting deals behind closed doors" (interview with Arnold Punaro, March 10, 2011).

Another argument focuses on efficiency. Whereas the entire markup process is usually completed in one week, there is general agreement that an open process would extend markup considerably. One MLA remarked that the two-day full committee markup could last for more than two weeks if it was opened to the public (interview with Senate staffer, January 20, 2011). Another staffer concurred: "The effect of the closed session is that the lobbyists don't know about the bill until it comes out. Coming up with a deal is a lot harder when an amendment is made public and circulates all over this town" (interview with Senate staffer, January 13, 2011).

Pushing It to the Limit: "Don't Ask, Don't Tell" and the Fiscal Year 2011 NDAA

Pressure to end the military ban on openly gay service members intensified after the 2008 presidential election. Candidate Barack Obama promised pub-licly during the campaign that he would end the Clinton-era practice of "Don't Ask, Don't Tell" (DADT) and support subsequent integration. By 2010, gay rights groups started to pressure the Obama administration for action on the issue. The president responded by including a statement of support for repeal in his 2010 State of the Union address. Soon thereafter, the chairman of the joint chiefs of staff, Admiral Mike Mullen, told the president he would support DADT repeal at an upcoming Senate hearing. During his opening statement, Mullen testified that DADT "forces young men and women to lie about who they are in order to defend their fellow citizens." He continued, "For me, per-sonally, it comes down to integrity" (Senate Committee on Armed Services 2010a). At the hearing, Mullen also revealed that a Pentagon report analyzing the impact of repealing the ban was scheduled for completion in December. After digesting the report, the plan was for Congress to move legislation re-pealing DADT in 2011 (Ambinder 2010).

However, political realities prevented a smooth execution of the plan. It soon became apparent that the Republicans had a good chance of taking control of the House in the upcoming election. The change in party control would make it nearly impossible to move a repeal of DADT in the upcoming 112th Congress. The House moved quickly, passing repeal language as a floor amendment to the NDAA in late May. On the same day, Senator Joe Lieber-man successfully offered an amendment in the closed full committee markup of the fiscal year 2011 NDAA to add DADT repeal language to the bill. The amendment was adopted by a vote of sixteen to twelve; SASC later approved its version of the NDAA with a vote of eighteen to ten (Senate Committee on Armed Services 2010b). For a bill that routinely garners unanimous or near unanimous support moving out of committee, the split support in markup indicated that floor adoption would be difficult.

Republicans organized a filibuster against the fiscal year 2011 NDAA, preventing Senate floor debate from moving forward on the bill. Due to a lack of support for DADT repeal and controversy surrounding the more restrictive NDAA amendment process proposed by Majority Leader Harry Reid, a cloture vote on the motion to proceed, requiring the support of sixty senators, failed on September 21, 2010, by a vote of fifty-six to forty-three.[7] At this point, passage of the fiscal year 2011 NDAA appeared unlikely. Since the bill had never proceeded to floor consideration, no senators had benefited from the opportunity to offer amendments to the NDAA, as had been routinely the case. With a long recess before the November election and the majority leader's legislative priorities focused elsewhere, the only chance of NDAA passage was during the lame-duck session (interview with Senate staff, January 20, 2011). The normal two-week floor process for the NDAA, which typically allows all senators to file amendments to the bill, seemed out of the question in an abbreviated lame-duck session. Given the opposition to the repeal of DADT and the proposed restrictions on the number of amendments that would be considered, the bill's passage seemed doomed.

However, the bill's prospects changed rapidly when the Pentagon released a survey of military service members on November 30. Its release was followed by two days of hearings in SASC on the report. While both proponents and opponents of the repeal cited findings that supported their own arguments, the survey showed that more than two-thirds of service members did not oppose openly gay men and women from serving in the military (Senate Committee on Armed Services 2010c). Those who supported the repeal of DADT believed that this finding would enable passage before adjournment. Nonetheless, when another cloture vote on the motion to proceed was taken, the tally fell three votes short of the required sixty needed to proceed to consideration of the NDAA on the floor.[8]

Senator Lieberman and Senator Susan Collins decided to file stand-alone repeal legislation. Besides the inclusion of the DADT repeal language, the fiscal year 2011 NDAA had been fraught with controversy concerning the process for considering amendments, and also contained a controversial provision concerning abortions in military hospitals. Senators Collins and Lieberman believed that if they could secure a vote before adjournment on the stand-alone repeal, they stood a better chance for passage. Also, using a separate legislative vehicle for DADT repeal would give the NDAA a better chance to move forward.

The strategic maneuvering enabled the repeal of DADT to pass the Senate on December 18 with a vote of sixty-five to thirty-one.[9] Even though the controversy over DADT had been removed from consideration of the fiscal year 2011 NDAA, there was very little time left before the adjournment of the 111th Congress (2009–2010). The only way forward was a last-ditch effort to pass the NDAA by unanimous consent (UC) on the Senate floor. The fact that the NDAA's survival relied upon the ability to secure support from every senator was astonishing.

Bills that pass the Senate under UC are usually uncontroversial bills with limited scope. The NDAA's final passage had never been secured in this manner.

Realizing this might become their only option, SASC staff had begun to work with House Democrats weeks earlier to prepare a stripped down version of the NDAA. All controversial provisions, including the language that would have allowed privately funded abortions in military hospitals, were removed. The danger of moving the NDAA by UC on the Senate floor was that any senator could object and prevent passage. Working closely with the Republicans in the Senate, SASC Chair Carl Levin moved toward crafting a bill that he believed would not raise an objection to a motion to move the bill by UC. On December 22, the fiscal year 2011 NDAA passed the Senate by unanimous consent. The exchange on the floor between Chair Carl Levin and Ranking Member John McCain in the *Congressional Record* is noteworthy. In their statements, both senators comment on the unorthodox procedural scenario required for the bill's passage:

Mr. LEVIN: Mr. President, in legislative session and in morning business, I ask unanimous consent that the Senate proceed to the immediate consideration of Calendar No. 717, H.R. 6523, the Department of Defense authorization bill, that a Levin-McCain amendment that is at the desk be agreed to, the bill, as amended, be read the third time and passed, the motions to reconsider be laid upon the table, with no intervening action or debate, and that any statements related to the bill be printed in the *Record*.

The ACTING PRESIDENT pro tempore: Is there objection?

Mr. McCAIN: Reserving the right to object, and I will not object, a lot of people may not understand that unanimous consent request that was just made by the chairman of the Armed Services Committee.

Am I correct, I ask my friend from Michigan, that this is in order to pass the National Defense Authorization Act? We have gone, I believe, 48 years and passed one, and there are vital programs, policies, and pay raises for the men and women in the military and other policy matters that are vital to successfully carrying out the two wars we are in and providing the men and women who are serving with the best possible equipment and capabilities to win those conflicts. Am I correct in assuming that is what this agreement is about?

Mr. LEVIN: The Senator from Arizona is correct. It is the bill—slightly reduced to eliminate some of the controversial provisions, which would have prevented us from getting to this point, but this is the Defense authorization bill, and 90 to 95 percent of the bill is the bill we worked so hard on in committee on a bipartisan basis. I am very certain that our men and women in uniform, as this Christmas season comes upon us, will be very grateful indeed that we did this in the 49th year—and if the House will move swiftly today and pass this bill, as we have done in the previous 48 years—passed an authorization bill—which is so essential to their success.

Mr. McCAIN: I will not object.[10]

Although the Senate had to resort to unconventional mechanisms, even the controversy generated by the repeal of "Don't Ask, Don't Tell" was unable to derail passage of the fiscal year 2011 NDAA. The factors that enabled passage of previous NDAAs played an important role. In particular, when it came down to the final days before adjournment and it was apparent that the bill could only move through the Senate by UC, staff needed to rely upon trusted relationships to make the negotiations work. The precarious nature of the situation can be appreciated in the words of one committee staffer, "When it goes to UC, you only have relationships and trust. The staff had to trust each other to put it together in the end" (interview with Senate staffer, January 4, 2011). Another staffer close to the negotiations called it a "Hail Mary pass" (interview with Senate staffer, January 13, 2011). Nonetheless, the persistence of the senators on SASC and committee staff mattered, because no one wanted the bill to fail in the end. "A sense of pride" in the passage of the NDAA helped to carry the day (interview with Senate staffer, January 13, 2011). Committee leadership also worked diligently to ensure final passage on a carefully negotiated, albeit pared down, bill. One staffer described Senators Levin and McCain as demonstrating "a desire and willingness to put the needs of the institution, of defense, of our service members, and the legacy of the committee, ahead of their own needs" (interview with Senate staffer, December 29, 2010).

The difficult passage of the fiscal year 2011 NDAA, however, forces hard thinking about the fate of future defense authorization bills. The controversy surrounding the fiscal year 2011 bill either solidifies the strength of the process used to pass the annual NDAA, or serves as an ominous indicator that yearly passage of the defense bill is surviving on borrowed time. Was the fiscal year 2011 bill and DADT the straw that broke the camel's back, or the straw that demonstrated the camel's strength?

Conclusion

It seems as though the answer to this question depends heavily on perspective. Staff involved currently or recently in the production of the annual NDAA diverged widely when asked about the future of defense authorization. One former staffer concluded, "I'm pessimistic about the future. What happened last year wasn't really a complete bill. If they can't return to full debate on the floor, the Senate is going to lose it [the NDAA] for a few years" (interview with Greg Kiley, March 8, 2011). A current staffer was more optimistic: "I honestly think we've weathered the worst. I could be wrong about that, but as I look to the new year, I think we'll have the same goal as we do every year—completing our bill to help the men and women in uniform" (interview with Senate staffer, December 29, 2010). Yet another staffer took a middle-of-the-road approach, concluding that the momentum for future defense authorization bills "may be slowly eroding" (interview with Senate staffer, January 6, 2011).

Overall, there is a sense that the past several years could be aberrations. There is considerable hope that the Senate can return to regular order when considering the NDAA in future years. Nonetheless, one certainty remains without question. Despite larger political forces that may conspire against it, the Senate Armed Services Committee is not planning to change the way it does business. Within the committee, bipartisan procedures and processes will continue as the mechanism for producing an annual defense authorization bill.

A harder question to answer is whether the SASC approach can be applied to other authorizing committees in the Senate. The four main explanations for SASC's success in producing an annual defense bill each year can be examined in turn. Perhaps the most important ingredient is bipartisanship. Such bipartisanship is displayed on a number of levels—among senators, committee staffers, and those who work in personal offices for senators on SASC. The issue of defense is also inherently bipartisan. The culture of bipartisanship among the people who work on the NDAA is a product of history and shared philosophy. For decades, staffers from both parties who work on the NDAA have considered themselves a unified entity. It would be difficult to replicate this culture in other committees where partisanship and an "us versus them" mentality are more pervasive. Of course, nothing prevents other committees from trying to adopt or mimic bipartisan practices, such as regularly traveling together on trips or receiving joint executive branch briefings. Personal office staff can also reach across party lines by creating their own ad hoc groups of legislative assistants to meet and discuss relevant committee business and upcoming policy debates. Current and former SASC staff credit the lineage of strong committee chairmen and staff directors for the bipartisan culture that has developed and persevered. This indicates that other Senate committees would need their top leadership to mimic SASC's bipartisan customs and invest considerable time in replicating them.

SASC utilizes a routine process to pass the NDAA each year, beginning with the construction of a robust hearing record that serves to inform the bill's composition. SASC focuses primarily on the passage of one bill each year, although certainly additional activities (particularly civilian and military nominations) require time and attention. Other committees may not be able to concentrate their efforts on the passage of a single bill. However, committees could adopt a more structured approach to hearings and attempt to replicate their legislative processes in a more predictable manner. Other committees could also choose, upon occasion, to focus solely on the drafting of one specific bill. When doing this, adopting some of the processes utilized by SASC may be possible, such as using the bipartisan "building-block" approach to craft the chairman's mark.

The closed full committee markup in SASC is the least likely practice that could be replicated in other Senate committees. Since classified information is sometimes discussed and debated during the NDAA markup, SASC is allowed to close its markup. Rule 26 of the Standing Rules of the Senate requires open committee meetings, except when a committee is scheduled to discuss matters in which national security, law enforcement, finance, or governmental security would be compromised. Other committees do not routinely require closed sessions. However, committees could arrange meetings between key senators prior to an open markup if committee staff could identify issues of contention. At those smaller, unofficial meetings, senators could perhaps move toward finding compromises that would result in a bill more amenable to a larger voting bloc on the committee.

The Senate's continued passage of the NDAA may represent the institution's last best hope. Several scholars, such as Tom Mann and Norm Ornstein (2006) in *The Broken Branch*, have acutely diagnosed what is wrong with Congress. But exposing Congress's flaws is only half the solution. Figuring out how to improve legislative debate in Congress also requires careful analysis to determine what is working well in Congress. Descriptions of Congress's demise are just one part of the story. The Senate Armed Services Committee's failsafe production of the NDAA presents an alternative to such pessimism and may provide a ray of hope for the future of Congress and legislative deliberation.

Notes

1. These interviews were completed during non-duty Library of Congress status.
2. There are some technical aspects of the NDAA that contribute to its "must-pass" status. For example, military construction projects must be authorized before funds can be expended. Also, military pay tables, which provide pay raises to service members, must be authorized. However, nothing prevents Congress from passing a short bill that makes these authorizations and achieves nothing else legislatively. Congress has not adopted this approach. Instead, a comprehensive policy bill is enacted each year.
3. It is worth noting that the author worked on three defense authorization bills (FY2006 through FY2008) as a staffer in the United States Senate, attending closed full committee and several subcommittee markups.
4. The names of current Senate staffers are withheld to preserve anonymity.
5. Two notable exceptions include the Goldwater-Nichols Act in 1986 and Wounded Warrior legislation in 2007.
6. For a different perspective on the House versus the Senate in conference, see James R. Locher, *Victory on the Potomac: The Goldwater-Nichols Act Unifies the Pentagon* (College Station: Texas A&M University Press, 2002), 187.
7. September 21, 2010. Senate roll call vote #238. All Senate roll call votes can be found using the Library of Congress's public legislative search engine, THOMAS. See http://thomas.loc.gov/home/thomas.php.

8. December 9, 2010. Senate roll call vote #270.
9. December 18, 2010. Senate roll call vote #281.
10. Congressional Record, 111th Cong., 2nd sess. December 22, 2010, p. S. 10936.

References

Ambinder, Marc. 2010. "Outing the Debate: An Inside Account of the Struggle to End 'Don't Ask, Don't Tell.'" *National Journal Online*, December 20. www.nationaljournal.com/magazine/the -battle-to-end-don-t-ask-don-t-tell--20101209. Accessed November 28, 2011.

Carsey, Thomas, and Barry Rundquist. 1999. "The Reciprocal Relationship between State Defense Interest and Committee Representation in Congress." *Public Choice* 99:455–63.

Dawson, Raymond H. 1962. "Congressional Innovation and Intervention in Defense Policy: Legislative Authorization of Weapons Systems." *American Political Science Review* 56:42–57.

Fisher, Louis. 2000. *Congressional Abdication on War and Spending.* College Station: Texas A&M University Press.

Fowler, Linda L., and R. Brian Law. 2008a. "Seen but Not Heard: Committee Visibility and Institutional Change in the Senate National Security Committees, 1947–2006." *Legislative Studies Quarterly* 33:357–85.

———. 2008b. "Make Way for the Party: The Rise and Fall of the Senate National Security Committees, 1947–2006." In *Why Not Parties? Party Effects in the United States Senate*, edited by Nathan W. Monroe, Jason M. Roberts, and David W. Rohde, 121–41. Chicago: University of Chicago Press.

Goss, Carol F. 1972. "Military Committee Membership and Defense-Related Benefits in the House of Representatives." *Western Political Quarterly* 31:372–80.

Koger, Gregory. 2010. *Filibustering: A Political History of Obstruction in the House and Senate.* Chicago: University of Chicago Press.

Mann, Thomas E., and Norm J. Ornstein. 2006. *The Broken Branch: How Congress Is Failing America and How to Get It Back on Track.* New York: Oxford University Press.

Price, David. 2011. "The Advantages and Disadvantages of Partisanship." *Boston Review*, May/June. http://bostonreview.net/BR36.3/ndf_david_ price_fixing_congress.php. Accessed September 14, 2011.

Rundquist, Barry, Jungho Rhee, Jeong-Hwa Lee, and Sharon Fox. 1997. "Modeling State Representation on Defense Committees in Congress: 1959–1989." *American Politics Quarterly* 25:35–55.

Senate Committee on Armed Services. U.S. Congress. United States Senate. 1959. *Military Construction Authorization for Military Departments, Fiscal Year 1960.* 86th Cong., 1st sess. S. Rept. 296. May 19. Washington, DC: Government Printing Office.

———. 2010a. *To Receive Testimony Related to the "Don't Ask, Don't Tell" Policy.* 111th Cong., 2nd sess. February 2, 2010. http://armed-services.senate.gov/Webcasts/ 2010/02%20February/ 02-02-10%20Webcast.htm. Accessed June 11, 2011.

———. 2010b. *National Defense Authorization Act for Fiscal Year 2011.* 111th Cong., 2nd sess. S. Rep. 201. June 4. Washington, DC: Government Printing Office.

———. 2010c. *To receive testimony on the report of the Department of Defense Working Group that conducted a comprehensive review of the issues associated with a repeal of section 654 of title 10, United States Code, "Policy Concerning Homosexuality in the Armed Forces."* 111th Cong., 2nd sess. December 2. http://armed-services.senate.gov/testimony.cfm?wit_id=9791&id=4879. Accessed June 11, 2011.

Towell, Pat. 2011. "Congressional Oversight of Defense: A Preliminary Assessment and Outline for Future Research," April 25, 2011. Unpublished manuscript.

11

Filibustering and Partisanship in the Modern Senate

Gregory Koger

I<small>N ANY PARLIAMENTARY SETTING</small>, there is the potential for some legislators to devise a way to drag out the decision-making process for strategic gain. In the American context, we call this *filibustering* or *obstruction* when it occurs on the floor of either chamber of the U.S. Congress or a state legislature, and this practice is currently strongly associated with the U.S. Senate.[1] It is a staple of Senate lore that the practice of filibustering has been tolerated since its earliest days. Yet the filibuster of today is a far cry from the obstruction of the nineteenth century and the first half of the twentieth century (Koger 2010). Today's filibuster requires much less effort. Senators do not consume the time of the chamber with endless speeches or repeated votes on procedural questions; they simply threaten to do so and force the other legislators to overcome a filibuster that never actually happens. Over the last five decades, the number of Senate filibusters has risen dramatically.

This pattern of increasing obstruction since 1960 has coincided with the partisan polarization of the Senate; senators are increasingly likely to vote with their parties and against members of the opposing party (Theriault 2008). While filibustering is not inherently partisan—it has been waged by single legislators, a fraction of one party, or a bipartisan group based on common views—the ability of the minority party to filibuster has led to a unique pattern of partisan interaction in the Senate. The Senate has a set of rules that forces senators to cooperate if they wish to accomplish anything, yet it is more and more difficult for senators to cooperate if doing so means that the other party gains a public relations "win."

This chapter explains how parties propose and contest the legislative agenda in the Senate, with a focus on the ability of the minority party to "veto" majority party proposals. I begin with a discussion of agenda-setting: the goals and strategies of the majority party and the available responses of the minority party. Next, I apply this framework to the Senate and explain how the majority party and minority party in the Senate compete for partisan advantage while they cooperate to run the chamber.

The Calculus of Partisan Agenda-Setting

In order to understand the partisan use of obstruction, we must begin by understanding how party leaders select which issues come up for discussion and action (Sinclair 2006, 258–63). I assume that the primary goal of party leaders is to help their members win reelection and increase their party's share of the chamber (Cox and McCubbins 1993, 2005; Lebo, McGlynn, and Koger 2007; Patty 2008). Individual legislators may have a broader set of goals, including making good public policy and advancing their careers inside and outside of their chamber, but it is fair to assume that they cooperate as parties to extend their careers and retain or gain majority party status. In preparation for the next election, each party strives to enhance its collective reputation, or *brand*.

Figure 11.1 illustrates one measure of the party brand, the average Democratic advantage (or deficit) on the generic ballot question from December 2008 to June 2011. The generic ballot question is some form of "if the Congressional election were held today, would you vote for the Republican or the Democrat?" Figure 11.1 displays the mean Democratic percentage minus mean Republican percentage per month, using polls aggregated by www.realclearpolitics.com.[2]

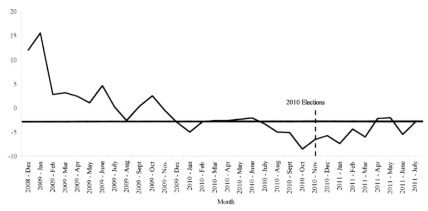

FIGURE 11.1
Democratic Party Advantage in Generic Ballot Polls

One main point of figure 11.1 is that the prospects of congressional parties vary a great deal. The Democrats began with a large advantage after their victory in the 2008 election, which quickly faded about a month into the 111th Congress (2009–2011). To some extent, the congressional Democrats probably suffered because voters held them responsible for the lagging economy, but the major shifts in approval from month to month suggest that public opinion is also responding to congressional actions on major legislation, nominations, scandals, or other events. For this reason, party leaders pay close attention to the issues that come before their chambers.

The Agenda-Setting Strategy of the Majority Party

Majority party leaders have three agenda-setting strategies. First, they try to help party members develop a portfolio of issue positions and personal accomplishments to help during reelection campaigns. Second, leaders seek to maintain and expand the coalition of organized groups and demographic subsets of the party. Toward this end, the leaders will introduce legislation to show support for group policies. Third, leaders seek to maximize the reputation or "name brand" of the party so that voters develop long-term loyalties or short-term biases toward their party (Cox and McCubbins 1993; Pope and Woon 2008, 2009), at least on specific issues (Petrocik 1996).

One implication of the first goal is that party leaders may be very selective about which issues come up for a vote, as a vote against a popular proposal or a powerful interest group can be used against party members in the next election cycle. By the same token, the majority party may try to maximize its relative brand advantage over the opposing party by scheduling proposals that are popular, supported by the majority party's coalition, and opposed by some portion of the minority party's base coalition. These "wedge" issues force minority party members to either cast an unpopular vote or disappoint some of their core supporters—perhaps leading to a challenge in their next party primary.[3] Finally, party leaders have an interest in addressing major national problems (e.g., the financial crisis of 2008) and performing basic obligations like appropriating funds for government operations and raising the debt limit to avoid default. Failure to do so could damage the majority party's reputation severely.

The modern U.S. House of Representatives offers a nearly pure case of majority party agenda-setting. Majority party leaders in the House enjoy a set of procedural advantages that enable them to dictate which issues come up, when they will be debated, and which amendments will be allowed. This can lead to much greater efficiency than the Senate, but it also means that major legislation—including the landmark health care reform law of 2009–2010—often passes after a few hours of debate and a single opportunity to amend the bill.

Minority Party Reponses to the Majority's Agenda

The minority party has several options when confronted with strategic agenda-setting by the majority party. The first strategy is to simply try to *defeat* the major proposals of the majority party. If the minority party succeeds, it denies the majority party a legislative success and makes it appear inept—this was the fate of Democrats in 1994 when their attempts to reform the health care system fizzled and failed. The risk of this approach is that the majority party might successfully blame the minority for blocking popular legislation; this criticism is dampened to the extent that the minority persuades majority party members to join the blocking coalition key votes.

Second, the minority party may respond to a popular proposal by the majority party by *raising a counter-issue* as a rhetorical alternative. If the majority party proposed a dramatic increase in spending on behalf of an influential constituency, the minority might respond by calling for a balanced budget amendment (highlighting the effect of the proposal on the federal budget) or campaign finance reform (if the organized interest gains its influence via campaign donations). The minority party may seek to offer its counter-proposal as an alternative agenda item, and failing that it may try to offer its counter-proposal as an amendment to the majority's bill.

Third, the minority party may simply *criticize* the majority's proposal to reduce the political benefits of passing the proposal. This is often the best the minority party can do in the House, and even then the floor time for its criticism may be limited. In extreme cases, the minority party may resort to stunts to attract media attention to its complaints. Alternatively, the minority party may *acquiesce* in the passage of the majority's proposal to avoid the blame for opposing it. This is a fair description of the Democrats' response to President Bush's request for a resolution authorizing the use of force against Iraq in October 2002—members of the party were divided but they did not want to oppose the proposal as a united party. When the minority party acquiesces, however, the lion's share of the credit will probably accrue to the majority party.

Filibustering and Agenda-Setting in the Senate

How does filibustering affect the majority party's efforts to set the agenda? I begin by discussing the basic features of Senate filibustering, then how the minority party uses obstruction to combat the majority party's agenda-setting. Under current rules, the majority party is forced to rely on the goodwill of the minority party, or to appeal its objections to the general public.

Filibustering as a Minority Party Veto

The distinctive feature of the modern Senate is that any senator can threaten to filibuster and it is difficult to overcome such a threat. Historically, the most common response to filibuster was a war of attrition: keeping a bill on the Senate floor continuously until either the obstructionists or the rest of the chamber was too tired to continue. However, during the mid-twentieth century Senate leaders decided that this approach was too costly to be effective, and switched to using the Senate's cloture rule (Koger 2010). This rule—Senate Rule 22—was first adopted in 1917, but rarely used over the next forty years. The cloture rule has always required a supermajority to limit debate (two-thirds of those voting in 1917–1949 and 1959–1975, two-thirds of the entire Senate in 1949–1959, and three-fifths of the entire Senate from 1975 to the present), with a two-thirds requirement for rules changes. It also mandates ample time for consideration: two days must elapse from the time a cloture petition is filed until a cloture vote is taken, and afterward there is guaranteed debate time. Currently, post-cloture debate is limited to thirty hours.

Filibustering is not necessarily a "partisan" tactic. Individual senators have long taken to the floor for solitary filibusters, and the current "hold" system (discussed below) institutionalizes obstruction by individual senators. When there is a broader coalition behind the filibuster, it could be a cross-party group based on ideology or region, or a faction of one party or the other. However, under the current cloture rule the necessary condition for a sustained filibuster is a coalition of forty-one votes against cloture and the parties provide a natural pool of senators with common political interests, a reservoir of trust, and perhaps a willingness to back each other on procedural votes. The more the Senate polarizes along partisan lines (see Theriault 2008), the more it seems that the general right of any forty-one-senator coalition to block legislation and nominations is a de facto minority party veto.[4]

Figure 11.2 traces the increasing partisanship of filibustering since 1969 (Binder and Smith 1997). The line indicates the mean Rice difference scores on cloture votes for each year. Rice difference scores measure the absolute difference in the percent of one party voting for cloture minus the percent of the opposing party voting "aye." Higher difference scores indicate elevated partisanship, with a maximum of 100. In 1969 (a low point for partisanship in Congress) the two parties were, on average, 15.1 percent apart on the two cloture votes held that year. By 2010, the two parties averaged an 80.0 percent difference on fifty-two cloture votes. Indeed, this may *understate* the partisan nature of filibustering in 2010 by including a few consensus votes. The *median* Rice difference score in 2010 was 91.2 percent.

In addition to the overall time trend, another pattern is that cloture partisanship tends to be higher during the first year of a Congress than the second year,

Gregory Koger

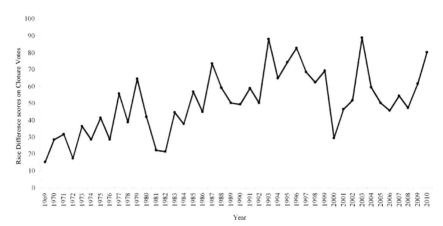

FIGURE 11.2
Average Partisanship on Cloture Votes by Year (mean Rice difference scores on cloture votes)

with the exceptions of 1996, 2002, and 2010, suggesting that legislators are less likely to vote with their parties during election years. Both these patterns are evident in the broader roll call record, but the fact that voting on cloture has become more partisan suggests that the minority party is increasingly likely to see filibustering as a party obligation.

Strategic Obstruction by Senate Minority Parties

The most obvious partisan use of filibustering is to block the majority party's major proposals. By doing so, the minority can limit the number of legislative victories scored by the majority party and foster the impression that the majority is hapless and ineffective. During the 111th Congress, the Senate Republicans blocked major initiatives on immigration reform, climate change and energy policy, and labor unions. In each case (particularly the latter), it is difficult to prove that a simple majority favored a specific proposal since no roll call votes were held, but it is clear that these issues were on the Democratic agenda and that Democratic senators sought to build a cloture-proof supermajority by negotiating with Republican senators. Senator Lindsey Graham was the lone Republican negotiator on climate change and immigration legislation, and his decision to back out of talks was considered a death knell for major policy change on both issues.

Since 1975, the minority party has almost always held enough Senate seats to defeat a cloture vote. During the 111th Congress, the Senate Democrats briefly held sixty seats in the Senate and could conceivably invoke cloture without Republican support. This is how the Democrats passed health care reform in

December 2009. However, as the health care reform bill demonstrated, it can be very difficult to muster every majority party member for a controversial bill. Democratic leaders were forced to "buy" the last few Democratic senators with state-specific provisions. Consequently, a united minority party can almost always block a cloture attempt.

Why, then, does the minority party not always pursue a strategy of pure obstruction? One constraint is that the majority party may successfully draw public attention to a minority party filibuster. While it may be difficult to convince the news media to pay attention to cloture votes, on highly salient issues the majority party can successfully "go public" and portray the minority party as blocking a popular and important proposal using illegitimate tactics (Canes-Wrone 2005; Kernell 2006).[5] When this occurs, the minority party may give in rather than allow its collective reputation to suffer. This was the case when the Senate Republicans initially blocked Democratic attempts to bring up financial reform legislation in the spring of 2010, only to relent as media attention increased and poll results worsened (Koger 2012). Or most of the minority party may hold firm while a few moderate members—perhaps from states that tend to support the opposing party in presidential elections—join the majority party rather than continue with a strategy that could cost them their seats.

While legislators have filibustered to kill individual bills throughout congressional history (Koger 2010), during the current era of polarized parties this tactic may be elevated to an overall strategy. During the 111th Congress, for example, Senate minority leader Senator Mitch McConnell rallied his party around a strategy of blanket opposition to Democratic initiatives and efforts to drag out debate and slow down the chamber to reduce its output (Hulse and Nagourney 2010, A13). For example, during the 2009–2010 health care reform debate the Republicans insisted on using all of the allotted post-cloture debate time, even though much of this time was spent on quorum calls instead of speaking or voting. The Senate floor debate on the banking reform bill was also prolonged several weeks by Republican obstruction against the motion to begin debating the bill, and then by the slow pace of negotiations between Mr. McConnell and Senate Majority Leader Harry Reid over the debate and amendment process (Koger 2012).

For the Democratic majority, these landmark bills were worth the time wasted by Republican foot-dragging. However, there were opportunity costs for this lost floor time (Den Hartog and Monroe 2011). Early on, President Barack Obama and Senator Reid expected that health care reform would pass the Senate by the end of summer or early fall, after which the Senate would debate climate change legislation. Since health care reform did not pass the Senate until December 2009 and another three months were devoted to finalizing the legislation, climate change was delayed until 2010. Senator Reid also planned to bring up climate change legislation (or a broader energy policy bill) after banking reform, but the long debate on banking pushed the energy policy debate into summer 2010, by which time senators were apparently too exhausted—and wary of tackling any more controversial legislation before the November elections—to debate another major issue.

The Republicans' obstruction was even more effective against legislation that was not worth the opportunity cost of overcoming a filibuster. While public attention is typically focused on major legislation, treaties, and nominations for the president's cabinet and the Supreme Court, much of the Senate's agenda is actually composed of less salient legislation and nominations. While these agenda items may be important to the functions of government and some senator's state, they typically do not offer enough political payoff for the majority to overcome an obstructionist minority willing to force multiple cloture votes and use all of its post-cloture debate time. For example, during the 111th Congress, only 36 percent (461 of 722) of bills passed by the House also passed the Senate. Some of these were major bills like climate change legislation, but most were minor bills that were easily blocked by a threat of obstruction or crowded out by lengthy filibusters on major bills. In comparison, the House passed 67 percent (115 of 172) of the bills passed by the Senate.

Less salient bills and nominations make easy prey for threats to filibuster, often referred to as "holds." Formally, a hold is a request by a senator to keep a bill or nomination off the Senate floor while the requesting senator gathers more information, prepares for a floor debate, or returns from travel. A short-term hold is usually quite benign and the delay is a small price to pay for full and informed participation. Senators, however, may ask to keep a measure off the Senate floor indefinitely, backed by a threat to filibuster the measure. Or a senator may hold a measure until he or she is satisfied with the debate agreement for a measure (e.g., if the senator would like a vote on an amendment he or she sponsored). Senators may even place holds on bills or nominations in order to gain bargaining leverage with other senators, executive agencies, or presidents on an entirely different issue. This is an especially useful tactic for minority party senators during periods of unified government. They may use holds to delay nominations in an attempt to force the executive branch to provide information or take some action that it otherwise would not take. In February 2010, for example, Senator Reid's office disclosed that Senator Richard Shelby had placed a hold on all pending nominations (around seventy) in an effort to force the executive branch to commence with two spending projects in Alabama (Wilson and Murray 2010, A3). While this was an extreme case—and a source of embarrassment for Mr. Shelby and Senate Republicans when it came to light—it illustrates how senators can take hostages to gain leverage. The Shelby case also illustrates the constraint on minority party holds: as with filibusters on major bills, the majority party may expose covert filibusters and portray members of the minority party as petty obstructionists working against the public welfare.

Filibustering and Bipartisan Compromise

Instead of trying to block a majority party proposal, the minority party may try to negotiate a bipartisan compromise. This is more likely when defeating the legislation would have a negative impact on the minority party's reputation, or when the national interest would suffer significantly if no legislation were enacted. For example, sooner or later appropriations bills must pass or the government will shut down, so eventually the two parties will agree on compromise funding plans.

While some of these bipartisan deals are worked out while a bill is pending on the Senate floor, many compromises are reached while bills are still in committee or awaiting floor consideration (Sinclair 2006). In the latter cases, the expectation of a possible filibuster provides an incentive for committee chairs and majority party leaders to compromise rather than provoke the inevitable floor fight.

Anecdotally, it seems that it has become more difficult for senators to compromise over the last decade. The fiscal year 2011 appropriations, for example, should have been enacted by October 1, 2010. Instead, the Democrats extended the deadline until after the election and then sought to compromise with the Republican minority in December. Senator McConnell backed out of a reported deal under pressure from conservative Republican senators (Rogers 2010). In the end, the operating budget was not resolved until April 15, 2011—six and a half months into the fiscal year—after seven extensions.

Filibustering and Minority Agenda-Setting

Another strategy the minority party might employ is to filibuster until the Senate votes on a particular minority party proposal. While one commonly thinks of a filibuster as a negative veto to keep proposals from progressing, senators have a long history of filibustering one measure as a "hostage" until the majority agrees to allow a vote on another measure (Koger 2010). In the contemporary polarized Senate, this often takes the form of the minority party insisting on a vote on its "message" proposals—measures that highlight unpopular positions of the majority party and/or promote divisions within the majority party (Evans and Oleszek 2001). This tactic is often used in response to the majority party scheduling its *own* message proposals, so both parties typically engage in a stylized political debate by voting on both message proposals and often shelving both matters (Evans and Oleszek 2001).

One recent example was a Senate vote to repeal the 2010 health care laws. The Senate Republicans insisted on this vote during the debate to reauthorize the

Federal Aviation Administration. While the proposal lost by a vote of forty-seven to fifty-one, the Republicans successfully put the Democrats on record supporting the controversial law while registering their continued opposition (Kim and Lesniewski 2011, 305). More recently, Senate parties sparred over oil policy in the context of rising gas prices and debate over how to reduce government spending. Senate Democrats brought up a bill to eliminate tax breaks for oil companies, and the Republicans responded by trying to bring up a bill to expand offshore oil drilling (Gardner 2011, 1133). Both proposals failed, but both parties got to make their political point. This stands in contrast to the Republican-controlled House of Representatives, which only voted on the offshore oil drilling bill.

Lessons for the Majority Party

The preceding paragraphs sketch a dim prognosis for the Senate majority party. The minority party now possesses a de facto veto over majority party proposals that can be used to block or moderate, or hold proposals hostage to force votes on minority party priorities. In addition to its procedural disadvantage, the Senate majority party is at a significant political disadvantage, as all else being equal, the majority party is often held responsible if the Senate fails to address major policy problems in a timely fashion. The gap between the majority party's public responsibility and parliamentary power enables the minority party to reap political gains by slowing the legislative process in the Senate.

The limit to minority party filibustering—whether of a specific bill or nomination or a general blockade of legislation—is the ability of the majority party to take its frustration to the general public. In response to each of the tactics above, the majority may publicly complain about the minority's obstruction and hold multiple cloture votes to prove how unyielding the minority can be (Sinclair 2006, 283–307). However, just as the president cannot go to the public on every issue that the executive branch considers important, the Senate majority party cannot attract media attention or public sympathy on every filibuster. Usually, only proposals that are intrinsically interesting and popular can be appealed to the general public. For example, in a tacit acknowledgment that the Senate Democrats could have benefited from a better "outside game" during the 111th Congress, they elevated Senator Charles Schumer to coordinate media strategy.

Conclusion

This chapter has explained how filibustering has empowered the minority party in the Senate and, consequently, become a flash point for the struggle between the Republicans and Democrats. To understand this, one must first consider the majority party's agenda-setting strategy: the majority party seeks to manipulate the set of issues that come before the chamber and the manner in which legislation is debated. In the House of Representatives, the minority party is virtually helpless to prevent this manipulation. In the Senate, however, the minority often uses the filibusters to ensure that its procedural rights are respected and its policy proposals are debated.

Needless to say, this competition over the agenda in the Senate leads to great tension. Members of the majority party and their supporters are keenly aware that the general public will hold the majority responsible if the Senate fails to enact legislation in a timely manner. This tension increases when the minority party uses its veto power for the *political* goal of depriving the majority party of a "win" rather than out of sincere policy concerns or to ensure a fair debate.

One offshoot of this tension is the call for cloture reform, including the abolition of filibustering completely. Critics of the contemporary Senate claim that, if the minority party is going to behave like a parliamentary party by voting with perfect cohesion, the majority should demand, and seize for itself, the strong procedural powers of a parliamentary majority. This view does not currently enjoy the support of a majority of the Senate, although this could change if the Senate becomes more dysfunctional in the future. In the meantime, senators seem willing to try to keep working in a polarized body with a set of rules that give power to both parties.

Notes

1. During the nineteenth century, filibustering was prevalent in the U.S. House, and has occurred in dozens of state and foreign legislatures.

2. For the raw poll data, see "Congressional Job Approval," *Real Clear Politics*, http://www.realclearpolitics.com/epolls/other/congressional_job_approval-903.html (accessed July 8, 2011).

3. However, in the interest of coalition maintenance a majority party may advance controversial legislation that is demanded by a core constituency as a condition of its support in the next election. During the 111th Congress, this dynamic played out as Latino and business leaders sought comprehensive immigration reform and labor union leaders insisted that passage of the Employee Free Choice Act was the reward for their support during the 2008 election.

4. This does not mean, however, that the polarization of the Senate has "caused" the increase in filibustering over the last fifty years. The Senate has experienced a similar period of high partisanship while obstruction remained low; a better explanation for the recent surge in filibustering is that the costs of obstruction have decreased because the majority does not have enough time to challenge threats to obstruct (Koger 2010).

5. Filibustering is "illegitimate" in the sense of "contrary to default norms of democratic decision-making"; while there are sophisticated arguments for tolerating obstruction (Koger 2010, chapter 9), many citizens may consider the Senate's rules an unexplained deviation from the norm of majority rule.

References

Binder, Sarah A., and Steven S. Smith. 1997. *Politics or Principle? Filibustering in the U.S. Senate.* Washington, DC: Brookings Institution Press.
Canes-Wrone, Brandice. 2005. *Who Leads Whom? Presidents, Policy, and the Public.* Chicago: University of Chicago Press.
Cox, Gary W., and Mathew D. McCubbins. 1993. *Legislative Leviathan.* Berkeley and Los Angeles: University of California Press.
———. 2005. *Setting the Agenda: Responsible Party Government in the U.S. House of Representatives.* New York: Cambridge University Press.
Den Hartog, Chris, and Nathan Monroe. 2011. *Agenda Setting in the U.S. Senate: Costly Consideration and Majority Party Advantage.* New York: Cambridge University Press.
Evans, C. Lawrence, and Walter Oleszek. 2001. "The Procedural Context of Senate Deliberation." In *The Contentious Senate: Partisanship, Ideology, and the Myth of Cool Judgment,* edited by Colton C. Campbell and Nicol C. Rae, 107–27. New York: Rowman & Littlefield.
Gardner, Lauren. 2011. "In Test Votes, Senate Backs Oil Subsidy But Rejects Expanded Offshore Drilling." *Congressional Quarterly Weekly Report,* May 23.
Hulse, Carl, and Adam Nagourney. 2010. "Senate G.O.P. Leader Finds Weapon in Unity." *New York Times,* March 17.
Kernell, Samuel. 2006. *Going Public: New Strategies of Presidential Leadership.* 4th ed. Washington, DC: CQ Press.
Kim, Anne, and Niels Lesniewski. 2011. "Democrats Stick Together to Stop Health Care Law Repeal." *Congressional Quarterly Weekly Report,* February 7.
Koger, Gregory. 2010. *Filibustering: A Political History of Obstruction in the House and Senate.* Chicago: University of Chicago Press.
———. 2012. "The Filibuster Then and Now: Civil Rights in the 1960s and Health Care, 2009–10." In *From Delay to Dysfunction: The U.S. Senate, 1960–2010,* edited by Burdette A. Loomis, 159–77. Washington, DC: CQ Press.
Lebo, Matthew J., Adam J. McGlynn, and Gregory Koger. 2007. "Strategic Party Government: Party Influence in Congress, 1789–2000." *American Journal of Political Science* 51:464–81.
Patty, John W. 2008. "Equilibrium Party Government." *American Journal of Political Science* 52:636–55.
Petrocik, John. 1996. "Issue Ownership in Presidential Elections, with a 1980 Case Study." *American Journal of Political Science* 40:825–50.
Pope, Jeremy C., and Jonathan Woon. 2008. "Made in Congress? Testing the Electoral Implications of Party Ideological Brand Names." *Journal of Politics* 70:823–36.
———. 2009. "Measuring Changes in American Party Reputations, 1939–2004." *Political Research Quarterly* 62:653–61.
Rogers, David. 2011. "McConnell with Tea Party on Budget." *Politico,* December 16. http://dyn.politico.com/members/forums/thread.cfm?catid=1&subcatid=1&threadid=4861999. Accessed July 6, 2011.
Sinclair, Barbara. 2006. *Party Wars: Polarization and the Politics of National Policy Making.* Norman: University of Oklahoma Press.
Theriault, Sean M. 2008. *Party Polarization in Congress.* New York: Cambridge University Press.
Wilson, Scott, and Shailagh Murray. 2010. "Sen. Richard Shelby of Alabama Holding Up Obama Nominees for Home-State Pork." *Washington Post,* February 6.

Section IV

LEGISLATIVE RECONCILIATION BETWEEN THE CHAMBERS

12

Ping Pong and Other Congressional Pursuits

Party Leaders and Post-Passage Procedural Choice

Barbara Sinclair

F OR A BILL TO BECOME LAW in a bicameral system, the two chambers must agree on identical language. Bicameralism can be shown as a consequence to have a status quo bias (Tsebelis and Money 1997). When, as is the case for the U.S. Congress, the chambers have differently constituted memberships, starkly different rules, and are nevertheless equal in power, that status quo bias should be especially strong.

The U.S. Congress has, in fact, often been accused of having a severe status quo bias (Krehbiel 1998; Binder 2003; Brady and Volden 2005). Many argue that the increase in partisan polarization in the last several decades has exacerbated Congress's tendency toward gridlock (Nivola and Brady 2008). One might then expect that the problem bicameralism presents for successful legislating would generally arise at the inter-chamber resolution stage; that is, it is after each chamber has passed its bill and the chambers seek to resolve their differences that the difficulties manifest themselves. And further, one might expect that resolution procedures have become less effective in the recent, more partisan period.

Yet most congressional insiders will tell you that, once a bill has passed both chambers, the prospects of inter-chamber agreement are considerably higher than a naive bicameralism theory would lead one to expect. For one thing, by that point a great many members have a stake in the legislation's success; for another, the legislation has surmounted a considerable number of obstacles. Congressional scholars have increasingly come to understand that Congress adapts its institutional and procedural arrangements so as to make it possible for its members to advance their goals, which, most scholars believe, include legislative success. From that perspective, we would expect that if traditional inter-chamber resolution procedures become less effective (due, for example, to heightened partisan polarization), other procedures might well be developed.

This chapter focuses on inter-chamber resolution processes in the U.S. Congress and on how they have changed in recent times. I first review evidence showing that, in fact, the House and Senate almost always do resolve their differences on legislation that has passed both chambers. I then show that the mix of procedures used to resolve inter-chamber differences on major legislation has changed significantly in recent years. These changes, I argue, are the result of the majority party leaderships' adaptation to changed circumstances; specifically, in their quest to satisfy their members' legislative goals in an altered political environment, majority party leaders found that they needed to involve themselves in the post-passage process more deeply and frequently and discovered that resolution procedures other than the traditional conference were often most effective for meeting their objectives. I substantiate my argument by developing and testing hypotheses about the sort of major measures on which one would expect alternative procedures to be used and by examining a number of illuminating examples.

The Frequency of Agreement

A naive bicameralism theory might posit that reaching inter-cameral agreement on legislation passed by both chambers presents a major barrier to enactment. After all, two chambers with differently constituted memberships and different rules can often be expected to pass quite different versions of a bill. On the other hand, legislators in the two chambers do not work in isolation from one another. As Elizabeth Rybicki (2007), a prominent student of the post-passage process, has argued, busy legislators are unlikely to spend their scarce time passing legislation on which inter-chamber agreement is perceived as unlikely. Further, a great many legislators have a considerable investment in a bill that has passed both chambers and thus are likely to be willing to expend further effort to bring it to a successful conclusion.

The most extensive data series on post-passage agreement of which I am aware is that of Elizabeth Rybicki (2003), who examines all public measures that passed both chambers for selected congresses from the 34th (1855–1857) through the 106th (1999–2000). Examining the proportion of public measures on which differences were not resolved, she finds some variation over time but around a low mean; that proportion never reaches 7 percent and in most of the congresses examined is below 4 percent.

These data demonstrate that the naive bicameral theory is wrong in the case of all legislation. Of special interest here, however, is major legislation that most members and the party leadership would care about and that might well present special problems. For this and most of the subsequent analysis, I use a dataset of major measures that I have developed.

My cases are the major measures considered during a Congress as defined by the list of major legislation in the *CQ Weekly* (before 1998 the *Congressional Quarterly Weekly Report*), augmented by those measures on which key votes occurred (again according to the *CQ Weekly*).[1] This definition yields for each Congress between forty and sixty bills (and some other measures such as budget resolutions) that close contemporary observers considered major. The dataset consists of such major legislation for sixteen congresses from the early 1960s (87th Congress, 1961–1962) through the 2000s (111th Congress, 2009–2010).[2] The number of cases is 814.

Of these 814 measures, 601 (73.8 percent) passed both chambers. The House and Senate failed to resolve their differences on 5.8 percent of these 601. Clearly the likelihood of resolution is not very different on major legislation than it is on all public bills. The hypothesis that resolution has become more difficult in the period of high partisan polarization does receive some support in these data; the rate of successful resolution is on average lower in the congresses of the 1990s and later than in the earlier congresses. Thus, for the selected congresses from the 87th though the 101st (1961–1990), the chambers failed to resolve their differences on 4 percent of the major measures; for the congresses from the 103rd through the 110th (1993–2008), failures double to 8 percent. Still, in absolute terms, the likelihood that a major bill passes both chambers and then fails because the House and Senate do not resolve their differences is low.

Two of the congresses in the dataset—the 97th (1981–1982) and the 107th (2001–2002) after Senator Jim Jeffords switched parties in early June 2001—saw split control of the House and Senate. It is in these that we would expect the greatest problems in reaching inter-chamber agreement. In fact, the proportion of major bills that passed both chambers in the 107th (69 percent) is considerably lower than the proportion (80 percent) that did for the other, non-split-control congresses. But once legislation did pass both chambers in the 107th Congress, differences between the chambers were even more likely to be successfully resolved (100 percent versus 95 percent). In the later, highly partisan period, the proportion of major measures that pass both chambers is considerably lower than in the less partisan preceding period, but there is no difference between the 107th (post-Jeffords switch) and the non-split-control congresses (68 percent versus 69 percent). Differences between the chambers were a bit less likely to be resolved in the 107th—11.1 percent failed—than in the other partisan congresses (7.7 percent), but, again, the proportion of failures at this stage is relatively small.

The Mechanisms for Resolving Differences

As any Congress text will explain, a number of alternative ways of reconciling House-Senate differences are available. One chamber can simply accept the other chamber's version of the legislation. Another procedure based on amendments between the chambers entails a kind of public bargaining back and forth: one chamber passes its bill and sends it to the other as an amendment to a bill that house has passed; that chamber then can accept the amendment or send it back with an amendment. Finally, a conference committee of members from both chambers can be appointed and charged with coming up with a compromise, which is then taken back to both chambers for approval.

Although typically most attention is given to the conference process, other procedures are used much more frequently. By far the most common way of "getting one bill" is by one chamber adopting the other's language. Data for selected congresses from the 1980s through the mid-2000s show that, usually, on over 70 percent of all public laws, this occurred (Oleszek 1996, 273; Oleszek 2008, 4; cq.com, January 5, 2009, 19). Amendments between the chambers—the so-called "ping pong" method—were used on average for 17 percent of all measures, with the range being from a low of 11 percent in the 108th (2003–2004) to a high of 24 percent in the 103rd (1993–1994) (cq.com). As these figures make clear, a conference committee is the least often used procedure; on average, for these congresses, only 8.2 percent of public laws went through conference.

The conference procedure receives so much attention because of the type of legislation on which conferences are used to resolve differences. Major legislation that is complex and contentious is much more likely to be sent to conference for resolution than the average bill. Of the 601 major measures in my dataset that passed both chambers, 64 percent were sent to conference and the differences between the chambers were successfully resolved.[3]

The rules governing the consideration of conference reports and those governing amendments between the chambers differ, most importantly in the Senate. Conference reports are subject to points of order on "airdrops" (earmarks inserted at the post-passage stage) and on scope (that the agreement goes beyond the scope of the differences between the House and Senate bills); amendments between the chambers are not. House amendments to Senate bills are privileged in the Senate, so no filibuster on the motion to proceed is possible; thus, the parliamentary situation is no worse than for conference reports, which are also privileged. A potential disadvantage to using amendments between the chambers rather than conference committees is that, while conference reports are not subject to amendment, House amendments to Senate bills are. However, the Senate majority leader can "fill the amendment tree" (that is, using his right of first recognition, offer amendments in all the parliamentarily permissible slots) and, if he has sixty votes to invoke cloture, prevent amendments. Majority Leader Frist employed this maneuver twice during the 109th Congress, seemingly the first time it had been employed. Majority Leader Reid used it eight times in the 110th, on major bills such as the reauthorization of the State Children's Health Insurance Program (SCHIP), the ethics reform bill, and the energy bill (Beth et al. 2009, 16).

TABLE 12.1
Resolution Procedures and How They Have Changed

Resolution Procedure	All Congresses	87th–105th	107th–111th
Total Major Measures passed by both chambers on which differences successfully resolved (N)	567	400	167
% Conference	68	79	43
Type of Alternative Procedures			
House and Senate pass same bill (percent of alternative procedures)	47	48	46
Amendments between the chambers	43	45	41
Informal agreement, inserted in another bill	10	7	13
Major Measures successfully resolved by alternative procedures (N)	180	85	95

Source: Compiled by the author

The frequency of the traditional conference procedure for major legislation has declined in recent years. Table 12.1 shows that conferences have been used considerably less often on major legislation in the period after 2000 than they were in the preceding period. In fact, the frequency of conferences decreases over the course of the decade; it is 50 percent in the last of the Republican-controlled congresses and averages only 25 percent in the two Democratic-controlled congresses. The data for all public laws show the same trend, but less clearly, because major bills are overwhelmed by the large but variable number of more minor bills.

By the early 2000s, partisan polarization is well advanced. I have used the early 1990s (103rd Congress) as the beginning of the era of high polarization in the past when a convenient two-part categorization was needed. However, the decline in the frequency of conferences comes quite distinctly with the 107th Congress (2001–2002) and that cut point is used here.[4] In terms of the frequency of conferences, the two split-control congresses are far more similar to the other congresses in their era than to each other; in fact, the 97th Congress used conferences—in every case successfully—on 85 percent of the measures that passed both chambers, a higher percentage than the other congresses of its era. The 107th Congress successfully used conferences on 54 percent (and unsuccessfully on 7.7 percent). The increased partisan polarization seems more influential than split control in terms of the phenomena under consideration here.

When conferences are not used, how are differences between the chambers on major legislation resolved? Beginning with the Congressional Research Service's categories that mirror the conventional description of resolution mechanisms, I examined in more detail resolution procedures on the major measures that passed both chambers and were resolved via a process other than conference. I found that to provide an accurate picture of what actually—as opposed to formally—happens to legislation, an additional mechanism needed to be added. In some cases, an agreement is reached through informal processes and the legislative language is put into a different bill altogether, which then becomes law (Rybicki 2003). Furthermore, the category "simple adoption by one chamber of the version sent to it by the other" (Oleszek 2008, 4) is sometimes, in the case of major legislation, anything but simple. That is, in a number of cases, an agreement is reached through informal processes, a clean bill reflecting the agreement is drafted and is passed by one chamber, then the second chamber adopts the same bill without change. I have labeled that category "House and Senate pass same bill" to indicate that more than simple agreement may be going on.

Table 12.1 shows that, for those major measures on which inter-chamber agreement was reached through procedures other than conferences, the House and Senate passed the same bill about half the time and amendments between the chamber were used about 40 percent of the time. In the remaining cases, the measure became law in another legislative vehicle altogether. The period of higher partisan polarization differs a bit from the period preceding it in the frequency with which this third option was employed. The two periods, however, do not differ much in the mix of alternative procedures employed when so categorized. The big difference is in how frequently alternative procedures have been used post-2000.

Why Alternative Resolution Procedures? Theory and Hypotheses

Congressional scholars have come to understand that, far from being static, Congress changes its institutional and procedural arrangements over time. Much of the literature argues that Congress adapts to changes in its environment so as to make it possible for its members to advance their goals, which, most scholars believe, include legislative success. The increase in the power, resources, and involvement in the legislative process of the party leadership, especially in the House, has been explained, in part, as a response to members' incentives and needs in a period of high partisan polarization (Rohde 1991; Sinclair 2006). The leaderships' increased capacity as well as the greater member demands upon them have made them innovators in the use of procedures for strategic purposes; they are, as I have argued elsewhere, often the orchestrators of unorthodox lawmaking (Sinclair 2007, 2008). I thus hypothesize that a significant part of the increase in alternative procedures to resolve differences between the chambers is leadership-directed. Traditional inter-chamber resolution procedures may have become less effective as a result of heightened partisan polarization, so leaders turned to other mechanisms. Other mechanisms may have provided leaders with strategic options and flexibility that conferences could not. Even the Senate majority leader, who lacks many of the enhanced powers and resources the Speaker commands, does have considerable say over post-passage procedures.

The alternative hypothesis is that the shift from conferences toward other procedures is primarily a response to time pressure; if time is scarce either because of increasing legislative demands or because of members' desires to spend more time in their constituencies and if conferences are more time consuming than the alternatives, one would expect such a shift.

As a first attempt to assess whether alternative procedures are mostly used just for convenience—to save time when the differences between the chambers are not very great, for example—I examined the situation surrounding the process of reaching inter-chamber agreement on each of the major measures on which a non-conference resolution procedure was successfully used. I relied primarily on the accounts in *Congressional Quarterly* but sometimes also consulted newspaper accounts. For each case, I judged whether the use of the alternative procedure was motivated by strategic considerations or not. Although that judgment is of necessity somewhat subjective, it was in most cases surprisingly easy to make. For example, in the 87th Congress, non-conference procedures were not often used on major measures, but, when they were, it was mostly for convenience. A bill extending current tax rates requested by President John Kennedy was not really controversial and required relatively quick action; the House passed the bill on June 8, 1961, and the Senate followed suit, passing the bill without amendments on June 22 by voice vote (*CQ Almanac* 1961, 465). Another example of nonstrategic use of alternative procedures in the 87th Congress was on the bill raising the debt limit in June 1962. In this case, as is usual, the votes, especially in the House, were close, but, since the language was not in question, the fact that the Senate passed the House bill without change was not coded as strategic. In contrast, the two instances of the strategic use of alternative procedures found were unambiguous. The Public Works Acceleration Act of 1962 was highly contentious and passed the Senate and then the House only after a series of compromises. As the *CQ Almanac* explained, "Although the House version differed substantially from [the bill] passed by the Senate, Democratic leaders asked for its adoption without change in order to avoid a conference with the House" (*CQ Almanac* 1962, 447). Thus the Senate agreed to the House amendments. The other case was the Communications Satellite Act. Liberals filibustered the bill and the Senate, for the first time in thirty-five years, invoked cloture. To avoid a conference and an opportunity for another filibuster, the House accepted the Senate amendments (*CQ Almanac* 1962, 546–58).

The use of alternative resolution procedures on major measures is more often motivated by strategic considerations than by simple convenience. On 61 percent of these major measures, the choice of non-conference procedures appears to have been motivated by strategic considerations. To be sure, the two chambers do sometimes produce even major legislation on which a conference would be time-wasting overkill: the legislative preferences within the two chambers are very similar, so one chamber willingly accepts the other's bill or the differences are easy to resolve through a straightforward exchange of amendments between the chambers. Strategic motivations loom larger in the more highly partisan period; in the pre-2000 period, 47 percent of non-conference procedures appear to have been motivated by strategic considerations, but, post-2000, 74 percent were strategic. The increase in the use of non-conference resolution procedures documented earlier is more than accounted for by strategy rather than convenience; the proportion of major measures successfully resolved through non-conference procedures chosen for strategic reasons increased from 10 percent in the pre-2000 period to 42 percent post-2000.

If this increased use of non-conference resolution procedures for strategic purposes is indeed leadership-directed as hypothesized, one would expect them to be especially evident on partisan measures. Measures that split the parties are more likely than others to be important to the majority party's members and to the party's reputation. Furthermore, because they do not have broader support, partisan measures are likely to be more difficult to pass. Both considerations suggest greater leadership involvement (see Sinclair 1995). As I have shown elsewhere, filibuster problems have become a significant barrier to legislative success in the partisan era (Sinclair 2009). One might, thus, expect that, as Senate passage becomes more difficult, leaders respond by altering resolution procedures in a way that mitigates the problem (Sinclair 2007, 73–90).

My measure of partisanship is based on the character of the legislation's drafting process. If a committee or committees reported the legislation, the character of the drafting and reporting coalition is determined by examining reports of committee action in *Congressional Quarterly* publications, *CongressDaily* where available, and newspaper articles and committee reports when necessary. Not all these major measures were reported from committee; for those bills, the drafting process, whether by the party leadership, committee leaders, or an informal coalition, was examined and coded. Here I simply use partisan versus other.

In the earlier, less polarized period, measures that were partisan in at least one chamber and those that were not partisan in either were similarly likely to go to conference and be resolved there (see table 12.2). Post-2000, both partisan and nonpartisan measures are less likely to be resolved in conference. However, measures that were drafted through a partisan process in at least one chamber were considerably more likely to trigger an alternative resolution procedure employed for strategic reasons. Further, in the latter period, measures that were partisan in at least one chamber make up 57 percent of the measures that passed both chambers and on which inter-chamber agreement was reached; that compares with 31 percent for the earlier period. Thus the number of partisan major measures on which inter-chamber agreement was reached through alternative procedures employed for strategic purposes is much larger in the latter period.

TABLE 12.2
The Impact of Partisanship on Post-Passage Resolution Procedures
in the Pre-2000 Period and in the Hyper-Polarized 2000s (%)

Resolution Procedure	87th–105th		107th–111th	
	Partisan in House or Senate	Not Partisan in Either	Partisan in House or Senate	Not Partisan in Either
Conference	76	80	38	50
Alternative—Strategic	14	8	52	28
N	123	273	94	72

Source: Compiled by the author

Legislation that encountered a filibuster-related problem (a hold, a filibuster threat, an actual filibuster) was just as likely to go to conference in the earlier period as legislation that did not, but it is much less likely to do so post-2000 (see table 12.3). In the latter period, filibuster problems are much more likely to beset major measures and, when they do, strategic alternative procedures are used over half the time.

In sum, in the post-2000 decade, alternative resolution procedures are far more frequently used on major legislation than in the earlier period and their use is most often strategic. Such procedures are especially likely to be employed on measures drafted through a partisan process and on those that encountered a filibuster problem, both characteristics that are far more frequent in the post-2000 period than earlier. These mechanisms do appear to have provided leaders with strategic options and flexibility that routinely using conferences did not.

Ping Pong and Other Congressional Pursuits: Choosing and Using Resolution Procedures

The considerations that determine the choice of procedure and how those procedures actually work are best understood by examining a number of cases in

TABLE 12.3
The Impact of Filibuster Problems on Post-Passage Resolution Procedures
Pre- and Post-2000 (%)

Resolution Procedure	87th–105th		107th–111th	
	No Filibuster Problem	Filibuster Problem	No Filibuster Problem	Filibuster Problem
Conference	79	78	51	36
Alternative—Strategic	8	17	30	54
N	312	88	83	83

Source: Compiled by the author

some detail; doing so provides a specificity not captureable in the necessarily broad coding on which the above qualitative study is based. These examples and mini–case studies illuminate the role of the party leadership in the choice and employment of post-passage resolution procedures, show how procedures are adapted to new conditions and needs and, further, make clear that the same procedure can serve multiple strategic purposes.[5]

Convenience

As the quantitative data have shown, alternative procedures are still used for convenience—to save time when a procedure as elaborate as a conference is deemed unnecessary. Even in a period of high partisan polarization, some major measures are not controversial—at all or by the time they reach the resolution process. When, in 2003, a federal court ruled that the Federal Trade Commission (FTC) had overstepped its authority in creating the enormously popular do-not-call registry, the House immediately passed a bill explicitly giving the FTC that authority and the Senate passed that legislation without change only hours later. In the 109th Congress, Senator Ted Stevens worked out a compromise on a rewrite of the fisheries law acceptable to all the major stakeholders. When the Senate attached that to a different House-passed bill, the House simply accepted the Senate amendment (e.g., the Stevens compromise bill).

In some cases, the measure itself is highly controversial, but House and Senate majorities are agreed on language, so the decision of one chamber to accept the other's bill lacks a strategic component. Thus, the bill intervening in the Terri Schiavo litigation was passed by the Senate on March 20, 2005; the next day the House passed the same bill without change. Although the bill was extremely controversial, the Republican majorities in the House and Senate agreed on the relatively simple language, there was no threat of a Senate filibuster, and there was some time pressure for getting the bill done. So the decision by the House to accept the Senate bill was not a strategic one.

In some cases, informal, behind-the-scenes negotiations between the chambers on legislative language prior to passage by either chamber or even prior to bill introduction does occur, though the frequency and the success of such conversations are impossible to gauge. Peak-level negotiations on top-priority, high-saliency measures—such as the bill establishing the Troubled Asset Relief Program (TARP) in the fall of 2008 or the debt limit increase in 2011—are highly visible, but other discussions that go on at the staff and to some extent at the member level occur "below the radar." Contact between the key players in the two chambers early in the process may facilitate agreement at the end of the process; it may even sometimes result in bills so similar that the second chamber willingly accepts the first's handiwork. The constraint on early cross-chamber negotiations is the inability of either to make a binding agreement. For example, the chairs of the relevant House and Senate committees may want to make a deal early in the process, but neither can guarantee that the deal will survive the legislative process in their own chamber.

What Goes to Conference?

The decline in conferences on major measures needs to be understood in context; much major legislation still does go to conference. Regular appropriations bills that become law as such are always the product of conference committees; it is when regular appropriations bills are bundled into an omnibus bill that differences may not be resolved through a formal conference. One of the reasons for the decline in the number of conferences is the difficulty that Congress has had since the mid-1990s enacting its regular appropriations bills.[6] From fiscal year 1996 through fiscal year 2008, 46 percent of regular appropriations bills were bundled into omnibus measures (Sanchez 2008, 7).

Budget resolutions and reconciliation bills always go to conference for the resolution of inter-chamber differences. To be sure, these are complex measures on which multiple differences between the two chambers' bills can be expected. Probably most dispositive, however, is the fact that budget resolutions and reconciliation bills are protected by the Budget Act from filibusters in the Senate. Thus, although these measures tend to be highly partisan, the majority party need not worry about having to muster supermajorities multiple time in the Senate if it decides to use conference procedures.

The annual Department of Defense Authorization bill, which is seldom strictly partisan, almost always goes to conference. In the 110th Congress (2007–2008), a number of other reauthorization bills were reconciled in conference: the 2008 intelligence authorization bill, the agricultural authorization bill, a big water projects authorization bill, the Head Start reauthorization, and the higher education reauthorization bill. Although a number of these bills had controversial provisions and in some cases were hard fought, on none of them was the drafting coalition partisan.

My emphasis on the use of alternative procedures for strategic purposes, primarily by the party leadership, should not be interpreted as implying a lack of leadership involvement in conference committee decisions. In fact, as I have shown elsewhere, the party leadership is now often deeply involved in conference deliberations (Sinclair 2006, 2007). Thus, Majority Leader Bill Frist and House Speaker Dennis Hastert made the final big decisions on the bill adding prescription drug coverage to Medicare in 2003 when the conference committee bogged down. Frist had, in fact, appointed himself to the conference committee. This was a signature bill for President Bush and the Republican Party and it fell to the leadership to get it done. The fiscal year 2007 supplemental appropriations bill funding the Iraq war was vitally important to the new Democratic majorities. Speaker Nancy Pelosi and Majority Leader Harry Reid were deeply involved throughout its legislative life, crafting withdrawal language, deciding what else to include, and making the key decisions on compromises. That involvement very much included conference proceedings.

Strategic Alternative Procedures and When They Are Used

Alternative resolution procedures are most often now employed for strategic reasons, my data show. Strategic motivations can, at least loosely, be categorized as defensive or offensive. Party leaders' uses of alternative procedures fall into both categories.

The leadership may employ alternative resolution procedures as defensive strategic maneuvers, often aimed at avoiding Senate obstructionism. The decision to use alternative procedures to reconcile House-Senate differences has, in recent years, frequently been motivated by direct minority party obstruction of going to conference. Three different motions are required in the Senate: to insist on its amendments, to request a conference, and to authorize the chair to appoint conferees. Although the three are ordinarily bundled together and agreed to by unanimous consent, they can be individually filibustered, thereby making going to conference a time-consuming process at best and impossible in many cases. When Senate Republicans used this strategy to prevent a conference on a campaign finance bill late in the 103rd Congress (1993–1994), it was, according to Majority Leader George Mitchell, an unprecedented move (Oleszek 2007, 262). That cannot be said today.

The 107th Congress (2001–2002) began with the Senate equally divided. Because the vice president has the constitutional authority to break ties, Republicans organized the chamber—chose the majority leader and the chairs of all the committees—but only after agreeing to equal numbers of Democrats and Republicans on each committee. No agreement was reached on the composition of conference committees and Democrats blocked conferences on all but those measures protected by the Budget Act. The effect was small because little legislation that Republicans wanted to send to conference was at that stage of the legislative process before Jim Jeffords switched to caucusing with the Democrats and thereby gave Democrats control of the chamber.

When Republicans took back the majority in the 2002 elections, they began to exclude minority Democrats from meaningful participation in conference deliberations. So, for example, only two Senate Democrats thought to be amenable to the Republicans' approach were actually included in the conference negotiations on the 2003 prescription drug bill; the other Democratic conferees were completely excluded. In response, Senate Democrats sometimes blocked conferences or extracted promises before agreeing to allow them. Thus, on the massive 2004 highway bill, Democrats allowed a conference only after Majority Leader Bill

Frist, in a colloquy on the floor, guaranteed Democrats that they would be full participants in the negotiations (Sinclair 2007, 83–84).

When the Democrats took a narrow majority in the 110th Congress, Republicans responded by sometimes blocking conferences. On two major bills, lobbying reform and a big energy bill, it was the right wing of the Republican party that objected. On energy in particular, many Senate Republicans wanted to go to conference. However, with any straightforward path to conference blocked, the party leaders reached agreement through informal negotiations. On the lobbying bill, the House passed, on a motion to suspend the rules, S. 1, the original Senate bill "as amended"—that is, with the compromise language. Then the Senate agreed to the House amendment. H.R. 6, the vehicle for the big energy bill, was initially passed by the House in January 2007 as part of the "six for '06" Democratic agenda; it passed the Senate in considerably different form (i.e., with amendments) in June. After informal negotiations produced a compromise, the House agreed with amendments (the compromise) to the Senate amendments; then the Senate concurred on the House amendment to the Senate amendment to the text of H.R. 6.

Minority opposition to going to conference can sometimes produce significant concessions from the majority. Thus, in 2007, Republicans refused to allow a bill implementing the 9/11 Commission's recommendations to go to conference until Majority Leader Reid promised to drop a provision giving airport screeners collective-bargaining rights. Senate minority opposition can occasionally kill legislation, as the Democrats' did on parental abortion notification in the 109th Congress. However, this is rare, as the data on failure at this stage make clear. In a very unusual case, House Republicans, then in the majority, refused to go to conference with the Senate on immigration legislation in 2006. President Bush supported the Senate-passed bill that House Republicans abhorred. By refusing to go to conference, House Republicans killed the bill. Most of the time when the minority blocks a conference, the majority leadership finds a way around the problem through alternative procedures. And, furthermore, such alternatives may well give the minority less influence on the legislative outcome than a conference would have.

When one chamber accepts the other's legislation for strategic reasons, it is now most often to avoid the possibility of delay or worse in the Senate. As the example for the 87th Congress discussed above suggested, in earlier times, it was just about as likely that the anticipated problem was in the House as in the Senate. Now that is much less the case. In the 108th Congress (2003–2004), minority Democrats had managed to derail bankruptcy and class action overhaul legislation, both high on the Republican majority's priority list. With a bigger Senate Republican majority, prospects seemed better in the 109th Congress; nevertheless, the Republican leadership wanted to avoid giving opponents any more opportunities for delay than absolutely necessary. Thus, Speaker Dennis Hastert and Majority Leader Frist agreed that the Senate would pass both bills first and the House would then pass the Senate bills without change. The strategy succeeded. Senator Frist got both bills through the Senate without killer amendments, though Republicans did have to invoke cloture on the bankruptcy bill, and the House accepted the Senate bills without change.

The legislative process may culminate with one chamber passing the other's bill, but that seemingly simple action may, in fact, hide a much more complex and strategically driven process. Extending and revising the Foreign Intelligence Surveillance Act confronted Democrats with a number of challenges during the 110th Congress. President Bush and most Republicans favored an extension that put few new limits on surveillance and that explicitly granted immunity to telecommunications companies for disclosing presumably private information to the government in the past. The majority of Democrats favored substantially greater restrictions and opposed immunity, but some moderate Democrats leaned toward Bush's position and red-district and marginal Democrats certainly did not want to open themselves to charges of being soft on terrorists.

On November 15, 2007, the House passed a Democratic bill that Bush strongly opposed and threatened to veto. The Senate Intelligence Committee meanwhile negotiated with the White House and reported a draft that Bush and most Republicans supported but many Democrats opposed. On February 12, 2008, after a protracted and parliamentarily complex fight on the Senate floor, the bill passed without any of the Democratic amendments to strip immunity. Following the usual procedure, the Senate struck all after the enacting clause and substituted the language of its bill (S. 2248) for the House bill (H.R. 3773); it then passed that bill and sent it back to the House.

Republicans tried in a variety of ways to force House Democrats to accept the "bipartisan" Senate bill. For example, they blocked another temporary extension, believing that the imminent expiration of the law would ratchet up the pressure, especially with Bush claiming that, without the law, the country would be in peril. House Democratic leaders refused to allow a vote on the Senate bill despite the expiration of the law. Instead House Democrats reworked their bill and "on a motion that the House agree with an amendment to the Senate amendment," the House agreed to the new version on March 14 and sent it to the Senate. Bush and congressional Republicans opposed the new version, claiming it was little better than the initial House bill, and continued to hold out for the Senate bill. Majority Leader Harry Reid never attempted to get the Senate to accept the House bill.

With moderate House Democrats becoming more and more nervous and pressuring their leaders to allow a vote, House Majority Leader Steny Hoyer engaged in negotiations for a compromise. Working with House Minority Whip Roy Blunt and the chair and ranking member of the Senate Intelligence Committee, he hammered out a deal that gave Bush much of what he wanted but did impose more restrictions than the Senate bill. The compromise was introduced as a clean bill (H.R. 6304) on June 19 and passed by the House on June 20. The Senate passed the bill without amendments on July 9.

Under certain circumstances, leaders' use of alternative resolution procedures is clearly an element of an offensive strategy. In early 2007, the House and then the Senate passed H.J.Res. 20, the continuing appropriations bill for the remainder of fiscal year 2007, in identical form, thus obviating the need for a formal resolution process. Doing so required adept leadership strategy. The continuing resolution (CR) was necessary because Republicans had not passed most of the regular appropriations bills in 2006 when they were the majority party. The new Democratic majority had to pass a bill before the Republicans' CR expired on February 15; the leadership wanted to pass one that shifted funds to Democratic priorities but did not add so much to spending it would give the Republicans a big political target. Appropriations Committee chairs David Obey and Robert Byrd negotiated a CR under leadership oversight. The House Democratic leaders brought it directly to the floor, bypassing committee, and had it considered under a closed rule, barring all amendments. With no procedure such as special rules available, the real problem was avoiding Senate amendments. Majority Leader Reid used his prerogative of first recognition to "fill the amendment tree" (offer amendments in all parliamentarily permissible slots) and so prevent Republicans from offering amendments; he then filed for cloture, a vote Democrats won. Reid was able to succeed with such aggressive tactics because the CR was must-pass legislation, the deadline was imminent, and Republicans were leery about calling attention to their own dereliction.

Resolving differences through amendments between the chambers—the "ping pong" method—may be part of a highly complex leadership strategy. Conflict between President Clinton and the new Republican majorities elected in 1994 led to a government shutdown over Christmas 1995. A stalemate had been reached over government spending and, without the necessary appropriations bills having become law, the U.S. government lacked the authority to spend on many programs citizens were accustomed to. When Congress returned to Washington in early January, Senate Majority Leader Bob Dole decided to act. The public was blaming Republicans far more than the president for the impasse. On January 2, Senator Dole pushed through the Senate a condition-free CR to fund the government until January 12, while budget talks between the congressional majority and the president proceeded. To move the legislation so quickly, Dole took up a most-favored-nation bill for Bulgaria that the House had already passed and offered the CR as a substitute amendment to it, a maneuver that the Senate's loose rules on germaneness made possible. When the Senate adopted the "amendment," the CR was substituted for the original bill.

Dole's move put the responsibility for the shutdown squarely on House Republicans, who had been much more enthusiastic than their Senate colleagues about the strategy. The House Republican leadership decided that House Republicans were in a politically untenable position; after some false starts and much heated argument with its members, Speaker Newt Gingrich brought up, under a rule, a motion that the "House concur in the Senate amendment [to the original bill] with (face saving) amendments," and this passed. The Senate then agreed to the "House amendments to the Senate amendment." The CR was thereby cleared for the president and the government shutdown ended (Sinclair 1997, 215–43).

In this case, although the two chambers were controlled by the same party, once the shutdown became a liability, the leaders did not agree on strategy. Dole's initiative forced Gingrich's hand, but certainly neither wanted a public standoff between the chambers. The procedures used allowed them to get the embarrassing episode behind them quickly.

Another case of highly strategic use of amendments between the chambers was the resolution process on the Iraq war supplemental appropriations bill in the spring of 2008; in this instance, the majority leadership decided to use alternative resolution procedures to bypass much of the usual legislative process. In the 110th Congress, these war supplemental bills presented the new Democratic majorities with significant challenges, but also offered them enticing opportunities. A substantial part of the Democratic membership strongly opposed the Iraq war and wanted to force Bush to end it; yet the leadership knew it lacked the votes to override the certain Bush vetoes of withdrawal language and was further convinced that, to protect the party's reputation and many of the freshmen from marginal districts, the bills funding the troops had to be enacted. But President Bush also had to have this legislation, so the supplementals offered Democrats opportunities to fund some of their domestic priorities that, had they been sent to Bush as free-standing legislation, he would have vetoed.

The Democratic House and Senate leaderships, as well as House Appropriations Chair David Obey, were convinced that their best strategy in the spring of 2008 was to send Bush a bill that funded the troops and also included funding for a carefully selected set of Democratic domestic priorities. These add-ons had to be broadly popular and thus easy to defend in the public arena and sufficiently limited in number and scope that they could not be easily labeled as pork by Republicans. Yet the demands for additional domestic spending from Democratic members were intense. President Bush had used his veto in 2007 to block many of the domestic spending increases Democrats favored, so the pent-up demand was even greater in 2008.

The leadership feared that the regular process, including a markup in the Appropriations Committee, would not only be too slow but, worse, would also add spending for a plethora of domestic programs and so produce a package that could neither be defended effectively in the public arena nor sustained against Bush's opposition. Keeping the bill focused on a few highly popular additions, notably veterans' benefits, gave Democrats their best chance of prevailing in the public relations war with Bush that was sure to come. Extraordinary procedure was necessary to produce such a tightly focused bill, the House Democratic leadership concluded.

Working closely with Chairman Obey, the party leaders decided to bypass committee consideration and then use a highly unorthodox procedure to block all floor amendments. The House leadership used as the base bill H.R. 2642, a military construction appropriations bill that had passed both the House and the Senate in 2007, but not in identical form, and had gone no further. The special rule made "in order a motion by the chairman of the Committee on Appropriations that the House concur in the Senate amendment [to H.R. 2642] with each of . . . three amendments" (www.rules.house.gov). The three amendments were the three components of the Democrats' 2008 supplemental. One appropriated funds for the Iraq war; the second consisted of Iraq withdrawal language; and the third appropriated funds for the carefully selected set of programs, including, most significantly, a major expansion of veterans' education benefits, and also extended unemployment benefits. Since technically the House was attempting to come to agreement with the Senate on a bill the House had already passed once, no regular floor amendments were in order, nor was the minority's traditional motion to recommit. By providing three separate votes on the three parts, the leadership gave its members the opportunity to vote for the popular domestic spending increases without voting for Iraq funding.

Republicans were outraged both at the committee being bypassed and at the floor procedure. In fact, they voted "present" rather than "yea" on the Iraq funding amendment and it failed to pass. However, the two other "amendments" did pass and the amended bill was sent back to the Senate.

Majority Leader Reid was unable to persuade Senate Appropriations Committee Chair Robert Byrd to forgo a markup and the committee added far more domestic spending than the House had. On the floor, the Senate considered the supplemental as a series of motions to concur with the House amendments to the Senate amendments with amendments. Domestic spending provisions, though not all of what the Senate Appropriations Committee had recommended, were added and some House provisions for offsetting the costs were deleted through this procedure. Additionally, an attempt to add war funding with war policy provisions that Bush strongly opposed was defeated. War funding was then added without the restrictions. The bill was then sent back to the House.

With President George W. Bush still threatening to veto the bill over the domestic add-on and yet the need for the funds becoming critical, House leaders and the White House reached a bipartisan deal in which Bush agreed to Democratic demands to include enhanced veterans' education benefits and a thirteen-month extension of unemployment benefits in exchange for a reduction in other domestic spending and no tax increases. Senate Democrats reluctantly endorsed the deal. The House approved and sent the bill with the deal to the Senate through two motions to agree to Senate amendments; first, by passing the motion "to agree to Senate amendment to House amendment number No. 1 to Senate amendment," the House approved the war funding that the Senate had approved and that had not passed the House; second, on a motion "to agree to Senate amendment to House amendment number No. 2 to Senate amendment with an amendment," the House approved the deal on domestic and veterans' spending. This way of structuring the vote again allowed anti-war Democrats to vote against the war spending while making it hard for Republicans to oppose it even though they thereby provided a majority; yet the procedure made it possible for those Democrats to vote for the popular domestic spending. Final action came when the Senate "agreed to the House amendment to the Senate amendment to the House amendment to the Senate amendment."

In recent years non-conference post-passage procedures have been used in a highly strategic—and most unorthodox—way to, in effect, achieve the initial passage of major legislation. The financial bailout legislation—the bill establishing the Troubled Assets Relief Program (TARP)—illustrates this use of alternative resolution procedures. With a financial crisis looming menacingly, Secretary of the Treasury Henry Paulson on September 19 called on Congress to pass rescue legislation immediately. The legislation Paulson proposed was so cursory and gave him so much untrammeled authority that leaders and members on both sides of the aisle balked. Still the pressure to act quickly was intense and the regular legislative process would take far too long. So a small bicameral and bipartisan group of congressional leaders and White House negotiators hammered out a bill in closed-door meetings over the course of a week.

To get it to the floor quickly and without the possibility of amendment and to then make swift Senate action easier, House leaders used a bill providing tax relief and protection to military personnel that had passed both chambers in 2007. Inter-chamber difference on H.R. 3997 had come close to being resolved through amendments between the chambers, but then the leaders had decided to include modified versions of various parts of it in other bills. So, while the substance of H.R. 3997 had become law, H.R. 3997 was still available as a vehicle.

On September 29, House Financial Services Committee Chair Barney Frank moved that the House "concur in the Senate amendment to the House amendment to the bill, with an additional amendment"—that additional amendment being the bailout package. If it had passed, the Senate could have simply accepted the House amendment and that would have cleared the bill for the president's signature. However, with public opinion running overwhelmingly against bailing out greedy banks seen as responsible for the financial mess, two-thirds of House Republicans and 40 percent of Democrats voted against the motion and it failed 205–228.

When the vote triggered a massive sell-off on Wall Street, the Senate leaders took over. They agreed on a package that added to the bailout language a number of "sweeteners"—provisions extending various popular tax breaks, expanding incentives for renewable-energy projects, limiting the reach of the alternative minimum tax for a year, and requiring insurance companies to offer mental health coverage on par with what they offered for other health problems (*CQ Weekly*, October 6, 2008, 2692–99).

The Senate used H.R. 1424, the mental health parity bill, as its vehicle. The House had passed this bill and the Senate had passed its own bill earlier, but no resolution of the two had been formally attempted because, by the time the significant differences between the two had been worked out informally, time had become short. The bill extending the popular tax breaks had stalled because the House insisted on paying for the revenue loss (PAYGO) and the Senate, with the need to get sixty votes, could not pass the bill with tax increases included. H.R. 1424 was brought to the floor under a unanimous consent agreement requiring that any amendments get sixty votes to pass; the first and critical vote was on the Dodd substitute for H.R. 1424. When that passed 74–25, the negotiated package—including the Senate's language on the tax extenders and the compromise on mental health—was substituted for the original House-passed bill. The Senate then passed the bill by an identical vote.

Although they had not been included in the negotiations and Senate language had replaced House language on several contentious issues, House Democratic leaders reluctantly accepted the deal. Time was of the essence and the sweeteners were likely to persuade some Republicans to vote for the legislation. On October 3, the House approved Frank's motion to concur in the Senate amendment to H.R. 1424 by a vote of 263 to 171, with Republicans splitting 91–108 and Democrats 172–63. That vote cleared the bill for the president's signature.

After Republicans took back the House in the 2010 elections, President Barack Obama negotiated a deal to extend the Bush-era tax cuts, unemployment insurance, and some other expiring tax provisions with Senate Minority Leader Mitch McConnell. Time was short and the agenda long in the lame duck session of the 111th Congress; many liberal Democrats and conservative Republicans were unhappy with the deal. So, to move legislation quickly and allow as little opportunity for opponents to unravel the deal as possible, the leadership used a bill that had passed both chambers. H.R. 4853 was the Federal Aviation Administration Act of 2010 when it initially passed the House in March and the Senate in September. Through a process of amendments between the chambers in December it had became the Tax Relief, Unemployment Insurance Reauthorization, and Job Creation Act of 2010 when it was enacted into law.

Both of these examples were to some extent bipartisan efforts, but, in the 111th Congress, with its big Democratic margins, the Democratic leadership was in several instances able to use the procedure on more partisan legislation as well.

On August 5, 2010, the Senate passed H.R. 1586, providing additional funding to the states to prevent teacher layoffs and shore up Medicaid; the Senate had imposed cloture by a vote of 61–39 with only the two Republican senators from Maine joining all Democrats in support. H.R. 1586, a bill funding aviation programs, had passed the House in March 2009. In March 2010, the Senate passed it with an amendment and then the House had sent it back to the Senate with an amendment. When Majority Leader Reid was able to put together a package of such funding for which he could get the necessary sixty votes, he used that bill as a vehicle. So in August, the Senate formally concurred in the House amendment to the Senate amendment to the bill with an amendment; that latter amendment was a substitute that incorporated the funding for teachers' jobs and Medicaid. Speaker Pelosi called the House back into session from its August recess and when the House agreed to the Senate amendment to the House amendment to the Senate amendment, it effectively agreed to new legislation (Lesniewski and Friel 2010, 1926; Goldfarb 2011, 1984–85).

A final example—the repeal of the "Don't Ask, Don't Tell" (DADT) for gays in the military—further illustrates the combination of offensive and defensive strategic consideration that often motivates the employment of alternative resolution procedures to pass legislation. President Obama had promised to repeal DADT during his presidential campaign, but various political considerations delayed the effort. With Department of Defense Secretary Robert Gates and Joint Chiefs Chairman Mike Mullen finally on board, the House passed repeal as a floor amendment to the Department of Defense authorization bill in May 2010. The Senate Armed Services Committee incorporated the identical repeal language in its bill, but a filibuster prevented floor passage; Reid attempted to impose cloture on September 21 and again in the lame duck session on December 9 but failed in both attempts. Republican supporters of repeal gave various reasons for voting against cloture on the Department of Defense bill with DADT included. Time was running out; given the Republican victories in the November elections, supporters of repeal knew their chances of success in the next congress were nil. So Speaker Nancy Pelosi used as a vehicle a small-business technology bill that had passed both chambers. On December 15, by a vote of 250 to 175, the House agreed with an amendment (the DADT repeal language substituted for the original bill) to the Senate amendment (the Senate-passed version of the bill). Not only did this maneuver speed up the process, but it also prevented Republicans from offering a motion to recommit with instructions, effectively an opportunity to amend the DADT language. When the bill was received in the Senate on December 16, Reid filed for cloture on the motion that the Senate agree to the House amendment to the Senate amendment. He then immediately filled the amendment tree to prevent any other amendments from being offered, as it was essential that the Senate not alter the language, both because this was the compromise language that had been agreed to in the summer and because time was so short. On December 18 the Senate voted 63–33 to cut off debate and the motion was approved by a somewhat surprising 65–31 vote. This sent repeal to the president, who signed the legislation on December 22 (*CQ Weekly*, December 27, 2010, 2918).

Conclusion

The mix of procedures used to resolve inter-chamber differences on major legislation has changed significantly in recent years. The decline in conferences and the more frequent use of alternative resolution procedures does seem to be linked to increased partisan polarization and the more central role of the party leadership in the legislative process. Whether on the offense or the defense, the majority party leadership often finds alternative resolution procedures useful for meeting its members' expectations of legislative success with the minimum feasible political pain.

Notes

1. Those key vote measures on which the controversy was about an amendment and the bill itself was not controversial were excluded, as were seven other measures for which the bicameralism analysis makes no sense.

2. The congresses included are the 87th, 89th, 91st, 94th, 95th, 97th, 100th, 101st, 103rd, 104th, 105th, 107th, 108th, 109th, 110th, and 111th.

3. An additional 1.7 percent went to conference, but the process was unsuccessful because either the conference failed to reach a resolution or one chamber refused to accept the agreement reached.

4. The 106th Congress was not initially one of my selected congresses and coding of the cases for the 106th is not complete. However, because the decline in the use of conferences came between the 105th and the 107th in my data, I did code resolution procedures for the 106th and found that the 106th was much more like the previous congresses than the following congresses; of major measures that passed both chambers and on which differences were successfully resolved, 72 percent went to conference. In sum, the 107th is the appropriate cut point.

5. Legislative language in quotation marks and without a source is taken from the Thomas Bill Status Reports for the legislation under discussion. The descriptions of the cases are based on original sources—Thomas, *Congressional Record*—or accounts in secondary sources, including *CQ Weekly Reports*, *CongressDaily*, *Roll Call*, the *Washington Post*, the *New York Times*, and my interviews.

6. This has little impact on my data because regular appropriations bills are not included in *CQ*'s list of major measures; they enter my dataset, if at all, via key votes.

References

Beth, Richard, Valerie Heitshusen, Bill Heniff, and Elizabeth Rybicki. 2009. "Leadership Tools for Managing the U.S. Senate." Paper presented at the annual meeting of the American Political Science Association, Toronto, Canada, September 1–4.

Binder, Sarah. 2003. *Stalemate: Causes and Consequences of Legislative Gridlock*. Washington, DC: Brookings Institution Press.

Brady, David, and Craig Volden. 2005. *Revolving Gridlock*. Boulder, CO: Westview Press.

CQ Almanac. 1961. "Tax Rate Extension." Washington, DC: Congressional Quarterly, Inc.

———. 1962. "Congress Enacts Communications Satellite Bill." Washington, DC: Congressional Quarterly, Inc.

CQ Weekly. 2008. "Highlights of Tax Provisions." October 6.

———. 2010. "2010 Legislative Summary: Don't Ask, Don't Tell." December 27.

Goldfarb, Sam. 2011. "Uphill Overhaul." *CQ Weekly*, September 26:1980–86.

Krehbiel, Keith. 1998. *Pivotal Politics: A Theory of U.S. Lawmaking*. Chicago: University of Chicago Press.

Lesniewski, Niels, and Brien Friel. 2010. "Rush and Rumbles Before the Break." *CQ Weekly*, August 9:1926–27.

Nivola, Pietro, and David Brady, eds. 2008. *Red and Blue Nation: Consequences and Corrections of America's Polarized Politics*. Washington, DC: Brookings Institution Press.

Oleszek, Walter. 1996. *Congressional Procedures and the Policy Process*. 4th ed. Washington, DC: CQ Press.

———. 2007. *Congressional Procedures and the Policy Process*. 7th ed. Washington, DC: CQ Press.

———. 2008. "Whither the Role of Conference Committees: An Analysis." *Congressional Research Service*. Washington, DC: Library of Congress.

Rohde, David. 1991. *Parties and Leaders in the Postreform House*. Chicago: University of Chicago Press.

Rybicki, Elizabeth. 2003. "Unresolved Differences: Bicameral Negotiations in Congress, 1877–2002." Paper delivered at the History of Congress Conference, University of California, San Diego, December 5–6.

———. 2007. "Bicameral Resolution in Congress, 1863–2002." In *Party, Process, and Political Change in Congress*, vol. 2, edited by David Brady and Mathew McCubbins, 323–44. Palo Alto, CA: Stanford University Press.

Sanchez, Humberto. 2008. "Lawmakers Increasingly Resigned to Breakdown of Regular Order This Year." *CongressDaily*, June 2:1, 7–8.

Sinclair, Barbara. 1995. *Legislators, Leaders, and Lawmaking*. Baltimore, MD: Johns Hopkins University Press.

———. 1997. *Unorthodox Lawmaking*. 1st ed. Washington, DC: CQ Press.

———. 2000. *Unorthodox Lawmaking*. 2nd ed. Washington, DC: CQ Press.

———. 2006. *Party Wars: Polarization and the Politics of the Policy Process*. Norman: Julian Rothbaum Lecture Series, University of Oklahoma Press.

———. 2007. *Unorthodox Lawmaking*. 3rd ed. Washington, DC: CQ Press.

———. 2008. "Orchestrators of Unorthodox Lawmaking: Pelosi and McConnell in the 110th Congress." *The Forum* 6, article 4.

———. 2009. "Partisan Polarization, Rule Divergence, and Legislative Productivity." Paper delivered at the Conference on Bicameralism, sponsored by the Political Institutions and Public Choice Program, Duke University, March 27–28.

Tsebelis, George, and Jeanette Money. 1997. *Bicameralism*. New York: Cambridge University Press.

13

Legislative Sausage-Making

Health Care Reform in the 111th Congress*

Mark J. Oleszek and Walter J. Oleszek

E NACTING CONSEQUENTIAL, CONTROVERSIAL, complex, and comprehensive public laws is typically not an easy task. Inevitably, such measures must surmount an array of legislative and political obstacles before they can be signed into law. President Barack Obama accomplished this feat in winning passage of landmark legislation in the 111th Congress (2009–2011)—P.L 111-148, the Patients' Protection and Affordable Care Act—that many observers believe is the signature achievement of his administration thus far. A companion measure, the Health Care and Education Reconciliation Act (P.L. 111-152), was also essential to enactment of health care reform. Many presidents before Obama tried and failed to overhaul the health care system; President William Clinton could not even persuade the Democratic 103rd Congress (1993–1994) to vote on his far-reaching health reform plan (Johnson and Broder 1996).

President Obama's health care initiative encountered numerous political and legislative hurdles before being signed into law on March 30, 2010. Among just a few of the obstacles were an electorate distrustful of the federal government; the emergence nationwide of a Tea Party movement filled with aggressive and assertive individuals who favor limited government, oppose President Obama's policies, and disapprove of Obama personally; public anxiety about escalating deficits and debt; a Senate in which sixty votes is the new normal for passing legislation; the worst economic downturn (the Great Recession) since the 1930s Depression; a largely unified GOP opposition in the Democratic House and Senate; the polarization between the parties and their intense electoral competition,

---

*This chapter reflects the views of the authors and does not reflect the views of the Congressional Research Service, the Library of Congress, or Albright College.

inhibiting bipartisan cooperation; and criticisms of the health plan organized and amplified by conservative media outlets and spokespersons, who called it "socialized medicine" and a "government takeover." Some erroneously claimed that various health proposals recommended "death panels." One House member even yelled, "You lie!" when President Obama referred to illegal immigrants and health coverage during his September 9, 2009, address to a joint session of Congress. The purposes of the president's speech were to outline his core health principles and to revive support for his ailing health care initiative after it was lambasted in numerous boisterous town hall meetings held by lawmakers during their traditional August recess.[1]

President Obama and the Democratic Congress overcame these obstacles because of countervailing forces and factors. These included a large Democratic majority in the House (257–178) and a sixty-vote, filibuster-proof majority in the Senate, at least until the surprise January 2010 special election victory of Republican Scott Brown. He won the Massachusetts seat held for decades by Democratic Senator Edward Kennedy (who died in August 2009). Another factor bolstering health reform was the resolve and determination of President Obama to prevail despite various setbacks, such as angry constituents shouting down lawmakers at town hall meetings for supporting the president's "socialist" agenda. The procedural and political leadership of Speaker of the House Nancy Pelosi and Senate Majority Leader Harry Reid were vital to the success of both measures. Importantly, there was growing realization that escalating health care costs—triggered by expensive medical advances for an aging society in which individuals live longer and die longer—could not go on indefinitely without threatening the solvency of the government.

To assess the whole array of forces and factors that influenced the enactment of health care—the people, the politics, the policies, and the procedures—is beyond the scope of this chapter. Instead, it largely focuses on many of the major procedures and political issues involved in moving health care reform through Congress. Senator Christopher Dodd, who served as acting chair of the Health, Education, Labor, and Pensions Committee in the absence of the ailing Senator Edward Kennedy, had a bird's-eye view of the entire process. "We all know what a painful process it was to come to a conclusion on the health care debate," Dodd said. "I am sorry it went through that process—not exactly a textbook version of how a bill ought to become law—but nonetheless an important contribution to our country" (Dodd 2010a, S5395; Dodd 2010b, S5657). An overview of this "painful" legislative sausage-making process is the chapter's principal focus.

Specifically, the chapter proceeds as follows. First, it highlights President Obama's strategic approach to health care reform. Second, it examines the major procedural and political issues that shaped consideration of health care reform in each chamber. The discussion for each chamber examines three overlapping topics: committee action, vote mobilization, and procedural maneuvers. Third, it addresses the impact of GOP Senator Scott Brown's special election victory on Democratic expectations for fairly rapid enactment of health care reform. Fourth, the chapter focuses on Democratic use of a two-step procedure to win passage of the landmark health overhaul measure. Lastly, the chapter closes with several summary observations. Discussion of the substance of health issues is limited, as is that of the important role of lobbyists and the Congressional Budget Office (CBO), which "scores" the cost of the various health initiatives.[2]

A Snapshot of President Obama's Strategic Approach

Health care reform was a top priority of Barack Obama's 2008 presidential campaign. He told his confidantes that he would stake his presidency on the outcome. Like many advocates of health care reform, President Obama emphasized a few key objectives: universal, or expanded, coverage (about fifty million people at the time lacked health insurance) and "bending the cost curve" of health's ever-rising financial trajectory. Moreover, the president expected to achieve these hard-to-reconcile goals without, as he said many times, "adding a dime to the deficit." To pay for health reform, which he pledged to keep at $900 billion over ten years, the president suggested such measures as finding savings in Medicare in the range of $400 to $500 billion, eliminating unnecessary medical procedures, and fostering market competition to give consumers a wider range of health insurance choices. To be sure, the debate on health care reform was replete with arcane terms, such as "insurance exchanges," "public option," and "individual mandate."[3]

In March 2009, the president launched his health care initiative at a White House conference with physicians, drug manufacturers, insurance executives, and health associations in attendance. The president's key objectives: win their general support and thus inhibit any early "attack ads" aimed at torpedoing the idea at its inception. On both counts, the president was successful. He did win the backing of many who played a large role in defeating the ambitious health overhaul proposed by President Clinton, drafted in large measure by the First Lady. In fact, some insiders suggest that President Obama learned too well the pitfalls that scuttled Clinton's reform proposal. Three "lessons" stand out.

First, President Obama heeded the advice of many advisors and officials who had witnessed firsthand the demise of President Clinton's health plan (several also serve, or have served, in top positions in Obama's administration, such as Secretary of State Hillary Clinton). They suggested that instead of sending a detailed health proposal to Congress, as President Clinton did, Obama should leave the detailed bill-writing process to the House and Senate. The advisors' general message: let Congress take the lead in drafting the legislation but then step in forcefully at the conference stage to shape the final bill. It was at the conference committee, said Vice President Joe Biden, that the "White House plans to really exert its voice" (Brown 2009, 21).

Second, President Clinton's health plan as chiefly drafted by the First Lady was an immensely complicated measure, difficult to comprehend and to explain in terms people could understand. A well-known television spot ("Harry and Louise"), paid for by the health insurance industry, ran for a year between 1993 and 1994. It featured a suburban couple who criticized Clinton's health proposal as bureaucratic (in July 2009, the same couple reappeared in a television ad, only this time they supported Obama's health initiative). Third, the Clinton plan was crafted in secret with no legislative input. As one observer noted, "Hillary Clinton refused to negotiate with Republicans who offered reasonable alternatives" (Drew 2009, 67).

Only months later, when the fate of health care reform looked bleak, did President Obama recognize that his reliance on Congress was not an effective strategy. The negative publicity surrounding Congress's role in drafting the health bill—the deal-making, closed-door negotiations, missed deadlines, and partisan gridlock—contributed to the public's dismay at Congress's messy and disorderly health care reform process. This legislative sausage-making gave many voters indigestion. Further, the intense media coverage of the legislative bickering and plotting undermined the president's campaign pledge to change the way Washington works. The result: the president altered his approach and took charge of pushing health care reform through the House and Senate. "In 2010, the president has to look like he is leading the process," declared Obama's communications director. We have to "change the narrative" from the deal-making on Capitol Hill to "Obama finally taking charge of health reform" (Connolly 2010, A6).

The president's "take charge" approach began when he attended and responded adroitly to Republican lawmakers' questions at a televised House GOP Conference meeting in Baltimore on January 19, 2010. As a next step, the president scheduled a televised White House Health Care Summit the next month (February 25) with key congressional Democrats and Republicans. He won no GOP converts, but the summit demonstrated his willingness to listen to and answer his critics. Moreover, the summit spotlighted on "national television precisely the bipartisan, high-minded debate that Congress's year-long process was not" (Hook 2010). In the view of Health and Human Services Secretary Kathleen Sebelius, who participated in the discussions, "In some ways, [the summit] really set the stage for what happened eventually" (Fritze, Page, and Wolf 2010, 8A). The summit, in short, showed Obama as "negotiator in chief," the leader in charge of overhauling the health care system.

It is reasonable to suggest that Obama wants to be a "transformational" rather than a "transactional" presidential leader in health care (Burns 1978). His goal, as he said, is to do "big things" and put the nation "on a fundamentally different path because the country [is] ready for it" (Condon 2011, 42). Unsurprisingly, the president expected to transform the country's health policy system and move it in a new direction (universal coverage, for example). Transformational presidents exploit the political context of the times to advance bold national policies. Crises, governing majorities in the House and Senate, public expectations, and persuasive skills are among the elements that enable presidents, such as Franklin Roosevelt, Lyndon Johnson, and Ronald Reagan, to win enactment of major changes that alter the nation's political, economic, and social life. "Transactional" presidents function in a more bounded context (smaller legislative majorities, for example), are unable to overcome such constraints through the force of their ideas or personal skills, and typically move policy incrementally, unless dramatic events intervene (9/11, for instance) to change the governing context.

Paradoxically, President Obama was able to advance comprehensive health care reform as a top national priority because lawmakers and the attentive public recognized that it required significant improvement. But even with his acknowledged oratorical skills, President Obama was unable to convince scores of people around the country who had adequate health coverage and opposed federal overreach that his reform objectives would be good for them. Citizens were also concerned that the government was trying to do too much, given its initiatives to bail out banks, address global climate change, and manage bankrupt automobile companies. At this juncture, it is too early to assess whether the Obama presidency transformed health care, in part because many of its key elements do not take effect until 2014 and others are subject to revision and ongoing court cases.

Action in the House

In 2009, legislative action on health care was largely shaped by three overlapping factors: the work of three committees, the coalition-building skills of Speaker Pelosi, and intricate legislative procedures. Of course, many other actions swayed House passage, such as periodic pep talks from the president. Bicameral dynamics also came into play. Some House members wanted the Senate to act first on health care. They remembered that after spending months passing a controversial "cap and trade" bill to address global climate change, which caused electoral grief back home for vulnerable House Democrats, the Senate did not act on the measure. House Democratic leaders, who consulted with their Senate counterparts, recognized that acting first on this high-profile measure would provide momentum to the often slower-moving Senate to develop a bill that it could pass. "There's no question that the House sets a different pace," exclaimed Speaker Pelosi (Dennis 2009b, 16).

Committee Action

Three House committees with substantial health jurisdiction were involved in the reform effort. They were: Education and Labor (family and medical leave;

health and workers); Energy and Commerce (health and health facilities); and Ways and Means (taxes and Medicare). Two of the three committee chairs— Representative George Miller, who chaired Education and Labor, and Representative Henry Waxman, who chaired Energy and Commerce—were especially close allies of the Speaker. Ways and Means Chair Charles Rangel played a less pivotal role in crafting the legislation, perhaps because of ethical issues associated with his personal finances (Dennis 2009a, 1).

All three panels were directed by the Speaker and the Democratic Caucus to avoid jurisdictional squabbles and to develop a consensus product to focus the work of their committees. On June 9, 2009, the three chairs announced an outline for overhauling the health system, which included a so-called "public option"—a government-managed health plan that would compete with private insurers. The public option divided Democrats, was opposed by Republicans, and remained a divisive issue in both chambers throughout the debate on health reform. Subsequently, on July 14, 2009, the Speaker, the three chairs, and other Democratic leaders unveiled a comprehensive (1,018 pages) health reform measure estimated by the Congressional Budget Office to cost just over $1 trillion. The measure (H.R. 3200) was titled "America's Affordable Healthy Choices Act." It included such features as the public option, a requirement that everyone have health insurance, and a restructuring of Medicare (Teske 2009, A24).

Three days later, two of the three committees—Education and Labor and Ways and Means—marked up (amended) their portions of H.R. 3200 after hours-long sessions. The vote to report the bill on July 17 was twenty-three to eighteen in Ways and Means and twenty-six to twenty-two in Education and Labor. Energy and Commerce, named the primary (lead) panel by the Speaker when H.R. 3200 was introduced, ran into significant opposition. Seven fiscally conservative "Blue Dog" Democrats on the panel were upset with the legislation drafted by the three liberal chairmen, such as a ten-year cost estimate over $1 trillion. Unless changes to H.R. 3200 were made, said the Blue Dogs, they would vote against committee approval of the legislation, administering a damaging, if not fatal, blow to health reform. Chairman Waxman and House Democratic leaders made adjustments to H.R. 3200 that won the votes of four of the seven Blue Dogs. Liberal Democrats on and off the committee "expressed outrage" over the deals made by Chairman Waxman (Armstrong 2009, 20). On July 31, Energy and Commerce reported H.R. 3200 by a 31–28 vote (Austin 2010, 13-4-13-5). Republicans on the three panels were uniformly against H.R. 3200.

Several fundamental consequences flowed from the committees' deliberations and, ultimately, President Obama's decision not to send the specifics of a health plan to Congress. First, there were now three versions of the same bill. It would be up to the Rules Committee and the Speaker to meld the three versions into a single measure. Second, it was more difficult for the president and Democratic leaders to educate their constituents and their colleagues about health reform with three versions in circulation (later, when the blended bill was released in late October, it was so complex that party leaders sponsored tutorials for their members). Third, congressional Republicans and their Tea Party supporters had a field day castigating and demonizing the Democrats' still-to-be-finalized health plan during the August 2009 recess. Finally, the committees' consideration of H.R. 3200 revealed large splits between liberals and conservatives within the Democratic Party. Nonetheless, given solid GOP opposition, majority party leaders understood that the votes needed to pass health care reform had to come mainly, even exclusively, from House Democrats.

Speaker Pelosi and Vote Mobilization

Many things can be said about the vote-gathering skills of Speaker Pelosi. A powerful Speaker, she is a determined, organized, patient, and results-oriented leader who spends considerable time meeting with, listening to, and wooing her rank-and-file colleagues to support party-preferred priorities. Two examples make the point. First, on a crucial health reform vote and with dozens of wavering Democrats worried about their reelection, a leadership aide told the Speaker that the party whips needed to get busy and lobby sixty-eight on-the-fence Democrats. "I'll take all sixty-eight," the Speaker responded (Stolberg, Zeleny, and Hulse 2010, 1).

When the fate of major health care reform looked bleak and White House aides were encouraging President Obama to back away from comprehensive change and propose a pared-back health bill, it was Speaker Pelosi who said no to any "kiddie care" bill. "We will go through the gate. If the gate is closed," she said, "we will go over the fence. If the fence is too high, we will pole vault in. If that doesn't work, we will parachute in. But we are going to get health reform passed" (Stolberg, Zeleny, and Hulse 2010, 1).

Speaker Pelosi functioned as a "transactional" leader—utilizing the bargaining tools at her disposal—to win votes. But the Speaker's leadership approach was more than that. She was willing to challenge the White House, her colleagues, and go for broke for comprehensive health care reform. No simple "agent" of her party followers, the Speaker moved many followers to risk their reelection by supporting health care reform.

For the next three months (August through late October, when the composite bill was publicly disclosed), the Speaker and other committee and party leaders worked to meld a health reform package from three disparate committee products. With Congress in its traditional August recess, Majority Leader Steny Hoyer explained that "staff would work first and present options to the committee chairmen and the leadership" (Rothman, Ferguson, and Nicholson 2009, GG-1). The fundamental leadership task was to draft a bill that could attract the majority support required to pass the House. This was an arduous task, as many lawmakers wanted to make adjustments to the legislation to suit their constituents and outside interests. When to bring the work-in-progress bill to the floor was a constant question that came from many quarters. A close ally of the Speaker's, House Rules Chair Louise Slaughter, New York, provided the answer: "When we have the votes, we are going" to bring it up (Ota and Roth 2009, 9).[4]

Gathering the votes meant accommodating the views of liberals and conservatives in the party, ensuring that a public option was included in the package (essential to liberal Democrats), and coming up with a price tag (revenues to pay for health care initiatives) viewed as reasonable to most of the fifty-five Blue Dogs in the House. All this required the Speaker to be involved in endless meetings with party factions; engage in one-on-one sessions with wavering Democrats; accommodate conservatives without alienating too many liberals; convene a health care forum where White House senior advisor David Axelrod urged Democrats to act soon on health care reform; and promise various Democrats that she would assist in meeting their constituency-based requests.

The issue of abortion merits mention because unless the views of pro-life lawmakers were accommodated in the health reform bill, they could have brought down the whole package. The issue also demonstrates the Speaker's pragmatic and tough-minded focus on winning votes despite her own pro-choice leanings. Anti-abortion Democrats, led by Representative Bart Stupak, insisted that the Speaker allow a separate vote on an amendment banning the use of federal funds for abortions under any new health care reform law. Without the votes of anti-abortion Democrats and Republicans, health care reform could not pass the House. Following repeated meetings with the Pro-Choice Caucus, and after one contentious three-hour session, the Speaker announced that she was "going to allow a vote on the Stupak amendment" (O'Connor and Bresnahan 2009, 12). Despite a yelling match between a female lawmaker and a Pelosi confidante, and other expressions of outrage by pro-choice members, the Speaker won the support of the forty or so lawmakers who, according to Stupak, supported the abortion ban. The U.S. Conference of Catholic Bishops endorsed and lobbied for Stupak's amendment, which the House agreed to include in the health bill by a 240 to 194 vote (Wallsten 2009, A4).

The push for votes involved more than the Speaker cajoling, challenging, or confronting her Democratic colleagues. With 258 Democrats, the Speaker could lose 40 Democrats (she lost 39) and still have the 218 votes to pass the legislation. As a result, the Democratic leadership was constantly fine-tuning the legislation to pick up votes, including modifying the public option, addressing Medicare reimbursement rates between rural and urban areas, and heeding the concerns of Hispanic members to allow undocumented immigrants—with no verification of legal status—access to health insurance under the proposed new law.

The Congressional Hispanic Caucus had a lot riding on this issue. According to one Caucus member, if it was not satisfied, "I guess [our Democratic leaders] won't have those 20 [Hispanic] votes" (Murray and Montgomery 2009, A4). Hispanic lawmakers also threatened to vote against the rule from the House Rules Committee if the bill prohibited undocumented workers from using their own money to purchase health insurance under the proposed new law.[5]

Speaker Pelosi had help in rounding up votes. The American Medical Association (AMA) and the American Association of Retired Persons (AARP) endorsed the House's health overhaul plan. President Obama journeyed to Capitol Hill the day before chamber consideration of health reform. He addressed the Democratic members during a closed-door session of the party's caucus to rally support for the landmark measure. House Democratic leaders devised a "ratcheting-up" strategy to persuade wavering members. Calls would come first from House Majority Leader Hoyer, "then the speaker, then White House senior adviser David Axelrod, then White House Chief of Staff Rahm Emanuel [now mayor of Chicago], and finally the president" (Weisman and Bendavid 2009, A7). The strategy did not work with every representative, but it did with enough to achieve House passage. Only one Republican voted with the Democrats: Louisiana Representative Anh "Joseph" Cao. The first Vietnamese American elected to Congress, Cao conversed with White House officials multiple times, "topped with new promises of support for his Katrina-ravaged New Orleans district" (Weisman and Bendavid 2009, A7). Cao was defeated in the November 2010 mid-term elections.

Procedural Politics

Representative John Dingell, the longest-ever serving House member, once said, "I'll let you write the substance on a statute and you let me write the procedure, and I'll screw you every time" (Committee on the Judiciary, Subcommittee on Administrative Law and Governmental Relations 1983, 312). There is little doubt that parliamentary procedures shape decision outcomes. On the other hand, if a determined majority of lawmakers in the House stay united, they can surmount any number of procedural obstacles. If there is adequate time, votes can trump procedure and push substance over the finish line. After months of meetings and negotiations, accommodations to party factions and individual members, the Speaker succeeded in mustering the votes to pass health care reform. Three key procedural-political elements facilitated House passage.[6]

New Bill and a "Manager's Amendment"

House Democratic leaders crafted a new health bill that reflected the numerous compromises and deals made during the vote mobilization process. In an October 29, 2009, ceremony at the Capitol, the new bill (H.R. 3962) was unveiled by the Speaker. The measure, which included many of the provisions in H.R.

3200, was nearly two thousand pages in length, with a cost of about $900 billion. Members could now determine whether their requests were included in the legislation. Stupak's abortion proposal, for instance, was not included in H.R. 3962. Once it became crystal clear a few days later that anti-abortion Democrats could kill the bill, the Speaker made sure that the Rules Committee—known as "the Speaker's committee"—would make the Stupak amendment in order. As the procedural resolution (H.Res. 903) stated, "The rule makes in order the amendment in part C of the [Rules Committee's] report if offered by Representative Stupak or a designee."

In addition, Democratic leaders developed a forty-two-page "manager's amendment"—a package of discrete provisions—whose purpose was "less an attempt to buy the votes of wavering members than an effort to firm up support among Democrats whose votes were probably never in doubt" (Wayne 2009a, 8). For example, the concerns of the Congressional Black Caucus were assuaged by including in the manager's amendment the creation of minority health offices in several federal agencies. Upon adoption of the rule by the House, the manager's amendment was automatically incorporated (or "self-executed") into H.R. 3962.

A "Structured Rule" from the Rules Committee

The procedural resolution (H.Res. 903) that made H.R. 3962 in order for floor consideration was a "structured" rule. This type of rule limits and specifies which amendments can be offered to a bill. Clearly, Democratic leaders did not want a wide-open amendment process that could pick apart the bill and unravel their hard-won winning coalition. In this case, setting aside the manager's amendment, only two amendments—out of more than 150 submitted—were made in order to H.R. 3962: the Stupak amendment and a GOP alternative called the "Common Sense Health Care Reform and Affordability Act," which was offered by Minority Leader John Boehner. The Stupak amendment, as noted, was adopted; the GOP substitute was rejected by a vote of 176 yeas to 258 nays.[7]

For months, congressional Republicans—and their outside supporters—had attacked the Democrats' health care plan. As Minority Leader Boehner told a November 5, 2009, rally of conservatives two days before the House enacted H.R. 3962, "This bill is the greatest threat to freedom that I have seen in the 19 years I have been here in Washington, taking away your freedom to choose your doctor, the freedom to buy health insurance on your own. Join us in rejecting Pelosi care" (Gruenwald 2009, 6).[8] To refute Democratic charges that Republicans were the "party of 'no,'" and mindful that voters expected the party to propose its own health plan, Republicans offered their proposal only a few days before the House took up H.R. 3962.

Some of the features of the GOP plan that were made in order by the Rules Committee—recall, this amendment was voted on after Stupak's—included limiting medical malpractice suits, allowing Americans to purchase health insurance outside the state where they live, and encouraging small businesses to band together to buy health insurance. The different goals of the two parties—comprehensive change for Democrats, incremental for Republicans—are underscored by the stark differences in their respective price tags. According to a preliminary analysis by the Congressional Budget Office (CBO), the ten-year cost for the Republican proposal was $61 billion; for the Democratic approach, nearly $1 trillion (Hook 2009b).

The Motion to Recommit

The motion to recommit, if adopted, means that either a bill is returned to the committee(s) that reported it (in effect, killed), or that the measure is changed substantively by requiring a committee to report back "forthwith" (instantly) to the chamber the minority party's policy alternative. Authorized by the House rulebook and in special rules issued by the Rules Committee, precedents stipulate that the motion is the prerogative of the minority party by someone who is opposed to the legislation. Traditionally used by the minority party to force the House to vote on its substantive alternative, recent congresses have also witnessed its use for political purposes, so-called "gotcha" amendments designed to undermine the majority party's bill and to force electorally vulnerable majority party members to vote on "hot button" issues (gun control, pornography, immigration, and so on) that might cause them political grief back home.

House Democratic leaders were worried that an artfully crafted GOP-offered motion, if adopted, could upend the bill. Their worry was that Republicans would force Democrats to vote on restricting the ability of undocumented immigrants to purchase health insurance under the proposed health overhaul. Instead, Minority Whip Eric Cantor offered a motion to recommit that would reform medical liability lawsuits and improve the Medicare payment system. Cantor's motion was handily rejected by a vote of 187 yeas to 247 nays.[9] Many Democrats expected that they would face a tough immigration vote. "Let's just say there could have been tougher motions to recommit," remarked House Democratic Campaign Chair Chris Van Hollen (Bendery 2009). A GOP leadership aide said Republicans offered the recommittal motion that they did because medical liability and Medicare cuts would be key issues in the 2010 elections. He opined that it was "a devastating vote for vulnerable Democrats" (Bendery 2009).

On November 7, 2009, in a rare Saturday session that started at 9 a.m. and ended at 11:33 p.m., the health reform bill passed by the narrow vote of 220 to 215.[10] After the months-long battle in the House, attention now turned to the Senate. Although health care was a top priority when the House started action, there was also heightened concern in the general public about double-digit unemploy-ment, a rising tide of red ink, and the expanding role of the national government.

Moreover, the months-long struggles and acrimonious battles required to pass the health bill in the House portended even larger difficulties in the Senate, where any senator has an array of parliamentary prerogatives to frustrate action on any measure or matter. Unsurprisingly, the two Senate parties viewed House passage of health care reform quite differently. A top aide to Senate Majority Leader Harry Reid said the House's action "gives us momentum in the Senate"; not so, declared GOP Senator Lindsey Graham—"The House bill is dead on arrival in the Senate." Added Republican leader Mitch McConnell, "Americans don't want a 2000-page, trillion-dollar government experiment" (Hook 2009c).

Action in the Senate

The House was the first chamber to pass health care reform, but the Senate Com-mittee on Health, Education, Labor, and Pensions (HELP) was the first to mark up and report a health reform bill (July 15, 2009). To be sure, each chamber's leaders were monitoring what the other's was doing and staking out positions to be resolved in the expected conference negotiations. Senate Majority Leader Reid announced on October 26, 2009, that he would include a government-run insurance plan in the Senate's health bill. Although his decision aroused the ire of several centrist senators, it eased the anxieties of many House Democrats who favored a robust public option. As House Majority Whip James Clyburn explained, "One thing that had been challenging on this side is that many of our members who feel good about a public option didn't feel good about walking the plank [to be heckled by right-wing groups back home for] voting on something the Senate wasn't going to consider" (Epstein 2009, 6).

Compared to the House, the Senate is a more floor- than committee-cen-tered institution. Every senator has wide opportunities to debate and amend measures reported from the various committees. This reality stems from the character and rules of the Senate. It is simply easier to bypass committees in the Senate either by offering non-germane amendments or by employing Sen-ate Rule 14. This rule allows any individual senator to have a bill placed on the legislative calendar rather than referred to committee.[11] Once on the calendar, the measure is positioned to be proposed to be called up for Senate consid-eration by the majority leader, who sets the chamber's agenda. The majority leader used Rule 14 to place the House-passed health overhaul bill (H.R. 3962) on the Senate's calendar. Accordingly, he had the option to offer a motion to proceed to it at a time of his choosing.[12]

Discussion of Senate action focuses less attention on committee action and more on Majority Leader Reid's efforts to mobilize the votes to pass the president's health overhaul initiative. Senator Reid also had to overcome scores of procedural hurdles because of the determined opposition of the forty-member GOP minority. Recall the well-publicized statement of GOP Senator Jim De-Mint, a Tea Party favorite: "If we're able to stop Obama on [health care reform], this will be his Waterloo. It will break him" (Smith 2009).

Committee Action

The Senate's two principal health committees are the aforementioned HELP panel and the tax-writing Finance Committee. The focus of the HELP Committee, a panel filled with liberal-leaning Democrats, was to produce a measure with provisions reflecting their goals, such as a strong government-run program (the public option) that could compete with private insurers. A concern of the Finance panel, with a more conservative Democratic membership, was to produce a deficit-neutral measure that cost less than $1 trillion. How to pay for expanding health care to millions of uninsured individuals was a source of considerable and continuing controversy. For example, some Democrats proposed a surtax on Americans making $250,000 or more per year; others urged taxing employer-based health benefits.

Senator Dodd, as noted earlier, served as acting chair of the HELP Committee in the absence of the ailing Senator Kennedy. In mid-June 2009, Senator Dodd stated, "My goal is to write a good bill. My goal is not bipartisanship" (Hunt 2009, 3). After sixty hours of debate and the consideration of hundreds of amendments, the HELP panel in mid-July approved its health reform measure on a party-line vote of thirteen to ten. Numerous GOP amendments were agreed to during the HELP markup, but Republicans contended that they were technical or minor rather than substantive. The HELP panel's bill (S. 1679, the Affordable Health Choices Act) was reported to the Senate in mid-September.

The Finance Committee, chaired by Senator Max Baucus, wanted to report a bipartisan health reform measure that could pass the Senate. Mindful that the House product was partisan, as was the likely HELP bill, in June 2009, Chairman Baucus put together a bipartisan group of Finance members who had a record of working across the aisle. The press dubbed the group the "gang of six." The three Democrats were Senators Baucus, Kent Conrad, and Jeff Bingaman. The three Republicans were Senators Charles Grassley, the former chair of Finance; Michael Enzi, the ranking member of HELP; and Olympia Snowe.[13] Snowe, a centrist lawmaker, was especially targeted by Baucus as someone who could be encouraged to vote with the Democrats.

The negotiating group met many times over the course of the next three months. Progress was slower than expected and deadlines for action by the group were rebuffed. The only deadline that really mattered to Democratic leaders was to finish the bill by the end of December 2009. The Finance Committee began its markup on September 23 and over the course of eight days conducted long markup meetings and considered over a hundred amendments. In a blow to liberal Democrats, the Finance Committee rejected an amendment to add a public option to Baucus's bill. On October 13, the panel voted fourteen to nine to approve the measure: the America's Healthy Futures Act (S. 1796). Senator Snowe was the lone Republican to vote for the measure. Widely reported in the media was her comment that a vote to report did not mean that she would vote the same way on the floor (Hook 2009a). Later, Majority Leader Reid said too much time was wasted trying to woo Senator Snowe: "As I look back it was a waste of time dealing with her, because she had no intention of ever working anything out" for floor consideration (Nagourney 2010, 30).

Following successful action by the two panels, two overlapping issues shaped the activities of the majority leader: developing a health reform measure acceptable to his sixty-vote Democratic majority—fifty-eight Democrats and two independents, Senators Joseph Lieberman and Bernie Sanders—and overcoming Republican procedural obstacles. Both posed difficult challenges for Reid. Worth mentioning is that Reid could have used a filibuster-proof procedure called "reconciliation" (discussed below) to move health care reform, but with a sixty-vote majority—at least on paper—he opted to follow the regular order for debating and amending the legislation. A bill of such importance deserved extensive and vigorous deliberation, he stated.

Vote Mobilization and Strategy

Senator Reid assumed control over merging the HELP and Finance Committees' products into one overhaul package. He consulted with Chairmen Baucus and Dodd and White House Chief of Staff Rahm Emanuel, among others, during this process. As Reid stated, "All four of us understand that legislation is the art of compromise, consensus-building, and we're going to do that. And of course—it's obvious that the president himself is going to have something to do with what comes to this bill that is brought to the floor" (Haberkorn 2009).

To take up a health reform measure that would inevitably contain tax provisions, Reid had to employ what might be called the "shell bill" strategy. Since the Constitution requires revenue-raising bills to originate in the House, Reid took a House-passed tax bill on the Senate calendar, deleted all the text following the bill's operative clause ("Be it enacted in the Senate and the House of Representatives of the United States of America in Congress assembled"), and substituted the composite measure fused from the work of the HELP and Finance Committees (Pierce 2009a). Reid selected a popular House tax measure (H.R. 3590) that passed 416 to 0 as his shell bill.[14] The bill was titled the "Service Members Home Ownership Tax Act," which provided homeowner assistance to the families of military, diplomatic, and intelligence community personnel. Recall that Reid used Senate Rule 14 to place the House-passed health bill on the legislative calendar of the Senate, but he chose not to use Speaker Pelosi's bill because it was anathema to many senators.

The majority leader recognized that passing health care reform hinged on winning the support of his party's liberal and moderate senators. Liberals disliked the omission of a public option in the Finance Committee's bill and moderates objected to the sticker-price of the HELP Committee's bill. Reid's fundamental goal was to produce a health bill that could attract under Senate rules the sixty votes required to overcome GOP filibusters. As Senate Republican leader McConnell revealed, "There's no question [health reform] will require 60 votes to get on the bill" (Hunter 2009a, 7). Reid also had other objectives, such as keeping a health reform bill at or under $900 billion, as the president promised, and, by the end of the year, passing the measure, which happened on December 24. Adding extra pressure on the majority leader was a tough reelection battle back home. The Senate's failure to pass health care could jeopardize his November 2010 reelection chances by angering various liberal groups (MoveOn.org, for example), which could advise their supporters not to work to energize Nevada voters to turn out for Reid.

The result: the majority leader employed the traditional tools of party leaders to win votes and to keep the process moving to a final conclusion. His actions and maneuvers epitomize those of a transactional party leader. As one analyst said about Reid's leadership approach, "While other lawmakers consider a bill on its policy merits, Reid views it first through the lens of how many votes he will need to enact it" (Friedman 2011, 39). The majority leader wanted to win on health care, and he went all out to achieve that result.

Gathering votes is additive, and in this case it proved to be an arduous and rather lengthy process. With Republicans solidly opposed to the Democrats' health reform plan, the hard bargaining and deal-making occurred among Senate Democrats. Three vote-gathering techniques on health care reform are illustrative of Reid's approach. They are one-on-one and small group meetings, policy concessions, and "gangs."

One-on-One and Small Group Meetings

The majority leader held scores of private meetings with individual or groups of Democratic senators to listen to their concerns and to try to respond to them in a way that was satisfactory to the lawmakers. Reid met many times with three moderate Democratic senators—Mary Landrieu, Ben Nelson, and Blanche Lincoln—as well as independent Joseph Lieberman, to try to allay their concerns. All had many issues with the health bill, particularly the inclusion of a public option, and Reid needed all four on board to approve the motion to proceed to the bill, to end debate on any amendments, and, finally, to vote for the health bill on final passage.

Policy Concessions

Reid made numerous policy concessions to on-the-fence, centrist senators. With every Democratic vote crucial, moderate members were favorably positioned to make demands that the majority leader could not ignore. The political reality: any member could be the sixtieth senator, threaten to derail health reform, and win concessions from the majority leader. For example, Senator Landrieu secured more Medicaid funding for Louisiana (dubbed the "Louisiana Purchase" by the press), and Senator Nelson received similar favorable treatment for Nebraska (called by critics the "Cornhusker Kickback"). Liberal Democrats were not happy with the use of such provisions to secure the votes of the party holdouts. "I don't want [a few] Democratic senators dictating to the other 56 of us and the rest of the country," remarked Senator Sherrod Brown (Fritze 2009, 15A). Despite their misgivings, liberal senators had little choice but to go along with the policy concessions; they needed their colleagues' votes to prevail. To be sure, Republicans said these deals were added to the health bill to "buy" the votes of the Democratic senators.

"Gangs"

Throughout the Senate's history, small groups of senators have come together to try to resolve knotty procedural, political, and policy issues. Today's press has dubbed these informal groups "gangs."[15] Finance Chairman Baucus, for instance, had his previously mentioned "gang of six." To meet the challenge of reaching a compromise of the contentious public option proposal, Reid directed Senators Charles Schumer and Mark Pryor "to convene negotiations with five moderates and five liberals to reach a deal on the public option" (Raju 2009, 12). This group became known as the "gang of ten." Strategically, engaging Democrats in the negotiating process gives them a personal stake in the outcome. There were a number of these groups formed during the health care debate. For example, Senator Mark Warner led a freshmen Democratic group working on a package of cost-containment proposals (Wayne and Hunter 2009, 4).

Procedural-Political Obstacles

On November 19, 2009, after weeks of negotiations concerning the cost of health care, the public option, and many other issues, Majority Leader Reid presented his merged bill to the Democratic Conference in a PowerPoint presentation titled "Health Insurance Reform: Highlights of Merged Democratic Bill" (Hunter 2009b, 4). Reid's measure was actually a 2,074-page substitute amendment to H.R. 3590 (aiding military home buyers) that he titled the "Patient Protection and Affordable Care Act." Thereafter, the majority leader confronted a large number of procedural and political issues that he ultimately overcame, ending in the successful Christmas Eve enactment of H.R. 3590.[16] The majority leader used his considerable parliamentary skills to move health reform through the Senate in several ways.

Calling Up the Measure

On November 20, Reid moved to proceed to H.R. 3590 under the terms of a unanimous consent agreement (UCA) reached the previous day.[17] The unanimous consent agreement stipulated that after debating the motion to proceed for two days, the Senate would hold a cloture vote on the evening of the second day. If cloture attracted the required sixty votes, the motion to proceed would be considered agreed to and the majority leader would be recognized to call up his amendment and make it pending before the Senate. Importantly, this meant that the Republicans were waiving their right under Rule 22 to have thirty hours of post-cloture debate. With Thanksgiving only a few days away, senators wanted to head home for the holiday rather than stay in session to consume the thirty hours (no doubt GOP leader McConnell surmised that Reid had mobilized the required sixty votes to invoke cloture on the motion to proceed).

Given unified GOP opposition to the Democratic proposal, why would Republicans agree to Reid's unanimous consent request? Two explanations appear relevant: first, to force moderate and electorally vulnerable senators (Blanche Lincoln, for example) to vote on the procedural motion to proceed to the bill. Their vote could then be framed as a vote on substance and not procedure. As GOP leader McConnell said, "Anyone who votes 'aye' [on the motion to proceed] is voting for all these things [higher taxes, hikes in health insurance premiums, and massive cuts in Medicare]" (Pierce and Stanton, 2009).

Second, Republicans wanted at least a full day (November 21) preceding the cloture vote to orchestrate a debate critical of the Democratic proposal and to use the time to try to turn a Democrat against cloture.[18] In fact, the UCA provided to each party blocks of controlled time to discuss health reform during Friday (November 20) and Saturday (November 21). As a senior Senate Republican aide explained, under Senate Rule 22, Republicans "would have only been entitled to one hour of debate before the [cloture] vote. Now we have all day [Saturday] to flip one Democrat. The reading [of Reid's amendment, threatened by GOP Senator Tom Coburn] would've been to an empty chamber after the vote had happened, press would have gone home, and Americans would have turned the channel. Now it's show time" (Pierce 2009b).

On November 21, the Senate voted 60–39 along strict party lines to invoke cloture on the motion to proceed to H.R. 3590 and, under the terms of the UCA, the motion to proceed was also agreed to. Majority Leader Reid knew that the vote to invoke cloture by several Democratic senators did not mean that they would do the same on various motions offered on the floor or on final passage. Moderate Senators Landrieu, Lieberman, Lincoln, and Nelson told Reid that unless the public option was stricken from Reid's amendment or modified to their liking, they would vote against the health measure on final passage. Liberal Senator Bernard Sanders responded that he, and other like-minded colleagues, "would not support final passage without a strong public option" (Wayne 2009b, 2).

Manager's Amendment

It was evident to Reid that the only way to win the backing of all the moderates and liberals was to draft a manager's amendment acceptable to the two party factions. Given President Obama's wish to wrap up health care by the end of the year—to avoid the election-year politics of 2010—and Reid's self-imposed Christmas deadline, there simply was not time for the Senate to consider separately each senator's amendment to alter the health reform legislation. As it was, Democrats were frustrated with the often slow pace of the proceedings, with GOP leaders unwilling at times to expedite action on amendments. "What's the rush?" was the view of GOP senators, who noted that key portions of the health plan would not take effect until 2014.

The GOP's goal was to force Reid to mobilize sixty votes over and over on substantive and procedural issues. Moreover, UCAs on amendments often required sixty votes for adoption, as Republicans hoped to win the votes of Democrats with artfully crafted amendments. Republicans also formulated amendments with themes in mind, such as "start over." Several times Republicans offered motions to commit (or send) H.R. 3590 to the Finance Committee with instructions rather than offer a health-related amendment. GOP lawmakers said they used the procedural tactic "to make the point that the Senate should go back to the drawing board on the health care bill" (Pierce 2009, 1).[19] None of the motions to commit were successful. If one had been, Majority Leader Reid would have had to start over and use time-consuming procedures to return the bill to the floor.

On December 19, Majority Leader Reid offered the manager's amendment to the Senate. After weeks of negotiations, and with the aid of President Obama and other party leaders, Reid secured the sixty votes needed to push health care reform over the finish line. But it still would not be easy to do given the array of procedural obstructionist tactics employed by Republicans. As indicated above, Senate rules require amendments to be read in full, unless unanimous consent is granted to waive that requirement.[20] GOP leader McConnell requested that the 383-page manager's amendment be read in its entirety. At the conclusion of the reading, Senator McConnell thanked the clerks for having "to read for the last 7 or 8 hours."[21]

Once the manager's amendment was before the Senate, Reid immediately used a procedural tactic that recent majority leaders have employed with increasing frequency. He "filled the amendment tree." The "tree" is a parliamentary chart that determines, depending on the nature of the amendment (to add new text to the pending measure, for example), how many amendments may be simultaneously pending to a measure. Using the majority leader's right of priority recognition by the presiding officer, Reid offered amendment after amendment until the "tree" was filled, closing off any opportunity for senators to propose changes to the manager's amendment that might cause Democratic defections. Reid also used tree-filling in mid-December to force favorable Senate action on the defense appropriations bicameral agreement, which GOP senators were stalling to prevent Reid from meeting his promised Christmas deadline for passing health care reform (Kane and Montgomery 2009, A1). (He also employed tree-filling on H.R. 3590 following a successful December 22 cloture vote.)

Angry at the tree-filling tactic, Republicans were also upset that Reid drafted the manager's amendment in secret with no input from the minority party. The manager's amendment was "written in secret for the last six weeks," declared Senate GOP Conference Chair Lamar Alexander. "So almost no one here knew what was in it. It was presented to us. Then the Democratic leader said: Well, we are going to start voting on it, and we are going to pass it before Christmas" (Alexander 2009, S13640). Senator Alexander's remarks turned out to be accurate since Senator Reid on December 19 also filed cloture to bring to a close debate on overhauling the health care system. In short, the "end game"—the vote on final passage—was just a few days away.

Strategic Use of Cloture

The Senate is an anti-democratic institution because a majority often cannot act when it wants to pass legislation. Rather, the reality or threat of a filibuster permeates Senate activities; hence the upper house is often called the "sixty-vote" Senate. Cloture is the Senate's formal way of ending filibusters, but it is a time-consuming process, taking three or more days. On day one, a cloture petition is filed on an amendment and/or the bill; on day two, germane amendments are filed; on day three, the cloture vote is held. If cloture is invoked, thirty more hours (day four and some of day five) of post-cloture debate is in order.

In today's ideologically polarized and sharply partisan Senate, cloture is a strategic procedural tool of all recent majority leaders, including Reid. Unable often to secure the unanimous consent of Republicans to proceed to legislation ("obstruction on steroids," he called it), Reid filed dozens of cloture motions in recent congresses with diverse purposes in mind, such as framing the minority party as obstructionist, imposing a germaneness requirement on amendments (required if cloture is invoked), or, as in the case of health care reform, expediting action on legislation. In this instance, the majority leader filed three back-to-back cloture motions on December 19 to bring Senate consideration of health care reform to a successful end.

The first cloture vote was on the manager's amendment. The second was on Reid's initial 2,047-page complete substitute amendment. And the third cloture vote was on H.R. 3590, the "shell" bill that Reid selected to carry his complete substitute.[22] After each cloture vote, Republicans usually insisted on the thirty additional hours provided under Rule 22 before the Senate could then vote on the next. There were early morning votes (1:00 a.m. and 7:00 a.m.) that captured the media's attention. This case explains why.

On Saturday, December 19, Senator Reid filed cloture on the manager's amendment. Under Rule 22, one day must pass before the cloture vote could occur on the manager's amendment, one hour after the Senate convenes. The Senate convened on Sunday (December 20) to debate health care reform. On Monday, December 21, the Senate convened at 12:01 a.m. and voted an hour later to invoke cloture (60–39) on the manager's amendment. Thirty hours of consideration remained before the Senate could vote on the manager's amendment. Thus, the Senate met at 7:00 a.m. on Tuesday (December 22) to adopt (60–39) the manager's amendment. Cloture was also adopted on Reid's complete substitute and H.R. 3590, each carried by a 60–39 vote.

During these final days, Republicans raised numerous points of order against the health care legislation, citing violations of Senate rules, laws, and constitutional provisions. All were set aside by vote of the Senate. With Democrats united behind health care reform, GOP leader McConnell knew he was fighting a losing battle. As he said in reference to Reid, "We are working on an agreement that will give certainty to the way to end this session" (McConnell 2009, S13717). Ultimately, certainty came when the Senate convened at 6:45 a.m. on December 24 and approved the health overhaul bill (H.R. 3590, as amended) by a 60–39 vote. Lawmakers quickly departed the Capitol for the holiday and New Year's recess.

The Outlook for Passage Suddenly Turns Bleak

When lawmakers returned to Capitol Hill in mid-January 2010, House and Senate Democrats wanted the two chambers to resolve their differences as quickly as possible. Congressional Democrats knew that with a slumping economy voters were more concerned about jobs and economic growth than health care reform. Moreover, overhauling the health care system was unpopular with many voters.

Resolving bicameral differences on legislation typically involves one of two formal methods: convene a conference committee or employ the exchange of amendment (or "ping pong") procedure. Press accounts indicated that Senate Republicans would filibuster each of the three steps required to create a health reform conference committee (Stanton 2009).[23] Majority Leader Reid had enough of GOP tactics and did not want to give Republicans additional opportunities to delay the enactment of health care reform. As a result, the formal conference process was bypassed; instead, Democrats used a de facto conference of top House and Senate party and committee leaders, with the participation of key White House officials (Allen and Young 2010, 3). The plan was for the House to amend the Senate version and then "ping pong" the negotiated compromise amendment between the chambers for adoption. The House would act first on the compromise amendment and then send the package to the Senate for final action. Senate Republicans might stall action on the negotiated compromise, but Democrats could stop a filibuster with their sixty-vote margin.

The de facto conference committee, led by Speaker Pelosi and Majority Leader Reid, had the job of melding the provisions wanted by the House, Senate, and White House into a compromise amendment to H.R. 3590 that could pass both chambers and be signed by the president. The procedural and policy struggles in the Senate implied that the negotiated health compromise would tilt more toward the Senate's version than the House's. Liberals in the House recognized this reality but insisted that the compromise amendment include provisions wanted by the House. "Merely to rubber-stamp what the Senate does is not enough," declared the co-chair of the Congressional Progressive Caucus (Pershing 2010, A8).

Although there were sharp differences of views on many health issues—amplified by the lobbying of numerous special interests—disagreements over contentious issues were defused by "the desire to avoid new brawls and finish healthcare—especially with polls showing that joblessness [was] weighing heavily on voters' minds" (Levey and Hook 2010). In an optimistic assessment of bicameral progress, Speaker Pelosi stated, "I think we're very close to reconciliation, respectful of the challenges, policy and otherwise, in the House and Senate" (Barr and Teske 2010, A14).

Congressional Republicans, angry that the Pelosi-Reid-Obama negotiations were being held behind closed doors, asked about the president's transparency pledge. On the campaign trail in Chester, Virginia, on August 21, 2008, Obama had promised that "we'll have [health care] negotiations televised on C-SPAN [the Cable Satellite Public Affairs Network], so the people can see who is making arguments on behalf of their constituents and who is making arguments on behalf of the drug companies or the insurance companies." Brian Lamb, the head of C-SPAN, asked the president to permit C-SPAN to televise the health negotiations. House Republicans even filed a discharge petition (a procedure to extract legislation stuck in committee) to bring a bipartisan resolution to the floor, urging the public broadcasting of the health negotiations (Bendery 2010). Needless to say, Democratic leaders rebuffed these requests. The compromise health bill, explained Speaker Pelosi, is being put together "behind closed doors according to an agreement by top Democrats" (Knickerbocker 2010).

Scott Brown's Surprise Senate Victory

On January 19, 2010, an electoral event occurred that stunned the president and congressional Democrats, upended their plan to move expeditiously to get health care reform signed into law, and revived GOP hopes that they could kill the legislation. Massachusetts voters sent Republican Scott Brown to the Senate in a special election to replace Democratic Senator Kennedy. Moreover, one of many issues that Brown campaigned on was that, as the forty-first senator, he would give Senate Republicans the chance to derail "the trillion-dollar health care bill that is being forced on the American people," a measure that will "raise taxes, hurt Medicare, destroy jobs and run our nation deeper into debt" (Tumulty 2010, 1; Nagourney 2010, A1). Although many factors influence election outcomes, the health overhaul issue did contribute to Brown's surprise upset victory. Three scholars, for example, asked this question: "How can a little known Republican [Scott Brown] run a competitive campaign in Massachusetts?" Their prescient answer: "The culprit is the unpopularity of health reform, and it means that Democrats will face even worse problems later this year [November 2010] in less liberal places than Massachusetts" (Brady, Kessler, and Rivers 2010, A17).

Brown's victory immediately changed the political calculus on Capitol Hill and caused congressional Democrats to ponder the fate of health care and their ambitious agenda. Without a filibuster-proof, sixty-vote supermajority in the Senate, congressional Democrats entered a period of intense negotiations to determine their course of action. Members raised many options, such as to complete House action quickly on Reid's Senate measure with no changes and send the measure to the president for his signature; expedite House-Senate bargaining and pass health care before Brown can be sworn in (on February 4, 2010); or work with the GOP to pass a smaller, consensus version of health care reform.

For the next several weeks, until mid-March 2010, private negotiations among the president, Speaker Pelosi, and Majority Leader Reid, along with others, consumed their time and effort. Policy and procedural issues dominated these discussions, not to mention the overlay of the fast-approaching 2010 mid-term elections. Despite opposition from various lawmakers, the Democratic leaders decided to pursue a dual-bill strategy. The House would pass the Senate's version (H.R. 3590) unchanged and then immediately pass a second bill—a filibuster-proof budget reconciliation measure (see below)—that would "correct" the provisions in Reid's measure that offended many House Democrats (including, for example, Medicaid benefits for a few states, such as Nebraska, but not all states). This approach avoided further Senate action on H.R. 3590, where Reid no longer had sixty votes, and it was the fastest way to get comprehensive health reform sent to the president.

Reconciliation and the "Two-Bill" Strategy

The two-bill strategy initially meant that Speaker Pelosi had to implement the plan. Pelosi and her leadership team struggled to put together the winning margin for H.R. 3590. They faced an array of difficulties, such as vulnerable Democrats worried about their 2010 reelection given Brown's victory in a normally "blue" state; members who wanted to set aside health reform because of sagging popular support and move to a jobs bill; liberal Democrats who opposed Reid's concessions to conservative Senate Democrats; and House concern about the trustworthiness of the Senate. With nearly three hundred House-passed measures languishing in the Senate, many Democrats wondered if the Senate would even consider a second bill once the House enacted H.R. 3590. To assuage House Democrats, Majority Leader Reid pledged in a letter signed by fifty-one Democratic Senators "to pass the modifications using the budget reconciliation process, which requires only a majority vote and would protect the second bill from a filibuster" (Hunter and Wayne 2010, 1). Reid's letter pledging to pass a health care reconciliation bill was never made public (Pierce 2010a).

"Reconciliation" is an optional process established by the 1974 Budget Act. It is made in order when Congress adopts, pursuant to the 1974 budget law, a concurrent budget resolution (Congress's fiscal blueprint) that includes specific reconciliation instructions. Reconciliation's basic purpose is to bring revenue and entitlement legislation (Social Security, Medicare, and Medicaid, for example) into conformity (or "reconciliation") with the fiscal targets established in the concurrent budget resolution. Procedurally, reconciliation is especially significant for the Senate (the majoritarian House employs the Rules Committee to structure floor decision-making). Measures governed in the Senate by this optional process are treated differently from other bills or amendments. They cannot be filibustered (twenty hours of debate are permitted) and, therefore, passage requires a simple majority. Hence, a reconciliation bill was an attractive way to revamp H.R. 3590 once that measure passed the House and was sent to the president. On March 17, 2010, the House Budget Committee reported a reconciliation bill (H. R. 4872). That bill would be the second, or trailer, bill, crafted to revise the Senate-passed health reform plan (H.R. 3590).

Two Bills Pass the House

As Speaker Pelosi closed in on a winning majority, the Rules Committee aroused the ire of House Republicans, various media outlets, and even some House Democrats. The panel suggested, among other options, that it might report a procedural resolution that would "deem" the Senate bill passed without a direct House vote on it. As explained by the ranking Rules Republican,

Representative David Dreier, the "so-called 'Slaughter solution' [after Rules chair Louise Slaughter] would allow the House to wait for the Senate to pass a fix-it package [the reconciliation bill] to their . . . health care bill. When the fix would be passed by the Senate, the [Reid] bill would magically be deemed passed by the House without our ever having a transparent up-or-down vote on the original [Senate] bill" (Dreier 2010, H1365). This procedure was not used for many reasons, including the Senate parliamentarian's statement that reconciliation in his chamber could only be used to change an existing law. Under "deem and pass," there was no health reform law to fix because the president had yet to be presented with any health reform bill to sign.[24]

On March 21, 2010, in a rare Sunday session, Rules Chair Slaughter called up a special rule that made in order back-to-back chamber consideration of the Senate amendment (the Reid health plan) to H.R. 3590 and a budget reconciliation bill (H.R. 4872). No amendments were made in order to either bill by the special rule. Republicans challenged the procedural resolution (H.Res. 1203) by raising two points of order against its consideration by the House—one for violating House rules concerning unfunded mandates on states and localities and another for waiving House anti-earmark rules. Each point of order was turned down by vote of the House, after which the House adopted H.Res. 1203. When it was time to vote on final passage of the two measures, the House concurred in the Senate amendment to H.R. 3590 by a vote of 219–212. After rejecting the GOP's motion to recommit (dealing with abortions)—Obama won the support of anti-abortion Democrats on this motion by issuing an executive order that no taxpayer funds would be spent for abortions in the new health care system—the House then agreed to H.R. 4872, the Reconciliation Act of 2010, by a 220–211 vote. Two days later, President Obama signed the landmark health overhaul bill (H.R. 3590) into law (P.L. 111-148).

The Senate Considers Reconciliation

The Senate had ample notice that a reconciliation bill would be coming its way from the House. On March 23, H.R. 4872 arrived in chamber. Majority Leader Reid, employing Rule 14, promptly placed it on the legislative calendar, fulfilling his commitment to House Democrats that the Senate would "fix" the bill (H.R. 3590) that the president signed into law. Just hours after the president signed health reform into law, the Senate voted 56–40 to take up the reconciliation bill.[25] Senate Republicans were ready with their parliamentary plans to slow down and create obstacles to the bill, such as forcing the House to revote on H.R. 4872 by making changes to it. Although reconciliation bills cannot be filibustered, the procedure's complex rules and precedents provide ample opportunities for opponents to stall, modify, or even defeat reconciliation measures.

The Senate parliamentarian, who would advise the presiding officer of the validity of the procedural objections that Republicans would surely raise, was consulted by senators of both parties to get a sense of whether the House-passed bill violated the rules and precedents that govern reconciliation (Pierce 2010b, 1). For example, if the presiding officer rules—based on advice from the parliamentarian—that certain provisions in H.R. 4872 are out of order, the measure could lose the "fast track" protection of reconciliation, opening the bill to lengthy debate and potentially requiring a three-fifths vote of the Senate to invoke cloture. Moreover, any change to H.R. 4872 would require further action by the House. In short, reconciliation can be a risky proposition.

Three procedural strategies were employed by Senate Republicans. The first was to consider raising a point of order that might kill the reconciliation bill. Under reconciliation rules, "extraneous" matter is to be excluded from these measures. What is extraneous is not always easy to determine. For example, certain changes to Social Security are extraneous and subject to a point of order. If this point of order is upheld by the presiding officer, the reconciliation bill would fall, since sixty votes would be required to overturn the chair's ruling. It is noteworthy that forty-one GOP senators signed a letter saying that "we are going to sustain [and not vote to overturn] the rules of Senate."[26]

Initially, GOP senators believed that a Social Security point of order could kill H.R. 4872 because a tax provision affected the Social Security trust fund. However, informal GOP discussions with the parliamentarian, who cited past precedents involving a Senate GOP chair of the Budget Committee in similar circumstances, said there was only an indirect effect on the Social Security trust fund. Hence, if called upon to provide advice to the presiding officer, the parliamentarian indicated it would be to rule against such a point of order. "The parliamentarian issued guidance on the [Social Security] point of order that would have brought down the entire bill," confided a Senate GOP leadership aide. "Not in our favor" (Wayne 2010, 6).

Second, GOP senators offered numerous amendments or raised points of order either to delete or add provisions to H.R. 4872 or to commit the bill to either the committees on finance or HELP. For example, there were amendments to eliminate the "sweetheart deals" provided senators from certain states (Nebraska and Louisiana, for instance) or to repeal the health care reform bill that the president had just signed into law. All amendments were tabled (killed) or ruled out of order by the presiding officer. The object of points of order against specific "extraneous" provisions in H.R. 4872 was, if they were sustained, to turn the legislation into "Swiss cheese"—replete with policy holes as key provisions were stricken from the bill.

Third, a formidable dilatory tactic involved lawmakers offering amendment after amendment after the statutory time limit of twenty hours had expired. The twenty hours provided in the Budget Act limit *debate* but not *consideration* of the bill. As a result, amendments can be called up indefinitely, in what is called a "vote-a-rama," and voted on with no real debate. Unanimous consent was obtained in the health debate to allow the sponsor of an amendment one minute to make his or her case and an opponent was provided one minute to respond. As a former Senate parliamentarian explained, lawmakers "could have amendment after amendment after amendment, and vote after vote after vote. It doesn't have to end. They could delay [health care], certainly, as long as they're willing to offer amendments" (Hunter 2010, 27).

The Senate considered forty-two amendments during a two-day vote-a-rama (Newmyer and Pierce 2010). Many of the GOP amendments were "gotcha," or political, proposals, designed to cause electoral grief in November 2010 for Democrats who voted them down. For example, amendments were proposed on same-sex marriage, to prohibit giving Viagra to rapists and child molesters, and to protect the Second Amendment (the right to bear arms). These amendments were all rejected by the Senate.

In the end, Republicans realized that it was time to bring things to a close. As GOP leader Senator McConnell said on March 24, "the majority leader and I have had a number of discussions off the floor, I say for the benefit of everyone in the Chamber, about some process to complete this bill" (McConnell 2010, S2005). Later that day, Majority Leader Reid asked and received the unanimous consent of the members to vote the next day on final passage of the reconciliation measure (McConnell 2010, S2012).

On March 25, the Senate agreed to H.R. 4872 by a vote of 56–43, but not before Vice President Biden, who was presiding, sustained two points of order against provisions in H.R. 4872, which caused them to be stricken.[27] As a result, the bill, as amended (due to the stricken provisions), was messaged to the House and taken up the same day. The procedural resolution from the House Rules Committee, which was subject to spirited debate, provided for ten minutes of debate, equally divided between the two sides, on the motion to concur in the Senate amendments to H.R. 4872. The motion to concur was agreed to by a vote 220–207, ending the policy, political, and procedural effort to enact the health care reconciliation measure. On March 30, the president signed the legislation into law (P.L. 111-152). The legislative struggle for health care reform was hardly over, however. Even before the bill was signed into law, congressional Republicans had introduced legislation to repeal it, and "repeal and replace" became a 2010 campaign message for Republicans.

Conclusion

Passing the landmark health overhaul legislation amid policy, political, and procedural twists and turns—recall the Christmas Eve vote in the Senate, the surprise election of Scott Brown, the use of reconciliation, the work of multiple committees, and much more—is a legislative story that scholars and commentators will analyze for years to come. The vitriolic debate and popular unease over health reform were factors that contributed to the defeat of various Democratic lawmakers in the November 2010 elections. The outlook for the November 2012 elections is that health overhaul remains an issue of political salience in many electoral contests across the country. With health reform as the backdrop, the two parties appear certain to clash over the size, reach, and proper role of the national government. Moreover, the reality of escalating health care spending—will the new law control costs?—is likely to keep the issue in the public spotlight for years to come.

Many implications and issues flow from legislative enactment of health care reform. Simply the sheer scope of the law—and the controversy it aroused—may give pause to future presidents who are keen on pushing complex, interdependent, and transformative changes in domestic policy. Surprisingly, it proved difficult for President Obama—who is known for his exceptional oratorical skills and who occupies the bully pulpit—and congressional Democrats to sell (explain and persuade) the health reform package to many segments of the general public. Voters heard much more about the federal power grab for health and death panels than they did about the law's positive benefits, such as expanding health care to thirty million uninsured people or allowing children up to the age of twenty-six to be covered by their parents' health insurance plans. The Democrats' lack of an effective messaging strategy enabled congressional Republicans, hostile media outlets, and many other critics to dominate the airways with negative (and often distorted) characterizations of the health overhaul plan. It seems that the White House and congressional Democrats spent too little time on their communication strategies, essential elements of legislative policymaking in this fast-paced, 24/7, competitive media environment (Sellers 2010).

Numerous other issues emerge from the enactment of health care reform. Three are briefly noted in closing.

Implementation

Enacting health care reform was an arduous process, but administrative implementation will be difficult as well. As the health advisor to the Colorado governor said, "Everybody forgets that you pass legislation and that's just the first part. There are years of rulemaking and negotiations and lobbying over the regulations and implementation" (Montgomery and Slevin 2009, A3). Numerous federal entities will issue scores of regulations—which have the force of law—to carry out the terms of the new health law. Meanwhile, opponents of the statute—inside and outside Congress—have launched a multi-front assault through legal suits, in the court of public opinion, and at the state level; various state officials (governors, state lawmakers, and attorneys general) are challenging or "slow walking" its implementation. And the GOP-controlled 112th House has utilized an array of legislative techniques to attempt to emasculate the administrative implementation, such as using the appropriations process to eliminate or reduce funding for regulation-writing by the federal health agencies.

Partisan or Bipartisan Governance

If only one opposition member supports health care reform, does that make it a bipartisan measure? Is bipartisan lawmaking something to be sought for its own sake even if issues are allowed to fester for years or decades? Is passage of landmark legislation consistent with party-line voting and with parliamentary procedures designed to facilitate that outcome? People would answer these and related questions in various ways, as in these two cases. Yale Professor David Mayhew put it this way: "Bipartisanship is a good thing in major welfare-state enterprises if they are to stick. Otherwise, they may suffer legitimacy problems and come apart" (Nagourney 2009, 16). David Axelrod, a long-time top aide to candidate and President Obama, provided another perspective. "Ultimately we are going to be measured by what we do, and not by the process. Process can't be more important than the outcome of the [health care] legislation" (Nagourney 2009, 16).

The Role of Party Leaders

The roles of Speaker Pelosi and Senate Majority Leader Reid were critical to the enactment of health care reform. Their parliamentary and political savvy, combined with their perseverance and determination to overcome various hurdles, produced a major victory for President Obama. Despite the large differences in the House and Senate versions of health care reform, and the intraparty policy divisions and reelection concerns of many in their ranks, they were able to bridge those differences through skillful strategizing, negotiating, and, fundamentally, knowing how to put together the compromises that led to a winning outcome. Reid clearly functioned as a transactional leader; Pelosi also functioned in that manner—making trades and bargains to win votes—but she also exhibited transformational qualities (Bzdek 2010, B1). When the legislative outcome seemed darkest after the election of Scott Brown, she acted to change those political circumstances by her passionate support for health care reform. "We're in the majority," the Speaker told the president. "We'll never have a better majority in your presidency in numbers than we've got right now. We can make this work" (Stolberg, Zeleny, and Hulse 2010, 1). And she was right.

The history of health care reform is still evolving, however. Its constitutionality is likely to be decided by the U.S. Supreme Court. Many people remain skeptical of or hostile toward the new law—derided as "Obamacare" by Republicans—but many of its provisions (improving access to health insurance, for example) are also supported by numerous individuals. The GOP strategy to "repeal and replace" may prove difficult to accomplish as popular features of the law take hold. Health care spending continues to increase, and it is unclear whether over time the cost curve will start to bend downward, or at least remain stable. In a law as significant as health care reform, mistakes will be found and changes will be made as it is implemented at the federal and state level. To paraphrase Yogi Berra, the former well-known New York Yankee baseball catcher, it is hard to make predictions, especially about the future.

Notes

1. Among the president's core principles were preventing insurance companies from denying health coverage to people with preexisting conditions and curbing the growth of health expenditures.

2. For an excellent analysis of the Congressional Budget Office (CBO), see Philip G. Joyce, *The Congressional Budget Office* (Washington, DC: Georgetown University Press, 2011).

3. In general, an "insurance exchange" is a program administered by the states where individuals and small businesses can choose from a menu of health insurance plans. If they cannot afford the price of insurance, the government would subsidize their purchase. A "public option" was a type of insurance plan available at the insurance exchange administered by the government. An "individual mandate" requires every individual to carry basic health insurance with provision made for the less well-off. There have been numerous federal court challenges involving the constitutionality of the individual mandate provision. It is evident that the U.S. Supreme Court will eventually render a decision on this issue.

4. Speaker Pelosi wanted the House to pass health legislation before the August recess. Splits within the party prevented that from happening. The result: Republicans and Tea Party activists had five weeks to foster negative public perceptions of the existing health proposals.

5. A "rule" from the Rules Committee is a procedural resolution that, if agreed to by the House, determines the conditions for debating a bill and whether amendments can be offered to it.

6. To be sure, there were other procedural-political elements that came into play on health care. For example, one was the calendar. The final vote on November 7, 2009, occurred just before the House was expecting to go home for the Veterans Day recess. As Majority Whip James Clyburn explained, scheduling the crucial vote for Saturday night helped because "it's always easier to whip when people want to go home." See Mike Soraghan, "Pelosi Predicts Victory," *The Hill*, November 6, 2009, p. 1. As another example, some House Republicans recommended that their party colleagues vote "present" on a controversial anti-abortion amendment, knowing that Democrats did not have the votes to pass it alone. The result: the GOP "present" strategy could have ended up killing the health care reform bill by angering many pro-life Democrats who wanted the abortion ban in the health legislation. The GOP plan was not carried out, in part because the anti-abortion amendment had the support of Catholic bishops and many conservative groups. See Molly Harper, "House GOP Mulled 'Present' Strategy on Abortion Amendment," *The Hill*, November 10, 2009, p. 10.

7. *Congressional Record*, November 7, 2009, pp. H12962–H12963.

8. *CongressDaily* is a publication of Washington-based National Journal, Inc.

9. *Congressional Record*, November 7, 2009, p. H12967.

10. The House took that long for various reasons: the rule was debated for an hour, and it provided for nearly six and a half hours of debate on health matters; there were also several votes in relation to health, five votes to suspend the rules and pass the uncontroversial measures, twenty one-minute speeches that preceded the health debate, and sundry parliamentary inquiries and actions that consumed additional time.

11. Under Rule 14, bills and joint resolutions, including House-passed measures, must be read twice on two different legislative days before they are referred to committee. If a senator interposes an objection between the first and second day, the measure will be placed on the legislative calendar.

12. *Congressional Record*, November 10, 2009, p. S11356, and November 16, 2009, p. S11359.

13. It was originally the "gang of seven," but Senator Orrin Hatch dropped out after he became unhappy with the negotiations.

14. *Congressional Record*, October 8, 2009, pp. H11126–H11127. Part of the reason for selecting H.R. 3590 would be its ease of reenactment by the House. Senator Reid's complete substitute for H.R. 3590 effectively made that bill an empty shell.

15. No doubt the term "gang" was popularized in the press and media during the 2005 battle in the Senate to end judicial filibusters. The "gang of 14"—seven Democrats and seven Republicans— came together to block a heavy-handed parliamentary maneuver that would have ended extended debate on judicial nominees.

16. The extent of potential procedural hurdles was clear; GOP Senator Judd Gregg even circulated a December 1 memo to his Republican colleagues outlining various ways Senate procedures could be used to stall or derail the health measure.

17. Frequently, the Senate dispenses with its formal rules and creates a negotiated, tailor-made procedure for the consideration of various measures or matters. They are called unanimous consent agreements (UCAs). UCAs are designed to expedite work in an institution known for extended debate, to impose a measure of predictability on floor action, and to minimize dilatory actions.

18. Rule 22 does provide a day for debate before the cloture vote. However, Reid could have made his motion to proceed on November 20—filed cloture and then withdrawn the motion—and sought unanimous consent for controlled time between the two sides. In recent times, it is not unusual for a majority leader to file cloture on a motion to proceed or to a measure and then bring other legislation to the floor, leaving the clotured matter in a state of parliamentary limbo (not subject to debate or amendment) until the Senate votes two days later on whether to invoke cloture.

19. In some cases, the motion to commit was made to avoid budget points of order that might have been made if the commit motion had been offered as an amendment.

20. On January 27, 2011, the Senate amended its rules to provide that a non-debatable motion can be made to waive the reading of an amendment if it has been publicly available for at least seventy-two hours.

21. *Congressional Record*, December 19, 2009, p. S13479.

22. Three cloture votes were required not only to stop a filibuster on each proposition but because once it is invoked by sixty votes, there is a strict post-cloture germaneness requirement for amendments. Cloture on the manager's amendment made it germane to Reid's complete substitute. Similarly, cloture on the complete substitute made it germane to H.R. 3590. Then cloture was required on the bill, as amended, to stymie any filibuster and move the legislation to final passage. Thus, for the manager's amendment and the complete substitute, two key votes had to be forged on each item: first, one to invoke cloture, and then, following any post-cloture debate, one to adopt the clotured amendment.

23. The three steps are as follows: the Senate majority leader asks the unanimous consent of the Senate to (1) "insist" in its amendment to a House-passed bill or, conversely, "disagree" to a House amendment to a Senate-originated bill; (2) "request" a conference with the other body; and (3) "authorize" the presiding officer to name conferees. Each of these parts is subject to extended debate, if made as separate motions.

24. Similar procedural actions ("deem and pass") were not infrequently taken in so-called "self-executing" rules in recent times.

25 The motion to proceed to the consideration of a reconciliation bill is not subject to debate.

26. *Congressional Record*, March 18, 2010, p. S1686.

27. The two minor provisions that were struck from H.R. 4872 involved the education program. The reconciliation directive in the 2009 concurrent budget resolution directed the House Education and Labor Committee to find savings in that substantive area. The points of order dealt with student loan provisions. The reconciliation bill, however, still included a little-noticed but major revamp of the college student loan (Pell grant) program. See Christi Parsons and Janet Hook, "Obama Signs Reconciliation Bill with Major Student Loan Change," *Los Angeles Times,* March 31, 2010, http://articles.latimes.com/2010/mar/31/nation/la-na-obama-reconciliation31-2010mar31 (accessed September 22, 2011).

References

Alexander, Lamar. 2009. "Service Members Home Ownership Tax Act of 2009—Resumed." *Congressional Record,* Senate, December 21, vol. 155, daily edition.

Allen, Jared, and Jeffrey Young. 2010. "Pelosi, Hoyer, Panel Chairmen Will Represent House on Health Reform." *Roll Call,* January 13.

Armstrong, Drew. 2009. "Waxman Blasted from Left over Health Care Compromise with 'Blue Dogs.'" *CQ Today,* July 31.

Austin, Jan, ed. 2010. *CQ 2009 Almanac.* Washington, DC: CQ-Roll Call Group.

Barr, Sarah, and Steve Teske. 2010. "House Democrats Staking Out Positions As Negotiations on Compromise Bill Continue." *Daily Report for Executives,* January 7.

Bendery, Jennifer. 2009. "Democrats Dodge Tough Immigration Vote." *Roll Call,* November 8. http://www.rollcall.com/news/-40406-1.html. Accessed September 16, 2011.

———. 2010. "GOP to File Discharge Petition to Broadcast Health Care Talks." *Roll Call,* January 12. http://www.rollcall.com/news/-42202-1.html. Accessed September 16, 2011.

Brady, David W., Daniel P. Kessler, and Douglas Rivers. 2010. "Health Care Is Hurting Democrats." *Wall Street Journal,* January 20.

Brown, Carrie Budoff. 2009. "Fate of Public Option Rests in Obama's Hands." *Politico,* September 30.

Burns, James MacGregor. 1978. *Leadership.* New York: Harper and Row.

Bzdek, Vince. 2010. "Why It Took a Woman to Fix Health Care." *Washington Post,* March 28.

Committee on the Judiciary, Subcommittee on Administrative Law and Governmental Relations. U.S. Congress, House of Representatives. 1983. *Regulatory Reform Act.* 98th Cong., 1st Sess., June 15. Washington, DC: Government Printing Office.

Condon, George, Jr. 2011. "The Whole Enchilada." *National Journal,* July 16.

Connolly, Ceci. 2010. "61 Days from Near-Defeat to Victory." *Washington Post,* March 23.

Dennis, Steven T. 2009a. "Rangel Plays Bit Part in Health Reform." *Roll Call,* July 23.

———. 2009b. "Pelosi Gets a Pre-Recess Deal." *Roll Call,* August 3.

Dodd, Christopher. 2010a. "Comprehensive Iran Sanctions, Accountability, and Divestment Act of 2010—Conference Report." *Congressional Record,* Senate, June 14, vol. 155, daily edition.

———. 2010b. "American Jobs and Closing Tax Loopholes Act of 2010." *Congressional Record,* Senate, vol. 155, daily edition.

Dreier, David. 2010. "Providing for Consideration of H.R. 3650, Harmful Algal Blooms and Hypoxia Research and Control Amendments Act of 2010." *Congressional Record,* House, March 12, vol. 156, daily edition.

Drew, Elizabeth. 2009. "Health Care: Can Obama Swing It?" *New York Review of Books,* October 22.

Epstein, Edward. 2009. "House Leaders Prep for Health Vote." *CQ Today,* October 28.

Friedman, Dan. 2011. "Patient Guy." *National Journal,* July 30.

Fritze, John. 2009. "Negotiations Begin Anew over Health Bill." *USA Today,* November 23.

Fritze, John, Susan Page, and Richard Wolf. 2010. "A 16-Month Drama, with 8 Key Moments." *USA Today*, March 26.

Gruenwald, Juliana. 2009. "GOP Rallies Conservatives against Health Bill." *CongressDaily PM*, November 5.

Haberkorn, Jennifer. 2009. "Reid Merging Senate Health Reform Bills." *Washington Times*, October 15. http://www.washingtontimes.com/news/2009/oct/15/reid-merging-health-care-bills. Accessed September 16, 2011.

Hook, Janet. 2009a. "Senate Finance Panel Nears Completion of Its Healthcare Bill." *Los Angeles Times*, October 3. http://articles.latimes.com/2009/oct/03/nation/na-health3. Accessed September 16, 2011.

———. 2009b. "House Republicans Offer Alternative Healthcare Proposal." *Los Angeles Times*, November 5. http://articles.latimes.com/2009/nov/05/nation/na-health-gop5. Accessed September 16, 2011.

———. 2009c. "Healthcare's Bill's Tough Sell in the House Signals Tougher Fight Ahead." *Los Angeles Times*, November 9. http://articles.latimes.com/2009/nov/09/nation/na-health9. Accessed September 16, 2011.

———. 2010. "Obama Helped Bring on the Healthcare Backlash." *Los Angeles Times*, February 22. http://articles.latimes.com/2010/feb/22/nation/la-na-obama-congress22-2010feb22. Accessed September 16, 2011.

Hunt, Kasie. 2009. "Dodd: 'My Goal Is Not Bipartisanship' on HELP Markup." *CongressDaily AM*, June 19.

Hunter, Kathleen. 2009a. "Moderates Remain Skeptical of Reid's Gamble for Party Unity on Procedure." *CQ Today*, October 28.

———. 2009b. "Reid's Measure Moves to the Middle." *CQ Today*, November 19.

———. 2010. "Republicans Prepare Amendments, Budget Points of Order against Overhaul." *CQ Today*, March 4.

Hunter, Kathleen, and Alex Wayne. 2010. "Democrats Eye Fixes for Health Bill." *CQ Today*, February 26.

Johnson, Haynes, and David S. Broder. 1996. *The System*. Boston: Little, Brown, and Company.

Kane, Paul, and Lori Montgomery. 2009. "GOP Senators Seek to Block Defense Bill to Delay Health-Care Vote." *Washington Post*, December 18.

Knickerbocker, Brad. 2010. "What Happened to Obama's 'Government Transparency' Pledge." *Christian Science Monitor*, January 9. http://www.csmonitor.com/USA/Politics/The-Vote/2010/0109/What-happened-to-Obama-s-government-transparency-pledge. Accessed September 16, 2011.

Levey, Noam, and Janet Hook. 2010. "Congress Fights Healthcare Fatigue to Finish Bill." *Los Angeles Times*, January 13. http://articles.latimes.com/2010/jan/13/nation/la-na-health-congress13-2010jan13. Accessed September 16, 2011.

McConnell, Mitch. 2009. "Service Members Home Ownership Tax Act of 2009." *Congressional Record*, Senate, December 22, vol. 155, daily edition.

———. 2010. "Health Care and Reconciliation Act of 2010." *Congressional Record*, Senate, March 24, vol. 156, daily edition.

Montgomery, Lori, and Peter Slevin. 2009. "States Likely to Shape Health Reform." *Washington Post*, November 1.

Murray, Shailagh, and Lori Montgomery. 2009. "Democrats Wary of Health-Bill Defections." *Washington Post*, November 6.

Nagourney, Adam. 2009. "Partisan or Not, a Tough Course on Health Care." *New York Times*, July 26.

———. 2010. "Harry Reid Is Complicated." *New York Times Magazine*, January 24.

Nagourney, Adam, Jeff Zeleny, Kate Zernike, and Michael Cooper. 2010. "How the G.O.P. Captured a Seat Lost for Decades." *New York Times*, January 21.

Newmyer, Tory, and Emily Pierce. 2010. "Health Care Reform Survives Final Vote." *Roll Call*, March 25. http://www.rollcall.com/news/-44722-1.html. Accessed September 22, 2011.

O'Connor, Patrick, and John Bresnahan. 2009. "Pelosi Turns Ruthlessly Practical in Getting Votes." *Politico*, November 9.

Ota, Alan, and Bennett Roth. 2009. "House Democrats Split on Whether to Wait for Senate to Act on Overhaul." *CQ Today*, September 16.

Pershing, Ben. 2010. "Democrats in House Weigh Strategies for Health Reform." *Washington Post*, January 8.

Pierce, Emily. 2009a. "Reid Committed to Health Care Timeline, Has Plan for Forthcoming Bill." *Roll Call*, July 16. http://www.rollcall.com/news/-36900-1.html. Accessed September 16, 2011.

———. 2009b. "Reid Tees Up Vote; GOP Drops Bill-Reading Plan." *Roll Call*, November 19. http://www.rollcall.com/news/-40804-1.html. Accessed September 16, 2011.

———. 2009c. "GOP Quickly Goes to War." *Roll Call*, December 2.

———. 2010a. "Senate Won't Release Letter to Calm Nervous House Members on Reconciliation." *Roll Call*, March 19. http://www.rollcall.com/news/-44408-1.html. Accessed September 22, 2011.

———. 2010b. "Parliamentarian Takes the Stage." *Roll Call*, March 23.

Pierce, Emily, and John Stanton. 2009. "Lincoln's Saturday Timing Puzzles Colleagues." *Roll Call*, November 21. http://www.rollcall.com/news/-40869-1.html. Accessed September 16, 2011.

Raju, Manu. 2009. "Reid Plays It Close to the Vest." *Politico*, December 18.

Rothman, Heather, Brett Ferguson, and Jonathan Nicholson. 2009. "House Leaders to Spend August Merging Health Bills; Senate Finance Still Working." *Daily Report for Executives*, August 3.

Sellers, Patrick. 2010. *Strategic Communications in the U.S. Congress*. New York: Cambridge University Press.

Smith, Ben. 2009. "Health Reform Foes Plan Obama's 'Waterloo.'" *Politico*, July 17. http://www.politico.com/blogs/bensmith/0709/Health_reform_foes_plan_Obamas_Waterloo.html. Accessed September 16, 2011.

Stanton, John. 2009. "GOP Blocks Appointment as Senate Adjourns." *Roll Call*, December 24. http://www.rollcall.com/news/-41873-1.html. Accessed September 16, 2011.

Stolberg, Sheryl Gay, Jeff Zeleny, and Carl Hulse. 2010. "The Long Road Back." *New York Times*, March 21.

Teske, Steve. 2009. "House Democrats Release $1 Trillion Package on Health Care Reform, Pledge Quick Action." *Daily Report for Executives*, July 15.

Tumulty, Karen. 2010. "Mass Mutiny." *Time*, February 1.

Wallsten, Peter. 2009. "Catholic Church Emerges as Key Player in Legislative Battle." *Wall Street Journal*, November 10.

Wayne, Alex. 2009a. "With Manager's Amendment, Leaders Seek to Allay Fears, Avoid Controversies." *CQ Today*, November 5.

———. 2009b. "Reid's Recruitment Must Start Over." *CQ Today*, November 23.

———. 2010. "Path for 'Corrections' Bill Is Cleared." *CQ Today*, March 23.

Wayne, Alex, and Kathleen Hunter. 2009. "Nelson Insists on Abortion Limits." *CQ Today*, November 19.

Weisman, Jonathan, and Naftali Bendavid. 2009. "In Final Hours, an Intense Push for 'Yes' Votes." *Wall Street Journal*, November 9.

Index

About the Contributors

Jennifer Hayes Clark is assistant professor of political science at the University of Houston. Her teaching and research interests include U.S. congressional and state legislative politics, the politics of health care reform, and quantitative research methodology. She received her PhD from Indiana University in 2007. In 2009–2010, she served as an American Political Science Association Congressional Fellow, where she was a legislative assistant for health care, education, and small business policy.

Matthew Glassman is an analyst with the Congressional Research Service, where he focuses on congressional operations and administration, legislative branch appropriations, and congressional history. His research interests include institutional design and nineteenth-century American political development. He received his PhD in political science from Yale University.

Aaron S. King is a PhD candidate at Duke University studying American institutions and methodology. His research focuses on political parties in Congress and congressional elections. His dissertation project investigates the timing of strategic candidacy announcements in U.S. Senate elections and the consequences on the progressive ambitions of other politicians.

Gregory Koger is associate professor of political science at the University of Miami. After earning his BA at Willamette University, Koger worked as a legislative assistant in the U.S. House for over two years, where he served as a liaison to the Defense Appropriations Subcommittee. Koger earned his PhD from UCLA in 2002. He is the author of *Filibustering: A Political History of Obstruction in the House and Senate* (2010), and his research on filibustering and the Senate has led to interviews with the *Washington Post* and *Fresh Air* with Terry Gross, as well as testimony before the Senate Rules Committee. Koger has also published research articles on parties, lobbying, and Congress in the *American Journal of Political Science, Journal of Politics, Legislative Studies Quarterly, American Political Research, British Journal of Political Science, PS: Political Science and Politics,* and *Journal of Theoretical Politics.*

Mark J. Oleszek is assistant professor of political science at Albright College, where he teaches courses in American politics and the policymaking process. He earned his PhD in political science from the University of California, Berkeley, in May 2010 and spent the following year serving as an APSA Congressional Fellow in the personal office of Senator Al Franken. His doctoral dissertation examines the importance of member-to-member collaboration to the Senate's lawmaking process, an interest borne from previous experiences working with the Senate Democratic Policy Committee under the direction of former Democratic Leader Tom Daschle.

Walter J. Oleszek is a senior specialist on the Congress at the Congressional Research Service (CRS). He has been at CRS since 1968 and worked closely with many lawmakers and on many House and Senate committee reform initiatives. The author or coauthor of several books on the Congress, he is a long-time adjunct faculty member at The American University. He received his PhD from SUNY Albany.

Francis J. Orlando is a PhD candidate at Duke University studying American institutions and methodology with a special emphasis on the United States Congress. He has researched party, procedure, and elections in both the House and Senate. His dissertation focuses on the strategic context surrounding agenda population in Congress and its electoral consequences.

Honorable Major R. Owens served in Congress for twenty-four years (1983–2007). The only librarian to ever serve in Congress, Owens has a master's degree in library science. He worked for the Brooklyn Public Library, served as NYC Commissioner for the Community Development Agency, and was elected to the New York State Senate for eight years before resigning to run for Congress. During his congressional career Owens served on the Education and Labor Committee and the Government Oversight Committee. In 2011, Owens wrote *The Peacock Elite*, a subjective case study of his years as a member of the Congressional Black Caucus. The study was completed during a year spent at the Kluge Center of the Library of Congress. Owens presently serves as a distinguished lecturer at Medgar Evers College in Brooklyn, where he resides with his wife, Maria.

David W. Rohde is Ernestine Friedl Professor of Political Science and the founder and director of the Political Institutions and Public Choice Program at Duke University. He specializes in American national politics. His research has included various subjects, including the Congress, the presidency, the Supreme Court, and presidential and congressional elections.

James V. Saturno is currently the research manager for the Legislative and Budget Process Section in the Government and Finance Division of the Congressional Research Service, where he also serves as a specialist in congressional history and procedure, especially the federal budget process and budget process reform. His work has previously appeared in *The Encyclopedia of Congress, Legislative Studies Quarterly,* and *Public Budgeting and Finance.* In the 103rd Congress, he was detailed to the Joint Committee on the Organization of Congress as a consultant on the budget process. He has taught courses on Congress as an adjunct professor at American University and the Boston University Washington Center. He earned a BA in history from the State University of New York (Albany) and an MA in history from the University of Rochester.

Colleen J. Shogan is assistant director of the Congressional Research Service (CRS). Previously, she was assistant professor of government at George Mason University, an American Political Science Association congressional fellow, and a legislative assistant in the Senate. The author of several journal articles and a book on presidential rhetoric, she currently teaches graduate courses in American politics at Georgetown University. She received her PhD in political science from Yale University.

Barbara Sinclair is professor emerita of political science at UCLA. She specializes in American politics and primarily does research on the U.S. Congress. Her most recent books are *Unorthodox Lawmaking: New Legislative Processes in the U.S. Congress,* third ed. (2007), and *Party Wars: Polarization and the Politics of National Policy Making* (2006).

Jacob R. Straus is an analyst with the Congressional Research Service at the Library of Congress. He earned his bachelor's degree from the University of Maryland, College Park, and his master's and PhD from the University of Florida. He was an assistant professor of political science at Frostburg State (MD) University and currently is an adjunct professor of political science at the Johns Hopkins University and at the University of Maryland Baltimore County's Shady Grove campus. His research focuses on Congress, lobbying and ethics, public policy, and American political development.

Jessica Tollestrup is an analyst in Congress and the legislative process at the Congressional Research Service. She received her MS in political science from Portland State University.

James Wallner has worked on both sides of Capitol Hill. He currently serves as legislative director for a member of the U.S. Senate. Previously, he worked as a legislative assistant in the House of Representatives and the Senate. He is also a lecturer in the Department of Politics and the congressional and presidential studies program at the Catholic University of America.

CPSIA information can be obtained at www.ICGtesting.com
Printed in the USA
BVOW011546070312

284649BV00001B/3/P